Nonprofit and Civil Society Studies

An International Multidisciplinary Series

Series Editors

Paul Dekker
Tilburg University, Tilburg, The Netherlands

Lehn Benjamin
Indiana University - Purdue University Indianapolis, Indianapolis, IN, USA

More information about this series at http://www.springer.com/series/6339

Benjamin Gidron • Anna Domaradzka
Editors

The New Social and Impact Economy

An International Perspective

 Springer

Editors
Benjamin Gidron
Professor Emeritus
Business Administration
Ben-Gurion University of the Negev
Beer-Sheva, Israel

Anna Domaradzka
Robert Zajonc Institute for Social Studies
University of Warsaw
Warsaw, Poland

ISSN 1568-2579
Nonprofit and Civil Society Studies
ISBN 978-3-030-68297-2   ISBN 978-3-030-68295-8   (eBook)
https://doi.org/10.1007/978-3-030-68295-8

This Springer imprint is published by the registered company Springer Nature Switzerland AG
The registered company address is: Gewerbestrasse 11, 6330 Cham, Switzerland

Foreword

How do we want to work in the future? How and in which way do we have to change the economy in order to be sustainable? The volume at hand addresses these most salient topics, particularly because we are currently confronted with numerous and overlapping crises: the crisis of global warming, the social crisis of increasing inequality, and the extremely dangerous crisis of a pandemic disease. The volume aims at addressing these pivotal issues by taking a closer look at social enterprises as a fruitful combination of two controversial logics, precisely the one of the market and of the community that might help to overcome the shortcomings of both economic activities and societal deficiencies.

There are 11 articles from countries and regions around the world providing a fascinating portrait of the multifaceted character of social enterprises and their embeddedness in very different environments. Many of the articles draw on the results of the EU-funded project "For a Better Tomorrow: Social Enterprises on the Move" (fab.move),[1] which from 2016 to 2018 provided 28 researchers, scholars, and practitioners from more than 17 countries, among those Argentina, Costa Rica and the USA in the Americas, China and Indonesia in Asia, South Africa, and many European countries, with the opportunity to investigate on-site the ecosystems and day-to-day routines of social enterprises. Fab-Move was inspiring, challenging, innovative, and financed through the European Union's RISE Program (Research and Innovation Staff Exchange). RISE is based on the idea that close cooperation and hands-on experience constitute the best way to build trust and confidence among researchers and professionals working in the same area and therefore allow a smooth and timely dissemination of research results.

However, the outcome of excellent research always leads to new questions and even more difficult problems and topics that have to be addressed. This has also been the case in Fab-Move. Doubtlessly, social enterprises provide new and innovative solutions for tackling salient problems for communities and constituencies in need. But from a macro-level perspective, it is not at all clear whether social

---

[1] https://fabmove.eu

enterprises open up avenues to overcome the current economic system that is based on an ideology of continuous growth and hence exploitation of the natural resources of our earth. More specifically, are social enterprises just another Band-Aid that helps to deal with minor social problems without endangering the overall capitalistic system and the globalized economy at large? Or do they represent a new way of combining the social and economic sphere, and therefore are first signs indicating a "new social and impact economy"? The chapters in the volume, particularly the introductory and closing chapters as well as the contribution by Michael Roy, reflect on this issue. For sure, we need more research and intense collaboration with policy experts and practitioners to further develop this topic. The same holds true for the micro-perspective on the functions and embeddedness of social enterprises. One might argue that social enterprises in the Global South do not primarily work on behalf of communities in need; instead, financed by and large through corporate social responsibility (CSR) programs, they are the outboard motors of large corporations and hence help to set up an investment-friendly environment for global enterprises. We should not forget that the modern welfare state has from the very beginning significantly helped the economy and the large companies to externalize costs that otherwise the corporations would have had to take care of in order to safeguard a stable environment for their economic activities. Public investments in infrastructure, for instance schools and education at large as well as the introduction of work injury insurance, are classical examples for the externalization of costs with the outcome of more profitability and competitiveness for large companies. Against this background, it might be questionable whether impact investment as a new mode of financing social enterprises will contribute to the overall reform of the current economic system. Again, further research is needed, in particular with respect to the aspirations of the companies, the new generation of managers, and their view on the future of our planet. All in all, it might be worthwhile considering a revival of Fab-Move, albeit with a slightly different perspective and a new setting that in-line with the "European Green Deal" should investigate at the macro and meso levels the role and function of the social economy and social enterprises as regards the transformation of the European economy towards sustainable economic development.

November 23, 2020   Annette Zimmer
                              Professor of Social Policy and Comparative Politics
                                                    Münster University, Germany

Information Text

This edited volume discusses the development of the new social and impact economy in ten countries around the globe. It is an attempt to conceptualize developments after the 2008 economic crisis, which emphasized the pitfalls of the neo-liberal economic system. In the aftermath of the crisis, new organizational entities evolved, which combined social and business objectives as part of their mission. Using data gathered by two recent international research projects—the ICSEM project and the FAB-MOVE project—the book provides an initial portrait of the forces at play in the evolution of the new social and impact economy, linking those to the past crisis as well as to Covid19 and comparing the emergence of the phenomenon in a varied group of countries.

The book begins with an overview of the classical definitions of social economy and proposes a comprehensive concept of new social and impact economy, its characteristics, and sources. Ten country chapters as well as a comparative chapter on international social economy organizations follow. The volume concludes with an overall analysis of the data from the country chapters, forming a typology of social economy traditions and linking it to recent post-capitalism trends.

Creating a conceptual framework to analyze the new phenomena in social economy, this volume is ideal for academics and practitioners in the fields of social economy; social, economic, and welfare policies; social and business entrepreneurship in a comparative fashion; social and technological innovation as well as CSR specialists and practitioners.

Contents

About the Editors

Benjamin Gidron is a Professor of Social Enterprises and the Head of the Research Authority at the College of Management Academic Studies (COLMAN) and Professor Emeritus at the Guilford Glazer Faculty of Business and Management in Ben Gurion University of the Negev (Israel). He pioneered the study of the Third (Nonprofit) Sector in Israel and was the Founder-President of the International Society for Third Sector Research (ISTR) 1992–1996. He founded the Israeli Center for Third Sector Research at BGU and directed it for 12 years (1997–2009).

Anna Domaradzka is a sociologist, Assistant Professor, and the Director at Robert Zajonc Institute for Social Studies, University of Warsaw (Poland). She currently serves as a board member of International Society for Third Sector Research (ISTR), and Research Committee 48 on Social Movements and Collective Action of International Sociological Association. At the moment, her main research focus is on civil society in the urban context, neighborhood associations, "right to the city" movement and social entrepreneurship in comparative perspective.

About the Authors

Mara Benadusi is Professor of Anthropology at the Department of Political and Social Sciences, University of Catania (mara.benadusi@unict.it). She has served as scientific supervisor for the IMPACT HUB network in the EFESEIIS Project, "Enabling the Flourishing and Evolution of Social Entrepreneurship for Innovative and Inclusive Societies," funded by the European Commission through the Seventh Framework Program. She also led the Catania University's team in the H2020-MSCA-RISE Project "FAB MOVE. For a Better Tomorrow: Social Entrepreneurship on the Move.

Gabriel Berger is an Associate Professor at the School of Business of Universidad de San Andrés (UdeSA), Buenos Aires, Argentina, and Director of its Center of Social Innovation. Dr. Berger's teaching and research focus on strategic management and governance of nonprofits, social businesses, corporate social engagement, and philanthropy. He has been the dean of UdeSA's School of Business (2013–2017). Dr. Berger was the founder and director of the Graduate Program in Nonprofit Organizations launched in 1997, the first of its kind in Latin America, and led it for 16 years. He is a former board member of International Society for Third-Sector Research (ISTR). Since 2001, he has been a member of Social Enterprise Knowledge Network (www.sekn.org) and served two terms as its general coordinator. He has collaborated as an advisor to NGOs, businesses, and foundations in several Latin American countries and in the USA. He obtained a PhD in Social Policy and a Master in Management of Human Services from the Heller School for Social Policy and Management at Brandeis University (USA).

Leopoldo Blugerman is a Professor at the Institute of Industry (IDEI) of the National University of General Sarmiento (UNGS). At UNGS, he is the Program Director in the BA in Business Administration. He is a member of the Advisory Council of the National Institute of Associativism and Social Economy (INAES), at the Ministry of Productive Development. He is also an External Researcher for the Social Enterprise Knowledge Network (SEKN). His national and international publications, and his research, are mainly focused on collaborative strategies in the third sector, socially inclusive business, private social investment strategies, and social economy. Leopoldo Blugerman holds a Master in International Relations (Università di Bologna) and a PhD (c) in Systems Science (Faculty of Business, Law and Politics, University of Hull).

Ignacio Bretos is Assistant Professor at the Department of Business Organization and Management, University of Zaragoza, Spain. His research interests include alternative organizations, critical management studies, cooperatives, social enterprises, organizational hybridity, multinational organizations, and human resource management. Ignacio's research outputs have been published in international refereed journals such as *Organization, Human Resource Management Journal, Industrial and Labor Relations Review, Review of Radical Political Economics, and Annals of Public and Cooperative Economics.*

Didier Chabanet is Dean of Research at IDRAC Business School and Senior Research Fellow at Triangle (Ecole Normale Supérieure) in Lyon. He is also Associate Researcher at Sciences Po-CEVIPOF, France. He previously delivered research and teaching in various leading universities and institutes across Asia, Europe, and the USA, including Georgetown University, the EUI, Hong Kong Baptist University, and the University of Oxford. His interest lies especially in the field of social movements, social exclusion, social entrepreneurship, and European integration.

Giulio Citroni is Associate Professor in the Department of Social and Political Science at the University of Calabria, where he teaches Political Science and Public Policy Analysis. His main research interests and publications concern local democracy, local government, and the governance of local utilities and public services.

Teresa Consoli is Associate professor in Sociology of Law at Catania University (Dept. of Social and Political Sciences). Her main research areas focus on sociolegal dimensions of welfare systems, on social policies, on social professions, and on characteristics of the migratory phenomena. She is a member of the National Scientific Committee of the National Federation of Services for Homeless people and since 2017 of the Executive Committee of the European Sociological Association.

Deborah De Felice is a Sociologist of law and deviant behavior at the University of Catania (Italy). Her main field of study and research regards decision-making processes in legal contexts, especially in children's rights implementation.

Millan Diaz-Foncea is Assistant Professor in the Department of Business Management at the University of Zaragoza (Spain). As member of the GESES-University of Zaragoza Research Group (geses.unizar.es), his research has focused on the study of social economy, collective entrepreneurship, social enterprises, and new economies (solidarity-based economy, sharing economy).

Anjel Errasti is a member of the Institute of Cooperative Law and Social Economy (GEZKI) and a senior lecturer in Strategic Management at the Faculty of Economics and Business of the University of the Basque Country (UPV/EHU) in Donostia-San Sebastian. His research interests focus on cooperatives and social economy, public policies, employment, Mondragon cooperatives, multinational corporations, and globalization.

Irene Falconieri is Post-doc Research Fellow in Cultural Anthropology at the University of Messina. Her interests concern the perception of risks and the study of the social consequences of disasters; territorial conflicts and legal disputes related to environmental issues, and the analysis of the relationships between migratory phenomena and changes in urban space.

Laurence Lemoine is Professor of Communication at IDRAC Business School (Montpellier, France). Her research focuses on the study of collaborative economy, social economy, and volunteerism.

Ronny Manos is Professor of Finance at the School of Business Administration, College of Management Academic Studies, Israel. She is currently heading the Thesis Program at the school. Her PhD is from the Birmingham Business School, University of Birmingham, UK. In recent years, Ronny's research has focused on microfinance social corporate responsibility, social businesses, and impact investment.

Carmen Marcuello is Professor in the Department of Business Management of the University of Zaragoza (Spain). She is President of the OIBESCOOP and Vice President of CIRIEC-Spain. She is a member of the International Scientific Commission "Social and Cooperative Economy" CIRIEC International and in the editorial board of *Annals of Public and Cooperative Economics* and CIRIEC-Spain, Revista de la Economía Pública Social y Cooperativa.

Francesco Mazzeo is an Associate Professor at the University of Catania, where he teaches evaluation research methodology. He is also an Affiliate Professor at the KTH, Royal Institute of Technology, Stockholm. Among the main research interests covered by publications are public policies evaluation, Big Data analytics in social research, and social and cohesion policy.

Carlo Pennisi is Full professor in Sociology of Law at the Department of Political and Social Sciences, University of Catania. In 2016 he was responsible for the "Context Analysis and Functional Investigations to the Assessment of OS2ON3" as part of the evaluation of the Asylum, Migration and Integration Fund (FAMI), for the Ministry of the Interior. He is Director of the Research Centre LAPOSS (Laboratory of Project Management, testing and analysis of public policies and services to people).

H. Thomas R. Persson is Associate Professor in Sport Management with a PhD in Ethnic Relations. He is Program Coordinator of the International Master, Sport Science: Sport in Society, and a lecturer in Sport Management at the Faculty of Education and Society, Malmö University, Sweden. His research interests include social responsibility: CSR; social entrepreneurship and social innovation: B2B; andsocial capital and governance, both within and outside of the world of sports. On these topics, he has published a number of articles, reports, and book chapters as well as co-edited the book Social Entrepreneurship and Social Innovation: Ecosystems for Inclusion in Europe.

Maria Rosaline Nindita Radyati is the founder of a master degree program with specialization in sustainability and the Executive Director of the Center for Entrepreneurship, Change, and Third Sector (CECT) at Trisakti University. CECT is a leading think-tank, research center, and consultant for CSR and sustainability in Indonesia. Maria was the chairperson of the Expert Team for the House of Representative and Consultant to the Ministry of State-Owned Enterprises (SOE) for the drafting of the "CSR Law" and "Ministry Law on CSR for SOE" in Indonesia.

Michael J. Roy is Professor of Economic Sociology and Social Policy at the Yunus Centre for Social Business and Health at Glasgow Caledonian University. His research focuses primarily on the health and well-being impacts of organizations in the social economy, particularly social enterprises. He also examines ways in which social enterprise "ecosystems" can be supported and enhanced.

Hanna Schneider works as a researcher at the Institute of Nonprofit Management, at WU, Vienna. Her research and teaching focus on social entrepreneurship and social innovation, corporate volunteering, and circular forms of organizing of non-profit organizations.

Ruth Simsa is Professor for Sociology at the Department for Socioeconomics at WU Wien (Vienna University of Economics and Business). She is Editor in Chief of VOLUNTAS: International Journal of Voluntary and Nonprofit Organizations and up to 2020 has been Director of WU's Institute for Nonprofit Research.

Aurélie Soetens holds a PhD in Economics and Management from HEC Liège, Management School of the University of Liège, in Belgium. She started her PhD as a part-time teaching assistant at the Centre for Social Economy (CES) of HEC Liège and then was awarded an Aspirante FNRS grant to conduct full-time research. Part of her PhD was completed while visiting the International Centre for Co-operative and Social Economy (CIESCOOP) of the University of Santiago de Chile. Her research interests include dynamics of workplace participation and democracy, paradoxes in democratic enterprises, and relationship between social enterprises and trade unions.

Jorge Sousa is a Professor of Adult, Community and Higher Education in the Department of Educational Policy Studies at the University of Alberta. Jorge received his PhD from the Ontario Institute for Studies in Education of the University of Toronto. His areas of research expertise all fall within the intersection of community development and community education. He is primarily engaged in research aimed at understanding and strengthening Canada's social economy. The specific topics that his research focuses on include strengthening Canada's social economy through member engagement; community education and pedagogy supporting community development practices; and public policy related to community development, nonmarket housing, and community economic development.

Benny Tjahjono is Professor of Sustainability and Supply Chain Management and the co-leader of the Sustainable Production and Consumption cluster at the Centre for Business in Society (CBiS) at Coventry University, UK.

Chapter 1
Introduction

Benjamin Gidron and Anna Domaradzka

This book was conceived and written against the background of first one and then a second major international crisis, which shook the world economic and social order in a major way. We refer of course to the 2008/2009 subprime mortgage collapse, which at the time led to a major international economic crisis, but was also a prelude for a renewed, creative thinking about the relationship between economy and society, as well as the more recent Covid-19 pandemic, which undoubtedly calls for further thinking and action along these lines.

We entitled the book *The New Social and Impact Economy: International Perspectives* to stress the focus on the social aspects of the economy, reflected in new organizational strategies, ways of generating social impact, and innovative financial tools. In our view this new ecosystem needs a common conceptual framework to catch/depict its core values and characteristics to inform potential policies or consulting efforts. We christened it *new* social and impact economy to underline its rootedness in social economy logic, but to also underline its new forms, guiding values and interactions.

The last phase of this book is being written during the global coronavirus pandemic which is leading to a major global economic crisis where major industries suffered a blow and will need to reinvent themselves. However, this book focuses on the aftermath of the previous global crisis.

Crises are not only phenomena that break certain patterns and structures creating havoc and suffering, but also opportunities to rethink predominant truisms and build new structures. A glance at history shows this clearly: from the claim that the Black

B. Gidron (✉)
Professor Emeritus, Business Administration, Ben-Gurion University of the Negev, Beer-Sheva, Israel

A. Domaradzka (✉)
Robert Zajonc Institute for Social Studies, University of Warsaw, Warsaw, Poland
e-mail: anna.domaradzka@uw.edu.pl

© Springer Nature Switzerland AG 2021
B. Gidron, A. Domaradzka (eds.), *The New Social and Impact Economy*,
Nonprofit and Civil Society Studies, https://doi.org/10.1007/978-3-030-68295-8_1

Death in the fourteenth century was actually leading to the Renaissance (because of the decline in the power of religion), to the aftermath of the Spanish Flu, which led to a series of international agreements and frameworks, to the 1929 stock exchange and economic collapse, which led to the New Deal in the USA and the Keynesian ideology, to the institutionalization of the human rights concept after the horrors of World War II, to the Oil Crisis of the 1970s, which led many governments to adopt conservative economic policies, to name a few.

In a 1959 speech, John F. Kennedy famously said: "When written in Chinese, the word 'crisis' is composed of two characters—one represents danger and one represents opportunity." Crises require us to find solutions to daily problems in a different context; they serve as a trigger for change which was blocked before and provide a context for creative thinking; crises may also overthrow predominant ideologies. According to a Brookings Report,[1] out of crises new opportunities can emerge, as traditional approaches and paradigms are questioned and challenged. During a crisis, incentives and motivations change, potentially leading to new cooperative behaviors and creation of novel systems or structures. Crises can get the collective adrenaline flowing, focusing minds to solve the problems the crisis created.

The major argument of this book is that the economic crisis of 2008 was a trigger for significant changes in the thinking about the relationship between economy and society. The crisis emphasized the negative impact of the neoliberal economy on the society and the environment, and gave rise to a change in conception regarding the relationships between these two domains: from a conceptual (and institutional) separation between society and economy to the idea of hybridity, which suggests that it is possible to pursue both social and economic objectives within the same organizational structure.

This realization created in effect the new field that we termed the "*New* Social and Impact Economy." That depiction links this development to the existing and known concept of "social economy," which has, as we will show, certain ideological underpinnings. Those who are reluctant to paint the same development in such ideological colors prefer to call it the "Impact Economy." This distinction is particularly relevant between countries where the concept of "social economy" is well known and clearly institutionalized and others where it is not.

In this introduction and in the country chapters we focus on the "social economy" concept, which has a long history that "impact economy" does not. We are asking whether the "New Social Economy" is actually a continuation of the "old" one or it represents a different phenomenon. Another focus is the underlying value base and the forces behind these developments. The international perspective gives us an opportunity to present the diverse approaches to social economy, particularly highlighting the new processes or forms that have developed in recent years. Our starting point is to reflect on these novel forms, in relation to economic crises, specifically the economic crisis of 2008/2009, that seem to stimulate new phases of

---

[1] Maria Langan-Riekhof, Arex B. Avanni, and Adrienne Janetti: Sometimes the world needs a crisis: Turning challenges into opportunities *Brookings Report*, April 10, 2017.

growth within the social economy spectrum. In the conclusions we link our findings with a more recent Covid-19 crisis to stipulate about new challenges and directions of social economy worldwide.

The collected chapters cover different geographical regions and welfare regimes and as such offer a wide comparative perspective. Importantly, in many countries we cannot apply the social economy concept developed in the European context, which forces us to go beyond a traditional approach to the idea of a *social* economy. This is in line with this book aim, which is to offer reflections on the novel and nontraditional processes within this domain. We posit that we can now observe the initial stage of *new social and impact economy* emergence, shaped by the development of information and communication technologies, new modes of funding, and a general crisis of traditional approaches to generating social impact through business activities.

We use the concept of *new social and impact economy* to depict the recent parallel developments in the arenas of *social enterprises* on the one hand and of *impact investment* on the other. This is predicated by a dual rationale: first, to develop a concept that will be able to include these two phenomena within a single framework, and second to link it to previous eras, where these two dimensions—the substantive and the financial—are linked in one general concept that enables the view of both sides of the same coin.

In our analysis we will try to position both traditional and new forms of the social economy in relation to a wider civil society field. The logic of the third sector, represented by civil society organizations like associations and foundations, remains basic for developing a social economy in its traditional European form. However, the main characteristics of the social economy actors nowadays are their hybridity and the tendency to exist in between the market, the public sphere, and the civil society. This may be one of the reasons why the social economy is not recognized as a sector, and it spurs diverse forms of socioeconomic activities.

While we cannot analyze the new social and impact economy as a sector (yet) we propose to use the concept of field to better understand its dynamics and map actors and norms shaping its development. We claim, after Defourny and Nyssens (2014), that what seems to be at stake within the social economy field is the place and role of social enterprises and other hybrid forms within the overall economy and their interaction with the market, civil society, and public policies. These adjacent and often overlapping fields have an impact in shaping strategies and norms within the social economy field, which still remains weak compared to the more established field structures. To shed some light on the nature of their hybridity we can therefore discuss the role of the social economy as complementary, substitutive, or innovative in state, civil society, and market contexts (Domaradzka & Żbikowska, 2017).

Using Fligstein and McAdam (2012) analytical frame of strategic action fields we point out that new social economy actors challenge traditional truisms within the social economy field. As challengers, many actors in that field face difficulties trying to take advantage of either market solutions or public subcontractor privileges, often paying the price for their trans-sectoral character.

In our view new developments within the social and impact economy field illustrate the challenges that this concept will always face. What seems to be crucial for these new developments to be recognized as a *new social and impact economy* is the proof of action. We hope that this collected volume will offer enough grounding for further developing this concept and giving it more traction. While this emerging phenomenon still needs to be studied and better understood, we hope that the concept of *new* social and impact economy will help grasp the nature of new (often ICT-fueled) social enterprises and impact investment practices.

For the sake of clarity, we also define different aspects of social and impact economy often mentioned in this book:

1. *Social entrepreneurship* is defined as a process and quality located in an individual (social entrepreneur).
2. *Social enterprise* is defined as an organization structure in which a combination of social objective and business activity takes place.
3. *Impact investment* refers to investments made into companies, organizations, and funds with the intention to generate a measurable, beneficial social or environmental impact alongside a financial return.
4. *Social and impact economy* encompasses the production of social value through business activities with financing mechanisms enabling its development.

Both those who enable change on the ground level (e.g., social enterprises) and those who finance it (e.g., impact investors) co-create the structure of a social and impact economy. Here, we underline the interdependence between the type of organization and the specific funding mechanisms: whereas social enterprises need investors to develop their activities or scale up their solutions, impact investors look for entrepreneurs that will create social impact with the investors' funding.

Based on the country chapters we want to reflect on the diversity of new social and impact economy placement within state-market spectrum, depending on the national context, type of economic environment, and presence of welfare state. We are investigating the challenges and opportunities arising from the current position of social entrepreneurs, who play the role of challengers at the crossroads of three main sectors—the state, the market, and the third sector.

The Concept and Role of the Social Economy: Origins and History

The term "social economy" came into usage at the end of the eighteenth century and refers to a theoretical approach that was first developed by the utopian socialists— the early founders of the cooperative tradition—Owen, Fourier, Saint Simon, and Proudhon. This laid the foundations for the first cooperatives, which were seen by economists Charles Gide and Léon Walras and sociologist Frédéric Le Play as the organizational forms of the social economy (Restakis, 2006, 4–5). As Restakis points out:

> "This early history framed later definitions that retained the emphasis on an alternative paradigm that challenged the classical understanding of capitalist economics, including the control of capital. Very quickly the concept came to be used to refer to collective enterprises and associations guided by *ethical and moral considerations, not just material gain* (italics added). The elements of mutuality, collective effort, and social control over capital have remained as the most constant traits of the term as it has evolved ever since" (Restakis, 2006, 8).

It is important to stress that moral aspects of the economy were also discussed by Adam Smith, who is known for his "invisible hand" theory of the economy, which laid the foundations for the free market economy. In his earlier book *The Theory of Moral Sentiment* (1759) he discusses the dangers of asset accumulation by individuals and their duty to share their wealth with others.[2]

Thus, the evolution of the social economy finds its historical roots within the thought and work of utopian socialists and early attempts to create alternative, communitarian responses to the mainstream capitalist economy through the use of the cooperative model.

The fact that the social economy was developed by socialist thinkers in the nineteenth century and evolved around cooperatives created a natural affinity between the two movements. A question that was often raised was the role of these cooperatives in the socialist revolution. This dilemma of socialist leaders regarding cooperatives as a means for societal change was already raised by Lenin. At the International Socialist Congress in 1910 in Copenhagen he stated:

> "It is quite clear that there are two main lines of policy here: one – the line of proletarian class struggle, recognition of the value of the co-operative societies as a weapon in this struggle …. and a definition of the conditions under which the co-operative societies would really play such a part and not remain simple commercial enterprises. The other line is a petty-bourgeois one, obscuring the question of the role of the co-operative societies in the class struggle of the proletariat …. defining the aims of the co-operative societies with general phrases that are acceptable even to the bourgeois reformers, those ideologues of the progressive employers, large and small" (Lenin, 1910).

In a recent publication of *Common Ground* (a food cooperative), the relationship between cooperatives and socialism receives the following characterization:

> "The cooperative movement and socialism are distinct from each other, but they are close cousins. Socialism demands a whole-scale transformation of society's productive forces, and to immediately end Capitalism. Cooperatives are a little different – they seek to do the best they can democratically within whatever economic system is present. So, cooperatives aren't necessarily socialist, but they share a common root and are, in some cases, fully compatible with a Socialist society" (Dodson, 2018).

---

[2] One of the book chapters is entitled: *Of the corruption of our moral sentiments, which is occasioned by this disposition to admire the rich and the great and to despise or neglect persons of poor and mean condition.*

The Context and Evolution of the Social Economy on the Basis of Cooperatives

Long before the 2008 crisis, it was clear that the emergence and re-emergence of the social economy—practice, concepts, and policy/institutions, are linked to periods of crisis: "the social economy is a way to respond to the alienation and non-satisfaction of needs by the traditional private sector or the public sector in times of socioeconomic crisis" (Moulaert & Ailenei, 2005, 2040–41). In other words, social economy hybrid and flexible nature make it a "quick-response" taskforce within turbulent socioeconomic conditions. For example, the first generation of cooperatives and mutual support organizations (*mutuelles*) appeared in the 1840–1850s in the context of the transition from the old regulation (through craftsmen corporations) to competitive regulation. The second generation relates primarily to agricultural cooperatives and mutual financial institutions ("savings and loans") that rose in response to the needs of small producers affected by the crisis of the extensive regime of accumulation that required heavy investments in agriculture and natural resources (1873–1895). The third generation emerged from the economic collapse of 1929–1932 and was to a large extent the result of the crisis in competitive regulation. Consumption cooperatives of that time responded to food and housing shortages and supported workers and unemployed people in acquiring basic goods and services at affordable prices.

One may say that the nature of the social economy during the roughly hundred years between the middle of the nineteenth century and the middle of the twentieth century evolved around the collective efforts by individuals to deal with adverse economic conditions by organizing and pulling together resources, which enabled them to compete with the power of capital.

This changed after World War II and the development of the Welfare State, when social economy organizations became partners of the system of social service delivery. This added a new facet to the social economy that in many countries became its defining trait. Whereas in the past the social economy was composed of producer and consumer cooperatives as well as financial mutual institutions, the partnership with the welfare state apparatus resulted in the addition of service delivery organizations for disenfranchised populations (the elderly, the mentally ill, etc.). This was the context for the formal creation of "social cooperatives" in Italy (Thomas, 2004), but also for the enlargement of the concept of social economy and the inclusion in it of *associations and foundations* that were also independent partners of the welfare state apparatus (Moulaert & Ailenei, 2005, 2041).

The changes in the mass production system and the overburdening of the welfare state in the 1970s brought about a new emphasis on local economic development and on structuring the work environment to focus on ecological and cooperative production, with "the goal (of establishing) a collective well-being and (recreating) social bonds between the people within their communities, in order to provide alternatives for services usually rendered by the state" (Moulaert & Ailenei, 2005, 2041).

According to Laville, Levecque, and Mendell (2008), cooperatives were integrated into the market economy; they could be found in areas where capitalist activity was weak. Certain types of cooperatives, such as agricultural cooperatives, emerged almost everywhere; other types were more country specific, such as consumer cooperatives in England and housing cooperatives in Germany, Great Britain, and Sweden. In their analysis, Laville et al. point out that

> "while cooperatives were able to benefit from certain arrangements negotiated with the State, for the most part they were subject to competition. In general, the logical consequence was to concentrate the means of production, which prompted them to specialize in major activities linked to the identities of their members" (Laville et al., 2008, 2–3).

The emerging social economy was much less interested in creating a systemic change in society; it proposed an original form of entrepreneurship. While it was involved in both market and nonmarket activities it still promised to operate differently from a business firm or a public agency. This way it generally relied upon a "resource-mix combining public support as well as market resources besides its more specific ability to generate nonmonetary resources (volunteer work) and private monetary non-market resources (gift)" (Bidet, 2010).

A different view of the role of the social economy is presented by Tremblay (2009) who offers arguments for the development of an economic order based on solidarity, participation, and cooperation as an alternative to the mainstream neoliberal capitalist economy. She contends that there is a "growing global movement to advance concepts and frameworks of the Social Economy as a way to address increasing inequality of social, health, economic and ecological conditions, to provide alternative solutions to the perceived failure of neo-liberal dominated globalization and to address the weakening social capital of communities" (9). This concept finds its continuation in the literature concerning well-being economy, as described in the first chapter of this volume.

The Nature of the Traditional Social Economy and Its Typical Organizations

The Encyclopedia of Civil Society defines the social economy as "a conceptual space that helps to bridge the distance between informal and formal organizations and between non-profits and business enterprise and which focuses on areas of social and economic well-being of individuals, communities and regions." This view sees the social economy as a "bottom-up" phenomenon. It evolves around place, community, and participatory democracy and it manifests itself in activities such as caring for community members and environment, creation of new projects to meet social need, providing equitable and accessible employment and leisure activities, community ownership and control of local amenities and services, campaigns to protect habitats and endangered species, and celebration and revitalization of communities and cultures. Social economy organizations share features that represent an original form of entrepreneurship: a voluntary participation, an autonomy of decision, a formal existence through a legal identity, an orientation towards an economic activity, a democratic governance, a nonprofit orientation, and a distribution of profits that is not directly linked to the capital. These features shape a part of the economy that aims to serve the man rather than the capital and distinguishes the social economy organizations from both public agencies that form the public sector and for-profit entities that form the business sector (Bidet, 2010).

Myers (2009) sees social economy organizations' primary characteristic as their social mission. She adds that this is geared "less towards transformative social change (the social economy as an alternative to neo-liberalism and capitalist ideology and systems) and more towards generative and incremental change (focus on social problems and solutions; well-being of specific groups)" (ibid. 20). It pertains specifically to *social goals that can be achieved through economic means*. Thus, the social economy contains organizations that are both market and nonmarket focused (and those that are a mix of both) to provide a range of goods and services often geared towards disadvantaged individuals and groups. She also talks about the innovative and entrepreneurial functions of these organizations (ibid. 21).

Moulaert and Ailenei (2005) agree that the term social economy designates the universe of practices and forms of mobilizing economic resources towards the satisfaction of human needs that belong neither to for-profit enterprises, nor to the institutions of the state. Essentially, the social economy is made up of the voluntary, nonprofit, and cooperative sectors that are formally independent of the state. "Their market activities are means of achieving social development goals that transcend the market per se. Thus defined, the social economy should be logically considered as a third sector" (Moulaert & Ailenei, 2005, 2042).

It is important to stress that the depiction of the social economy as a *separate, third sector* of organizations that includes cooperatives, mutuals, nonprofit organizations, and foundations raises a cultural controversy: In the French tradition these organizations belong to the same sector, whereas in the Anglo-Saxon tradition, primarily the USA and the UK, the third sector does not include organizations with the legal form of cooperative as these do not prescribe to the nondistribution constraint, namely, they are allowed to distribute their profits to their members. Laville et al. (2015) suggest that while cooperatives and mutual societies stem from the same roots as associations, this common origin has been forgotten in certain countries. Thus, the reference to the social economy as a distinct sector is not a consensual one in Europe, and it emanates primarily from the French-speaking countries (ibid. 4).

Thus, these two views—the social economy as a *sector* of organizations or as a *facet* of the economy and society, not limited to a defined group of organizations but designating a social and moral approach in managing economic processes—dominate the debate on the concept.

Originated from the French experience, the social economy concept has successfully spread to other European countries that basically share many common historical, cultural, and political features. On that point the report by the CIRIEC offers a global view of this sector, its success, and the main trends and challenges it is facing in Europe (Chaves-Avila & Monzon-Campos, 2007). Interestingly, the report shows that the concept of social economy as a sector including cooperatives, associations, mutual benefits, and foundations is now well acknowledged in academic, political, and institutional circles in most of the European countries with the exception of a few that favor rival concepts such as Germany, the Netherlands, and the UK, and to a smaller extent Austria and Denmark. Yet, social economy remains largely under-considered in EU members from Central and Eastern Europe (Bidet, 2010).

Originally, the social economy hinged on four main families of organizations: cooperatives, mutual societies, associations, and foundations, although it is questionable whether they share all the core features, namely a democratic governance, an orientation towards an economic activity, and a voluntary participation. The non-profit nature of cooperatives has been questioned as well by the advocates of the nonprofit approach, but those of the social economy consider that the limited distribution of profit by cooperatives and their obligation to allocate a part of their surpluses to collective reserves make them nonprofit organizations in nature and undoubtedly organizations closer to nonprofits than to for-profits (Bidet, 2010).

Borzaga and Defourny (2001) presented an operational definition of social economy activities, distinguishing economic and social criteria. From an entrepreneurial perspective, social enterprises are therefore defined by high levels of autonomy, availability to take risks, and engagement of waged workforce. From a social perspective, the main objectives of their activity must be the following: a defined (local or trait-oriented) community must benefit, the stakeholders must be allowed to participate, and the governance must be based on democratic principles instead of ownership. Importantly, the distribution of profit must be limited, so that the capital can be reinvested in socially meaningful activities.

The scope and characteristics of the social economy vary according to each national context, but these organizations are generally engaged in, and play a prominent role in, market-oriented activities such as agriculture, credit and banking, insurance or commerce, as well as predominantly nonmarket-oriented activities that have been proved socially useful but not profitable, such as the provision of health and social services and education (Bidet, 2010).

The European Commission (2014) acknowledged that despite interest in fostering social economy and "inspirational and 'disruptive' social enterprises," there is still relatively little known about the scale and characteristics of the "sector" as a whole. While some studies distinguish these developing forms from both the social and mainstream economy, the diversity of national economic structures, welfare, and cultural traditions as well as legal frameworks means that measuring and comparing social economy activities across the world remain a challenge.

As Lipparini and Phillips (2018) point out, in spite of the political interest, 21 out of 28 EU countries do not have specific legislation or policy frameworks supporting the social economy. However, in many countries we can find legal forms and funding schemes for work integration social enterprises (WISEs) and social cooperatives or other traditional social economy organizations. This is because WISEs, in line with a long EU tradition, represent the most common form of social enterprises often heavily subsidized by the public sector.

The Emergence of the New Social and Impact Economy

The emergence of what we term the *new* social and impact economy can be traced to developments following the 2008 economic crisis. Whereas in the past there was a clear institutional separation between economic activity (primarily within the business sector) and social activity (within the public and the nonprofit sectors), the world crisis emphasized the interrelatedness between the economy and society and the injustices the neoliberal economic regime causes.

The economic crisis has shocked the world economy in a way that reminded people of the 1929 stock market crash. The crisis came after a decade of criticism against the globalized economic order of consumerism, which created growing gaps between the rich and the poor on the national as well as the global levels, and also emphasized the danger to the environment.[3] The popular reaction to the crisis has evolved, especially in 2011, to a wave of riots and demonstrations (the Occupy Movement) of millions of people around the globe that started in the Zuccotti Park in New York and spread to hundreds of cities around the world from London to Auckland, from Copenhagen to Seoul—demanding social justice and change of a system that benefits the few and endangers the many (Della Porta, 2015; Rogers, 2011).

After the wave of demonstrations subsided, the demand for change evolved into a different form: social and business entrepreneurs translated their frustrations with the existing economic order into a creative process of designing and leading organizations that expressed a new balance between business and social orientation. The main thrust of this trend was the idea introduced by the 2006 Nobel Laureate Muhammad Yunus, of a *social business*—a business enterprise that entails social and/or environmental objectives as part of its mission, which challenged the philanthropic as well as the Corporate Social Responsibility (CSR) approaches.

A new creative phase of popular anger was expressed in innovative entrepreneurial activity of individuals all over the world who developed a wide variety of *social enterprises*—organizations, in a wide variety of legal forms, that defied the previous separation, combining social and business objectives within the same entity. In a parallel development in the field of finance, an arena of *impact investment* developed, creating innovative platforms for investors to seek not only financial return on their investment but social impact as well. These two developments are in fact two sides of the same coin, which we term the *new social and impact economy*. It is important to stress that the initiative for these developments came primarily from those advocating social and business entrepreneurships, much less from the social economy actors.

As a result of this wave of entrepreneurial activity all over the world, we observed the evolution of a large variety of innovative and creative frameworks that provide new solutions to diverse social problems. These social enterprises are based, at least

---

[3] In a series of recent books, it is claimed that these gaps, especially the accumulation of tremendous riches in the hands of a small number of billionaires, form a danger to democracy (Piketty, 2020; Saez & Zucman, 2019; Stoller, 2020).

in part, on commercial activities with focus on employment of different marginalized groups,[4] creation of new ventures in social tourism, initiating cultural activities among minorities, and much more.[5] Many of these new ventures are technology based, using new Information and Communication Technologies (ICT) to collect resources (e.g., Polish *"Food cooperative Dobrze" crowdsourcing campaign*); connect people and services; gather data (e.g., Indonesian *"Telepak" fighting with illegal logging*) to reach, access, and connect between people; collect data on their health or social condition, etc. Another line of ICT-based social innovations focuses on specific populations and creates formats based on smart telephone applications, to deal with their specific predicament: for example, AngelSense, which developed a device to ensure the safety and independence of children on the autistic spectrum, or MyndYou, which improves the quality of life and independence of elderly adults with a cognitive decline. As several authors point out (Fisac-Garcia et al., 2013; Frączkiewicz-Wronka & Wronka-Pośpiech, 2014) ICT has significant economic advantages (see Dolgin, 2012), and it can help social enterprises create or scale up their social impact. The flexibility of ICTs makes them powerful tools for creating relationships between organizations and their beneficiaries, sharing knowledge, and disseminating social innovations (Ashoka, 2014).

Combining business and social orientations within the same organizational framework and demonstrating the ability of a business entity to successfully deal with social problems led to a parallel development in the field of finance: *new investment mechanisms* were created with the goal of seeking not only financial returns on their capital but social impact as well, and existing investment firms were transformed to include social impact. This trend started with the Grameen model (Yunus, 1989) turning microcredit into a global tool for poverty alleviation, specifically for rural women (with mixed results, see Bateman, 2014). A further development took place in Latin America (e.g., Americans for Community Co-operation in Other Nations), which introduced a business approach to microcredit, through cost recovery and management as well as individual lending within the group (Berenbach & Guzman, 1999). The newest development created a field of *impact investing*, which is developing a wide variety of innovative tools that provide investors the option to invest in projects in which they can obtain a financial return on their investment while creating a social impact (e.g., *Social Impact Bonds*). Guided by the concept of ESG (Environment, Social, Governance), major investment companies around the world, including BlackRock, the largest asset manager in the world, are moving in

---

[4] For example *L'Arcolaio* social cooperative from Siracusa—promoting the social and working reintegration of prisoners through production of traditional Sicilian sweets; *Mujeres Supervivientes* nonprofit from Sevilla—supporting women experiencing violence and discrimination through soup kitchen, training, and counselling; *Call Yachol* from Israel—company specialized in setting up outsourced call centers staffed mainly by people with disabilities.

[5] For example *Conflict Kitchen* restaurant in Warsaw, Poland—offering food from different parts of the world together with individual stories of employed migrants to help multicultural integration; *Caminos de Osa* in Costa Rica—a training program for rural micro-entrepreneurs geared towards helping them modernize and professionalize their business in sustainable tourism.

the direction of impact investment, and their portfolios include more and more companies that demonstrate commitment to these values (see Salamon, 2016 for a comprehensive discussion of the various tools for impact investment). These developments defy the common practice of investment companies, which see profits as the sole aim of their endeavor.

We argue that these two developments—the introduction of business orientations to the arena of social intervention and the introduction of social considerations to the field of financial investment—are in fact two sides of the same coin and it is not surprising that they develop in a parallel fashion. This is based on the premise that there is a fit between the nature of the organization and the sources of funding it uses. Such a fit existed of course during the height of the Welfare State era, when welfare organizations (in the broad sense) were based on public funding sources. Similarly, when privatization of public services took place with the thriving of the third sector, philanthropy and philanthropic foundations became a leading funding source of the nonprofit organizations.

The new types of hybrid social enterprises have legal limitations in using certain public and/or philanthropic funding sources when they base themselves on commercial activities. Therefore, they need funding sources that are sensitive to their special mission and nature and are willing to take a higher level of risk and accept a lower level of return given the creation of social impact. Thus, it seems that in the postcrisis period we witness an evolution of a new organizational and institutional reality, which is characterized by a mix between the social and the business worlds that in the past were very careful to remain separated. We suggest that this development provides the building blocks of a *new* social and impact economy.[6]

All these new developments can only be understood against the background of a changed outlook on life on our planet by the new, millennial generation. In contrast with the previous "Me generation," this generation is characterized by a different attitude to "personal success," which is no longer their leading value. Care for the planet and for more social equity, which are expressed in their eating patterns, lifestyles, and purchasing choices, are among their major characteristics. Such trends are then transpired to the general public opinion. The abovementioned patterns in the economy and society would not have been possible without this support from such a social dynamic.

Concluding Remarks

With this volume we want to open the debate concerning the *new* forms of social economy that in our view have grown distinctive enough to be perceived as a topic in itself. We link the emergence of these new social economy practices with the

---

[6]A book by the title *The New Social Economy* was published in 1992. It deals with the issue of divisions of labor in households, corporations, and multinational networks (Sawyer & Walker, 1992).

2008 economic crisis that created opportunity structures for new entities to establish themselves in between civil society and market actors. Hybridity being their main trait, they are more flexible and focused on creating targeted solutions and solving ad hoc problems than traditional social economy actors. They often emerge as a response to new societal challenges, like global warming, difficult access to fresh and healthy food produce, or unethical production and employment practices. These new themes can also be linked to generational shift as they represent new lifestyles and values typical for younger cohorts of millennials. These new social entrepreneurs are more open to tackling issues like refugee integration, discrimination, fair trade, ecological awareness, socially responsible lifestyles, co-ownership, or youth empowerment. Some of them are direct response to negative processes related to neoliberal order, allowing for acting out alternative lifestyles and individual choices.

Our major premise is that the 2008 crisis created ripple effect expressed in different forms of collective action, *which stressed the relationship between the economy and society*, linking poverty, inequality, and environmental issues with the unsatisfactory public and philanthropic interventions. As a result of the global market struggles, we observe new forms of engagement, which depart from the traditional cooperative movement or third-sector structures. Due to the crisis disruptive nature, a new opening emerges, spurring the plethora of different activities focused on creating social impact through business activities. Among their main features are hybridity, development of ICT-based activities or business models, individualism reflected in management modes and work arrangements, and its relation to new forms of consumption and needs that did not exist in the "old" social economy.

We also stress the importance of several factors that are in the background of these recent developments—the fast-developing ICT technologies, millennials' lifestyles, and a search for meaning, along with the development of hi-tech and start-up culture and entrepreneurship. As a result, in the context disrupted by the crisis, new forms have developed that are characterized by hybridity and defy previous categorizations (of welfare and business, philanthropy, and investment). The *new* social and impact economy is also characterized by individual (not collective) entrepreneurs and high involvement with ICT tools and is not linked to any overarching ideology.

Generally speaking, we can say that the *new* social and impact economy reflects a deeper societal change that in turn shapes economic behaviors, clients' preferences, and modes of production of goods and services. Democratization and self-organization are important traits of these new entities. We also observe a certain evolution of guiding values of social enterprises—it is not wrong anymore to make money while helping society. Due to globalization, both the markets and the audience have changed and by employing different communication technologies, new social economy actors can reach different and scattered audiences.

The driving values behind practices of both entrepreneurs and investors seem to include structural independence, creating decent employment conditions, investing in quality and design of products, and meaning-making as an important service. Building of flexible management structures makes them yet another niche where noncorporate work styles and business approaches can flourish, presenting an alternative to the economic mainstream.

This results in an emergence of service-oriented rather than production-oriented social economy actors, who could not compete with mass production but can offer added value aligned with individual preferences. The so-called digital revolution was crucial in stimulating some of these services or building new collaborative structures. As Lipparini and Phillips (2018) also point out, social enterprises and impact investment mechanisms seem to be particularly well placed to facilitate the transition towards a hyper-connected society and economy. Their hybrid nature and deep local roots predestine them to develop bridges between the public and private sectors and to foster social and technological innovation.

The following chapters provide an overview of the global new social economy landscape and examine how social enterprises are already using ICT to foster social investment approaches—by increasing the sustainability of existing welfare systems, fostering social and economic inclusion, and investing in lifelong learning and personal development.

It is obviously too early to characterize in detail the phenomenon that we term the *new social and impact economy*. Indeed, in most countries these new organizations are loosely connected to each other; in some countries they are in the process of developing an ecosystem of their own. Also, in countries with a tradition of a social economy and a strong cooperative presence, the tendency is to integrate the recent developments in some ways into existing social economy structures. Still, it seems that we are witnessing the nascence of a new era in economic and social development, which is important to record.

While systematic data on the evolution of the new social and impact economy around the globe cannot currently be obtained, two recent international research projects—the ICSEM project https://www.iap-socent.be/icsem-project/ and the FAB-MOVE project https://fabmove.eu/—gathered data, pertaining both to the history and policy environment of the *new social and impact economy* (without using that term) as well as case studies, which together provide an initial portrait of the forces at play in the evolution of the phenomenon in a particular country studied. Many of the book's contributors participated in one or both of these projects. As to impact investments, several Internet websites are devoted to this field, which is clearly growing.[7]

What can be learned from these studies is that the *new social economy* is obviously developing differentially in different countries. The country chapters focus on the process of evolution of the *new social and impact economy* against the background of that country's social and economic history, its welfare policies (or lack thereof), the existence of an entrepreneurial spirit in the population, political support of the social economy, and other institutional contexts (Kerlin, 2017).

---

[7] See for example: https://thegiin.org/impact-investing/need-to-know; https://www.ifc.org/wps/wcm/connect/8b8a0e92-6a8d-4df5-9db4-c888888b464e/2020-Growing-Impact.pdf?MOD=AJPERES&CVID=naZESt9

Structure of the Book

We begin this collection with Michael Roy's chapter, where he points out that building a new social economy designed to address twenty-first-century challenges requires new methods and approaches, as well as new conversations and alliances. His contribution focuses on the novel idea of "well-being economy" and the role social enterprises may have in maximizing well-being, particularly for vulnerable communities and individuals. This is particularly relevant in the Covid-19 pandemic, which hits the more vulnerable populations everywhere. The author claims that the promise of this new type of economy addresses the needs of everyone and as such have the capability to mediate both current and future crises.

From this inspirational contribution we then move to a series of country chapters describing non-European examples and trends within social economy sector.

The chapter on Argentina authored by Gabriel Berger and Leopoldo Blugerman presents the new social and impact economy as embodied by the new hybrid forms of engagement, creating social value through sustainable business models. The Argentinian model results from involvement of international actors, strengthening of an entrepreneurial culture, as well as new public policies financing start-ups. Moreover, the growth of impact economy could be observed in recent years, leading to the development of private sector support ecosystem, promoting hybrid forms of organizations and financing.

In their analysis of Israeli case, Ronny Manos and Benjamin Gidron recall the emergence and demise of the kibbutz model of social economy and the follow-up neoliberal model of a start-up country. The authors characterize the new social and impact economy by three features: individual rather than collective entrepreneurship, often taking the form of social-tech entrepreneurship (in line with a flourishing high-tech industry), and the focus on solving concrete social or environmental problems instead of pursuing the ideological goals. They also point out the importance of crisis in the development of the new socioeconomic landscapes, predicting that Covid-19 pandemic will be a catalyst for creative solutions. It is their belief that the ideas developed around the former crises will now be a part of the corona-crisis recovery.

The contribution from Indonesia presented by Maria Radyati and Benny Tjahjono reflects on the challenges the development of social economy faces in the non-welfare state context, where private companies are crucial actors. According to their analysis, the new social economy in Indonesia is clearly marked by the digital technology and strong participations of the private sector involved in creating non-financial values in line with Sustainable Development Goals. The highly diverse and vibrant ecosystem of Indonesian social economy is mainly shaped by Corporate Social Responsibility programs, crowdsourcing, crowdfunding, fintech, and impact investing, which aim to build financially sustainable local communities and create impact through innovative investment strategies.

The following chapter by Jorge Sousa describes how the social economy in Canada has changed from the cooperative model to social enterprise model, which reflects the shift from communal towards individualistic orientation informing new social economy actors. With the restructuring of the traditional pillars, the new social and impact economy is emerging in a supportive policy environment defining social enterprises as actors of social innovation. In Canada, the reduction of the welfare state leads towards accepting the dominance of the market-based approaches, changing the face of social economy in the country. However, as the example of Quebec illustrates, market-based and nonmarket-based activities can coexist and complement each other for the benefit of the society.

Moving to the European context, we open with the chapter on France, which has the longest tradition of social economy policies in Europe. In their contribution, Didier Chabanet and Laurence Lemoine point out that in France, the social economy sector is now in a crucial phase of its evolution, which puts the values upon which the social contract is founded under question. They also analyze three sequences of renegotiating the role of social economy creating a new balance of power which today shapes the field of social economy in France.

In Austria, we find a split between a network of new actors and institutions, and the much longer existing work integration social enterprises. Describing these developments, Hanna Schneider and Ruth Simsa refer to a "burst within the social economy," with new institutions entering the scene within the last decade. The number of specialized support institutions has been found to strengthen the new social economy and many new social enterprises evolved, while existing organizations adopted the SE label. Social enterprises have gained importance as institutions that are not dependent on government money, but able to forge networks with profit-oriented enterprises. This means they are incentivized to adopt a management or investment logic and expected to expand their impact in the foreseeable future.

In their chapter on Spain, Millán Díaz-Foncea and Carmen Marcuello take a long perspective on the development of social economy where some of the new forms and types of cooperatives emerge to cover nascent needs. Among factors related to the development of new social economy they enlist different funding instruments promoted by public and private organizations, including ethical banking and social or impact investing. As the authors point out, the developing new social economy is deepening the values and principles of the social and solidarity economy like democracy, solidarity, cooperation, and mutual support.

In the following contribution, Mara Benadusi et al. provide an overview of an evolving field of social economy in Italy, defined by the tension between traditional cooperatives and work integration social enterprises and the social start-ups, where innovation is a strategic asset, while social impact remains peripherical. However, between these extremes, several examples of hybrid organizations can be observed in Italy, seeking to minimize environmental impact, operating in the space between the WISE and proto-social entrepreneurship models. For these successful cases, the crisis, according to Benadusi, can be an occasion to better identify market opportunities and develop a more aware business and revenue model.

The analysis of the Polish case, presented by Anna Domaradzka, addresses the validity of the postcrisis social economy concept, analyzing the new directions within the national field. The recent changes in forms of activity (renewal of cooperative ideas with a start-up twist) as well as modes of financing (including crowdfunding or impact investment) are slowly changing the local ecosystem.

However, the evolution of social and impact economy in Poland remains primarily a response to specific threats and negative processes that have been going on for centuries. Despite the growing popularity of the renewed cooperative movement, restrictions in access to financing constitute one of the basic barriers to the development of new social and impact economy. While mixed with risk aversion, the distrust towards business as well as authorities also severely blocks the potential to innovate, develop, and scale up the successful new initiatives.

In the Swedish chapter, Thomas Persson points out the difficulties of defining the new social and impact economy in the context of a Swedish melting pot of numerous organizations emphasizing social values. However, he points out the existence of new forms of organizing activities and new types of collaboration and cooperation within the social economy and across economies. In the case of Sweden, this has less to do with the financial crises and more with finding new means to enable organizations to achieve their goals. What is new in social economy field is cyberorganizing and switching identity, with social media becoming a platform to share knowledge and experience, but also to find inspiration and building bridges between sectors.

The final contribution in the volume discusses the roles and strategies of international social economy organizations, shaping the context of the new social economy. The authors, Ignacio Bretos, Anjel Errasti, and Aurélie Soetens, show that international expansion has become a key trend in the evolution of the social economy sector. Organizations that operate across borders play a key role in addressing global environmental and social issues, such as poverty, health and living conditions, social and labor market exclusion, and climate change. As the authors show, some high-profile SEOs operating on a global scale engage in communitarian purposes, social values, and cooperative practices. They also point out their adaptation since the Covid-19 pandemic and their modes of interventions on the international level. By deploying hybrid strategies these organizations combine social welfare and market logics in their international expansion and seem to seek both scaling of social impact and enhancing of financial performance.

References

Ashoka (2014). Social innovation mapping: Social entrepreneurs changing lives through ICT. Retrieved from https://www.ashoka.org/files/ICT-Based-Social-Impact_09-2014-report.pdf

Bateman, M. (2014). The rise and fall of Muhammad Yunus and the microcredit model. *International Development Studies Working Paper* #001.

Berenbach, S. & Guzman, D. (1999). Are solidarity groups successful in poverty outreach? Accion International.

Bidet, E. (2010). Social economy. In H. Anheier & S. Toepler (Eds.), *International encyclopedia of civil society*. New York: Springer.

Borzaga, C., & Defourny, J. (2001). *The emergence of social enterprise* (Routledge studies in the management of voluntary and nonprofit organizations) (Vol. 4). London: Routledge.

Chaves-Avila, R., & Monzon-Campos, J. L. (2007). *The Social Economy in the European Union*, CIRIEC, The European Economic and Social Committee (EESC).

Defourny, J., & Nyssens, M. (2014). The EMES approach of social enterprise in comparative perspective. In Defouny, J, Hulgard, L. & Pestoff, V. (eds.) *Social Enterprise and the Third Sector: Changing European Landscapes in a Comparative Perspective*, Routledge.

Della Porta, D. (2015). *Social movements in times of austerity: Bringing capitalism Back into protest analysis*. Cambridge: Polity Press.

Dodson, C. (2018). Cooperatives and socialism, Common Ground Newsletter.

Dolgin, A. (2012). *Manifesto of the New Economy*, Springer.

Domaradzka, A., & Żbikowska, A. (2017). *Dancing with the state or the market? Social enterprises relation to other sectors in international perspective*. Report for "Fab Move" For a Better Tomorrow: Social Enterprises on the Move.

European Commission (2014). A map of social enterprises and their eco-systems in Europe.

Fisac-Garcia, R., Acevedo-Ruiz, M., Moreno, A., & Kreiner, T. (2013). The role of ICT in scaling up the impact of social enterprises. *Journal of Management for Global Sustainability, 1*(2), 83–105.

Fligstein, N., & McAdam, D. (2012). *A theory of fields*. New York: Oxford University Press.

Frączkiewicz-Wronka, A., & Wronka-Pośpiech, M. (2014). The use of ICT for achieving the objectives of the business model: Social enterprise perspective. *Polish Journal of Management Studies, 10*(2), 33–42.

Kerlin, J. (2017). Shaping social enterprise: Understanding institutional context and influence, Emerald.

Laville, J. L., Levecque, B. & Mendell, M. (2008). The social economy: Diverse approaches and practices in Europe and Canada.

Laville, J. L., Young, D., & Eynaud, P. (eds.) (2015). *Civil society, the third sector and social enterprise*. Routledge.

Lenin, V. I. (1910). *The question of co-operative societies*. Copenhagen: The International Socialist Congress.

Lipparini, F. & Phillips, J. (2018). The role of ICT-enabled social enterprise for promoting social investment, PlusValue.

Moulaert, F., & Ailenei, O. (2005). Social economy, third sector and solidarity relations: A conceptual synthesis from history to present. *Urban Studies, 42*(11), 2037–2053.

Myers, J. (2009). *In Search of... Exploration of the boundaries, scope and definitions of the social economy*, discussion paper, Halifax, Social Economy and Sustainability Research Network, Saint Vincent University.

Piketty, T. (2020). *Capital and ideology*. Cambridge: Harvard University Press.

Restakis, J. (2006). Defining the social economy - The BC context, British Columbia Co-operative Association.

Rogers, S. (2011). Occupy protests mapped around the world. *The Guardian*, Oct. 18.

Saez, E., & Zucman, G. (2019). *The triumph of injustice: How the rich dodge taxes and how to make them pay*. New York: Norton.

Salamon, L. M. (Ed.). (2016). *New frontiers of philanthropy*. New York: Oxford University Press.

Sawyer, A., & Walker, R. (1992). *The new social economy: Reworking the division of labor*. New York: Wiley.

Stoller, M. (2020). *Goliath*. New York: Simon & Schuster.

Thomas, A. (2004). The rise of social cooperatives in Italy. *VOLUNTAS: International Journal of Voluntary and Nonprofit Organizations, 15*(3), 243–263.

Tremblay, C. (2009). Advancing the social economy for socio-economic development: International perspectives, Canadian Social Economy Research Partnerships.

Yunus, M. (1989). Grameen bank: Organization and operation. In Levitsky, J. (ed.) *Microenterprises in developing countries*. London: Intermediate Technology Publications.

Chapter 2
The Evolution of the Social and Impact Economy in Argentina

Gabriel Berger and Leopoldo Blugerman

Introduction

This chapter describes the evolution of social and impact economy organizations and the emergence of new social economy and impact enterprises in Argentina and analyzes its features and drivers. Its past dynamics and prospective derive from disparate tensions in the economic and political dimensions (whether national, regional, and international). Specifically, it is possible to say that the new social and impact economy (henceforth NS&IE) in Argentina is the result of both the evolution of local social purpose organizations as a response to local economic, social, and political changes and the influence of international networks operating in the region. Understanding the development of both the social economy (SE) and the NS&IE in the context of an emerging economy with a significant international presence shed some light on how local and global factors contribute to the consolidation of the innovative institutional actor. The research presented in this chapter is based on a literature review and on secondary analysis of documents produced by organizational actors engaged in these processes.

To introduce the context of this chapter it is useful to have some basic indicators in mind. Argentina is a federal presidential republic in the southern cone of South America and is divided into 23 provinces and 1 autonomous city, Buenos Aires, which is its capital. In its 2,780,000 square kilometers, in 2019 it had an estimated population of 44.7 million people, and approximately one-third of its population lived in Buenos Aires metropolitan area. A Spanish colony in the beginning of the

G. Berger (✉)
School of Business, Universidad de San Andrés, Buenos Aires, Argentina
e-mail: gabrielberger@udesa.edu.ar

L. Blugerman
Institute of Industry (IDEI), Universidad Nacional de General Sarmiento,
Buenos Aires, Argentina

© Springer Nature Switzerland AG 2021   19
B. Gidron, A. Domaradzka (eds.), *The New Social and Impact Economy*,
Nonprofit and Civil Society Studies, https://doi.org/10.1007/978-3-030-68295-8_2

nineteenth century, it is a Spanish-speaking country, mostly catholic but with a fast-growing evangelical protestant sector. Migration came especially from European countries (until the post WWII period) and from other Latin American nations (in the last decades). Its population life expectancy reaches at 77.5 years. As the World Bank states "Urban poverty in Argentina remains high and reaches 35.4% of population, while poverty in children rises to 52.6%. To deal with this situation, the country has prioritized social spending through various programs, including the Universal Child Allowance, a cash transfer program that reaches approximately four million children and adolescents up to age 18, 9.3% of the population."[1]

According to the World Bank, with a gross domestic product (GDP) of approximately US$470 billion as of 2019, Argentina is the third largest economy in Latin America. Argentina has vast natural resources in energy and agriculture, is endowed by all accounts with extraordinary fertile lands and gas and lithium reserves, and has great potential for renewable energy. In addition, Argentina has significant opportunities in some manufacturing subsectors, and innovative services in high-tech industries. However, the historical volatility of its economy and the accumulation of institutional obstacles have negatively affected the country's development. By the end of 2019, Argentina was confronting a precarious economic situation. Argentinian currency exchange rate significantly fell after primary elections in August, annual inflation was over 50%, and GDP contracted 2.5% in 2018 and another 2.5% in the first half of 2019, and amidst a financial crisis,[2] Argentina became the recipient of the largest IMF loan in its history.[3]

Local social economy (hereinafter SE) organizations, mostly co-ops and mutual, but also some civil associations and foundations, could be characterized as value driven, based on the ideas of solidarity, democratic participation, collective effort, and alternative economic models. Starting in the last decade of the twentieth century the landscape of the sector began to change. After a severe national crisis during the 2001–2002 period the scene started to change and newer SE ventures emerged addressing socioeconomic problems (workers recovered factories, barter clubs, microcredit funds, and new grassroots organizations promoting income generation for their members). In parallel, international organizations began the promotion of local social entrepreneurship with a focus on financial sustainability using commercial and industrial activities. Public policies in the 2003–2015 period encouraged the creation of new SE organizations in the form of worker co-ops that engaged in basic local public works and other forms of income generation activities, which received the name of popular economy organizations. Between 2015 and 2019, when a new political party changed the direction of the federal administration, a different stream of public policies and programs started to emerge, promoting the development of NS&IE and the social enterprise ecosystem. Lastly, since December

---

[1] https://www.worldbank.org/en/country/argentina/overview. Accessed 22 Nov 2019.

[2] https://www.wsj.com/articles/why-argentina-faces-an-economic-crisis-again-11569422388. Accessed 22 Nov 2019.

[3] https://www.theguardian.com/world/2018/sep/26/argentina-imf-biggest-loan. Accessed 22 Nov 2019.

2019, the federal administration returned to the political party that ran the country in the 2003–2015 period, and thus the road ahead on the next policies regarding the sector remains uncertain.

The chapter begins with a description of how the concept of SE has been understood in Argentina. It continues with a discussion of how SE emerged and evolved in the national context, in relation to the social welfare system and political trends in the country. Next, the chapter analyzes the impact of the severe 2001–2002 economic, social, and political crisis on the SE sector and the influence of public policies during the 2003–2015 period. The chapter later continues with a discussion of how the NS&IE developed in Argentina, its driving forces and the role of different actors within the emerging ecosystem. In the last section, the chapter explains the legal framework that regulates both SE and NS&IE organizations. Finally, the chapter presents its conclusions on the challenges confronting the new social economy in Argentina.

The Concept of SE in Argentina

The Latin American context in general and the Argentinian in particular exhibit some particular features (Berger & Blugerman in Marquez, Reficco, & Berger, 2010, Kerlin, 2010, Roitter, 2007, Vuotto, 2011). The evolution of the local welfare system, although one of the most developed in Latin America, did not take the level of capillarity that was a common trait in the most advanced European areas analyzed in this volume. In particular, the political instability, recurrent military coups, and a restrictive democracy negatively affected the development of SE organizations.

Therefore, after the transition to democracy in 1983 the local debates around the social economy concept were (and still are) somewhat different than the ones in Europe. In this sense, García (2010) highlights that the academic debates in the field appeared just in the late 1980s, even though local organizations reflecting SE principles—mostly co-ops and mutual associations—appeared well before that. The Argentine academic thought about SE mostly conceives the economy as a domain that must be oriented by ethic, environmental, political, and social principles and not just by the pursuit of profits (Coraggio, 2007). Thus, the fundamental focus of the academic debates around SE in this country centered on a vigorous criticism of the capitalist system. In this critical view, markets governed by mere maximizing principles expelled many out of the formal economy and therefore SE field and SE organizations were considered a response to the dominant discourse about how the economy should be organized. Furthermore, due to the ideological dynamics, discussions were framed against prevailing neoliberal policies (Abramovich et al., 2003; Marzi & Vázquez, 2009).

Thus, overall, in Argentina, the SE concept has multiple meanings (García, 2010), involving social and solidarity economy actors with disparate legal figures. This comes as no surprise since, as expressed in the introduction of this volume, the

SE concept is a changing *social construct* related to disparate social and political realities. In the same vein, the local academic debates also show a tension between considering the SE as an approach to the socioeconomic dimension of society and as a *sector* of organizations with particular common traits.

In this sense, according to Pastore (2010), when reviewing different local authors and experiences on the topic, in addition to the historic forms of SE organizations, new kind of social organizations emerged in the late 1990s and in the first decade of the century under the concept of social and solidarity economy. This comprehensive term encompassing organizations guided under the broad ideals of solidarity and participation ended up including both the experiences of co-ops and mutual associations (the "traditional" SE in the Argentinian legal setting), and what at those times were the newer organizational forms. Thus, in Argentina the more established SE and other newer forms of the SE have been coexisting since the late 1990s.

As for the SE, whether the sector is called social economy (Coraggio in Di Stéfano, Sábato, Romero, & Moreno, 2002) or social and solidarity economy (Abramovich & Vázquez, 2007) the actors of the local SE have the organizational forms of cooperatives, mutual associations, foundations, and associations with an inclusive socio-productive purpose. According to these authors, the Argentinian SE is composed of a group of organizations neither in the public nor in the private sector economy, and oriented towards the following principles:

- Primacy of organizational social purpose over profits.
- Voluntary and open membership.
- Democratic control by its members.
- Conjunction of the interests of the members and the general interest.
- Defense and application of the principles of solidarity and responsibility.
- Management autonomy and independence from public authorities.
- Allocation of the majority of surplus to the achievement of goals related to social development and inclusion, the improvement of services to members, and the general interest.

In sum, analysis of the SE concept reflected how the actors in the local arena remained highly inspired by values of solidarity, social support, and collective effort and, to some extent, it confronted with the traditional capitalist logic of profit maximizing (Coraggio, 2007). However, in the social realm, especially as the 2010s decade evolved, these solidarity and social economy values alongside with the cooperative ones started to coexist with more pro-market values and organizational practices represented in several—and more hybrid—organizational forms, more akin to what is referred to as the NS&IE. NS&IE organizations started to emerge in the 2010s due to a large extent to the influence of international organizations promoting social entrepreneurship, social innovation, and impact investment in the country. As it can be seen, both the evolution of the SE and the emergence of the NS&IE seemed to be rooted on different dynamics and disparate drivers than in other countries, and tensions between older and newer forms of what constitutes the social arena, especially regarding values, meanings, and organizational practices and forms, still remain.

The Emergence and Evolution of SE in Argentina

The Argentinian Social Welfare System

In Argentina, the social welfare system underwent several phases that reveal the complex relationships between government and private and social actors amidst political, social, and economic changes of varying magnitudes.

Argentina's national state consolidated in the period 1860–1880. Then, a plural, non-planned social service scheme emerged (Arce, 2013), with the central government (re)acting as planner and organizer only when faced with some specific healthcare crises, as it was the case of yellow fever epidemics that affected the country between 1850s and 1870s. A notable exception was the field of education: public schools expanded across the country since the 1860s as a result of the central administration public policy focused on building the nation-state. Only around 1946, when the *Peronist* party rose to power, some centralized state planning became apparent (Arce, 2013) in these areas, representing the local adaptation to the welfare state. Thus, the federal government started to have a greater presence as a healthcare service provider and planner; charity was cast aside, and some workers' mutual organizations, organized per industry, and union social service providers (*Obras Sociales* in the local context) emerged to offer healthcare, tourism, sports, and housing.

A military *coup d'état* brought an end to the *Peronist* government in 1955. Since then, until 1983, the country witnessed political instability. This affected the social realm (with lapses of restricted democracy and recurrent military coups and army-controlled governments). In this context, social services began to grow somewhat decentralized, especially in the healthcare sector. At the same time, union social service providers expanded and became mandatory for employees, with compulsory contributions from workers' wages established by law. In the early 1970s, the funding system for active retired workers' healthcare became universal, financed with separate mandatory contributions from registered workers' salaries and employees' contributions (the [National] Program of Integral Medical Assistance, PAMI, in 1971). In the mid-1970s as the latest military coup unfolded, the public sector began a withdrawal process from direct social service delivery, and private players and civil society organizations became more active.

The return to democracy in 1983 brought a change in state's intervention, as it sought to play an active role in social policies. However, with inflation soaring and Argentina's sovereign debt straining national accounts, these attempts proved mostly unfruitful.

Nevertheless, the landscape did not change much for SE organizations until the next decade, when the local translation of international and regional processes—globalization and the neoliberal economic policies emerging from what was called *Washington Consensus* (Williamson, 2009)—started to change the shape and the dynamics of the local SE. In this vein, with the rapid withdrawal of the public sector from the social and economic realms, SE organizations had to respond to the consequences of these processes and cover the service gaps created. In order to face these opportunities, they had to professionalize their operations and pay more attention to achieving economic sustainability as well. Complementarily, the private sector gained a new momentum in social areas, with public reform and privatization processes that encompassed, for example, social security contributions (capitalization system known as *AFJP*) and work hazard coverage (private labor insurance providers called *ARTs*). At the same time, a new decentralization dynamic from the federal government to province administrations began in social areas, such as healthcare and education.

That was the policy context when a severe local crisis emerged in 2001–2002, and it changed the SE landscape, as it will be shown below.

A Brief History of SE in Argentina

The first local social charitable organizations were the result of the Spanish colonial rule (strongly related to the Catholic Church) and the donations and involvement of wealthier families (Di Stéfano et al., 2002). After the national independence in 1816, the consolidation of the nation-state took several generations of civil internal struggles and wars (until mid-nineteenth century). Soon after this process concluded, the country started to attract European immigration, mainly from the south (Italy and Spain) but also from Eastern European countries—and to a lesser extent, from Northern Europe, and the Middle East.

Between the end of the nineteenth century and the first part of the twentieth century, the immigrant groups were the driving forces in the emerging social sector (Plotinsky, 2015). As large groups of European immigrants settled in Argentina, a number of mutual organizations emerged to provide several kinds of services (healthcare, financial support, culture, etc.) to the members of their respective communities. Their associations had an impact in the economic domain (e.g., work cooperatives in the dairy industry), the educational and health realms (e.g., schools and hospitals created by the country of origin), and the political levels (e.g., the anarchist and socialist ideas brought by Jewish migrants coming from Eastern Europe, and by republicans coming from Spain).

In this evolution, it is worth mentioning the path of mutual and co-op organizations. To begin with, mutual associations: the first organization of this kind was founded in 1854 by French émigrés, called *Union et Secours Mutuels* [Union and Mutual Help] (Otero, 2009). Other immigrant groups developed strong organizational networks based on solidarity through mutual associations: for example, the Italians created, among many others, *Unione e Benevolenza*[4] [Union and Benevolence], still active nationally; Spanish migrants created *Asociación Española*

---

[4] https://www.buenosaires.gob.ar/areas/cultura/cpphc/sitios/detalle.php?id=29. Accessed 20 Nov 2019.

de Socorros Mutuos [Spanish Association of Mutual Help] among many hundred entities. Another example worth to mention is the *Asociación Mutual Israelita Argentina* (AMIA), founded in 1894[5] in Buenos Aires with the goal of promoting the welfare and development of the Argentine Jewish community.[6] As of 1914 there were 1200 mutual help societies placing themselves as an important provider of welfare services in the local arena, with more than half million associates, 38% from Italian associations, 20% from Spanish, and 7% from French institutions. More than half a century later, in 1977, 13% of the national population were associates of mutual associations (reaching 35–40% in Buenos Aires and Santa Fe provinces) according to Di Stéfano et al. (2002, 258). As of 2020 there were 3523 active and registered mutual associations[7] with more than ten million associates.[8]

As for co-ops, they were one of the main and oldest players in the Argentinian SE sector. The first Argentinian cooperatives were born on rural landscapes, with the first one being founded in Paraná (Entre Rios province) in 1857. Other examples of this kind were an apiarian co-op founded by French émigrés in 1865 (also in Entre Rios) and a Swiss-German émigré settlers' co-op in Esperanza (Santa Fe province) in 1878 (Plotinsky, 2015).

Complementarily, one of the hallmarks among the co-op local institutions was *El Hogar Obrero* [The Worker's Home], founded in 1905, with the purpose of contributing to the solution of housing problems of workers. Later on, it also developed credit services, the widely known supermarket chain (over 300 branches), and other services; however, in the 1990s it experienced serious financial problems when the country confronted a hyperinflation period that led to a bankruptcy process and later to a remaining residual activity.[9] Additionally, the co-op movement gained impact on the public utilities field, especially in rural areas. Thus, as a result, in 1939 the Argentine Federation of Cooperatives of Electricity and Other Public Services Ltd. was born,[10] a federation that brings together more than 240 public service cooperatives in 15 provinces, exercising its representation in defense of the principles and cooperative action.

As Plotinsky (2015, 164) mentions, "Very early, agrarian cooperativism started a process of cooperative integration that led it to create federations and/or second-degree cooperatives," starting in 1913. According to the same author, between 1930 and the early 1950s the rural co-op sector kept on growing, especially in the geographic and economic center of the country (Buenos Aires, Santa Fe, and Córdoba provinces) and in the north-east. An example of that was SanCor, a dairy co-op

---

[5] https://www.amia.org.ar/historia/. Accessed 20 Nov 2019.

[6] Suffering a terrorist attack in 1994 is still one of the main players amidst the mutual local associations.

[7] https://vpo3.inaes.gob.ar/Entidades/BuscarEntidades. Accessed 15 Apr 2020.

[8] https://ansol.com.ar/2019/06/13/el-inaes-presento-los-datos-nacionales-actualizados-de-mutuales-y-cooperativas/. Accessed 13 Nov 2019.

[9] https://www.clarin.com/economia/evitan-quiebra-hogar-obrero_0_rkDvqkJLnl.html.   Accessed 20 Nov 2019.

[10] https://face.coop/index.php/institucional/acerca-de. Accessed 22 Nov 2019.

founded in 1938 in Santa Fe: it was one of the leading dairy producers and exporters until it was finally sold in 2019.[11] Since 1956 on, the rural co-ops were mainly represented by CONINAGRO (Di Stéfano et al., 2002, 359).

Complementarily, in 1950 the Argentine Federation of Loan Cooperatives was born, reaching 292 co-ops in the 1960s (later on, with changes in the regulation of financial institutions, the sector shrunk). Additionally, in 1986 the Fund for Cooperatives' Education and Promotion was created.[12]

Some other co-ops, mainly in the agroindustry sector, insurance, and financial services, both in metropolitan and rural zones, became major players in their respective sectors. For example, Group San Cristobal was one of the most important actors in the insurance field, also founded in Santa Fe in 1939[13] (eight in the ranking of insurance companies in 2018). Last, Credicoop Bank was founded in 1979 when several co-op credit funds were pressured to merge[14] as they were suffering the financial policies of the military government, which tried to eliminate credit funds organized as co-ops but allowed them to convert into cooperative banks under banking regulations (in 2019 Credicoop Bank was in the eighth place of local banks by deposits[15]). We will return to the co-op sector below.

Finally, some SE organizations registered using other legal forms of nonprofit organizations: civil associations and foundations; however it is hard to assess their scale and scope as previous studies did not distinguish SE organizations within the wider nonprofit sector. However, it is worth to keep in mind one of the conclusions of the Nonprofit Sector Comparative Study when referring to the civil society sector or the nonprofit sector in Argentina: "The civil society sector in Latin America is slightly larger than the developing countries average, though this is largely due to the inclusion of Argentina, which has a civil society sector on a parity with that in many Western European countries" (Salamon, Sokolowski, & List, 2003, 50).

The 2001–2002 Crisis and Its Impact on the SE

Between 2001 and 2002, after a decade of neoliberal policies ending in high levels of poverty, unemployment, and social exclusion, Argentina suffered one of its worst economic depressions and social turmoil. A deep social, economic, and political crisis exploded. In this period, the inflation rate increased reaching 40% and the GDP per capita fell almost 20%. In 2002 the unemployment rate peaked at 20%,

---

[11] https://www.lanacion.com.ar/economia/campo/se-firmo-traspaso-plantas-lacteas-marcas-sancor-nid2219312. Accessed 30 Oct 2019.

[12] Law N° 23.427. http://servicios.infoleg.gob.ar/infolegInternet/anexos/20000-24999/22268/texact.htm. Accessed 30 Oct 2019.

[13] https://www.sancristobal.com.ar/institucional/nosotros/. Accessed 30 Oct 2019.

[14] https://www.bancocredicoop.coop/nuestrobanco/institucional/mision. Accessed 30 Oct 2019.

[15] https://www.archicoop.org.ar/el-cooperativismo-de-credito-en-la-argentina. Accessed 31 Oct 2019.

about a quarter of the population lived with less than US$2 a day, the average income fell more than 20%, and the Gini index soared (Doyran, 2015, 164). Finally, the poverty rate increased from 38.8% of households in October 1999 to 65.5% in October 2002.[16] Moreover, early in 2002 Argentina defaulted on its foreign debt, while the exchange rate jumped almost 400%. Not surprisingly, this desperate socioeconomic scene, in turn, led to institutional instability (five presidents between the last days of 2001 and the beginning of 2002), and a serious political deadlock, which created virulent manifestations, with a civic claim for a complete political renovation—"all politicians must leave the scene" was the popular cry.

This turbulent local landscape led to the emergence of a slightly diverse type of SE: different than the traditional ones (co-ops, mutual associations), but still far from the NS&IE logic. They encompassed a wide landscape of new organizational forms created to provide assistance and to promote self-help among lower income groups (Berger & Blugerman in Marquez et al., 2010), among them microcredit initiatives, grassroots organizations developing income-generating projects, and *empresas recuperadas* [recovered enterprises].[17] The latter were mostly local SMEs abandoned overnight by the owners usually after a severe financial crisis, taken over by their workers who transform them into workers' co-ops.[18]

Other type of organizations created in this period were *clubs del trueque*, or barter clubs (Pearson, 2003), which appeared in 1995 and grew to operate as a network.[19] Additionally, other low-income groups developed ventures such as urban waste recyclers' co-ops (Berger & Blugerman, 2006), consumer co-ops such as Consol,[20] and solidarity market fairs (Abramovich & Vazquez 2007). Corporations started to develop—or took part in—several bottom-of-the-pyramid initiatives in this period (Marquez et al., 2010) that in many cases worked together with these new SE organizations.

What Pastore (2010) referred to as traditional and "new" forms of SE (by late 1990s and the following decade) responded to the Argentinian reality in political, economic, social, and institutional terms. These low-income social ventures expressed responses from different actors with the mere intention of survival to the pressures of a context of poverty increase. Therefore, as Roitter (2007, 1) mentioned:

---

[16] https://www.cippec.org/wp-content/uploads/2019/07/El-desafio-de-la-pobreza-en-Argentina. pdf. Accessed 10 Nov 2019.

[17] A wide array of academic works dealt with in this period, among them Atzeni & Vieta, 2013, Fajn & Rebón, 2005, Fields, 2008, Marzi & Vázquez, 2009, Palomino, 2003, Pastore, 2010, and Rebón & Salgado, 2009. In addition to the latter, the documentary La Toma [The Take] can be mentioned, written and produced by Naomi Klein. It narrates the story of national workers who demand control of the closed industrial plants where they once worked, to turn them into worker cooperatives. The main ideas of these workers are summoned up in phrases such as "Fire the boss" and "Occupy, resist, produce." See https://www.imdb.com/title/tt0426596/. Accessed 30 Oct 2019.

[18] Around 300 of these organizations, with more than 13,000 workers overall. Among them Bauen Hotel, La Casona Restaurant, and Chilavert Press (http://www.elsalmoncontracorriente.es/?Que-se-vaya-el-patron-3-ejemplos. Accessed 10 Nov 2019.

[19] http://www.appropriate-economics.org/latin/argentina/quees.htm. Accessed 10 Nov 2019.

[20] https://tercersector.org.ar/otro-modelo-es-posible/. Accessed 21 Apr 2020.

... due to a relatively high capacity for self-organization and the survival of productive skills in important segments of its population, social strategies that emerged with more force in this period were autonomous ventures driven from the popular economy, which generated economic activities with the possibility of being self-sustaining, among which we place social enterprises.

This development of new forms of social and solidarity economy organizations (referred to as popular economy by some authors and community activists) received attention in the academic circles as well (Coraggio, 2018). Institutions such as Universidad Nacional de General Sarmiento (UNGS)[21] and Universidad Nacional de Quilmes (UNQ)[22] started to promote between the 1990s and the 2000s the study of (and the articulation with) the social and solidarity organizations. As an example of this work, but created more recently, UNQ promoted a Latin American Meeting of Social Cooperation and Solidarity Economy alongside with a National Meeting of Health Care Social Enterprises,[23] or the Project CREES (Building Entrepreneurial Networks in Social Economy), which aims to support the promotion of SE ventures.[24]

Some of these actors, such as the recovered factories and the barter clubs, lost relevance later on due to the improved economic conditions and new social policies enacted in the Kirchner era (2003–2015). In 2003, the country returned to institutional normalcy, and the economic activity reactivated. In this context, the Kirchner and Fernández de Kirchner's administrations (one presidential mandate the former, and two mandates the latter) had an important focus in shaping the dynamics of the SE, with a strong promotion of workers' cooperatives with low-skilled unemployed people to carry out basic public works projects. Complementarily, the public policies supporting organizations with a more traditional SE view were mainly channeled through another public assistance program: *Plan Manos a la Obra* [Hands to Work public program], addressing in 2007 up to 535,000 people on 56,000 projects supported by the Secretary of Social Policies and Human Development within the Ministry of Social Development.[25]

The historical evolution of the co-ops in Argentina (whether in their traditional forms or as more recent ones such as worker co-ops' *empresas recuperadas*, urban recyclers' co-ops) showed disparate trends (Acosta, Levín, & Verbeke, 2013). As Table 2.1 indicates, until 1998 the public works co-ops accounted up to a third of the total (1046 out of 3031), and as it was mentioned earlier is was just in the end of the 1990s the worker co-ops became the largest sector within this organizational population. In 2013, the focus of registered co-ops was worker related, followed by housing, agricultural, public works, and service provision.

[21] https://www.ungs.edu.ar/. Accessed 11 Oct 2019.

[22] http://www.unq.edu.ar/. Accessed 11 Oct 2019.

[23] http://encuentrocooperacionsocial.observatorioess.org.ar/acerca-de/. Accessed 31 Oct 2019.

[24] http://www.unq.edu.ar/proyectos-programas/84-crees%2D%2D-cooperaci%C3%B3n-social-y-salud.php. Accessed 17 Apr 2020.

[25] https://www.pagina12.com.ar/diario/suplementos/cash/17-2835-2007-02-11.html. Accessed 10 Oct 2019.

Table 2.1 Active co-ops by type and period of matriculation

Type	1927–1998	1999–2004	2005–2009	2010–2012	2014
Agricultural	548	272	550	125	1297
Consumer	37	9	24	72	195
Credit	66	90	105	37	290
Service provision	218	228	478	133	1582
Insurances	17	0	0	0	19
Public works	1046	52	67	15	1167
Workers	579	2538	7473	4487	22,516
Housing	520	348	760	108	1787
Total	3031	3537	9457	4977	28,853

Data extracted from Acosta et al. (2013) for the period 1927–2012, while for 2014 it was extracted from https://www.vocesenelfenix.com/sites/default/files/pdf/46_5_fenix38%20baja.pdf. Accessed 15 Apr 2020

According to official statistics,[26] between 2001 and 2014 the number of registered co-ops in the country rose from 16,059 up to 28,853 (with 78% of them being workers' co-ops in 2014 versus 42% in 2001). In 2014, almost 8000 workers' co-ops were linked to one of the key public social programs, *Argentina Trabaja* [Argentina Works] which operated with organizations representing the unemployed and poor. However, as of April 2020 there were just 10,484 co-ops included in the public open-access database of the federal control agency.[27]

Infrastructural or Umbrella Organizations for SE

Across the Argentinian SE landscape there are several organizations claiming representation of different subsectors. The more representative umbrella organization in the local SE setting is *Cooperar* (Argentinian Cooperative Confederation),[28] a third-level entity founded in 1962 and formed by federations of co-ops, gathered around 70 entities which represent nearly 5000 co-ops. The *Instituto Movilizador de Fondos Cooperativos* (IMFC),[29] an entity founded in 1958, which in 2019 gathered 158 co-ops is another relevant umbrella SE organization. The founding objectives of IMFC were to spread the principles and values of cooperation, to represent its associated cooperatives before the public authorities, to promote the creation of cooperatives, and to mobilize through a solidarity network the idle funds of cooperative credit funds, from some regions of the country to others, according to the seasonal

---

[26] https://www.vocesenelfenix.com/sites/default/files/pdf/46_5_fenix38%20baja.pdf. Accessed 15 Apr 2020.

[27] https://vpo3.inaes.gob.ar/Entidades/BuscarEntidades. Accessed 15 Apr 2020.

[28] https://rutacoop.com.ar/cooperativas/cooperar-confederacia-sup3-n-cooperativa-de-la-repa-ordm-blica-argentina-.html/1222. Accessed 31 Oct 2019.

[29] http://www.imfc.coop/modules/home/. Accessed 11 Oct 2019.

requirements. Finally, as previously mentioned, the *Federación Argentina de Cooperativas de Electricidad y otros Servicios Públicos* (FACE) is another umbrella organization in the Argentinian SE field.

As for the Argentinian mutual associations, its umbrella organization is the *Confederación Argentina de Mutuales* (CAM).[30] This organization gathers 39 federations that bring together more than 3000 mutual associations. CAM work is based on the contribution of its associates and provides expert advice, assistance, and training in legal, administrative, and financial matters to its members.

Complementarily, in 2011 PROFAESS (Alternative Finance for the Social and Solidarity Economy Promotion[31]) emerged as an organization dealing with SE issues. Founded by AVINA Foundation,[32] *La Base* and *Nuestras Huellas* Foundations, and other key professionals in the Argentinian SE field, PROFAESS worked on the identification, promotion, and design of alternative financing models for projects governed by the principles of the social and solidarity economy. However, after 4 years of operations (and the finalization of its initial funding obtained) it showed no further activities.

Two other networks in the SE arena are worth mentioning. First, Red *Encuentro de Entidades No Gubernamentales para el Desarrollo* [Meeting of Development NGOs Network] was founded in 1977, with the purpose of providing training, promoting exchanges and cooperation, and acting in public policy issues such as solidarity economy, new financial architecture, housing, and habitat..[33] Later, in 2004, RADIM (the Argentinian Network of Microcredit Institutions)[34] was created. Formalized in 2007, its mission is to enable the articulation of institutions of the microfinance sector, their strengthening, and their active participation in policy proposals to the state and to civil society.

Finally, two umbrella organizations in the CSO realm include some SE organizations among their membership. These are the *Red Argentina de Cooperación Internacional* (RACI) and *Foro del Sector Social*. RACI[35] is a federation of 150 CSOs. Created in 2004, RACI aims to strengthen the social sector by building connections between the Argentinian CSO sector and the local and international actors that make social investment in development projects and initiatives in Argentina. Finally, the *Foro del Sector Social*,[36] a Federation of Civil Associations and Foundations, was launched in 1994 (and formally established in 1996), whose purpose is to articulate, integrate, and enhance the actions of its nonprofit members.

In sum, the local SE sector was born as a creature of both solidarity and organizing efforts of migrant currents, and initiatives in different production and service

---

[30] https://camargentina.org.ar/. Accessed 11 Oct 2019.

[31] http://profaess.com.ar/. Accessed 11 Oct 2019.

[32] https://www.avina.net/. Accessed 22 Nov 2019.

[33] https://www.facebook.com/encuentrodeongs/. Accessed 31 Oct 2019.

[34] http://www.reddemicrocredito.org/. Accessed 31 Oct 2019.

[35] https://raci.org.ar/. Accessed 13 Nov 2019.

[36] https://www.forodelsectorsocial.org.ar/. Accessed 13 Nov 2019.

sectors that demanded cooperation to be viable, in a context of a weak presence of the state in the social realm. With the emergence of the *Peronism*, the federal government gained more social welfare presence, but later on the trend was somewhat erratic, since in several periods afterwards the public sphere was more or less protagonist, according to several regime changes and electoral choices. In any case, the local SE sector was mostly conformed to co-ops and mutual associations, but this arena grew in its complexity as a result of the 2001–2002 crisis, when new organizational responses to the socioeconomical emergency appeared. A strong state presence in the SE realm in the 2003–2015 period, especially via workers' co-ops, brought a new configuration to this sector. However, the 2016–2019 period, under a different political orientation, gave greater visibility to a parallel development: the emergence of NS&IE actors and ecosystem.

The New Social and Impact Economy in Argentina

The roots of what has been defined as the NS&IE can be related in Argentina to the local introduction and development of four new concepts and organizational forms in the late 1990s and early 2000s (in a partial overlap with what is mentioned in the introduction of the volume): social entrepreneurship, social enterprises, social businesses, and, to some extent, microcredit institutions. In addition, the emergence of the NS&IE can be related to three other processes: the growth of the entrepreneurial activity in the country, the influence of other international developments in the world sustainability agenda expressed with greater visibility since the beginning of the 2010s, and finally changes in national public policies promoted between 2015 and 2019.

While in other countries the NS&IE emerged in the context of the pervasive effects of the subprime crisis that affected international financial markets in the latest years of the 2000s, this was not the case in Argentina. The 2008/2009 worldwide crash had a limited effect in the country, due in part to a lower exposition to international financial markets. At that time, Argentina had a very limited access to international capital markets as it was still negotiating with holdouts of its 2001-defaulted sovereign debt.[37] The country had, right before the 2008–2009 crisis, trade and fiscal surpluses, and this situation made it to some extent unnecessary for the public sector to access international financing sources.[38]

It is worth mentioning that one of the most important influential leaders of President Cristina Fernández de Kirchner's opposition, Mauricio Macri, was the governor of Argentina's capital and wealthier city, Buenos Aires. Since he took office in 2007, his local administration became an active promoter of entrepreneurship

---

[37] https://elpais.com/internacional/2001/12/23/actualidad/1009062002_850215.html. Accessed 22 Nov 2019.

[38] https://www.clarin.com/opinion/diferencias-superavit-gemelos_0_HyM-ZbTAaFx.html. Accessed 22 Nov 2019.

policies and support programs for entrepreneurs. In 2015, Macri became the leader of the national opposition that put an end to the 12 years of the ruling party, and was elected president. Throughout his federal administration (which ended in December 2019), business and social entrepreneurship were intensively promoted.

Tracing the Early Developments of the Local NS&IE

The introduction of the concept of social entrepreneur was mainly made by international actors, such as Ashoka,[39] Schwab Foundation for Social Entrepreneurship,[40] and NESST,[41] and the idea was amplified by local media such as La Nación,[42] Clarin, and El Cronista.

Ashoka started a long-lasting activity in the country supporting innovative social entrepreneurs since the mid-1990s. Ashoka's approach was oriented towards providing financial support to their fellows, promoting their visibility in the media, building a network, and creating partnerships with corporate leaders. One of Ashoka's local initiatives was the *Premio Moviliza* [Mobilize Prize][43] launched in 2004 with support from McKinsey & Co, to promote commercial initiatives in local nonprofit organizations as an alternative source of funding. This award contributed to launching social businesses within several nonprofit organizations and encouraging some nonprofit leaders to create new social enterprises. Some of the initiatives recognized by Moviliza became mature social businesses that scaled up their operations and impact. Two such examples are *Sume Materiales*, a program related to *Fundación Sagrada Familia*[44] (later rebranded as *Vivienda Digna* [Decent Housing]) which runs a building materials business for low-income families, and *Granja Andar,*[45] which operates an industrial bread factory and a catering service employing special-needs youth in addition to therapeutic, sports, and educational programs for this population.

Other institutions such as Schwab Foundation for Social Entrepreneurship and the local business newspaper El Cronista Comercial launched a similar competition to recognize social entrepreneurs (Social Entrepreneur of the Year Award). In 2005, the Swiss bank UBS[46]—in partnership with Ashoka—launched a similar award to

---

[39] https://www.ashoka.org/es/country/argentina. Accessed 20 Nov 2019.

[40] https://www.lanacion.com.ar/editoriales/premios-a-emprendedores-sociales-nid751940. Accessed 10 Oct 2019.

[41] https://www.nesst.org/. Accessed 10 Oct 2019.

[42] https://www.lanacion.com.ar/comunidad/emprendedores-sociales-nid971420. Accessed 10 Oct 2019.

[43] https://www.lanacion.com.ar/sociedad/premio-para-estrategias-innovadoras-nid794261. Accessed 10 Oct 2019.

[44] https://www.viviendadigna.org.ar/. Accessed 30 Oct 2019.

[45] http://www.granjaandar.org.ar/. Accessed 22 Nov 2019.

[46] https://www.lanacion.com.ar/comunidad/emprendedores-sociales-nid971420. Accessed 10 Oct 2019.

outstanding social entrepreneurs in Argentina called Visionaries[47] (also ran in Mexico and Brazil, but in Argentina was interrupted in 2008).

Another actor that promoted the development of social businesses within non-profit organizations was NESST, which in 2008 launched a seed fund (*Fondo Nido*) to support commercial activities of nonprofit organizations and ran a number of competitions to select its grantees.[48] Its activities received support from the Multilateral Investment Fund of the Inter-American Development Bank, and from JPMorgan Chase Bank.

The development of social entrepreneurship in the country can be analyzed as well as part of the growth of the entrepreneurial culture in the country with organizations such as Endeavor,[49] which opened its first office in Buenos Aires in 1998. Other organizations contributed as well to the promotion and educational work that established a very active entrepreneurial environment in the country (such as *Inicia* mentoring program, or *Naves* Competition by IAE Business School) to support the evolution of general entrepreneurship in the country. The rate of entrepreneurial activity showed its largest growth ever between 2001 and 2003, with a fall in 2004–2005, recovering slowly in the following years and with a new high increase from 2010 to 2011 (Cohen Arazi & Alonso, 2016; Torres Carbonell, 2019).

Some social entrepreneurs influenced by personal experiences overseas or by their connections with international networks first introduced the social enterprise idea. These social entrepreneurs aspired to create inclusive, compassionate, self-sustained, and independent organizations through their own market-based activities. One example was the organization called *Hecho en Buenos Aires*[50] [Made in Buenos Aires], one of the first organizations that defined itself as a social and solidarity enterprise, founded in 2000 as a local adaptation of the UK SE Big Issue.[51] It seeks to support the labor and social inclusion of homeless people by producing and selling a magazine and by providing them with social services.

The initially self-defined social enterprises, around 20 organizations, gathered on RedESA (the acronym of Argentinian Social Enterprises Network), created also in 2000 (Pastore, 2010), a network built upon the need to participate in active policies for sustained and supportive development, creating spaces for co-management between the state and community organizations.[52] As the goal of RedESA stated, the role of the public sector in the development of what was called social enterprises was deemed both relevant and desirable. The organizing effort of this network was

---

[47] https://www.alliancemagazine.org/news/ubs-partners-with-ashoka-in-latin-america/. Accessed 30 Oct 2019.

[48] https://www.lanacion.com.ar/comunidad/las-ong-buscan-nuevas-fuentes-de-financiamiento-nid1119059; https://noticiaspositivas.org/nesst-premia-con-apoyo-financiero-a-cuatro-nuevas-organizaciones-de-la-sociedad-civil/. Accessed 22 Nov 2019.

[49] http://www.endeavor.org.ar/. Accessed 22 Nov 2019.

[50] https://www.pagina12.com.ar/diario/sociedad/3-45274-2004-12-27.html. Accessed 10 Oct 2019.

[51] www.bigissue.com. Accessed 10 Oct 2019.

[52] https://www.youtube.com/watch?v=Of_OAAOGFYI. Accessed 10 Oct 2019.

supported by COSPE Conosur, an Italian-based NGO cooperation. After a few years of exchanges, RedESA ceased to exist.

As for the microcredit sector, the first programs focused on creating financial services for the poor in the country were launched in the late 1980s (PNUD, 2005), but they were interrupted as a result of the hyperinflation process that affected the country. In the early 1990s, new organizations emerged focusing on microcredit as a tool for poverty alleviation, but applying a commercial approach to it. The Ford Foundation and Action International were two organizations that provided support for the development of microfinance institutions in the country. In April 1999, Muhammad Yunus visited for the first time Argentina and the experience of Grameen in Bangladesh received an important media coverage. In the same year, Argentine Grameen Foundation[53] was born and several other microcredit institutions emerged as well. During Menem's administration years (1989–1999), a private-public organization was created to provide support and funding to the microcredit industry, FONCAP.[54] In 2004, a number of these microcredit organizations decided to create RADIM (Argentine Network of Microcredit Institutions), and in 2007 it was formally registered as a legal entity.[55]

The New Wave of Organizations with Social Purposes

The level of awareness and visibility of entrepreneurship in Argentina has steadily increased in the last two decades,[56] reaching a peak in the period 2016–2019, due in part to federal policies and initiatives. These policies built on previous work by Buenos Aires City Government during Macri's local administration (2007–2015).

The development of a social entrepreneurial ecosystem seems to be a partial result of the important promotion work carried out not only by the state, but especially by a group of private entities specifically focused on supporting social entrepreneurship or social innovation. In addition to those organizations that began their promotion activities in the late 1990s, other initiatives also played a relevant role in the second half of the 2000s: Mayma,[57] Socialab,[58] Center of Social Innovation at the University of San Andrés,[59] Inclusive Business Space (ENI) at Torcuato Di Tella

---

[53] https://www.pagina12.com.ar/diario/suplementos/cash/17-2835-2007-02-11.html. Accessed 10 Oct 2019.

[54] https://www.foncap.com.ar/. Accessed 22 Nov 2019.

[55] http://www.reddemicrocredito.org/index.php/preguntas-frecuentes. Accessed 10 Nov 2019.

[56] To give a sense of local interest, Endeavor 2018 annual conference gathered 3500 young people interested in learning about entrepreneurship, https://www.lanacion.com.ar/economia/experiencia-endeavor-unas-3500-personas-fueron-parte-del-mayor-evento-de-emprendedores-nid2141124. Accessed 13 Nov 2019.

[57] https://mayma.org.ar/mayma. Accessed on 10 Nov 2019.

[58] https://ar.socialab.com/. Accessed 10 Oct 2019.

[59] https://www.udesa.edu.ar/centro-de-innovacion-social. Accessed 10 Oct 2019.

University,[60] impact investment funds such as *Equitas Ventures*[61] or OikoCredit,[62] and specific service providers such as NESST, *Emprediem*,[63] *Njambre*, or *Sistema B*.

These organizations and projects were influenced and inspired by international events and processes that had a turning point with the conference named Rio + 20. The United Nations Conference on Sustainable Development—or Rio + 20—took place in Rio de Janeiro, Brazil, in June 2012 and it resulted in a document that contained clear and practical measures for implementing sustainable development. This conference sparked a process that led to the launch of the UN Sustainable Development Goals (SDG) in September 2015. In parallel, by the end of 2015 the 21st Conference of the Parties (COP21) took place in Paris that concluded with a new global climate change agreement (known as the Paris Agreement) to reduce gas emission by countries with a goal of stopping global temperatures from rising more than 1.5 °C. These two processes and outcomes had an intense media coverage in the country and had an important influence in NGOs and corporations, and served as well to inspire organizations promoting NS&IE.

Several of these actors share a vision of a new way of organizing principles of economic activity. They tend to refer to this as "impact economy": "a system in which institutions and individuals give equal priority to social impact and financial impact when making decisions about how to make decisions about to allocate resources" (McKinsey & Co, 2018, 5). In this impact economy, social entrepreneurs and social enterprises are key stakeholders. While the idea of impact economy has been first used in the context of impact investment, the recent Global Summit of GSG in November 2019 held in Buenos Aires became an important local milestone for the movement, and contributed to disseminating the concept. In that event for example, its manifesto stated: "The call for the 'Impact Economy' makes traditional capitalism more humane, by embedding impact in every business, investment and consumption decision. An impact economy is designed to deliver social, environmental and economic justice for people and the planet."[64] Some local actors also referred to a similar term: "new economy" (Sistema B, Mayma, Njambre). This concept is applied to a development paradigm that searches for modes of production and service that seeks not only profits but also service for humanity without social or environmental costs.[65]

Mayma is an annual acceleration program for positive social and environmental impact enterprises. It provides tools to entrepreneurs engaged in the impact econ-

---

[60] https://www.utdt.edu/ver_contenido.php?id_contenido=11120&id_item_menu=21522. Accessed 10 Oct 2019.

[61] https://equitasventures.wordpress.com/quienes-somos/. Accessed 10 Oct 2019.

[62] https://www.sasr.oikocredit.coop/es/donde-trabajamos/oficinas-de-pais/argentina. Accessed 10 Oct 2019.

[63] https://emprediem.com/. Accessed 10 Oct 2019.

[64] See https://gsgii.org/2019/11/sir-ronald-cohen-calls-for-overthrowing-the-dictatorship-of-profit-and-putting-impact-by-its-side-at-the-gsg-impact-summit-2019-in-buenos-aires/. Accessed 30 Mar 2020.

[65] https://sistemab.org/nueva-economia-para-nuevas-sociedades/. Accessed 30 Mar 2020.

omy for the growth of their projects. Since 2007, Mayma has been promoting and encouraging entrepreneurs who create companies or organizations *with purpo*se.[66] From 2007 to 2012, the program received support from Business in Development Network (BiD), a Dutch-based association, and since then it began a process of geographic expansion and program elaboration moving from an award format to a program that includes training, technical assistance, networking, and access to potential investors. In 2019, Mayma began a partnership with *Mercado Libre Corp* (the company with the highest market value in the country) to offer an online training program targeting social and environmental entrepreneurs in six Latin American countries called *Emprender con Impacto*[67] [Enterprising with Impact].

Another important player in this ecosystem, *Njambre* was born in 2012 with the purpose of developing social impact enterprises and since then has been incubating five startups and providing technical assistance and training to many others. In 2019, *Njambre* (with the support of Facebook) launched an incubation program for impact ventures called *Miel* [Maturing Impact, Entrepreneurship and Leadership], an annual program aiming to select 30 of these ventures located in Buenos Aires, Cordoba, and Mendoza provinces.[68] Its goal is to promote and professionalize social and environmental businesses.

A very active organization in this ecosystem is *Sistema B Argentina*, the local chapter of a regional organization that has been promoting the B Corp movement in Latin America since 2011. *Sistema B* operates all over Latin America to "work for an economy where success is measured by the well-being of individuals, societies and nature"[69] and that promotes B Lab certification. As it is also explained in its website: "B Lab is a non-profit organization that was born in the United States and Canada in 2006 with the aim of re-defining the sense of success in the company: Solving social and environmental problems from the products and services that are marketed. Companies are certified as B companies and change their bylaws." By mid-2019 the subcontinent has 350 B-certified companies, 101 of them being from Argentina.[70] *Sistema B* has established several alliances with key actors specially in business media. For example, it launched the award called "Protagonists for a New Economy" with the business magazine *Apertura*, with the purpose of recognizing companies that seek to create social and environmental value and not only profits demonstrating that the transition to a "new economy" was already taking place. The award had three editions (2015–2017).[71] As an example of its mobilization capacity,

---

[66] https://www.premiosmayma.org/edicionesanteriores. Accessed 10 Oct 2019.

[67] https://www.dossiernet.com.ar/articulo/mercado-libre-y-mayma-lanzan-emprender-con-impacto-un-nuevo-ciclo-de-formacion-online/19512. Accessed 20 Nov 2019.

[68] http://www.njambre.org/miel/. Accessed 20 Nov 2019. Examples of these projects are in Buenos Aires, En Buenas Manos [In Good Hands], a WISE, or Feboasoma (Urban Solid Waste research lab); in Cordoba, Ondulé (recycled toys); and in Mendoza, Rañatela (a textile co-op).

[69] https://sistemab.org/movimiento-global/. Accessed 10 Oct 2019.

[70] https://sistemab.org/empresas-b-america-latina/?fwp_presencia=argentina. Accessed 10 Oct 2019.

[71] https://sistemab.org/protagonistas-de-una-nueva-economia-se-acerca-la-3-edicion/. Accessed 20 Apr 2020.

in September 2019, Sistema B organized its annual event in the city of Mendoza, with support from the local municipality, gathering more than 1000 entrepreneurs.

In the same period emerged the first local experiences of funding social businesses and social enterprises with the logic of private investment. One such experience was Equitas Venture Fund, which started in 2010 to create and manage projects and instruments that contribute to finance and growth of companies with impact on sustainable development. During its short life, it launched two rounds of investments with the support of a local bank (Banco Columbia).[72] A few years later, in 2016, Argentina witnessed new efforts to promote impact investment in the country: *Grupo de Trabajo de Inversión de Impacto Cono Sur* [Southern Cone Impact Investment Working Group][73] was launched with members from the financial, corporate, civil society organizations, academia, and triple-impact companies. It aims to consolidate the development of the impact investment in Argentina mobilizing financial markets towards economic, sustainable, social, and environmental business. Alongside with a similar group in Uruguay, they became the regional node within the Global Steering Group for Impact Investment (GSG) established in 2015.[74]

Complementarily, corporate actors have been increasingly developing social impact programs (ENI, 2016) and as part of their sustainability strategies many companies have propelled purchasing programs that prioritize sustainable and inclusive suppliers, and in some cases provide financial and technical support for their development. Examples of this approach to community engagement are the national oil company YPF[75] and Arcor,[76] one of the leading world candy manufacturers. By and large, inclusive purchasing programs are focused on including more traditional SE organizations in value chains. But, on the other hand, some companies have launched initiatives promoting NS&IE organizations such as EcoFriday,[77] an annual campaign to promote responsible consumption, which was started in 2016 by Mercado Libre and Sistema B, and supported by the Secretary of Environment and Sustainable Development of the federal administration. Other companies have in turn become sponsors of training programs for entrepreneurs with social and environmental purpose (as in the case of the previously mentioned corporate partnerships of Mayma and Njambre).

Other initiatives serve to illustrate the increasing visibility and interest in promoting and recognizing NSE organizations. For example, *Amcham Argentina* [American Chamber of Commerce in Argentina], the largest bilateral exchange

---

[72] https://equitasventures.wordpress.com/quienes-somos/. Accessed 04 Nov 2019.

[73] http://inversiondeimpacto.net/. Accessed 10 Oct 2019.

[74] https://gsgii.org/. Accessed 22 Nov 2019.

[75] https://www.ypf.com/Proveedores/Paginas/Compras-Inclusivas.aspx. Accessed 20 Nov 2019.

[76] https://www.arcor.com/sustentabilidad/el-vinculo-entre-arcor-y-los-emprendedores-de-la-economia-social. Accessed 20 Nov 2019.

[77] https://ideas.mercadolibre.com/cl/noticias/mercado-libre-lanza-cuarta-edicion-del-ecofriday-en-el-taller-de-joya-plastica/. Accessed 20 Nov 2019.

business association in the country, introduced in 2017, within its Corporate Citizenship Award (the oldest and most sought-after initiative in the areas of corporate responsibility and sustainability), a new category called "New Enterprise Paradigm," to publicly recognize new impact companies that are disruptive in the way they approach sustainability and that demonstrate commitment to create value for societies, communities, and respect for the environment, while rewarding appropriately financial investment.[78] In addition, several entrepreneurship competitions have emerged in the last years that are focused on new social and environmental impact companies or that include such a category, such as *Emprende Conciencia* launched by one of the most respected technological companies in the country (INVAP), or Startup Competition launched by Universidad de San Andrés.

Recognizing the context of emerging actors within the NS&IE, a network of support institutions to social enterprises, social entrepreneurs, and social businesses was launched in 2012 under the name of RAAES[79] (acronym for Argentinian Social Enterprises Supporting Network), with the purpose of promoting collaboration and information sharing among several organizations working with social businesses and social enterprises. Although this network had a brief life, it reflected to some extent the new dynamics of the sector—e.g., a demand for changes in the legislation and the fiscal treatment of the NS&IE.

Conclusively, the NSE support ecosystem in Argentina is composed of more than 20 institutions according to Roure, de San Jose, and Segurado (2016), offering different types of support (whether financing, training, counseling to entrepreneurs; promotion of the venture and/or the sector; networking between entrepreneurs or coworking), and targeting ventures at different stages (idea/seed, startup, consolidation, growth). In spite of failure to institutionalize a support network, most actors within the NS&IE support ecosystem maintain frequent dialogues and informal exchanges.

The Public Sector Promoting Local New Social and Impact Economy

As for public policies related to the NS&IE, Macri's administration put entrepreneurship promotion and support as one of its top economic development priorities. In 2017, National Congress passed a federal law that established funding for entrepreneurial support.[80] The authority of application of this law was the Small and Medium Size Enterprise Secretary (SEPYME) within the Ministry of Production. In

---

[78] http://www.premiociudadania.com.ar/trayectoria.asp. Accessed 20 Apr 2020.

[79] https://www.comunicarseweb.com/biblioteca/se-creo-la-red-argentina-de-apoyo-las-empresas-sociales-raaes. Accessed 10 Oct 2019.

[80] Law No 27,349: http://servicios.infoleg.gob.ar/infolegInternet/anexos/270000-274999/273567/norma.htm. Accessed 10 Oct 2019.

addition to providing tax benefits, and simplifying accounting and bureaucratic procedures to create new companies (called SAS, simplified shares society), the law established a Trust Fund for the Development of Entrepreneurial Capital (FONDCE), through which emerging enterprises and startups can apply for nonreturnable grants and obtain matching public and private sector investments. Its federal advisory council has representatives from the provinces (states) and the main support institutions for entrepreneurship. The SEPYME established different financing programs for entrepreneurs throughout the country, such as the Seed Capital Fund, Incubators, Accelerators, and Funds of Entrepreneurial Capital Investment, both for profit-oriented entrepreneurs and for those who primarily seek social impact, including cooperatives.[81]

Another public initiative developed by Macri's administration was PROESUS (National Entrepreneur Program for Sustainable Development), at the Secretary of Environment and Sustainable Development.[82] Since 2016, PROESUS has been seeking to promote and consolidate the framework for the development of sustainable enterprises that provide innovative solutions to environmental challenge, working with all the actors of the entrepreneurial ecosystem (incubators, civil society organizations, universities, etc.). As of mid-2019, there were 61 ventures labeled as *outstanding* and 85 *sustainable ventures* recognized by PROESUS, and more than 1200 registered ventures in PROESUS platform.[83]

In the city of Buenos Aires, another NS&IE-related public initiative launched by the local administration is IncuBAte,[84] which is a program started in 2009 that stimulates the strengthening and consolidation of local innovative ventures, through personalized support, and the possibility of accessing a nonrefundable contribution and a workspace. This program targets commercial, productive, or social, technological, and/or high-impact entrepreneurs seeking advice and mentoring and/or financial assistance and/or physical incubation to start their projects or strengthen existing ventures.[85] Similar programs aimed at promoting entrepreneurs in general with special recognition to those seeking social and environmental impact are found in several Argentinian provinces, such as in Mendoza (*Mendoza Emprende* under the

---

[81] https://www.infobae.com/economia/finanzas-y-negocios/2018/01/15/quienes-estan-detras-de-los-fondos-de-inversion-que-son-socios-del-estado-en-el-impulso-de-los-emprendedores/. Accessed 20 Apr 2020.

[82] https://www.argentina.gob.ar/ambiente/sustentabilidad/innovacion-para-el-desarrollo/proesus. Accessed 10 Oct 2019.

[83] Ibid.

[84] https://www.buenosaires.gob.ar/innovacion/emprendedores/capacitacion-e-incubadoras/incubate. Accessed 20 Nov 2019.

[85] https://www.buenosaires.gob.ar/innovacion/emprendedores/capacitacion-e-incubadoras/incubate. Accessed 20 Nov 2019.

motto "incubating sustainable processes"[86]), Córdoba (*Agencia Cordoba Innovar + Emprender*[87]), and Santa Fe (*Crear comunidad emprendedora*[88]).

Additionally, there are public competitions run by the public sector, both in several state governments and nationwide aiming to promote NS&IE. In the capital city, *Vos Lo Hacés*[89] [You Do] is an innovation public competition that seeks to foster the entrepreneurial, creative, and productive spirit, by identifying, enhancing, and rewarding ideas that, in addition to being innovative, become sustainable ventures. At the national level, in addition to those already mentioned, another initiative is the National Innovation Award *INNOVAR*. The federal Secretary for Science, Technology and Productive Innovation has been organizing this contest for the last 15 years. The main objective of *INNOVAR* is to promote the innovative culture in the different productive areas of the country and to develop projects aimed at improving the quality of life of the society. This award competition considers projects for its novelty, and its social and commercial impact, with one of its categories being "companies and third sector."[90] In 2019, 34 initiatives received awards and funding within this initiative.[91]

However, at the federal public policy level, these NS&IE promotion and support programs and awards coexisted with initiatives that continue to provide assistance to more traditional SE organizations. For example, *Ellas Hacen* [Women do] is a program of the federal Ministry of Social Development that seeks to encourage initiatives that create both job opportunities and training to women in vulnerable situations[92] and promotes solidarity and social economy organizations among women. The beneficiaries of the program reached 1,800,000 people in 2018 (Ferrari Mango & Campana, 2018, 10). In the city of Buenos Aires, a program that targets low-income individuals and promotes entrepreneurial activities among them is the Entrepreneurial Pact, a local 5-month mentoring program that aims to expand the social capital of entrepreneurs in vulnerable situations (microentrepreneurs) and follow them in the process of developing their microenterprises.[93]

---

[86] http://mendozaemprende.org/. Accessed 22 Nov 2019.

[87] http://innovaryemprendercba.com.ar/mas-empresas/. Accessed 22 Nov 2019.

[88] https://www.santafe.gov.ar/index.php/web/content/view/full/223835/(subtema)/192166. Accessed 22 Nov 2019.

[89] https://www.buenosaires.gob.ar/economia-y-finanzas/emprendedores/promocion/vos-lo-haces. Accessed 10 Oct 2019.

[90] https://www.conicet.gov.ar/convocatoria-abierta-para-el-concurso-nacional-de-innovaciones-innovar-2019/. Accessed 10 Oct 2019.

[91] https://www.argentina.gob.ar/noticias/en-su-15deg-aniversario-innovar-premio-al-talento-argentino. Accessed 22 Nov 2019.

[92] https://plataformacelac.org/programa/1269. Accessed 10 Oct 2019.

[93] https://www.buenosaires.gob.ar/innovacion/emprendedores/pacto-emprendedor. Accessed 10 Oct 2019.

The Evolution of the Legal Framework for SE and NS&IE Organizations

As explained above, the traditional legal forms for SE organizations in Argentina have been cooperatives, mutual associations, civil associations, and, to a lesser degree, foundations. The legal and tax framework for them has evolved over time and regulators have shown a restrictive view towards commercial and production activities of nonprofit organizations (other than cooperatives) which have negatively affected their development.

While the oldest reference to a co-op was from 1857,[94] the first legal mention to the cooperative form was from 1884. Later, the first Commercial Code (1889) addressed essential concepts of cooperatives, but some confusion around co-op bylaws remained until a Congress commission introduced a new bill, passed in 1926. This legal framework governed the Argentinian co-op life until 1973 when a specific legal law was approved. On the other hand, from 1945 until 1969, mutual associations were ruled by the first legal framework directed to them, and from 1969 began a process to establish a new legal corpus, leading to a new law in 1973 (later reviewed in 2001).

The differences between co-ops and mutual associations in Argentina are worth noting. In the former, members equally share ownership, organizational governance and management are democratic, and if there are surplus they can be distributed according to the contribution of each member. On the other hand, the aim of mutual associations is to provide mutual help through periodic contributions of their members. Additionally, there are multiple membership categories and it is not possible to distribute profits. Surplus of mutual associations are utilized to increase the capital and create reserve funds. Nowadays, both co-ops and mutual associations operate under the oversight of INAES[95] (National Institute of Associativism and Social Economy), a decentralized agency created in 2000 that in 2020 started to report to the National Ministry of Production.[96]

In spite of having a more favorable tax treatment than associations and foundations regarding commercial and production activities, co-ops and mutual associations feel that there is a need for a more enabling environment for their activities. For example, prior to last national elections, the representative entities of both co-ops and mutual associations made public a manifesto to the candidates, expressing: "Federal and state taxes and municipality fees must recognize that cooperative and mutual actions, clearly established in their specific laws, solidarity work and the

---

[94] Asociación Panadería del Pueblo, a Consumer's Co-op from Entre Ríos Province, according to Bazan (2012), in Plotinsky (2015, 160).

[95] https://www.argentina.gob.ar/inaes. Accessed 10 Oct 2019.

[96] https://www.cronista.com/economiapolitica/Traspasaron-el-INAES-a-la-orbita-de-Produccion-y-ya-financia-a-cooperativas-con-fondos-mutuales-20200217-0046.html. Accessed 11 Mar 2020.

nonprofit nature of coops and mutual entities, and that there should not be taxable consequences in the relationship between the entity and its associates."[97]

Other organizations, within the SE arena, adopted the legal forms of civil associations or foundations (Campetella, González Bombal, & Roitter, 2000) and therefore suffered some limitations and restrictions to maintain the tax exemption status when they carried out commercial and productive activities, given the nature of laws and regulations focusing on these two legal forms.

Since 2014 the legal framework for both civil associations[98] and foundations[99] has been set in the Civil and Commercial Codes, when they underwent a major revision. The reform of these codes tried to deal with some gaps and limitations of disparate previous laws.[100] Regarding the nonprofit sector organizations in general, this reform introduced several advancements as compared to previous legislation, but at the same time, it falls short, as it fails to provide a harmonious, systematic framework that matches best international standards. As a recent study (ACIJ, 2015) states:

The regulation of CSOs is scattered, outdated and unsystematic, which hinders the development of the sector and, therefore, of participatory democracy … Advancing in agile regulation that facilitates the emergence, development and coordination of CSO in Argentina is necessary to strengthen the participation of civil society, and in this way a greater plurality of voices is expressed in the public debate, thus improving and making democracy more robust.

The new legislation did not explicitly mention these organizations' ability or lack thereof to operate commercial or production activities, but it does curtail their options, as it does establish that conducting business operations may cause foundations and civil associations to lose its income tax exemption.

However, this last reform gave legal recognition to a long-due claim of the nonprofit sector: it incorporated the "simple associations" form. They only require a public or a private contract, certified by a public notary for their incorporation, with no need to register them in a public records office, which implies a more expensive and laborious process. This new legal form is seen as more suitable for emerging grassroots organizations.

In general, the application and enforcement authority of these norms has maintained over time a very strict position against associations and foundations that carry out commercial and productive initiatives, and nonprofit organizations conducting earned income activities are exposed to losing of their tax-exempt status granted by the Federal Tax Authority (*Administración Federal de Ingresos Públicos*, or AFIP). Recent changes introduced in regulations indicate that civil associations have no restriction on the percentage of their income that may originate from

---

[97] "Mensaje de las cooperativas y mutuales argentinas a los candidatos en las próximas elecciones nacionales" https://www.cooperar.coop/elecciones-2019-mensaje-del-cooperativismo-y-el-mutualismo/. Accessed 30 Mar 2020.

[98] Articles 30 to 50, and 168 to 192 (Thomson Reuters Foundation, 2016, 27).

[99] Articles 193 to 224 (Thomson Reuters Foundation, 2016, 22).

[100] http://servicios.infoleg.gob.ar/infolegInternet/anexos/235000-239999/235975/norma.htm. Accessed 10 Oct 2019.

commercial or productive activities (but these activities must be related to their public interest purpose). Foundations, in turn, can only obtain up to 30% of their income from these activities without putting at risk their tax exemption on income taxes.[101] Nonprofit organizations and civil associations registered as commercial societies are also exempt from the VAT on their sales if they received the tax-exempt status on income taxes.

On the other hand, as part of public policies of the 2016–2019 period, the national legal structure tried to adapt to changes in the emerging new social and impact economy scene, but with mixed results. Argentinian laws are running behind the blurring organizational reality and still do not embrace the complexity of hybrid organizations (Battilana & Lee, 2014, Defourny & Nyssens, 2017, Santos, Pache, & Birkholz, 2015, etc.). Despite some inconsistent efforts in changing the legal framework, it comes as no surprise that under the current Argentinian legal system NS&IE organizations can choose to obtain the legal form either as a nonprofit organization (with restrictions to commercial and production activities even when they contribute directly to achieving their purpose, as explained) or as a commercial for-profit entity (Thomson Reuters Foundation, 2016).

In this vein, among commercial figures deemed suitable for NS&IE (Thomson Reuters Foundation, 2016), the first to mention is civil association registered under the form of a commercial society,[102] be that an LLC or a corporation. Through this form, an organization can produce goods and provide services without profit distribution, but in the bylaws, it must establish its public purpose and a nondistribution of profits agreement. For example, the legal form adopted for civil associations registered as commercial societies can be an LLC such as *Libértate*[103]—a WISE organization—or the corporation legal form, as the case of *Njambre*. Organizations registered as civil associations registered as commercial societies can also theoretically obtain the tax-exempt status for the federal income tax, but AFIP hardly has granted it. NS&IE organizations can also adopt any for-profit form (LLC or corporations mainly), and there are growing examples of companies created to achieve social and environmental impact and to address sustainable development challenges that are taking this path, with no restriction on profit distributions (Thomson Reuters Foundation, 2016), and this is the case of most B-certified companies.

Additionally, in this effort to try to grasp the growing hybrid landscape, legal initiatives arise promoting new types of legal recognition that combine the pursuit of both social-environmental impact and profitability, such as Collective Interest Benefit (BIC) Societies. On December 6, 2018, the Chamber of Deputies voted affirmatively on the so-called BIC Law that seeks to give a framework to companies "with purpose," with the aim of encouraging a new paradigm of doing business with a focus on social and environmental impact. This law has been promoted by an

---

[101] Law No 27.430: http://servicios.infoleg.gob.ar/infolegInternet/anexos/4000044999/44911/texact.htm. Accessed 22 Nov 2019.

[102] Law No 19,550 on Commercial Societies, Article 3: http://servicios.infoleg.gob.ar/infolegInternet/anexos/25000-29999/25553/texact.htm. Accessed 13 Nov 2019.

[103] http://libertate.com.ar/. Accessed 13 Nov 2019.

informal group called B Lawyers, associated with *Sistema B*, and is inspired by the model of B Corp. However, the Senate did not vote on it, and given lawmaking procedures making provisions, the bill must be introduced again for discussion in Congress. The bill does not define tax benefits or grant preferential treatment over traditional commercial legal forms of societies, but it seeks to establish a first step to implement future measures from the state, aimed at encouraging their creation and development (for example, preferential public purchasing programs, facilities for access to credit, among others).

In sum, by the end of 2019, the local legal framework has not yet been adjusted to encompass the new realities and complexities of new social and impact organizations, and there is still no specific legal form to establish organizations pursuing a social mission in a profitable way (Thomson Reuters Foundation, 2016). Nevertheless, there have been recurrent efforts to move forward towards a more favorable NS&IE-enabling environment. However, with changes occurring in the political orientation of the federal administration since December 2019, the financial crisis confronting the country since 2019, and the new scenario created by the Covid-19 pandemic, it is unlikely that advancements in this front will take place in the coming months.

Conclusions

The developments described in this chapter reflect a dynamic scenario for the new social economy in Argentina. Several international actors working in the country since the beginning of the last decade; the growth of an entrepreneurial culture among young professionals in general and among those socially and environmentally concerned; the influence of international processes putting in the center stage the sustainability, social inclusion, and climate change agenda; and public policies and programs supporting and financing startups have all been influential forces behind these local hybrid new forms of engagement, reflecting the general trend explained in the introduction of this volume.

However, government incentives and support for the new social economy reflect contradictory messages. On the one hand, during the period of the federal administration that ended in December 2019, ventures focused on social and environmental impact have received recognition and financial assistance as never before. On the other hand, the legal and tax regulations have not given special recognition to for-profit organizations pursuing social and environmental impact, and bureaucratic discretion has been pervasive in granting tax-exempt status to civil associations and foundations engaged in commercial and productive activities that address social and environmental problems. Behind these mixed approaches and "messages" are different ideologies regarding the role of the nonprofit sector and private companies with social and environmental driven purposes. For some, private initiatives can play an innovative role in creating sustainable innovations to societal problems and these private organizations are considered key partners in social and human development. For others, the public sector should focus its efforts in strengthening the social and solidarity economy (organized in general as co-ops and mutual associations) and in implementing social protection programs, while other organizations (be that civil associations, foundations, and certainly for-profit organizations) must have more regulations and controls.

In addition, the volatile features of Argentinian economy become a barrier for entrepreneurial activities as the Global Entrepreneurship Monitor concludes (Torres Carbonell, 2019), even though Argentina is considered a regional hub for entrepreneurs.[104] All in all, taking into account the opposite ideological views found, the mixed attitudes of government, and the recurrent economic crises affecting Argentina, the enabling environment required for a new sector such as the NS&IE to blossom confronts important limitations and restrictions.

As of midst 2020 it is too early to attempt to assess the orientation of the new federal administration policies on this arena, especially in the context of very active public sector efforts to respond to the Covid-19 pandemic in the health and economic fronts. Early on, the federal Ministry of Social Development has announced its commitment to support social economy initiatives by grassroots organizations as part of the national poverty alleviation strategy. In addition, the INAES began a broad consultation process to articulate actors within the traditional social economy, but efforts to deal with the economic consequences of the pandemic among the most vulnerable populations and the lockdown measures taken by government make this articulation process an aspiration for the near future. On the other hand, institutional actors within the new social and impact economy have reacted to the new context with renewed efforts to promote initiatives through virtual channels and several business plans competitions have adapted by focusing them on finding entrepreneurial responses to the emerging needs caused by the coronavirus. Entrepreneurs and enterprises focusing on impact find opportunities to advance innovations in response to emerging social needs using ICT technologies.

In spite of the lack of an enabling environment, the creative and innovative spirit is pervasive among the actors of Argentinian new social and impact economy. This inner energy, together with the influence of international actors and processes, makes it possible to anticipate its growth as a driving force for social and economic inclusion, and sustainable development in the coming years. However, the dynamics of the social arena, and how the shape of the local topography of the NS&IE is about to emerge in this new decade, is still unknown. These local tensions may converge with global pressures on the one hand for a more active public sector deriving from the pandemic crisis and on the other hand for a more innovative and disruptive private sector engagement to address the social and environmental challenges that confront the country and the world.

---

[104] https://www.thebubble.com/argentina-regional-hub-entrepreneurship. Accessed 22 Nov 2019.

References

Abramovich, A. L, Cassano, D. Federico-Sabaté, A. M., Hintze, S. Montequín, A. & Vázquez, G. (2003). *Empresas sociales y economía social. Una aproximación a sus rasgos fundamentales.* Los Polvorines: Instituto del Conurbano-Universidad Nacional de General Sarmiento.

Abramovich, A. L., & Vázquez, G. (2007). Experiencias de la Economía Social y Solidaria en la Argentina. *Estudios fronterizos, 8*(15), 121–145. http://www.scielo.org.mx/scielo.php?script=sci_arttext&pid=S0187-69612007000100005&lng=es&tlng=. Accessed 21 Apr 2020.

Acosta, M. C., Levín, A., & Verbeke, G. E. (2013). El sector cooperativo en Argentina en la última década. *Cooperativismo & Desarrollo, 21*(102), 27–39.

Arce, H. E. (2013). *Evolución histórica del Sistema de Salud argentino a lo largo del Siglo XX. Rasgos, tendencias e influencias en los planos internacional, nacional y hospitalario* (PhD Dissertation). Buenos Aires: Fundación H. A. Barceló.

Asociación Civil por la Igualdad y la Justicia-ACIJ (2015). Condiciones institucionales y normativas para el funcionamiento de las organizaciones de la sociedad civil. Un aporte para su fortalecimiento. https://acij.org.ar/condiciones-institucionales-y-normativas-para-el-funcionamiento-de-las-organizaciones-de-la-sociedad-civil-2/. Accessed 30 Mar 2020.

Atzeni, M., & Vieta, M. (2013). Between class and the market: Self-management in theory and in the practice of worker-recuperated enterprises in Argentina. In G. Cheney, P. Parker, V. Fournier, & C. Land (Eds.), *Routledge companion to alternative organization* (pp. 47–63). Abington: Routledge.

Battilana, J., & Lee, M. (2014). Advancing research on hybrid organizing – Insights from the study of social enterprises. *The Academy of Management Annals, 8*(1), 397–441.

Bazan, R. C. (2012, September). Paraná, cuna del cooperativismo latinoamericano y del Caribe. Panadería del Pueblo. In: *La Economía Social y Solidaria en la historia de América Latina y el Caribe. Cooperativismo, desarrollo comunitario y Estado. Congreso Internacional de la Asociación de Historiadores Latinoamericanos y del Caribe (ADHILAC).* Buenos Aires: Centro Cultural de la Cooperación "Floreal Gorini".

Berger, G., & Blugerman, L. (2006). Recover them from oblivion. Recover the community's ability to produce. In C. Lescano & E. Ceibo (Eds.), *ReVista. Harvard Review of Latin America. Fall* (pp. 26–28). Cambridge, MA: David Rockefeller Center for Latin American Studies.

Campetella, A., González Bombal, I., & Roitter, M. (2000). *Definiendo el Sector Sin Fines de Lucro en Argentina.* Buenos Aires: CEDES.

Cohen Arazi, M., & Alonso, A. L. (2016). *La actividad emprendedora en Argentina.* Documento de trabajo. Año 22 - Edición N° 148. Córdoba: IERAL. Fundación Mediterránea. http://www.ieral.org/images_db/noticias_archivos/3298-La%20actividad%20emprendedora%20en%20Argentina.pdf. Accesed 30 Mar 2020.

Coraggio, J. L. (2007). *Economía Social, Acción Pública y Política (Hay vida después del neoliberalismo).* Buenos Aires: Editorial CICCUS.

Coraggio, J. L. (2018). ¿Qué hacer desde la economía popular ante la situación actual? *Revista Idelcoop, 224,* 13–26.

Defourny, J., & Nyssens, M. (2017). Mapping social enterprise models: Some evidence from the "ICSEM" project. *Social Enterprise Journal, 13*(2), 318–328.

Di Stéfano, R., Sábato, H., Romero, L. A., & Moreno, J. L. (2002). *De las Cofradías a las Organizaciones de la Sociedad Civil. Historia de la Iniciativa Asociativa en la Argentina. 1776–1990.* Buenos Aires: GADIS.

Doyran, M. A. (2015). Argentina y su desarrollo posterior a la crisis financiera. *Problemas del Desarrollo, 46*(180), 151–174.

Espacio de Negocios Inclusivos/ENI-Universidad Torcuato Di Tella (2016). Primer relevamiento de actores de los negocios inclusivos en Argentina, segunda parte: Programas con impacto social de las grandes empresas. 2014–2016. https://www.utdt.edu/listado_contenidos.php?id_item_menu=26052. Accessed 10 Oct 2019.

Fajn, G. & Rebón, J. (2005). El taller ¿sin cronómetro? Apuntes acerca de las empresas recupera-das. *Revista Herramienta, 28*. https://www.herramienta.com.ar/articulo.php?id=300. Accessed 21 Apr 2020.

Ferrari Mango, C. & Campana, J. (2018). *Informe N° 11. Del "Argentina Trabaja - Programa Ingreso Social con Trabajo" y el "Ellas Hacen" al "Hacemos Futuro". ¿Integralidad o desintegración de la función social del Estado?* Buenos Aires: OPPRE-FLACSO Argentina. http://politicaspublicas.flacso.org.ar/wp-content/uploads/2018/07/Informe-OPPRE-N%C2%B0-11.pdf. Accessed 20 Nov 2019.

Fields, Z. (2008). Efficiency and equity: The empresas recuperadas of Argentina. *Latin American Perspectives, 35*(6), 83–92.

García, A. T. (Ed.). (2010). *Repensando la economía social. Cuaderno de trabajo* (Vol. 86). Buenos Aires: Ediciones del CCC-Centro Cultural de la Cooperación Floreal Gorini.

Kerlin, J. A. (2010). A comparative analysis of the global emergence of social enterprise. *Voluntas: International Journal of Voluntary and Nonprofit Organizations, 21*(2), 162–179.

Marquez, P., Reficco, E., & Berger, G. (Eds.). (2010). *Socially inclusive business. Engaging the poor through market initiatives in Iberoamerica.* Cambridge, MA/London: Harvard University Press.

Marzi, M. V. D., & Vázquez, G. (2009). Emprendimientos asociativos, empresas recuperadas y economía social en la Argentina. *Iconos. Revista de Ciencias Sociales, 33*, 91–102. https://doi.org/10.17141/iconos.33.2009.300.

McKinsey & Co (2018). Catalyzing the growth of the impact economy. https://www.mckinsey.com/industries/private-equity-and-principal-investors/our-insights/catalyzing-the-growth-of-the-impact-economy. Accessed 30 Apr 2020.

Otero, H. (2009). El asociacionismo francés en la Argentina. Una perspectiva secular. In: *XII Jornadas Interescuelas/Departamentos de Historia.* San Carlos de Bariloche: Universidad Nacional del Comahue. http://www.aacademica.org/000-008/181. Accessed 13 Nov 2019.

Palomino, H. (2003). Las experiencias actuales de autogestión en Argentina. *Nueva Sociedad, 184*, 115–128.

Pastore, R. E. (2010). Un panorama del resurgimiento de la economía social y solidaria en la Argentina. *Revista de Ciencias Sociales. Segunda época, 2*(18), 47–74.

Pearson, R. (2003). Argentina's barter network: New currency for new times? *Bulletin of Latin American Research, 22*(2), 214–230.

Plotinsky, D. (2015). Orígenes y consolidación del cooperativismo en la Argentina. *Revista Idelcoop, 215*, 157–178.

Programa de las Naciones Unidas para el Desarrollo-PNUD (2005). Microfinanzas en la Argentina. https://avanzar.org.ar/wp-content/uploads/2018/02/Microfinanzas-en-Argentina.pdf. Accessed 20 Nov 2019.

Rebón, J., & Salgado, R. (2009). Desafíos emergentes de las empresas recuperadas: de la imposibilidad teórica a la práctica de la posibilidad. *Observatorio de la Economía Latinoamericana, 119*, 1–15.

Roitter, M. (2007, November). Nuevas experiencias de economía social en la Argentina. In: *VI Conferencia Regional de ISTR para América Latina y el Caribe.* Salvador de Bahía: ISTR & CIAGS/UFBA. http://biblioteca.municipios.unq.edu.ar/modules/mislibros/archivos/051.pdf. Accessed 01 Nov 2019.

Roure, J., de San Jose, A., & Segurado, J. L. (2016). *Aceleradoras para emprendimiento social. Modelos de aceleración y ecosistemas de apoyo en América Latina y el Caribe.* Washington, DC: IESE Business School & BID-FOMIN.

Salamon, L. M., Sokolowski, S. W., & List, R. (2003). *Global civil society: An overview.* Baltimore, MD: Center for Civil Society Studies, Institute for Policy Studies, The Johns Hopkins University.

Santos, F., Pache, A. C., & Birkholz, C. (2015). Making hybrids work: Aligning business models and organizational design for social enterprises. *California Management Review, 57*(3), 36–58.

Thomson Reuters Foundation (2016). Guía legal para emprendimientos sociales en Argentina: ¿Qué figura jurídica elegir para crear empresas de impacto social? https://www.utdt.edu/listado_contenidos.php?id_item_menu=26052. Accessed 10 Oct 2019.

Torres Carbonell, S. (2019). Resumen Ejecutivo - GEM – Argentina 2018. Centro de Investigación Entrepreurship-IAE Business School & GEM - Global Entrepreneurship Monitor. https://gem-consortium.org/economy-profiles/argentina. Accessed 23 Apr 2020.

Vuotto, M. (2011). Organizational dynamics of worker cooperatives in Argentina. *Service Business, 6*(1), 85–97.

Williamson, J. (2009). A short history of the Washington consensus. *Law and Business Review of the Americas, 15*(1), 7–23.

Chapter 3
The Restructuring of the Social Economy in Canada

Jorge Sousa

Introduction

The social economy has had a long and varied history in Canada. Historically, the state has seldom led the way to supporting the growth and entrenchment of the social economy in Canadian society. In fact, the social economy has emerged largely in response to poor government efforts to address challenging social issues and to address the failures of the private sector. As a result the social economy has been perceived as being comprised of a set of fringe activities aimed at helping the disadvantaged, as an extension of the welfare state, or a response to crises.

Since the late 1960s governments have supported social economy actors and organizations to deliver social programs that have been strongly linked to the welfare state, in particular those activities aimed at supporting vulnerable populations. However, there have been concerted efforts by academic researchers and practitioners to strengthen the role of the social economy in Canada by stressing the potential for it to operate in place of or complementary to the public and private sectors of the economy. The message has been that because the activities are more inclusive and organizational practices reflect principles that are qualitatively different than what characterizes the public and private sectors, the social economy exists for the public good. These efforts involve the legitimization of citizen-led interventions and the development of businesses with a social purpose, which are integral features of the social economy.

When describing the social economy in a Canadian context, the preferred approach has been to include cooperative and nonprofit organizations as the fundamental pillars of this sector of society. Over the last 20 years the prominence of the role of these pillars has shifted in significant ways, and as a result there has been an

J. Sousa (✉)
Department of Educational Policy Studies, University of Alberta, Edmonton, AB, Canada
e-mail: sousa@ualberta.ca

© Springer Nature Switzerland AG 2021
B. Gidron, A. Domaradzka (eds.), *The New Social and Impact Economy*,
Nonprofit and Civil Society Studies, https://doi.org/10.1007/978-3-030-68295-8_3

inadvertent reshaping of what constitutes the social economy. The shift has largely been found in the increased adoption of more market-based approaches across the sectors to generate the revenue needed to achieve social change. One outcome of implementing conventional market-based approaches to business is measuring of the impact that these organizations reflect on the expectations of private sector businesses, a point that I refer to later.

As explained in the introductory chapter to this book, the new social economy is a recent term to characterize a movement away from the communal orientation of the social economy to one that embraces more individualistic patterns of economic exchange as the means to achieve some form of social change. The individualism is manifested in a shift to a greater recognition of individual efforts supporting social change through traditional business practices.

In Canada, the distinction between the "old" and the "new" social economy is more likely to be associated with the development of the social economy in the province of Quebec (Charron, 2012). In Quebec, the notion of a new social economy is meant to demonstrate the inclusion of more community service organizations, social economy enterprises, nonprofits, and new approaches to financing (Charron, 2012). The existence of the social economy in Quebec is much more advanced when compared to the rest of Canada. Across Canada, there has been a greater plurality of perspectives associated with the social economy. This plurality exists because there is a lack of coherence and agreement with respect to what role social economy activities and organizations can have within the economy. To that end, the term new social economy is a useful heuristic to explain how the traditional pillars of the social economy have diminished and resulted in a shift towards one that is increasingly supportive of the social enterprise model and funding of social innovation. The traditional pillars are cooperative and nonprofit organizations, as well as community economic development activities. For the purpose of this chapter, I will focus on cooperative and nonprofit organizations.

In this chapter I will explore the transition of the social economy in Canada towards being more individualistic oriented businesses dominated by market-based practice from the collectivist-oriented approaches of organizations that provide services with a social objective. Including the introduction, there are five sections to this chapter. In the second I will explore the nature of the welfare state in Canada. In the third section I will explore the development of the social economy in Canada. In the fourth section I will describe the current state of the traditional pillars of the social economy. In this section I will explore the shift of Canada's social economy towards what is being referred to as the new social economy. Additionally, I will also explore the unique means taken by the province of Quebec to integrate the social economy into the broader society. What makes the case of Quebec unique is how different stakeholders associated with the social economy work collaboratively to develop an ecosystem that relies on the co-production and co-construction of public policy. I conclude this chapter with a brief discussion on some of the benefits and challenges of a shift towards a new social economy.

The Welfare State in Canada

Canada is a constitutional monarchy and functions as a federation with two levels of government (federal and provincial) identified in the constitution, including the distribution of legislative powers (Department of Justice, 2019). The federal government is expected to work with the ten provinces and three territories[1] in sharing responsibilities,[2] while respecting the jurisdictional autonomy of the provinces and territories as laid out in the constitution (Department of Justice, 2019). For example, in the case of taxation, each level has its own power to tax. The federal government is responsible for taxation across the country, while the provincial governments are responsible for taxation within the province. Needless to say, the power to tax has been a source of tension between the two levels.

As with many Western countries, the welfare state is known to be a significant part of one's national identity. The welfare state in Canada has developed over a period of 150 years through a variety of citizen-directed practices, which led to establishing public and social policies aimed at responding to social needs of various sorts (Moscovitch, 2015; Wallace, 1950). In essence, the evolution of the welfare state was never driven by a specific political ideology of a government in power, as successive governments representing different political parties would support social programs of various types as long as they responded to an urgent need or crises.

Canadians often describe the welfare state as a distinctive feature of the country's history. However, the welfare state only formally emerged in the 1960s as an agglomeration of social programs and services (Moscovitch, 2015). The federal government took on the active role of supporting key social programs and services as funder and regulator. Moscovitch (2015) describes that governments' efforts to provide social programs have to be considered carefully in order to avoid the risk of disrupting the market—a position that has crossed ideological boundaries—as well as crossing into the jurisdiction of the provinces and territories. In essence, the welfare state in Canada can be seen as the outcome of a set of negotiations between levels of government (Banting, 2004). To that end, establishing the welfare state has created tensions between federal and provincial governments.

One tension can be seen as ideological, for example, when a federal program is seen as too intrusive to both individual rights and freedom of the market (e.g., housing). A second tension can be grounded in constitution, for example, when the federal government tries to dictate how the provinces spend federal transfer grants for healthcare. Due to the jurisdictional differences, the welfare state emerged as the

---

[1] The territories of Yukon, Northwest Territories, and Nunavut were established as an act of parliament and are governed by the federal government, whereas the governing power of the provinces is outlined in the Canadian Constitution. Municipal level governments are creatures of the provinces.

[2] Articles 91 to 95 of the Canadian Constitution clearly lay out the different responsibilities and jurisdictions of the two levels of government (Government of Canada, 2019).

result of negotiations between the provinces and the federal government (Banting, 2004; Lightman & Irving, 1991). Banting (2004) refers to this process as a form of "Joint-Decision Federalism" and uses the Canada Pension Plan as an example.

In Canada the welfare state can be understood as falling within two major categories: income assistance and social services. Each category includes a variety of programs aimed at supporting the precariousness and volatility of capitalism. Successive federal governments have demonstrated a belief that the role of government is to support the security of the general public while supporting market mechanisms to address the shortcomings of capitalism (Moscovitch, 2015). Moscovitch (1983) states that traditionally, charities and community-based organizations provided much of the services that helped shape the priorities associated with the welfare state. One can speculate that it is for that reason that nonprofit organizations and other community-based organizations became the primary source to deliver social services that are funded by government.

There appears to be a consensus that the dismantling of the welfare state started in the mid-1970s, which seems to follow a global pattern (Pierson, 2011). It was during the mid-1970s that both levels of governments started to embrace austerity as a fundamental public policy, and it reflects a monetarist approach to managing the economy. While there has never been a systematic effort to erase social policies and programs, the dismantling effort was more related to changing the conditions and eligibility of certain social programs. For example, the principle of universality of social programs that became a core idea from the 1960s started to shift towards it perceiving the social problems as residual to the organization of society, and any response should be targeted with precision. In a sense, the purpose of the welfare state was to serve as a social safety net for individuals who were unemployable and those that were employable (e.g., seasonal workers or those that faced loss of jobs because of changing industries) but transitioned to work. Other forms of access to these programs would become based on means testing rather than being universal (Moscovitch, 1986).

As the welfare state was starting to be being dismantled by the federal government in the 1970s and into the 1980s, the provinces were expected to take on many of the responsibilities that were once shared (Lightman & Irving, 1991). An example was the provision of social housing, which was downloaded by the federal government to the provinces in the 1980s, which resulted in an increased divestment by the provinces. While the consequences of these decisions were clearly felt by the public, it also had a profound impact on the social economy as social housing was one of the areas in which nonprofit and cooperative organizations were able to grow the social economy. However, that was not a primary concern for governments who were more intent on reducing government spending on social programs.

Explaining the Social Economy in Canada

In Canada there is no consensus to a definition or usage of the term social economy. One perspective views the social economy as comprising of a variety of organizations (e.g., cooperative, mutual associations) that share a set of social objectives (Mook & Quarter, 2018) and provide services that share the characteristic of mutuality for the purpose of meeting the social and economic needs of individuals and communities (Quarter, Mook, & Armstrong, 2009). This characteristic of mutuality helps to humanize economic practices as well as ensure communication towards greater communalization, a feature that is part of the ethos of the cooperative movement (Craig, 1993).

While elements of the social economy have always been understood to include specific organizational forms that are geared to meet a social need, there is an absence of coherence of usage and understanding across the country. There are significant regional differences when determining the nature of the social economy; thus developing of an agreed-upon definition is very challenging to achieve (Quarter, 2000). Accordingly, the definition of the social economy is highly contested within academic and practitioner communities (see Fontan & Shragge, 2000; Lévesque & Mendell, 2005; Restakis, 2006). There are a number of obstacles that have made developing a common definition problematic. First, there is lack of a standard approach to organizing and accounting for the multitude of and emerging organizational forms. Secondly, the availability and absence of aggregate information that recognizes the breadth of the social economy across the country have ensured that making comparisons is virtually impossible. The absence of information is more pronounced in instances where businesses are present in the market-based economy while striving to achieve a social mission. Thirdly, the activities of different organizations can be so infused within the broader economy, thereby making it very difficult to determine how society is benefiting by having a robust social economy rather than supporting a reformed market-based economy (Fontan & Shragge, 2000).

While engaging in a debate as to the meaning of the social economy within a Canadian context can be interesting, it can limit efforts to develop processes and practices aimed at helping those people who benefit from the work of these organizations. Thus, there are a number of different definitions that reflect regional or ideological differences. I present two of the more commonly understood definitions used across the country, and each presents a different emphasis and reflects regional differences. First, according to Neamtan and Downing (2005) the social economy encompasses a wide variety of activities (e.g., community development and entrepreneurship) undertaken by individuals and organizations that operate from the following principles:

1. A social economy enterprise serves its members or the community rather than to simply make profits.
2. It operates at arm's length from the state.
3. It promotes a democratic management process involving all users and/or workers through its statutes and the way it does business.
4. It defends the primacy of individuals and work over capital in the distribution of its participation and individual and collective empowerment.

The definition provided by Neamtan and Downing (2005) reflects the development of the social economy in the province of Quebec, a point that I elaborate on later in this chapter. The key feature of this definition is the social movement orientation or reformist orientation (Fontan & Shragge, 2000).

A second definition that has emerged from central Canada takes more of a pragmatic approach when explaining the social economy. Quarter et al. (2009) state the following:

> *Social economy* is a bridging concept for organizations that have social objectives central to their mission and their practice, and either have explicit economic objectives or generate some economic value through the services they provide and purchases that they undertake. (p. 4).

Quarter et al. (2009) have chosen to take a utilitarian rather than a social movement orientation to the social economy, but it can complement the latter perspective.

While not explicit in the two definitions, there is an underlying agreement that sources of revenue and the diverse business and organizational forms contribute to the formation of the social economy. While there lacks clear consensus on a definition, there is widespread agreement that conceptually, the social economy is a robust organizing framework that recognizes activities and initiatives that fall outside the public and private sectors (Sousa & Hamdon, 2010). For the purpose of this chapter the operational definition of the social economy[3] is characterized as:

> encompassing the range of ways people exchange goods and services (often based on the principle of reciprocity) with each other and distribute profit as surpluses through various mechanisms, including: the family or household economy; local volunteer activities and opportunities; and the wide range of more formally structured organizations, (such as charities or member based associations) that explicitly pursue social goals using business oriented approaches.

As implied in this chapter, the social economy in Canada has developed through circumstance rather than as a planned process; however, the exception has been in the province of Quebec. An initiative in 2005 was developed by the federal government to both clarify and support the scaling of the social economy (Hall, 2011). This support came in the form of a federal investment to create a special investment fund as well as conduct a scoping exercise to get a sense of what exists in the country. This was referred to as the Social Economy Suite, and resulted in the establishing of six research centers and one coordinating group out of the University of Victoria.[4] One of the legacies that emerged was the effort to map social enterprises across the country (Thompson & Emmanuel, 2012), which has provided both a methodology and evidence of the varieties that exist across the country.

---

[3] This description of the social economy is paraphrased from the Mike Lewis (August 2006) discussion paper "Mapping the Social Economy in B.C. and Alberta: Towards a Strategic Approach." (Lewis, 2006)

[4] These research centers were funded with federal dollars for 5 years. Unfortunately, the funding was significantly reduced with the election of a conservative government in 2008. The newly elected government decided to withdraw the development finance fund, but the research funding remained (Hall, 2011).

The Cooperative Model and the Social Economy

As with many countries that recognize the social economy, the success of the cooperative model within the various sectors of the economy has been positively acknowledged by the Canadian public. There is a common understanding and broad agreement that the cooperative model operates with a social purpose; however, the social purpose can be narrowly applied, and is more often associated with serving the needs of a defined membership than benefiting broader society. The cooperative model exists in different sectors of the Canadian economy, including finance, agriculture, retail, and housing. The purpose of the cooperative and the motivations of the membership will reflect the issues or needs the organization is intended to address (see Sousa, 2013).

The origin of the cooperative movement in Canada was largely from a response to the negative consequences of the market-based economy. The best known and early examples of the application of the cooperative model could be traced to Atlantic Canada with the Antigonish movement in the province of Nova Scotia in the early 1930s (Dodaro & Pluta, 2012). The movement was the outcome of the work of two catholic priests, Moses Coady and Jimmy Thompkins, who worked with fishermen to develop cooperatives in order to get better prices for their catches. One of the key features of the Antigonish movement was the recognition that cooperative development relies on effective community development (Dodaro & Pluta, 2012).

Out of the Antigonish movement was the legitimization of the cooperative model as a competitive force in market transactions. Furthermore, efforts to reform the traditional business model through the incorporation of cooperative practices may have a wider social impact. While the Antigonish movement was monumental, there were parallel efforts underway across Canada. Most notable was the development of the Caisse Populaire, or Credit Unions, in Quebec by Alphonse Desjardins (Dodaro & Pluta, 2012). Presently, Desjardins is a well-established Credit Union, and has holdings that match what is found within the traditional banks. Resulting from the many successes of the cooperative movement has been the legitimization of the cooperative organization as an option to deliver particular social services rather than government. Examples include nonmarket housing and health services.

One of the primary strengths of the cooperative model is that it can meet a social need of a community or group through the business model. In this case, it is a social issue that drives the creation of the cooperative organization. The cooperative model became institutionalized through legislation at both the federal and provincial levels, and operates as a nonprofit or redistributes the profits (or surplus) to the membership. In both instances, a cooperative business will still adhere to a set of values and principles that distinguish it from similar businesses that operate solely in the private sector. Examples of these principles and values include:

- The provision of affordable goods and services
- Support the needs of a well-defined membership
- Generate revenue and redistribute to the members through patronage dividends

- Not intended to meet a broader social purpose, although social goals can align with social movements and advocacy groups
- Align with the values of the welfare state

In Canada there is quite a variety of cooperatives, which are found across all sectors of the economy, and are usually divided into nonfinancial (e.g., housing, consumer) and financial (e.g., credit unions) entities. As of 2018 there were 7794 nonfinancial cooperatives in Canada (Industry Canada, 2019). As shown in Fig. 3.1, there was a steady decline of cooperatives from 2009 to 2011, with a peak of 8042 in 2013.

What is clear is that there has been a decline in the number of nonfinancial cooperatives since 2009, a pattern that has been consistent since the 1990s. The reasons for the decline are not uniform across the sectors and are quite complex. Case studies have shown that the lack of member engagement and access to capital have been key contributors to increased incidences of demutualization among cooperatives into for-profit investor-owned firms (Fulton & Girard, 2015; Sousa, Pattison, & Herman, 2012).

Credit unions in Canada were born out of the Antigonish and Desjardins movements. Like all cooperative organizations, the model of the credit union was intended to be community based and member driven. The primary purposes of the credit union movement are the need to develop an alternative to the profit-driven services of regular banks and create a source of capital (i.e., for mortgage or loans) for community businesses and cooperatives. In essence, the credit union was intended to be the financial institution of the social economy.

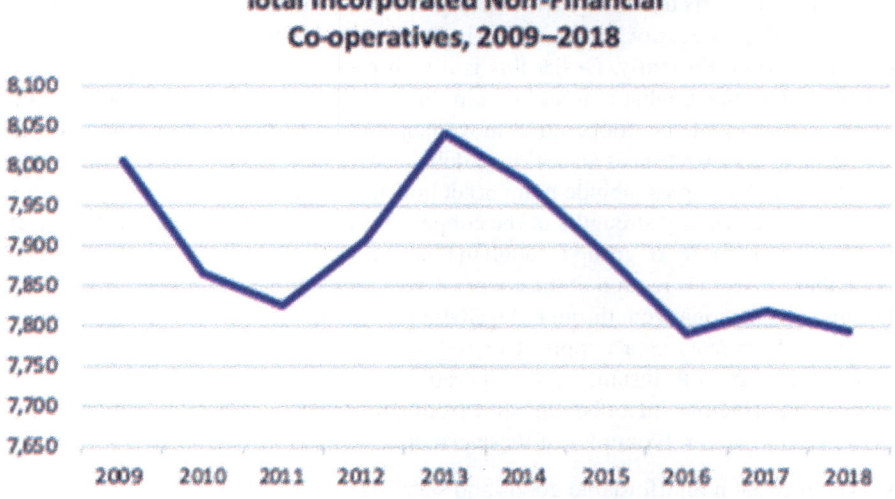

Fig. 3.1 Change in number of cooperatives. Source: Industry Canada, https://www.ic.gc.ca/eic/site/106.nsf/eng/00149.html

Credit unions have had to compete with regular banks[5] in terms of investments and attracting customers (referred to as members) and providing services. The outcome of this competition has resulted in the credit union resembling a regular bank. Consequently, the credit union is no longer the first place that social economy organizations will go to for financial support because they often do not meet the level of risk tolerance criteria that resembles regular banks. These organizations have had to seek other sources of capital and investment, resulting in the development of new funding sources in the form of investments that focus more on the impact of the business.

There has been a significant reduction in the number of credit unions in Canada. In the financial sector, as of 2018 there were slightly over 500 credit unions across the country. As shown in the data provided by the Canadian Union Association, there has been a notable change in the number of credit unions in Canada (see Fig. 3.2). It is notable that the decline became more pronounced after 2008, when the impact of the global economic crisis forced financial institutions to reconsider their investment strategies and there were mergers of credit unions.

Some features of credit unions shown in Table 3.1 can also help show some of the changes. Two points that stand out are the significant reduction in the number of credit unions and a modest decrease in membership levels.

The decline of financial cooperatives can be attributed to a variety of factors, including response to market forces; waning public awareness and interest; generational and demographic shifts; increased consolidations or mergers; and demutualization into for-profit investor-owned firms (Fulton & Girard, 2015). The global economic crisis in 2008 revealed that the investment strategies used by credit unions

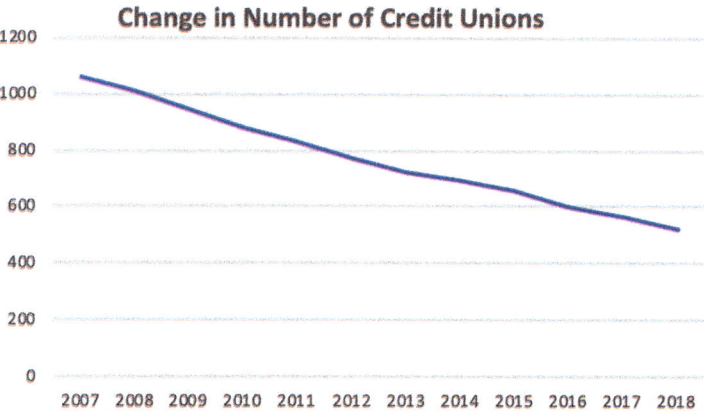

Fig. 3.2 Change in number of credit unions in Canada from 2007 to 2018. Source: Canadian Credit Union Association

[5] In 2017 the Canadian Office of the Superintendent of Financial Institutions (OSFI) directed credit unions to not use the term "bank" in any medium, including referring to the services provided as a form of "banking." See http://www.osfi-bsif.gc.ca/Eng/fi-if/app/rla-prl/Pages/adv-2017-01.aspx.

Table 3.1 Changes in features of credit unions in Canada from 2007 to 2018. Source: Canadian Credit Union Association

	2007	2018	Percentage variance
Number of credit unions	1061	521	−50.90
Members	10,672,481	10,426,636	−2.30
Deposits	$176,732,303,428	$329,139,954,940	86.24
Loans	$174,826,062,854	$352,148,105,095	101.43
Assets	$209,283,152,886	$416,746,350,214	99.13

resulted in significant losses because the investments were transnational; however, credit unions were found to have fared better than banks during and post-global financial crisis (Birchall, 2013). As shown in Table 3.1, deposits, loans, and assets all increased during a period when big banks were faced with significant challenges.

Out of those factors, the biggest concern seems to be a lack of awareness as well as a changing demographic of the membership and potential members. One is left to wonder that if the cooperative sector in Canada is decreasing, has the need for these organizations changed or is no longer a factor in Canadian society? This question is difficult to answer since there has been little empirical research that critically explores the incidences of these reductions across sectors. What has become clearer over the last 20 years is that the cooperative model is resilient and alternative models have emerged. For example, the new-generation cooperatives or limited-liability cooperatives rely on the capital of nonmember investors (Sousa et al., 2012). These new forms of cooperatives have become a form of social enterprise, and the non-member investors may be investing in the impact of the business, but what is more likely is that they are seeking a high rate of return on their investment.

While the cooperative model has changed, it continues to be an integral and successful feature of the social economy. The model is adapting, but arguably the cooperative is not the panacea when considering impact investing. The other area that comprises the social economy includes nonprofit and charity organizations that will be explored in more detail in the next section.

Nonprofit and Charity Organizations and the Social Economy

In Canada, the third sector[6] is deemed to be a central part of the social economy, and includes nonprofit organizations (e.g., charities and voluntary organizations). Nonprofit organizations have had a tremendous impact on Canadian society, likely due to the reliance of these organizations to provide services and activities associated with the welfare state. As in many countries, nonprofits have been integral in

---

[6] The third sector is often used as a synonym for the social economy (Fontan & Shragge, 2000).

providing a safety net for disadvantaged communities and has focused on the delivery of social services, either independently or as a proxy for government.

According to Faul (2014) there are over 170,000 nonprofit organizations in Canada, with over 80,000 being charities. Collectively, the activities generate $176 billion in economic activity and employ over two million employees. Over 13 million volunteers contribute over two billion hours annually, which is the equivalent to over one million full-time jobs. Figure 3.3 shows the range of activities that are undertaken by nonprofit organizations.

A framework developed by Quarter et al. (2009) divides nonprofits into the following categories: commercial nonprofits, social economy businesses, civil society organizations, and public sector nonprofits. There is some overlap when considering how each operates within the social economy, but a key defining feature is that they function with a social purpose. Nonprofit organizations have traditionally had the following sources of revenue: government grants and contracts, fees for services, and donations. The reliance on a particular source of revenue has traditionally reflected the type of nonprofit organization being referred to.

As with most countries that have a robust nonprofit sector, alternate means to generate revenue has become a priority. This priority became particularly poignant during and after the global financial crisis of 2008, and Canada's nonprofit sector was not immune to the adverse outcomes that were so common around the world. The effects of the crisis included the following:

- Decline in individual and corporate donations
- Increased demand for services
- Reduction in government funding
- Negative impact on foundation investments and endowments
- Elimination of some foundation granting programs
- Declines in earned income

These effects resulted in nonprofit organizations having had to change how they approach their mission as well as how they raised revenue, both of which were dependent on each other. In the matter of how organizations approached their mission, the need to implement budget cuts resulted in reduced staffing levels, and a

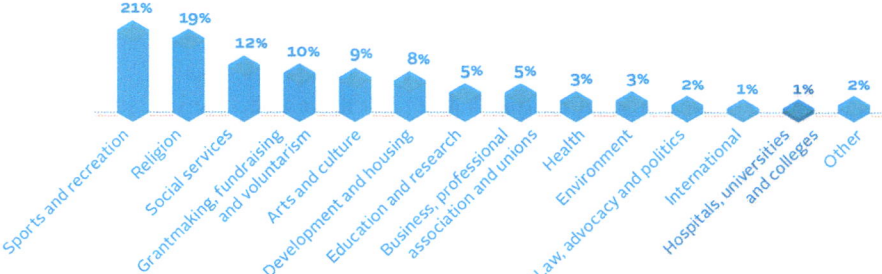

Fig. 3.3 Range of activities of nonprofit organizations. Source: Faul, 2014

greater focus on volunteers. The matter of generating revenue was more compli-
cated given the legislative limitations associated with nonprofits and charities.
One approach was to diversify the sources of revenue by being less reliant on external funders. Mulholland, Mendelsohn, and Shamshiri (2011) have developed tools
and resources aimed at helping nonprofit organizations to diversify its sources of
revenue. One statement is particularly revealing:

> These indicators point to the fundamental challenge faced by Canada's charities and non-
> profits—how to fulfill their missions on a sustainable basis, in the face of uncertain support
> from governments and donors and certain growth in demand for many of their services?
> This raises the further question of what governments can do to ensure that these organiza-
> tions continue to fulfill their vital mandates and meet growing demand. (p. 5)

A key message from this statement is that nonprofit organizations need access to different sources of revenue as governments reduce funding and the expectations of
donors have changed. Mulholland et al. (2011) do see that governments can play a role
in supporting nonprofit organizations and suggest that governments can make better
use of existing policy levers (e.g., tax code) to enable these organizations to better
compete in market-oriented activities. The authors also called for nonprofit organizations to make greater use of the social enterprise model as a way to fund programs and
services, as well as ensure the long-term sustainability of the organization.

However the social enterprise model is not foreign to the nonprofit sector as
many nonprofits are themselves social enterprises (e.g., the salvation army thrift
stores). What is new is the expectation that nonprofit organizations need to be more
self-sufficient and resilient to changes that occur in the economy, which can be
either cyclical or the result of a crisis. I now turn to the role of the social enterprise
model in Canada's social economy.

The Social Enterprise and the Social Economy

The introduction of the social enterprise model in the 1990s has contributed to the
public at large to pay greater attention to the social economy by focusing on social
purpose businesses. There are several reasons for this. First, social economy organizations and activities contributed to the development of the Canadian welfare state,
and there have been many documented cases of successful social economy activities
supporting disadvantaged populations and communities of different sorts, and many
of these activities were related to business in one form or another (e.g., consumer
cooperatives). However, with the dismantling of the welfare state in Canada, traditional social economy organizations have had an increasingly more challenging
time to access revenue sources and, in some cases, to remain relevant. Second, the
social enterprise model has introduced a unique perspective to the discourse of the
social economy, such that the social enterprise model has become the term of choice
when referring to the social economy. The popularity of the social enterprise model

is based on the idea that they can be responsive and resilient to the changing nature of the economy. Consequently, the prominence of the social enterprise model has resulted in proponents of the communal orientation to the social economy to reconsider the traditional or essential pillars of the social economy.

Third, the social economy has been increasingly defined as an inclusive concept that encompasses existing organizational forms, and the social enterprise is one of many options. Fourth, government has increasingly seen that the social economy can have a role in forwarding both a progressive and neoliberal agenda, rendering them no longer mutually exclusive, by supporting social enterprises as a form of social innovation. Taken together, these four points demonstrate how the social economy has changed from being a fringe alternative to the mainstream economy towards greater integration by adopting more market-based approaches to running a business. In essence, the current understanding of the social economy has shifted from having a communal focus to being more individualistic in operation and intentions; the latter point aligns well with the notion of the new social economy, as explored in this book.

The social enterprise model in Canada has increasingly become the predominant way that the social economy is understood. Consequently, as a result there has been a shift in the perception of the social economy being of organizations whose social priorities are achieved through market-based activities. The social enterprise business model started out as a source of revenue for nonprofit organizations, where the nonprofit is the parent organization and the social enterprise would be either a program or merely a source of revenue. Most often, the social enterprise's mission or purpose would align with the nonprofit or parent organization. However, there have been new forms of social enterprises developed while existing organizational forms are increasingly considered to be social enterprises.

The social economy has formed as a result of networking across groups, and there have been efforts to learn what is working, or develop best practices; several key realities have emerged as a result. Elson, Hall, and Wamucii (2016) reported on a national survey of social enterprise activities, which included a sampling frame of 7000 and responses from 1350 organizations. Some key findings from the research follow. According to the report, social enterprises in Canada exist for a variety of purposes (p. 9):

- 26% provide employment development.
- 19% provide training for workforce integration.
- 19% generate income for a parent organization.
- 81% operate to achieve a social mission.
- 45% operate to achieve a cultural mission.
- 27% operate to achieve an environmental mission.
- 43% address poverty reduction.

As shown in the findings, the social enterprise model has significantly departed from the welfare state approach that characterized the social economy. Another outcome of the research was the realization that social enterprises have been narrowly defined, and may not reflect the reality of the practice. For the purpose of the research, they defined social enterprise as follows:

> A business venture owned or operated by a non-profit organization that sells goods or provides services in the market for the purpose of creating a blended return on investment, both financial and social/environmental/cultural. (p.8)

The findings from the research reveal that far fewer than expected (68%) are directly associated with a nonprofit organization, revealing the need to reconceptualize how social enterprises are defined to reflect what is happening on the ground.

The broadening of the social objectives expected from a traditional social economy organization has helped the social enterprise model gain greater traction. From one perspective, departing from the welfare state approach legitimized it as a progressive business model. Relatedly, traditional organizations of the social economy tend to be focused too closely on problems and needs that affect a portion of the population, whereas social entrepreneurs see themselves as operating to the benefit of the broader society rather than solely for a defined group or as a revenue stream for a nonprofit organization. Whatever the reason, the opportunity for a business to be more flexible and responsive to needs not addressed by government programs has become a selling point for the social enterprise model (Mulholland et al., 2011).

In Canada, the social enterprise model was intended to serve as a revenue source for nonprofit organizations. As the social enterprise model has continued to gain broader acceptance, new forms have emerged that are outside the expectation that all social enterprises are associated with a nonprofit organization. McMurtry et al. (2015) describe five forms of social enterprise in Canada: cooperatives, nonprofit organizations, community development/interest organizations, First Nation businesses, and business with a social mission. The authors explain that these models "have clear, if diverse, fields of activity, distinct social missions and target groups, legislative supports, and governance models. Perhaps most importantly, they are almost exclusively the organizational forms that social enterprises take in the Canadian context" (p. 12).

Much of what has been written in this chapter implies that there is a uniformity to how the social economy is understood and practiced in Canada. The reality is that much of what has been written applies to English Canada. Social economy actors in the province of Quebec have been much more active in developing a social economy that works with the public and private sectors. Therefore, it is important to briefly describe some of the features of the social economy in Quebec.

The Social Economy in Quebec

One of the exceptions to the pattern described above in Canada has been the development of the social economy in the province of Quebec. While the components of the social economy are quite predictable across Canada, the social economy has been an integral part of the socioeconomic infrastructure in the province of Quebec. The social economy has been a key part of the history of Quebec (Bouchard, Paulo, & Zerdani, 2015; Mendell & Neamtan, 2010), and is closely aligned with Europe in supporting the social economy as an economic sector within society.

As with other parts of Canada, the social economy was once found to be located at the periphery of society (Bouchard et al., 2015). The key difference in Quebec is that different stakeholders or social actors (e.g., labor groups) have traditionally played a significant role in developing or entrenching the social economy into Quebec social and public policy (Bouchard et al., 2015; Mendell & Neamtan, 2010). A new impetus to see a better integration of the social economy into Quebec society took place in 1996 at the *Socio-Economic Summit*. The summit was intended to build on the successes from tripartite agreements developed by government, cooperatives, and the private sector, and the labor movement by including social movements as a key stakeholder (Charron, 2012; Mendell & Neamtan, 2010). The intention was to develop a single strategy that consolidated the different areas of the social economy in order to ensure that the greatest impact could be made on Quebec Society (Mendell, 2009). The outcome of the summit was the establishing of an infrastructure to support and sustain the social economy as a unique sector in society. The infrastructure consists of the following: development finance from a solidarity fund; establishment of an organization and building space in the form of the Chantier de l'économie sociale, which has become a critical voice on issues related to the social economy; and creation of local investment funds and local development centers.

The social economy looks quite different than the rest of Canada because the process was the outcome of a co-construction and co-production of public policies. Categories of public policies included:

- Territorial policies that support local communities through intermediaries
- Generic development and access to finance, HRD, research and education, and public procurement
- Sectoral policies that support enterprise development to meet particular needs
- Policies for target populations that integrate individuals into the economy

The implementation of these policies resulted in a clearer pathway for social economy organizations to be better integrated into the broader economy. According to the Government of Quebec (2019), the following characteristics of the social economy are evident in Quebec:

- Quebec has 11,200 social economy enterprises. 75% are nonprofit organizations (NPOs), 22% are nonfinancial cooperatives, and 3% are financial cooperatives or mutual insurance companies.
- Most social economy enterprises are small businesses: 65% have fewer than ten payroll employees and 64% have revenues below $500,000.
- There are also large enterprises among them: 2.3% have 100 or more payroll employees and 3.5% have revenues of $10 million or more.

A relatively large proportion of social economy enterprises have existed for over 30 years (39%), while 15% have been in existence for less than 10 years, and 46% for 10–30 years. The social economy is found in the following sectors: home care services (7000 employees), parent-controlled daycare (35,000 employees), funeral cooperatives, health cooperatives, and multiservice solidarity cooperatives:

- Housing: cooperative and nonprofit
- Tourism and recreation
- Environment (waste management, etc.)
- Alternative agriculture and forestry
- Culture
- Financial services: 671 credit unions
- Worker cooperatives
- Worker-shareholder cooperatives
- Community real estate

What makes Quebec's approach to the social economy unique in Canada? According to Mendell (2009) the experience in Quebec has resulted in a level of coherence that is not found elsewhere in the country. She refers to three pillars that have contributed to the current existence of the social economy: (1) the social economy enterprises; (2) an enabling policy environment; and (3) leadership. As stated by Mendell (2009): "Co-existence underwrites the agenda in Quebec and is built on established practices" (p. 39). Mendell details three key elements that have contributed to this success:

- Development finance: solidarity finance with a distinct investment fund
- Institutionalized partnerships that reinforce the co-production and co-creation of policy and programs
- Political and practice-based role of intermediaries, for instance Le Chantier which is a network of networks

These elements have resulted in a well-organized ecosystem that supports future development while sustaining existing enterprises. This support is evident in the existence of impact investment funds; social economy enterprises provide services for the broader public; and the Chantier de l'économie sociale can respond to urgent and emerging needs.

The social economy in the province of Quebec is an integrated strategy that demonstrates the presence of the social economy as a sector of Quebec's economy, and functions in a way that complements the public and private sectors, rather than being an alternative. However, Quebec remains quite unique in Canada, where there seems to have been a greater willing to adopt elements of the new social economy.

(Re) Structuring of the Social Economy in Canada

As described in this chapter, there has been a restructuring of what constitutes the social economy in Canada, and arguably, the idea of the new social economy can help explain how this occurred. Although the term is not commonly used[7] in the way that is described in the introductory chapter, the concept can help to explain how the social economy in Canada has changed. The role of the social enterprise, as described in the introductory chapter of this book, does not always take the communal qualities that were part of the pillars of the social economy. I am not basing this view on any specific source, but present more as a reflection of the reduction of the number of key organizations associated with the social economy (e.g., cooperatives) as well as how nonprofit organizations have had to adapt to economic crises by seeking alternative sources of revenue and restructuring operations in order to sustain themselves.

In Canada, the federal and provincial levels of government have traditionally supported the development of the social economy through activities and programs associated with the welfare state. Accordingly, support has largely been intended to maintain the sector's initiatives by aligning with a government's priorities. The support has been in place because of a desire by the government to offer social programs and services that are affordable (e.g., housing and healthcare) and respond to a social need. In the province of Quebec, the social economy is more entrenched in society because of the active collaboration of social economy actors, social economy enterprises, government, and the private sector to provide social programs and services that are best found in the market while others are more appropriate as nonmarket.

A key challenge for social enterprises has been access to capital since they are unable to accrue debt and there is limited investor interest if the return on investment is uncertain. As the social purpose of the social enterprise model is to operate within the market and compete with private sector businesses, the two levels of government have increasingly become supporters through public policy initiatives and legislation. Governments across the country have started to develop new funds aimed at supporting the social innovation brought about by social enterprises.

In 2018, the federal government announced the creation of a social finance fund with the following purpose:

> To encourage innovative approaches to persistent and complex social challenges, the Government of Canada is creating a Social Finance Fund. This will give charitable, non-profit and social purpose organizations access to new financing to implement their innovative ideas, and will connect them with non-government investors seeking to support projects that will drive positive social change (Government of Canada, 2018).

According to the Government of Canada (2018) the social finance fund provides $755 million dollars over 10 years to support the development of social pur-

---

[7] Fontan and Shragge (2000) make a reference to the new social economy in their chapter, which very much resonates with how the idea is used in this book.

pose organizations in Canada. There is an additional fund referred to as a capacity-building Investment and Readiness fund of $50 M over 2 years. This announcement was greeted with much enthusiasm from practitioners. According to (Williams, 2018):

> There are so many people who are working to put people and planet before profit. We need to help them become investment ready and scale their impact" said Centre for Social Innovation CEO Tonya Surman. "The Social Finance Fund could unlock the potential of social entrepreneurs to solve real problems. This will result in things like fewer people living in poverty, less polarization, and curbing climate change.

What is clear is that the purpose of the social finance fund is to support individual initiatives rather than being a part of a larger project, which is a very specific area within the social economy. In fact, the social economy is not mentioned in the material at all, which is in stark contrast to how the federal government announced a similar initiative in a 2004 Speech from the Throne:

> And the Government will help communities help themselves. One of the best ways to do this is to get behind the remarkable people who are applying entrepreneurial skills, not for profit, but rather to enhance the social and environmental conditions in our communities across Canada. These new approaches to community development – sometimes referred to as the "social economy' are producing more and more success stories about a turnaround in individual lives and distressed neighbourhoods – communities working to combat homelessness, address poverty and clean up the environment. The Government of Canada wants to support those engaged in this entrepreneurial social movement. It will increase their access to resources and tools. The Government will, for example, work to widen the scope of programs currently available to small and medium-sized enterprises to include social enterprises (Chantier de L'économie Sociale, 2005, p. 5).

While the federal social finance fund is aimed at supporting national level projects, there are also new forms of investment funds or equity tax credits emerging in Canada. One of the more successful examples is the Community Economy Development Investment Funds (CEDIF) in the province of Nova Scotia (Nova Scotia Co-operative Council (2019)). According to the Nova Scotia Securities Commission (2019):

> A Community Economic and Development Investment Fund (CEDIF) is a pool of capital which is raised from individuals within Nova Scotia to invest in for-profit entities within a defined community. These funds are controlled by a local group of officers and directors, who may be chosen by the founders and promoters of the CEDIF or by the CEDIF's investors at an annual general meeting. To establish a CEDIF offering the applicants must prepare and file the Form 1 Simplified Offering Document and receive from the Director of the NSSC as well as an Equity Tax Credit (ETC) from the Minister of Finance. Once these are in place, the CEDIF can raise capital through an exempt public offering in Nova Scotia and advertise its shares to the public in Nova Scotia.

These examples of investment funds are a significant departure for how the social economy and organizations have been represented, including the absence of a focus on community-level activities. This shift towards supporting individual organizations and initiatives with a social purpose assumes that the social purpose is in the public interest. In effect, the role of social economy organizations associated with a more communal orientation as the vehicle for social change has been reduced, which has resulted in a weakening of the significance of the social economy in Canada.

Another way of understanding the development of special investment funds is to see them as operating in a similar way as the solidarity fund in Quebec. In other words, these funds are examples of developing a nationwide ecosystem supporting social innovation. One would expect that those who access the funds will begin working with community economic development that exists across the country. However, this emerging ecosystem is supporting social enterprise development rather than the social economy. It is unclear what impact this trend will have on the other elements of the social economy.

What is clear is that the movement towards impact investing is gaining traction in Canada, and both federal and provincial governments see this as an opportunity to foster some form of social change by being a part of the impact investing trend, which has a substantial amount of money to invest into the social economy. For instance, according to the Responsible Investment Association (2019), "Impact assets under management (AUM) in Canada now total $14.75 billion, $14.75 billion, up from $8.15 billion reported 2 years prior" (p. 6). It is too early to tell both the benefits and consequences this trend will have on the social economy.

Conclusion and Looking Forward

My objective in this chapter was to demonstrate how the social economy has changed in Canada, with the most significant change being the increased legitimization of what has been seen as organizations working on with the margins of society by transforming into organizations that increasingly adopt private sector practices. As shown in this chapter the social economy has had an important place in Canadian society, but there is no consensus as to whether its impact has been positive, negative, or neutral. Efforts to build greater coherence have been met with what are perceived as insurmountable challenges, including absence of a supportive public policy infrastructure and a perception that the social economy activities and organizations exist to respond to a social need or to a failure in the market. Consequently, is the new social economy the best way to conceptualize how the social economy exists in the Canadian context?

In its aggregate form, the social economy is not seen as its own sector within the Canadian economy. The social economy is currently pluralistic, but what is shared across organizations and initiatives is a desire to reduce reliance on the state and challenge the dominance of the private sector as the means for daily living. However, social economy organizations and businesses have fared well on an individual level because they have been able to show their impact in comparable terms to private sector business. For instance, measuring and assessing impact will more often reflect economic indicators (e.g., employment, contribution to the GDP) that are similar to those expected from private sector business rather than socially oriented ones (e.g., health, happiness). Yet, community service-oriented and less market-oriented elements of the social economy have flourished over the last 100 years in Canada, but are most often seen as operating on the fringes of the social economy.

I have chosen to problematize the shift from a collectivist or communal orientation towards individualistic efforts when operating a business with a social purpose. This shift is a form of restructuring that can lead towards accepting the dominance of the market-based approaches, which is a significant departure of how the social economy has come to be represented in the public discourse in Canada. Yet, as shown in the case of Quebec, market based and nonmarket based can be complementary and do not need to be rivals. Accordingly, in the province of Quebec, the social economy has evolved to become part of a "plural economy" (Mendell & Neamtan, 2010).

The absence of such coherence across the rest of the country has resulted in an assortment or mishmash of strategies and initiative. In Canada, the social economy is not uniformly counter hegemonic or oriented towards social change. Some social economy organizations were created to challenge the dominant hegemony of the private sector (Carroll & Ratner, 2010) as highlighted in the Antigonish movement. Other organizations have been created to work with government to provide social services and other programs. These organizations form partnerships with government, and are a key part of the modern welfare state (Hunter & Miazdyck, 2004; Moscovitch, 1983). However other organizations aim to meet their social objectives by working in the market in competition with private sector businesses. Unfortunately, these organizations do not always fare well in the market. If they are unable to successfully compete in the market as their own entity they may demutualize (Sousa et al., 2012), may transform into a private sector business through some form of mission creep (Grizzle & Sloan, 2016), or may be purchased by a fund associated with private sector investment (Nair, 2020), as in the recent case of Mountain Equipment Co-operative (MEC) sold to an American-based private equity firm. It should be noted that failure to compete in the market is not necessarily an indication that the business cannot be successful. However, such failure can result when a business entity is not feeling a part of or supported as a sector that is distinct from the public and private sectors.

It is too early to determine whether the further entrenchment of more individualistic approach to the social economy can actually benefit Canadian society, so more research, tracking, and discussion are needed as there can be unforeseen consequences of the shift. What has become clearer recently is that the resiliency of social economy organizations is being tested. One of the unexpected outcomes of the coronavirus pandemic (referred to as COVID-19) has been its impact on raising the profile of areas associated with the social economy, for instance, government reliance on nonprofit organizations and foundations to deliver social services and serve as intermediaries for income-related programs. However, the capacity of the traditional pillars of the social economy has reached its peak as well. Some provinces are projecting a significant reduction of the nonprofit organizations, for example 20% in Alberta (Kaufmann, 2020). Furthermore, *Imagine Canada* has reported a significant reduction in volunteer contributions as well as the adverse effects of health requirements aimed at dealing with COVID-19 (e.g., social distancing) on the demand for services.

Fortunately, there are other signs that the crisis associated with COVID-19 is initiating discussions and reintroducing solutions to social ills that predate the pandemic (Lasby, 2020). COVID-19 has reintroduced elements or aspirations of the welfare state into the public discourse that had largely been eliminated, neglected, or forgotten. There has been a robust discussion of whether the federal government can introduce new income security programs, such as providing a guaranteed income for all citizens. It is important to note that these discussions may inadvertently reinforce the idea that social economy and organizations therein exist because of market failure. An additional phenomenon is the appearance of efforts that are grounded in solidarity and cooperation rather than competition (for example, Pillar Nonprofit Network, n.d.) to support the work of individual social enterprises. In essence, COVID-19 has brought out the strengths of the traditional social economy, but has tested the resiliency of the new or impact social economy.

Finally, the difficulties of building a coherent approach to integrating the social economy into society can be seen as an opportunity, in particular in times of crises. Embracing diverse practices and business models is a starting point, and what should follow should be efforts to bridge those differences rather than seeing them as competing models. There are many international examples of such efforts successfully occurring, and future priorities should aim to better integrate these differences to support greater solidarity and cooperation rather than competing visions of a better world.

References

Banting, K. (2004). *Canada - nation-building in a federal welfare state.* (ZeS-Arbeitspapier, 6/2004). Bremen: Universität Bremen, Zentrum für Sozialpolitik. Retrieved from https://nbn-resolving.org/urn:nbn:de:0168-ssoar-109350

Birchall, J. (2013). *Resilience in a downturn: The power of financial cooperatives.* Geneva: International Labor Organization.

Bouchard, M., Paulo, C., & Zerdani, T. (2015). Social Enterprise in Québec: Understanding their "Institutional Footprint.". *Canadian Journal of Nonprofit and Social Economy Research Revue canadienne de recherche sur les OBSL et l'économie sociale, 6*(1), 42–62.

Carroll, W., & Ratner, R. S. (2010). Social Movements and Counter-Hegemony: Lessons from the Field. *New Proposals: Journal of Marxism and Interdisciplinary Inquiry, 4*(1), 7–22.

Chantier de L'économie Sociale. (2005). Social Economy and Community Economic Development in Canada: Next Steps for Public Policy. Retrieved from https://ccednet-rcdec.ca/sites/ccednet-rcdec.ca/files/Issues%20Paper_Sept_2005.pdf

Charron, A. (2012). The growth of the social economy in Quebec through the unification of the movement since 1996. The Canadian CED Network. Retrieved from https://www.ccednet-rcdec.ca/sites/ccednet-cdec.ca/files/ccednet/Alex_Quebec_paper.pdf

Craig, J. (1993). *The Nature of Co-operation.* Montréal, QC: Black Rose Books LTD..

Department of Justice. (2019). *The Canadian Constitution.* Retrieved from https://www.justice.gc.ca/eng/csj-sjc/just/05.html

Dodaro, S., & Pluta, L. (2012). *The big picture: The antigonish movement of Eastern Nova Scotia.* Montréal, QC: McGill-Queen's University Press.

Elson, P., Hall, P., & Wamucii, P. (2016). *Canadian National Social Enterprise Sector Survey Report*. Calgary, AB: Institute for Community Prosperity.

Faul, S. (2014). *Narrative core resource: The beginnings of a new discussion with Canadians about the charitable and nonprofit sector*. Toronto, ON: Imagine Canada.

Fontan, J. M., & Shragge, E. (2000). Tendencies, tensions and visions in the social economy. In J. M. Fontan & E. Shragge (Eds.), *Social economy: International debates and perspectives* (pp. 1–15). Montreal: Black Rose Books.

Fulton, M. & Girard, J.-P. (2015). Demutualization of Co-operatives and Mutuals. Report for Co-operatives and Mutuals Canada.

Government of Canada. (2018). *Backgrounder: The Social Finance Fund*. Retrieved from https://www.canada.ca/en/employment-social-development/news/2018/11/backgrounder-the-social-finance-fund.html

Government of Canada. (2019). *Justice Laws Website*. Retrieved from https://laws-lois.justice.gc.ca/eng/const/page-4.html

Government of Quebec. (2019). Québec has 11,200 social economy enterprises. Retrieved from https://www.stat.gouv.qc.ca/salle-presse/communique/communique-presse-2019/avril/avril1929_an.html

Grizzle, C., & Sloan, M. F. (2016). Assessing changing accountability structures created by emerging equity markets in the nonprofit sector. *Public Administration Quarterly, 40*(2), 387–408.

Hall, P. (2011). Introduction: Learning from the Social Economy Community-University Research Partnerships. In P. Hall & I. MacPherson (Eds.), *Community-University Research Partnerships: Reflections on the Canadian Social Economy Experience* (pp. 1–22). Victoria, BC: University of Victoria.

Hunter, G. & Miazdyck, D. (2004). Current Issues Surrounding Poverty and Welfare Programming in Canada: Two Reviews. Retrieved from https://www.policyalternatives.ca/sites/default/files/uploads/publications/Saskatchewan_Pubs/poverty_welfare.pdf

Industry Canada. (2019). *Total Incorporated Non-Financial Co-operatives, 2009–2018.*. Retrieved from https://www.ic.gc.ca/eic/site/106.nsf/eng/00149.html

Kaufmann, B. (2020, September 16). As many as 20 per cent of Alberta's non-profits could fold due to the pandemic. The Calgary Herald. Retrieved from https://calgaryherald.com/news/local-news/as-many-as-20-per-cent-of-albertas-non-profits-could-fold-due-to-the-pandemic

Lasby, D. (2020). Charities & the COVID-19 Pandemic. Imagine Canada's Sector Monitor. Retrieved from https://imaginecanada.ca/sites/default/files/COVID-19%20Sector%20Monitor%20Report%20ENGLISH_0.pdf

Lévesque, B., & Mendell, M. (2005). The Social Economy: Approaches, Practices and a Proposal for a New Community-University Alliance (CURA). *Journal of Rural Cooperation, 33*(1), 21–45.

Lewis, M. (2006). *Mapping the Social Economy in B.C. and Alberta: Towards a Strategic Approach*. Victoria, BC: The B.C- Alberta Research Alliance on the Social Economy (BALTA).

Lightman, E., & Irving, A. (1991). Restructuring Canada's Welfare State. *Journal of Social Policy, 21*(1), 65–86.

McMurtry, J. J., Brouard, F., Elson, P., Hall, P., Lionais, D. & Vieta, M. (2015). Social Enterprise in Canada: Context, Models and Institutions. ICSEM Working Papers, No. 04, Liege: The International Comparative Social Enterprise Models (ICSEM) Project.

Mendell, M. (2009). Three Pillars of the Social Economy: The Quebec Experience. In A. Amin (Ed.), *The Social Economy: International Perspectives on Economic Solidarity* (pp. 176–207). London: Zed Books.

Mendell, M., & Neamtan, N. (2010). The Social Economy in Québec: Towards a New Political Economy. In L. Mook, J. Quarter, & S. Ryan (Eds.), *Researching the Social Economy* (pp. 63–83). Toronto, ON: University of Toronto Press.

Moscovitch, A. (1986). The Welfare State Since 1975. *Journal of Canadian Studies, 21*(2), 77–94.

Moscovitch, A. (1983). *The Welfare State in Canada: A Selected Bibliography 1840 to 1978*. Waterloo: Wilfred Laurier Press.

Moscovitch, A. (2015). Welfare State. The Canadian Encyclopedia. Retrieved from https://www.thecanadianencyclopedia.ca/en/article/welfare-state

Mulholland, E., Mendelsohn, M., & Shamshiri, N. (2011). *Strengthening the Third Pillar of the Canadian Union: An Intergovernmental Agenda for Canada's Charities and Non-Profits.* Toronto, ON: Mowat Centre for Policy Innovation, The University of Toronto.

Nair, R. (2020, September 14) MEC to be acquired by private U.S. investment firm. CBC News. Retrieved from https://www.cbc.ca/news/business/mec-acquired-private-investment-firm-1.5723934

Neamtan, N., & Downing, R. (2005). *Social economy and CED in Canada: Next steps for public policy.* Montreal: Issues paper prepared for Chanter de l'economie sociale in collaboration with CCEDNet and ARUC-ES.

Nova Scotia Co-operative Council. (2019). *Community Economic Development Investment Funds.* Retrieved from http://www.novascotia.coop/programs/community-economic-development-investment-funds/

Nova Scotia Securities Commission. (2019). *Community Economic Development Investment Funds.* Retrieved from https://nssc.novascotia.ca/corporate-finance/community-economic-development-Investment-funds

Pierson, P. (2011). The welfare state over the very long run, ZeS- Arbeitspapier, No. 02/2011, Zentrum für Sozialpolitik, Univ. Bremen, Bremen.

Pillar Nonprofit Network. (n.d.). Social Enterprises Open During COVID 19. Retrieved October 20, 2020, from https://pillarnonprofit.ca/news/social-enterprises-open-during-covid-19

Quarter, J., Mook, L., & Armstrong, A. (2009). *Understanding the Social Economy: A Canadian Perspective.* Toronto, ON: University of Toronto Press.

Quarter, J. (2000). The Social Economy and the Neo-Conservative Agenda. In J. M. Fontan & E. Shragge (Eds.), *Social Economy: International Debates and Perspectives* (pp. 54–64). Montreal, QC: Black Rose Books.

Quarter, J., & Mook, L. (2018). The social economy: An international comparison. In B.A. Seaman and D.R. Young (eds). Handbook of Research on Nonprofit Economics and Management: Second Edition (pp. 428–441). Cheltenham, UK: Edward Elgar Publishing Ltd.

Responsible Investment Association. (2019). *2018 Canadian Impact Investment Trends Report.* Retrieved from https://www.riacanada.ca/research/2018-impact-trends-report

Restakis, J. (2006). *Defining the Social Economy – The BC Context.* Prepared for the Social Economy Roundtable. Retrieved from http://www.msvu.ca/socialeconomyatlantic/pdfs/DefiningSocialEconomy_FnlJan1906.pdf

Sousa, J. (2013). *Building a co-operative community: The conversion of Alexandra park to Atkinson housing co-operative.* Toronto, ON: The University of Toronto Press.

Sousa, J., & Hamdon, E. (2010). *Preliminary Profile of the Size and Scope of the Social Economy in Alberta and British Columbia.* Victoria, BC: The B.C- Alberta Research Alliance on the Social Economy (BALTA).

Sousa, J., Pattison, D., & Herman, R. (2012). Thematic exploration and looking forward. In J. Sousa & R. Herman (Eds.), *A co-operative dilemma* (pp. 271–310). Saskatoon, Canada: Centre for the Study of Co-operatives.

Thompson, M. & Emmanuel, J. (2012). Assembling Understandings: Findings from the Canadian Social Economy Research Partnerships, 2005–2011. Retrieved from https://ccednet-rcdec.ca/sites/ccednet-rcdec.ca/files/Assembling_Understandings.pdf

Wallace, E. (1950). The Origin of the Social Welfare State in Canada, – 1900. *The Canadian Journal of Economics and Political Science, 16*(3), 383–393.

Williams, A. (2018). *New Federal Fund Will Make Canada A Leader in Social Innovation.* Retrieved from https://Socialinnovation.Org/New-Federal-Fund-Will-Make-Canada-A-Leader-In-Social-Innovation/

Chapter 4
The New Social Economy in Indonesia: Features, Recent Development and Challenges

Maria R. Nindita Radyati and Benny Tjahjono

Introduction

This research was part of FAB-MOVE project, funded by the European Union, conducted between 2016 and 2018. It uses a qualitative method: to get primary data, interviews have been completed to 22 social entrepreneurs and 15 companies that have conducted Corporate Social Responsibility (CSR) programmes. Desk research was done to investigate among other things the history, previous researches and current development of social economy. Content analysis was conducted to scrutinise the data. The objectives of the research are to investigate the history and context, issues, current development and challenges that are faced by those who are participating in social economy and new social economy in Indonesia.

Social economy in Indonesia follows features of those in Europe (Liger, Stefan, & Britton, 2016), where the participants are mainly non-profit organisations, cooperatives and associations. They also apply democratic principles, self-help and governance self-regulations. However, one of the biggest challenges of many non-profit organisations in Indonesia is to maintain its sustainable growth (Davis, 2015; Radyati, 2010).

Cooperative has been treated as a very special form of people's economic organisation, by the first Vice President of the Republic of Indonesia, Dr. Mohammad Hatta, who was also named the "Father of Cooperative in Indonesia" (Suhendra, 2016). He included Cooperative in the 1945 National Constitution,

M. R. N. Radyati (✉)
Center for Entrepreneurship, Change, and Third Sector, Trisakti University, West Jakarta, Indonesia
e-mail: maria_nr@trisakti.ac.id

B. Tjahjono
Centre for Business in Society (CBiS), Coventry University, Coventry, UK
e-mail: ac8300@coventry.ac.uk

© Springer Nature Switzerland AG 2021
B. Gidron, A. Domaradzka (eds.), *The New Social and Impact Economy*, Nonprofit and Civil Society Studies, https://doi.org/10.1007/978-3-030-68295-8_4

particularly Article 33, that described Cooperative as an organisation that meets the needs of Indonesia's economy which is based on democratic economy; it is the prosperity of the people that should come before the prosperity of individuals Azis (2017). According to Mohammad Hatta, cooperative is not only an economic organisation, but also a way of social life, which involves values, souls and spirits based on a sense of brotherhood, kinship, togetherness and mutual cooperation (Pulungan, 2019).

The main driver for social economy in Indonesia is fulfilling the social gap, i.e. social issues in which the government does not have enough budget to solve, and there is no interest from the private sector and state-owned enterprises (SOEs) to address (Radyati & Simmonds, 2018a, 2018b).

The uniqueness of Indonesia's social economy is the implementation of local wisdom in organisations' activities. The first local wisdom is collective actions or mutual help (*gotong-royong*). This means "to bear" and to provide "shoulder" together, in other words mutual help (Badaruddin & Ermansyah, 2017). *Gotong-royong* actually means working in the farms without pay, but then it is expanded into other areas, which involve collective social activities and are considered as Javanese culture, but it is in fact practised in other ethnic groups (Bowen, 1986).

The second local wisdom is familial values (*asas kekeluargaan*). Asas means principle and *keluarga* means family; *kekeluargaan* is the adjectival form of family which represents family values. Therefore, *asas kekeluargaan* means family value principle. This means a cooperative should operate like a family where each member of the family helps each other. Based on the family value principle, a cooperative is considered to be a collective business. This system of managing the business collectively is also called gotong-royong (Radyati, 2010).

The third local wisdom is the collective decision-making (*musyawarah untuk mufakat*) to produce solutions in acclamation. However, this is enabled by equality of rights and obligations, as well as individual sovereignty (Radyati, 2010; Suparman, Supriyatni, Ratnasari, & Sofianto, 2018).

These three local wisdoms are reflected in Pancasila, the Indonesian ideology, which consists of five principles (*sila*), which according to Ir. Soekarno, Indonesia's first president, cannot be separated but must be applied in our way of life altogether (Pulungan, 2019). The principles of Pancasila are embedded in the cooperative principles; those are: (1) The Divinity of Almighty; (2) Just and civilised humanity; (3) The unity of Indonesia; (4) The people who are led by wisdom, discernment in collective decision-making (*musyawarah*) and representation; and (5) Social justice for all Indonesian people. According to Dr. Mohammad Hatta, the most appropriate economic system in Indonesia is Pancasila economy Jelani (2016); however, up to now, it has failed to be practised because the Indonesian economy so far tends to lead to liberalism (Mubyarto, 2002). Fortunately, these local wisdoms are still rooted in Indonesian people's way of life and implemented in the practices of many types of organisation.

Hitherto, traditional and informal not-for-profit organisations are still in existence in the country that exercise significant influence on people's lives such as subak[1], arisan,[2] mapalus[3] and others. However, these informal organisations will not be discussed at length in this chapter.

The later section elaborates further on the national context of social economy in Indonesia, its history, legal environment, welfare system and funding instruments for social economy.

History of Social Economy in Indonesia

In its history, the main motivation of the emergence of actors in social economy was helping the poor to address social issues in the era of the Netherlands colonial government (Radyati, 2010). There are many types of actors in social economy in Indonesia which are included in third sector organisations, such as foundation, associations, forum, alliances, mass organisations and cooperative. Some of the NPOs are registered and others are unregistered to the government, or informal organisations. The organisations are formed based on common goals and needs and sometimes by those who come from the same ethnic group but live not in their hometown.

Dutch Colonisation Era (Before 1900s): In the beginning of the social economy history, the non-profit actors were motivated by their members' or constituents' motivation to solve the socio-economic problems of Indonesian people who were the subject to the occupying of the Netherlands colonial government.

It is estimated that the oldest NPO was established in 1848. This is due to the fact that the Netherlands Government put a new article in the Civil Law in 1848, i.e. no. 1653 which states that any organisation which does not perform anything contrary to the law is acknowledged and considered legal by the government. This Civil Law is still applied in Indonesia as the basis for establishment of an association.

National Movement Era (1908–1930): In this era, the Netherlands colonialists applied "Ethische Politiek" in Indonesia, where the Netherlands Government introduced the programme of "Trias Politica", and one of the programmes was increasing education activities for indigenous people. In 1908 two prominent indigenous leaders, Dr. Wahidin and Dr. Sutomo, pioneered the Boedi Oetomo movement, engaged in providing free quality education, art and culture to economically poor Indonesians who did not have access to education (Poesponegoro & Notosusanto, 1984). Boedi Oetomo was considered by many as the first NGO/NPO in Indonesia

---

[1] *Subak* is a way of water management system for farming in Bali (World Culture Forum, 2016).

[2] *Arisan* is a gathering of people who know each other well to collect money and at a certain period they come together to draw lots in order to decide who has the right to get the money. This gathering is quite common in Java.

[3] *Mapalus* comes from Manado, North Sulawesi, which means "working and helping each other". Thus mapalus means working together deliberately for reaching a certain aim, e.g. mapalus to grow rice or build a bridge (Wuryaningrat & Kumajas, 2017).

(Budairi, 2002). *Sarekat Islam*, established in 1913, was the first association, whose mission was to improve the economic and trade relationships between the indigenous Indonesian businessmen and the Chinese traders and to promote Islamic teachings (Pusponegoro & Notosusanto, 1984).

After that, several youth organisations from various Indonesian islands, such as Java and Sumatra, began to emerge. This period is identified as the "*Youth Movement Era*" having a focus on improving the education and cultures within each island. The first youth movement was *Tri Koro Dharmo*, established on 7 March 1915, which was then followed by *Jong Java* on 12 June 1918, and the other youth movements such as *Jong Islamieten Bond, Pasundan,*[4] *Jong Sumatranen Bond, Jong Minahasa* and *Jong Batak* (Pusponegoro & Notosusanto, 1984).

Japanese Occupation Era (1942–1945): During the World War II, the Netherlands colonial government in Indonesia was defeated by the Japanese. Under the ensuing Japanese occupation, all the NPOs were dissolved and liquidated. All workers became *romusha* (forced workers). Not a single NPO, even traditional organisations, was able to survive (Kartasasmita et al., 1980a, 1980c).

Independence Era (1945): On 17 August 1945 Indonesia proclaimed its independence and became a new, free and sovereign country. The independence triggered many NPOs to re-emerge. Ir. Soekarno, the first president of the Republic of Indonesia, supported the establishment of organisations formed by the society, including political parties, with the main purpose being to defend independence and protect the population's welfare and security (Pusponegoro & Notosusanto, 1984). In this era, social economy started to grow.

Liberal Era (1950–1959): In 1950, the Round Table Conference between the Indonesian and the Dutch governments took place in the Hague, where the Netherlands acknowledged the independence of Indonesia and gave way to the authority of the new Indonesian Government (Pusponegoro & Notosusanto, 1984). In this era, the first regulation that was enacted based on the constitution, specifically RIS (Republic Indonesian State) constitution, was the Cooperative Law ratified in 1958 (Kartasasmita et al., 1980b, 1980c).

Old Order Era (1955–1965): During the old order era, Indonesia adopted the so-called Guided Democracy (*Demokrasi Terpimpin*), where the most influential political party was the Indonesian Communist Party (PKI)[5] that used NPOs, specifically cooperatives and labour unions, as tools for flourishing communist idealism.

The cooperatives were influenced by the communism through the enactment of Law of Cooperative No. 14, 1965, in which one of the articles stated that to become a member, they must understand the communism principles. However, this regulation did not take long to implement, because a year later the government changed into the New Order, so a new Cooperative Law was formulated.

---

[4] These youth groups were formed based on their similarities of Ethnic Group. They want to ensure the welfare of their members are met and they would provide help to each other whenever they can.

[5] PKI is the substitution of ISDV (Indische Sociaal-Democratische Vereniging) established on 9 May 1914, a political organisation that adheres to communism. The official change of name was made in December 1920 (Kartasasimta, et al., 1980c; Poesponegoro & Notosusanto 1984c, p. 200).

New Order Era (1966–1998): In this era, non-profit organisations with a popular name of *Lembaga Swadaya Masyarakat* (LSM)[6] grew and developed relatively fast, due to the increased number of international donor agencies giving funding to Indonesia (Budairi, 2002). The government implemented a very strict control over the movement and development of NPO through a regulation, Mass Organisation Law no. 8, 1985, that stated that the government can dissolve an organisation at any time if it is deemed to carry out activities and have values that are contrary to the government. Nevertheless, many NPOs (LSM) contributed to social economy in the programmes of fulfilment of peoples' grassroots needs, such as health and nutrition services, clean water facilities, family planning advice and environmental preservation.

In the 1990s, along with the growing awareness of human rights protection and global democracy, many NPOs became involved in human rights advocacy, monitoring human rights' violations.

The next Cooperative Law was enacted in 1967, although the cooperative was under the tight control of the government. In villages, the government only allowed one type of cooperative, namely KUD (*Koperasi Unit Desa*), with farmers as the members but the KUD was managed by government employees (Kawai & Inoue, 2011). One of the main objectives was to control the farmers, price of fertilisers and production of rice for food self-sufficiency. The Cooperative KUD was given the monopoly right to sell fertilisers whose price was controlled by the government. This had caused many corruption practices in KUD which then created a bad image of cooperatives in Indonesia (Kawai & Inoue, 2011).

The credit unions (CUs) started to grow in the 1970s. Unlike KUD, the CUs are a bottom-up movement of member-based organisations. The establishment of CUs was encouraged by activists concerned to reduce poverty and combat the practice of so-called loan sharks, people lending money at a high rate of interest (Kawai & Inoue, 2011; Setiawan, 2015). The emergence of credit union was aimed to eradicate poverty by introducing the behaviour of saving. This CU is a saving-lending cooperative that has five pillars, namely education, self-reliance, solidarity, innovation and unity (CUCO Indonesia, 2020a, 2020b).

The development of CU in Indonesia was initiated with the establishment of Credit Union Counselling Office (CUCO) Indonesia. This organisation prepared training programmes for the communities and was managed by volunteers and led by a Roman Catholic priest, *Romo* Albrecht (CUCO Indonesia, 2020a, 2020b). Since only KUD could be established in villages, CU's development was more in the form of community movement, informal but well managed (Kawai & Inoue, 2011).

The Cooperative Law was then revised in 1992. The main difference is that previously cooperative was considered as people's economic organisation with social character. According to the revised law, cooperative is considered as a business entity through people's economic movement (Rubiyanto & Darmawan, 2006).

---

[6] LSM (*Lembaga Swadaya Masyarakat*) is a self-reliant non-profit organisation, which engages mostly in advocacy activities.

However, both state that cooperative has family value principle, which is consistent with Indonesia's ideology, Pancasila, particularly principle no. 2 (Noventari, 2016). This Cooperative Law no. 12/1992 is still being applied.

Reformation Era (1998 Up to Now): Within this reformation era, former president, Dr. Ing. B.J. Habibie, signed a presidential decree on the rights for establishing organisations and freedom for expressing ideas in public (specifically for demonstrations). Habibie's successor, Abdurrahman Wahid, reconstituted the Cooperative Department into the Ministry of Cooperative in order to return the autonomy of cooperatives, because it had been misused by the previous government in the New Order Era (Sulistyowati, 2003).

In the Reformation Era, the government generally did not perceive NPO or NGO (non-government organisations) as anti-government, nor as an opposition force, and for that reason the government no longer supervises and interferes with the NPOs' activities (Ibrahim, Suryaningati, & Malik, 2003).

Foundation Law was enacted in August 2001 in order to restore the function of all foundations into its original role, which is for a social purpose. Prior to the enactment of Foundation Law, many non-profit organisations received donations for purposes other than social good, for instance, political campaigns, business activities or other unrelated social activities, yet they were not obliged to report their financial accountability to public or the government (Wahyono & Margono, 2001). Yayasan (foundation) is a legal entity with separate assets established for the purpose of dealing with social, religious and human affairs issues.

An association is a member-based organisation. They are frequently formed by those with similar interests or professions. Based on their activities, foundations and associations usually perform activities in education, advocacy, society and religion, and art and culture.

Special Cases of Credit Union and Women Mutual Liability Credit Unions

Credit unions (CUs), as one type of cooperatives, have a noteworthy role in the economic aspect in Indonesia. The largest credit unions in Indonesia is in West Kalimantan with a total asset of more than USD 570 million (Walfajri, 2017). Credit unions' organisational performance in West Kalimantan exceeds that of banks (Redaksi, 2019). Particularly in West Kalimantan, the initiation of credit union was driven by enhancing the dignity of Dayak people, who are the indigenous ethnic groups there (Achwan, 2007). Therefore, the increase in the number and financial performance of CU in West Kalimantan is the most significant in Indonesia. This is due to the existence of social capital which strengthens trust in CUs. The other aspects that have boosted CU's development are competitive deposit rates, easy loan application procedures and distribution of surplus (dividend) to the members every end of the year (Santika, 2017).

Credit unions have helped alleviate poverty and keep economic durability of micro, small and medium enterprises strong during the global economic crisis. The total asset of all CUs in Indonesia in 2017 was more than USD 2000 million (Gutomo, 2017).

According to the Law of Cooperative no. 25/1992, cooperatives in Indonesia are divided into primary and secondary cooperatives. Primary cooperatives consist of a number of people (minimum 20), while secondary cooperatives consist of a minimum of 3 organisations. Based on the type of business or economic interests of its members, cooperatives are divided into producer cooperatives, consumer cooperatives, service cooperatives, savings and loan cooperatives, i.e. credit unions, and marketing cooperatives.

The number of cooperatives in Indonesia to date is about 123,000 (Kementerian Koperasi, 2019). The contribution of cooperatives until June 2019 alone reached 5.1% of Indonesia's GDP, compared to 2014 which was around 1.7% (Rahayu, 2019).

Another important contribution of CUs is the women empowerment. There is a strong traditional women cooperative network in Indonesia that, through its traditional system namely *tanggung-renteng* (mutual liability), has helped many women participate actively to save household economy during national economic crisis in 1998 (Radyati, 2010). They originated in Malang, East Java, established by Mrs. Mursia Zaafril whose main intention was to help women who were trading in the traditional market, in need of borrowing some money from "loan shark" and had to pay them a very high daily interest rate. She developed a unique way of raising funds through a saving-lending cooperative, namely Tanggung-Renteng Credit Union (TR CU).

Tanggung-renteng means "sharing the burden" or mutual liability. A TR CU consists of groups of people. The maximum number of people in one group is 15. The members are well acquainted with each other and live close to each other. To become a member, one has to have a recommendation from someone known to the TR CU. The reason for this is credibility, ensuring that any loan is given only to people who have the financial capacity to repay it in full. The process of giving credit/loan approval is carried out at monthly members' meetings. Each member must explain their reason for applying for a loan. The other members will discuss the loan application and decide whether it should be approved or rejected. If a member fails to make an instalment payment in the previous month due to financial difficulty, then other members will take on the member's liability by collecting money to make the due loan instalment on behalf of the member who thereby falls into arrears. In the following month, the defaulting member repays the money advanced by the other members, thereby having to pay double the usual instalment payment.

The prominent feature of this traditional cooperative is the system of "sharing the burden", which promotes values such as togetherness, thoughtfulness, openness, discipline, tolerance and honesty. One of the leaders of mutual liability CU, Mrs. Yoos Lutfi, described that the main objective to establish this type of cooperative was to change the behaviour of its members, from ignorant into persons who have the aforementioned characteristics (Radyati, 2010). Its unique system, which members are forced to follow, will change their behaviour to become caring and good persons.

This mutual liability system is now being adopted by a fintech (financial technology-based) social enterprise, namely Amartha, which will be elaborated later.

It appears that CUs have created significant positive impacts on social economy, particularly on its members on aspects of welfare, dignity and even changing their behaviour to become better people. Unfortunately the development of cooperatives like this is still inferior to banks, some of the reasons being that they are not fast enough to follow the development of technology, and many people still do not understand the prominent features of cooperative system and the benefit of becoming cooperative members (Indra, Mardiyah, Ajeng, & Desi, 2020).

Legal Environment

There is no specific law that regulates the social enterprises (Pratono, Pramudija, & Sutanti, 2016). However, these are types of social enterprises in Indonesia, based on their legal entities: Yayasan (foundation),[7] association,[8] cooperative, private limited companies[9] and commanditaire vennootschap (CV)[10] (Radyati & Simmonds, 2018a, 2018b). The differences are based on its source of funds, ownership/control and distribution of profit/surplus (Table 4.1).

All the aforementioned legal entities (social enterprises) must pay tax, e.g. income tax generated from the selling of products and services. If a social enterprise receives donations to maintain its working operations, this source of funds must be treated as income, and is thus subject to income tax. However, if the donations received are solely used for conducting social activities for identified beneficiaries, then they can claim the tax-free allowance (Radyati & Simmonds, 2018a, 2018b).

Welfare System

There are several welfare support systems that have been created by President Joko Widodo in the area of health and education, which are *Kartu Indonesia Sehat (for health)*, organised by BPJS (Badan Penyelenggara Jaminan Sosial), and popular as

---

[7] The related regulations are: The Law no. 16 about Foundation, year 2001 (Undang-Undang No. 16 tentang Yayasan, Tahun 2001), the Law no. 28, year 2004 about the Amendment of Law no. 16 about Foundation, year 2001 (Undang-Undang No. 28 Tahun 2004 tentang Perubahan UU No. 16 Tahun 2001), and Government Regulation no. 63, year 2008 about the Implementation of the Law on Foundation (Peraturan Perintah no. 63 Tahun 2008).

[8] The basis for establishment of this type of enterprise is Civil Law inherited from the Dutch colonial time (Burgerlijk Wetboek voor Indonesie) Article No. 1652.

[9] The Law of Private Limited Company No. 40, 2007 (UU PT.no.40 tahun 2007).

[10] A CV is regulated under the Trade Law inherited from the Dutch colonial time (Wetboek van Koophandel voor Indonesie S.1847–23), particularly in the Articles 19 until 21.

Table 1 The different features of social enterprises in Indonesia, based on legal entity

Legal entity	Source of funds	Ownership or control	Distribution of profit/surplus
1. Foundation	1. Founders 2. Donors	Founders	1. No distribution to founders or board members 2. Used to fund activities
2. Association	1. Members 2. Donors	All members	1. No distribution to founders or board members 2. Used to fund activities
3. Cooperative	1. Members 2. Donors	All members	1. No distribution to founders or board members 2. Distribution of the surplus to members based on their activities 3. The rest of the surplus is used to fund activities
4. Private limited company	1. Shareholders 2. Commercial loan 3. Donors	Shareholders	1. Distribution to shareholders 2. Mostly used to fund activities
5. CV	1. Founders 2. Donors	Founders	1. Distribution to founders 2. Mainly used to fund activities

"BPJS programme" and *Kartu Indonesia Pintar/KIP (for education)*. In previous years, there were other welfare systems created by several mayors/governors in several cities in Indonesia, including Jakarta. However, since there has been changing of leadership, they do not exist anymore. Hence, hitherto only national level welfare systems prevail.

This BPJS programme is part of the implementation of Law No. 40 of 2004 about the National Social Security System. Those who can join BPJS programmes are the citizens of Indonesian and foreign nationals who stay in the country for more than 6 months. BPJS covers work accident, health, pension and death, which basically follows the ILO Convention (Rolindrawan, 2015). There are standard insurance and premium insurance in BPJS, and those who need premium services will need to pay for additional fee per year. However, the quantity of public services for premium class is limited, compared to those covered by private insurance programmes. Those who come from medium and upper classes of economy still tend to pay for and join insurance programmes from private companies. Nevertheless, BPJS is considered successful in increasing the use of public health facilities by many people (Rolindrawan, 2015).

Indonesia Smart Card (KIP) is the implementation of "Presidential Instruction No. 7 of 2014 concerning the implementation of the Welfare Family Savings Program, the Healthy Indonesia Program to build Productive Families". It is distributed to students between the age of 6 and 21 years from poor families, who have registered themselves and get the Prosperous Family Card (*Kartu Keluarga Sejahtera*). This programme is a collaboration between the Ministry of Religion, the Ministry of Education and Culture and the Ministry of Social Affairs. Those who are granted KIP can join free education until university level. However due to bad administration system (Cahyaningsih, 2018) and perhaps geographic factors, where Indonesia has more than 17,000 islands and many remote areas, the registration of poor families is very difficult to do, so there are many young people who come from poor families who could not get access to KIP (Cahyaningsih, 2018).

It is quite obvious that government's welfare system is not adequate to support the needs of all Indonesia's population of unfortunate people. Therefore, Indonesia's society strives to create an ecosystem that enables the people to achieve better well-being and welfare.

New Social Economy

The new economy in Indonesia is indicated by active participation of many sectors, namely private, government and civil society, including social entrepreneurs. Social entrepreneur is *an individual or organisation that makes a change for the betterment of a marginalised group or an ecosystem, and whose main objective is to fill the "Social Gap" and where its operation is sustained by means of business activities* (Radyati & Simmonds, 2018a, 2018b). There are more than 340,000 social entrepreneurs in Indonesia (British Council & UNESCAP, 2018).

There are many regulations rectified by the government to encourage partnership between all sectors. In the area of palm oil plantation, government requires direct business partnerships between companies and cooperatives[11]; in the area of natural environment conservation, the partnership is between government and civil society[12]; in the area of social responsibility, the government encourages all private companies to participate in community development programmes and environmental preservation[13]; the Ministry of State Owned Enterprises (SOEs) gives mandate to all SOEs to conduct community development programmes.

After the United Nations formulated the Sustainable Development Goals (SDGs) (UN, 2015), the Indonesian Government took the country's contributions to the achievement of SDGs very seriously. The government rectified Presidential Regulation No. 59/2017 Concerning Achievement of Sustainable Development Goals, and through the Ministry of National Development Planning, the government also formulated the National Action Plan to achieve SDGs and required all local governments to make Regional Action Plans (Bappenas Admin, 2018).

---

[11] Law No. 20 of 2008 concerning micro, small and medium enterprises (Article 27) and PP No. 44 of 1997 concerning partnerships.

[12] Regulation of the Director General of Conservation of Natural Resources and Ecosystems, No. P.6/KSDAE/SET/Kum.1/6/2018 Concerning Technical Guidelines for Conservation Partnerships in Nature Reserve Areas and Nature Conservation Areas.

[13] Limited Liability Company Law no. 40/2007 Article 74 and Government Regulation on Social and Environmental Responsibility no. 47/2012.

All publicly listed companies are required to make Sustainability Reports[14] which must elaborate their contributions to SDGs, including highlighting the partnership they have made.

Inclusive Business in New Social Economy: New social economy in Indonesia has similarities to what has been described by Rymsza (2015), that is, in terms of the business inclusion of the excluded or underprivileged, such as lack of access to education and labour market (Rymsza, 2015). This inclusive business model involves low-income communities in their value chain, namely **SIPOC (Suppliers, Input, Process, Output and Customers)** (Mishra & Sharma, 2014), as suppliers, distributors, employees, retailers and consumers of their products and services (Simani, 2020).

An example can be given in the supplier side, in the area of providing employment,[15] which is supported by incentive provided by the government regulation[16] by cutting the gross income tax by maximum of 200% if a company is providing vocational education to communities. Many companies through their CSR activities provide vocational education for local communities offering trainings on specific skills that the company needs; once they are graduated, they are not obliged to become employees to the company. Some examples include the Polytechnic Gajah Tunggal established and funded by PT. Gajah Tunggal, the biggest tire manufacturer (Akhmad, 2020); Polytechnic Petrokimia established and funded by 14 chemical companies (Maskur, 2019), etc. There are many CSR investments made in the area of education; one of the biggest CSR education funds is made by Adaro Group, about USD 100 million in 2018 (Kunjana, 2018). These CSR activities contribute to new social economy environment in Indonesia.

In the area of input (raw material), palm oil companies that are practising sustainable palm oil are also in partnership with farmer cooperatives through the mechanism "Inti-Plasma", which is mandated by the Law.[17] Other examples include East-West-Seed Group, an agriculture company who is partnering with groups of farmers as their direct suppliers, not through mediators (Tutwiler, 2016), and Unilever, who is in partnership with soybean farmers (Susilowati, 2018).

The following examples of social enterprises and their direct collaborations with communities to solve social, environmental and economic issues in the area of SIPOC are those who have won some competitions organised by credible organisations in national as well as international levels.

---

[14] Through Financial Services Authority's regulation (OJK = Otoritas Jasa Keuangan), POJK No. 51/POJK.03/2017, all publicly listed companies must publish Sustainability Report.

[15] The government through the Ministry of Industry (Kemenperin) continues to encourage the development of the quality of human resources in the industrial sector through the implementation of vocational education and training programmes (Siregar, 2019).

[16] The Government of the Republic of Indonesia Regulation No. 45/2019 About "Amendment to Government Regulation Number 94 Year 2010 Concerning Calculation of Income Taxes and Repayments Income Tax".

[17] Regulation of the Minister of Agriculture No. 26/2007 concerning Guidelines for Plantation Business Licensing.

- In the **input** side within SIPOC, many social entrepreneurs are using eco-friendly or certified materials for their productions, such as Javara, which helps farmers to get organic certification for their agricultural products and then build the brand and export them (Mahita, Rifa, & Taruli, 2015).
- In the **process** side, social enterprises practise socially responsible business process, such as SukkhaCitta, a social entrepreneur that produces international standard clothing, using traceable natural dyes, zero waste practice and free repairs; promotes environmentally friendly practices; and also preserves culture through a modern reinterpretation of Indonesian heritage; the enterprise also provides access to marginalised craftsmen (Kujana, 2018); "PT. SOBI (Social Business Indonesia)" in collaboration with TELAPAK, an association of environmentalists, helps farmers of teakwood to conduct sustainable logging and get FSC (Forest Stewardship Certification), so they can export certified wood to European markets (Radyati & Simmonds, 2018a, 2018b).
- In converting the **output** side of value chain, there are "Waste4Change" that offers waste management services from upstream to downstream with the aim of changing people's behaviour towards waste and "SMASH", an online waste management system, that connects people with their nearest "trash bank", so they can exchange trash with savings and become a customer of the "trash bank" (Andriani, 2018).
- For the **customer** side, there are social enterprises that connect customers directly to producers, such as "Agromaret" that connects customers directly to farmers and "Alodokter" that provides information about health through mobile apps, where users can also ask the doctor directly using mobile apps, regarding health advices.

Private Sector's Contribution to New Social Economy: Corporate sectors have been involved in solving social/environmental issues through Corporate Social Responsibilities (CSR) activities in the area of, among other things, health, education, entrepreneurship, religion, infrastructure development, philanthropy and culture (Radyati, 2014).

As previously explained, CSR activities are mandatory in Indonesia. State-owned enterprises (SOEs), under the Law of Ministry of SOE, must set aside 4% from their total net income to conduct CSR/Community Development activities, namely PKBL[18] (*Program Kemitraan dan Bina Lingkungan*) funds. The total amount of PKBL funds from all SOEs in 2019 reached 20 million USD (Sunaryo, 2019). These PKBL funds must be invested to the communities in two forms: low-interest loan (soft loan) to micro-small-medium enterprises and non-financial support activities, such as training, mentorship and other non-financial supports such as providing seeds and fertilisers; building infrastructure; and providing access to mar-

---

[18] SOE Minister Regulation PER-02/MBU/7/2017 dated July 5, 2017, concerning Second Amendment to Regulation of the Minister of Business Owned by State Number PER-09/MBU/07/2015 Concerning Partnership Program and Program for the Development of Environmental Business Entities.

ket through conducting exhibitions for SME's products to those who are their CSR beneficiaries. These types of support are very useful for social entrepreneur developments in Indonesia.

For private companies, CSR mandatory is regulated under the Private Limited Law (Act) no. 40/2007, Article 74. This article stated that only those companies that are conducting business in the extractive industry (e.g. oil and gas, mining) must conduct CSR activities to the communities. However, in the explanation section of the Act, it is stated that companies whose business activities have impacts on the community and the environment must carry out CSR.

Many companies in Indonesia doing CSR have been involved in collaborations with social entrepreneurs or local champions, from the local area where the company operates. The term "local champion" is widely used by companies which are doing CSR; it refers to a local person who has high motivation to make a change towards betterment and solve social/environmental issues in the area where they live. This local champion is appointed as partner or facilitator by the company in carrying out their CSR programmes, and then groomed by the company through trainings and partnership activities that enable them to become a change maker or social entrepreneur in their hometown.

In the banking sector, the Indonesian Federal Reserve Bank (Bank Indonesia/BI) enacted Bank Indonesia Regulation No. 17/12/PBI/2015 about "Changes to Bank Indonesia Regulations Number 14/22/PBI/2012 Concerning the Provision of Credits or Financing by Public Banks and Technical Assistance in the Development of Micro, Small and Medium Enterprises" which mandated all banks to provide loan to micro, small and medium enterprises (MSMEs) amounting to 20% of total loan distributed to the public. Whenever the bank is unable to reach this amount, a fine of one million USD will be imposed. However, the bank can convert this fine into community development activities for MSMEs. Unfortunately, even this effort experienced many obstacles to success, due to the lack of personnel from the banks to provide optimal assistance to MSMEs. Therefore, there are many situations where banks distribute the remaining "fines", which must be paid to BI, into loans to cooperatives.

Because the nature of the banking business is to uphold prudence, which must request collateral for all loans, many social entrepreneurs who are MSMEs do not have sufficient collateral to get the loan amount according to their needs, which is usually called "not bankable". Consequently, many Islamic banks offer Syariah loans, where prospective customers do not need to provide collaterals, but the system is *murabaha* or buying and selling, *ijarah wa iqtina* or leases with changes in ownership and *musharaka mutanaqishah* or capital sharing. With this system SME/social entrepreneurs do not need to provide guarantees, and the bank is willing to share risk with customers.

Large companies, especially publicly listed companies in the Indonesia Stock Exchange, are competing to show potential investors and the public that they have contributed to the achievement of the Sustainable Development Goals (SDGs). Therefore publicly listed companies are keen on being included in the Sustainable and Responsible Investment (SRI) KEHATI Index. It is an index that consists of companies that have operated in sustainable ways. This index is issued yearly by a trusted Grant-Making Foundation, Yayasan KEHATI (*Keanekaragaman Hayati*). Those companies which are included in the index have passed a thorough scrutinisation by a group of professional researchers in Kehati Foundation. It is a prestigious position to be included in the SRI KEHATI Index, which reflects a corporate's contribution to Sustainable Development Goals. Impact investors are usually keen on investing their money to buy their stocks.

The Role of Impact Investment in New Social Economy: **Impact investing** is capital invested in enterprises that create social and environmental benefit in addition to financial return (Pandit & Tamhane, 2018). A report by Global Impact Investing Network and Intellecap shows that there are two types of impact investors in Indonesia, which are private impact investors (PIIs) and development finance institutions (DFIs). During 2007–2017, the total amount invested by PII amounted to USD 148.8 million, and DFI reached USD 3.6 billion. The main areas of investment are agriculture, workforce development, fisheries, financial services, energy and manufacturing (GIIN & Intellecap, 2018).

Other impact investments are encouraged through investing in Sustainable and Responsible Stocks listed in Indonesia Stock Exchange, included in SRI KEHATI Index, Green Bond (total value by 2018 was 6, 3 million USD) and *Sukuk Mudharabah Berkelanjutan* (total value in 2018 was USD 191 million) issued by PT Sarana Multi Infrastruktur (SMI) (Kencana, 2018). The creation of ecosystem for impact investment has encouraged corporates and individuals to participate in creating impact through investment activities. This provides supports to creation of social innovation that will contribute to Sustainable Development Goals.

Community as Shareholders—Community Enterprises (CE): CE main characteristic is community or collective ownership of an enterprise. In Indonesia some community enterprises are established by a cooperative; thus the cooperative is part of the shareholders. One of the biggest cooperative-owned enterprises is PT Asuransi Jiwa Syariah Jasa Mitra Abadi Tbk. It is owned by Kospin Jasa (Kospin Cooperative) based in Pekalongan, Central Java, and was established in 1973. The cooperative is now one of the cooperatives with the largest assets, more than Rp 7 trillion in early 2017.

Another CE success story is Community Economic and Business Incubation (IBEKA) initiated by Tri Mumpuni and Iskandar Budisaroso. This social entrepreneurship provides solutions for dozens of villages in remote areas in Indonesia to create their own microscale power plants by utilising their energy sources from local water sources. They invited the community to directly involve in developing and managing micropower plants in their respective villages. Villagers are required to pay their electricity usage to their own cooperative. The money collected is used to maintain the power plants and village activities. The IBEKA programme has also been successful in encouraging local residents to actively protect the forest so that their electricity sources remain sustainable (Cannon, Thrope, & Emili, 2020).

There is a new social enterprise (www.punyabersama.id) that provides a platform for society to own several business alternatives. Even though the business choices are regular business practices, the effort to provide opportunities for community at large to become shareholder is noteworthy. This social enterprise provides services to seek other investors and take care of legal requirements when an entrepreneur wants to buy a business, for example a franchise company, and is in need of additional funding. The uniqueness is that this social enterprise will seek and gather maximum of 300 investors to buy/own one business entity. For example, an entrepreneur intends to own a franchise supermarket worth USD 120,000, and then punya-bersama.id will find 300 investors to make collective investment. This means an investor only needs to invest USD 400 to own a supermarket. The maximum number of shareholders allowed by the Government of Indonesia's regulation to own one business entity is 300. After that, they create a smartphone application that will provide information to the shareholders about the value of transactions in the supermarket, which is updated every minute. This way they are able to provide business opportunities to many people in the society and enable timely accurate monitoring system (Radyati, 2019). This shows that collective ownership or community ownership is encouraged with the help of digital technology.

Industry 4.0 in Indonesia: Welcoming the fourth Industrial Revolution, Indonesia set several aims to achieve the great national aspirations, which are bringing Indonesia upward to reach ten biggest economies by 2030. Indonesia's target is to reach the industry net export rate to 10%, doubling the labour productivity rate over the labour costs, allocating 2% of GDP to R&D and technology innovation fields (or seven times higher than current allocation) and creating 10–15 million new jobs in 2030.

Crowdsourcing in Indonesia: Crowdsourcing has been harnessed as a way to broadcast design problems to people all over the world in hopes of receiving creative solutions and innovative ideas from motivated participants (Enrique & Fernando, 2012; Howe, 2006). One of the earliest crowdsourcing businesses in Indonesia is Gojek (Go-Jek), a technology company that serves transportation through motorbike or motorcycle taxi services, founded in 2010 by Nadiem Makarim. Not just for business, crowdsourcing in Indonesia is also used to advance and strengthen democracy. In the 2014 presidential election, Ainun Nadjib initiated the site "kawalpemilu.org" which invited the public to get involved in monitoring the results of voting at the polling stations (TPS) in their area. In the 2019 election, KawalPemilu.org inspired the same platform for monitoring the results of democratic party in Indonesia, such as *Jaga Suara 2019* and Jariungu.

Crowdfunding in Indonesia: Crowdfunding in Indonesia is growing rapidly amid the difficulty of accessing funding from formal financial institutions. All crowdfunding activities on the Internet must obtain permissions from the Ministry of Social Affairs (Ministry of Social Affairs, 2018). Since 2012, local crowdfunding start-ups have begun to emerge and cover a variety of initiatives, like business funding, small medium enterprise, social projects and creative industries. For example, "Kolase.com" is the first crowdfunding site in Indonesia that presents a variety of campaign choices for creative industry players, be it musicians, event activists, book writers or other creative planners. Another example is "Gandengtangan.co.id" being a crowdfunding site that brings together social problems and provides solutions to social activists, sponsors and donors. "KitaBisa.com" is one of the most famous fundraising sites in Indonesia. It has been a fundraising platform for various humanitarian donations and major projects since it was founded by Muhammad Alfatih Timur in 2013.

Fintech in Indonesia: Fintech industry is growing rapidly in Indonesia; it is estimated that there are around 235 fintech companies. In fact, Indonesia is one of the countries with the highest market growth rates in fintech services in the Asia Pacific region (Nizar, 2017). The Financial Services Authority of Indonesia (OJK) said that, per November 2019, the accumulation of loans through fintech in Indonesia had reached USD 384,031,021,570. CNBC Indonesia recorded that the fintech business in Indonesia was dominated by fintech payment which served 39%, followed by fintech lending (24%). The Angel Investment Network Indonesia (ANGIN) with the United Nations Development Programme (UNDP) report in 2017 stated that fintech social mission covers 20% of the total social enterprises in Indonesia.

The start-up business in technology-based financial services (fintech) will continue to grow in Indonesia. This is due to the fact that the roles of banks are not yet optimal in the financial services sector and there are still many people who have not been able to access the banking services. Nonetheless, Indonesia's fintech industry continues to face challenges such as mitigating the risks of user's personal data abuse, money laundering and domination of a handful of e-commerce platforms.

Peer-to-peer (p2p) lending: "Amartha", "Akseleran" and "Gandengtangan" are three of many social enterprises in the financial sector that, through mobile apps, connect directly those who have money with those who need loans, such as through peer-to-peer (P2P) lending and other types of loan.

Amartha is a fintech pioneer who specifically helps capitalise on women's micro-businesses in rural areas. Founded in 2010, Amartha is a pioneering online lending peer-to-peer (P2P) technology that serves micro-entrepreneurs in rural areas. In 2019, Amartha had a lent of IDR 1.6 trillion [US $113 million] to over 343,000 partners across 5200 villages in Java and Sulawesi. Amartha adopts the system of "mutual liability" practised by women credit union. They mentor the women entrepreneurs who need financial support, to form a group lending with 15–20 members, and then apply this system. In the process of selection to analyse whether an entrepreneur is feasible to get loan, Amartha uses an algorithm to identify the "character and capacity" of the individual, based on her answers to a set of interview questions that they prepare before. If the individual is not eligible to get loan straight away, she will have to join a "changing-behaviour" class programme carried out by Amartha's team. This proves to be a very effective way to reduce the financial risk of non-performing loan.

Challenges: There are several challenges faced by social enterprises to participate in new social economy, inter alia: access to financial capital, access to CSR programmes, agility to adapt with fast-changing technology and global trends, and knowledge, skills and attitudes of a successful entrepreneur. Social entrepreneurs need to be able to gain trust from the corporate sector, so they can be included as their partners in CSR programmes so as to get resources. This means they need to act professionally. Therefore, education related to social enterprise and digital technology is very important for social entrepreneurs.

Impact investing has contributed to supporting many social enterprises; nevertheless they are still puzzled as to where to find the impact investors. This is because the information about impact investment practices is still not clear to public; hence people prefer to participate through fintech companies.

Collective ownership through credit union (CU) and community enterprise, where the cooperative becomes one of the shareholders of an enterprise, is evidenced to be able to increase society's welfare; however to encourage its development is challenging, because the system is still new to many people.

Corporations find it challenging to adapt quickly with the global demand regarding sustainable development to solve social issues. Corporate people find it perplexing to convince their Board of Directors (BOD) to invest in social programmes, because it is difficult to measure non-financial returns.

Government also finds it very challenging to be agile in promulgating regulations related to sustainability and digital technology-based business swiftly. The government realises the need to gain updated knowledge and skills regarding sustainable development and digital technology. Hence the Ministerial Office of National Development is collaborating with UNDP and Tanoto Foundation to establish SDG Academy. This Academy prioritises in educating government employees about SDGs. However, they also provide opportunities to public to register and join the education for free for certain curriculum related to general knowledge about SDGs (UNDP, 2019).

Support for Victims Affected by the Impact of COVID-19 in Indonesia

After the COVID-19 outbreak, the significant impact was on health and economic aspects. The number of companies that have collapsed has caused more than six million people to be laid off in Indonesia since March 2020. Direct assistance has been channelled by individuals, the private sector, SOEs and the third sector. By using the Indonesian keyword "covid victim assistance", there are more than 16,000,000 news and stories about this. Crowdsourcing also plays a significant role, recording that within 3 days in early March 2020 USD 300,000 was collected through "Kitabisa.com", one of the crowdsourcing platforms, to help the victims of COVID-19. Thus, it appears that the spirit of "gotong-royong" (mutual help) is getting stronger due to this pandemic.

Conclusion

In conclusion, there are several key points that we learnt from our investigation:

1. Local wisdom of gotong-royong (helping each other), tanggung-renteng (mutual liability), family value system (asas kekeluargaan) and collective decision-making (musyawarah untuk mufakat) is embedded in the practices of third sec-

tor organisations, such as NPOs, cooperatives, foundations and associations in the social economy. Corporate sector also instils local wisdom in their collaborative actions to solve social issues and SDGs.

2. Third sector organisations and social enterprises mainly possess social capital, but they are in need of financial capital. On the other hand, private sector has much financial capital but needs social capital to help them carry out their mandatory CSR activities successfully. These two sectors can actually complement each other, but they rarely communicate with each other. Social entrepreneurs also need education to become professionals in conducting their activities; hence they need intellectual capital. This is where educational institutions as centres of intellectual capital should bridge the two sectors in order to communicate and work together.

3. Credit union (CU) can become a priority choice of an organisation that can contribute significantly to social economy. The impact can be boosted by establishing a community enterprise where CU/cooperative becomes one of the shareholders. Unfortunately, its development is still hindered by lack of public knowledge about the CU system and its benefits. Consequently, not many CSR programmes are focused on providing technical assistance to communities to establish CU. In fact, CSR programme has been one of the most significant sources of funding for community development activities that can contribute to social economy. If the company helps the community establish a CU or cooperative, then the company has prepared an exit strategy for its CSR programme and prepares the community to rely on self-help, maintain social cohesion and become independent financially.

4. The new social economy in Indonesia has been very interesting in its development, since it involves many initiatives from various sectors to help improve the welfare of society. These initiatives have been driven by inadequate welfare system. It is also noteworthy that many initiatives have been inspired by the 17 Sustainable Development Goals (SDGs).

5. Companies have been involved in new social economy through their CSR activities and practising inclusive business where they include the communities in their value chain (SIPOC). On the other hand, the banking industry is taking part by practising sustainable banking to provide more access to those who are not "bankable" to get loan or other services. Individual and institutional investors are allocating their money to projects that are contributing to SDGs through impact investing. Social enterprises have been using digital technology to include all individuals to participate directly in new social economy (e.g. crowdsourcing, crowdfunding, fintech, p2p lending). Consequently, CU is challenged to quickly adapt to technology and increase collaboration with companies through CSR programmes to increase its presence.

6. The Indonesian Government is always playing catch-up by introducing lagging legislation, after other sectors and industries have taken actions. For example companies had been making Sustainability Reports for 2 years and then the government issued a regulation to make it mandatory. Similarly lagging legislation

were introduced in the area of impact investing, start-up business, fintech, crowdfunding and crowdsourcing.

This study is only limited to investigate the history, general description and trends in organisations' participations in social economy. Consequently, it does not provide a detailed context about each participant that takes part in contributing to solving social issues.

It is recommended to conduct further research using case study methodology, to observe in depth the context, challenges and strategies of social enterprises in contributing to new social economy. It is also important to investigate why companies and impact investors are keen on solving social issues where the return and direct benefit are uncertain. Other methodologies such as quantitative or mix methods will be useful as well to investigate relationships among many indicators of sustainability to the performance of new social economy.

References

Achwan, R. (2007). Microfinance Institution, Social Capital and Peace Building: Evidence from West Kalimantan, Indonesia. *the 3rd International Conference on Gross National Happiness* (pp. 22–28). Bangkok: University of Chulalongkorn.

Akhmad, N. (2020, February 6). *CSR Gajah Tunggal Berdampak 4 Kali Lebih Besar dari Investasi.* Retrieved April 2020, from www.topbusiness.id; https://www.topbusiness.id/30338/csr-gajah-tunggal-berdampak-4-kali-lebih-besar-dari-investasi.html.

Andriani, D. (2018, August 10). *8 Sociopreneur Indonesia Tembus Kompetisi Seratus Wirausaha Sosial se-Asia.* Retrieved April 2020, from www.entrepreneur.bisnis.com.; https://entrepreneur.bisnis.com/read/20180810/265/826454/8-sociopreneur-indonesia-tembus-kompetisi-seratus-wirausaha-sosial-se-asia.

Azis, S. (2017). Design building of Indonesian economic politics. *European Research Studies, 20*(3), 890–904.

Badaruddin, B., & Ermansyah, E. (2017). Proposing a model for law number 6 of 2014: Evidence from North Sumatra. *Journal of Economic & Management Perspectives, 11*(4), 188–198.

Bappenas Admin. (2018, July 9). Sosialisasi Rencana Aksi Nasional (RAN) Tujuan Pembangunan Berkelanjutan (TPB/SDGs) 2017–2019. Retrieved April 2020, from www.sdgs.bappenas.go.id: http://sdgs.bappenas.go.id/sosialisasi-rencana-aksi-nasional-ran-tujuan-pembangunan-berkelanjutan-tpbsdgs-2017-2019/

Bowen, J. R. (1986). On the political construction of tradition: Gotong royong in Indonesia. *The Journal of Asian Studies (1986–1998), 45*(3), 545.

British Council, & UNESCAP. (2018). Building an Inclusive and Creative Economy: The State of Social Enterprise in Indonesia. British Council.

Budairi, M. (2002). Masyarakat Sipil dan Demokrasi.. Yogyakarta.

Cahyaningsih, R. I. (2018). Pendistribusian Kartu Indonesia Pintar (KIP). *Didaktik: Jurnal Ilmiah PGSD STKIP Subang, 4*(1), 147–162.

Cannon, M., Thrope, J., & Emili, S. (2020, April 18). IBEKA: Community-owned and Managed Mini Grids in Indonesia. Retrieved May 2020, from www.opendocs.ids.ac.uk; https://opendocs.ids.ac.uk/opendocs/bitstream/handle/20.500.12413/15261/Case_18_IBEKA_FINAL.pdf?sequence=1

CUCO Indonesia. (2020a). *Historis Perjalanan Gerakan Koperasi Kredit Indonesia (GKKI).* Retrieved April 2020, from https://cucoindo.org/; https://cucoindo.org/sejarah/

CUCO Indonesia. (2020b). *Pilar Credit Union*. Retrieved April 2020, from www.cucoindo.org; https://cucoindo.org/lima-pilar-credit-union/

Davis, B. (2015). *Financial Sustainability and Funding Diversification: The Challenge for Indonesian NGOs*. Retrieved April 2020, from https://www.ksi-indonesia.org/; https://www. ksi-indonesia.org/assets/uploads/original/2020/02/ksi-1580493181.pdf

Enrique, E.-A., & Fernando, G.-L.-d.-G. (2012). Towards an integrated crowdsourcing definition. *Journal of Information Science, 38*(2), 189–200.

European Union Commission. (2013). *Social Economy and Social Entrepreneurship: Social Europe Guide* (Vol. 4). Brussels: Director General for Employment. Social Affairs and Inclusion.

GIIN, & Intellecap. (2018, August). Retrieved March 2020, from www.thegiin.org; https://thegiin. org/assets/Indonesia_GIIN_SEAL_report_webfile.pdf.

Gutomo, A. (2017, October 25). *Aset Koperasi Kredit/CU Se Indonesia Rp 30,645 Triliun*. Retrieved March 2020, from https://pipnews.co.id/nasional/aset-koperasi-kredit-cu-se-indonesia-rp-30645-triliun/

Howe, J. (2006, June 14). The rise of crowdsourcing. Retrieved April 2020, from ww.wired.com; http://www.wired.com/wired/archive/14.06/crowds.html

Ibrahim, R., Suryaningati, A., & Malik, T. (2003). Governance, Organizational Effectiveness and the Non-Profit Sector – Indonesia Country Report. Makati City, PH: APPC Conference on Governance, Organizational Effectiveness and the Non-Profit Sector.

Indra, N., Mardiyah, T., Ajeng, S., & Desi, L. (2020). Peluang Dan Tantangan Perencanaan Pembentukan Koperasi Mitra Gojek di Era Milenial. *Fair Value: Jurnal Ilmiah Akuntansi dan Keuangan, 2*(2), 111–142.

Jelani, A. (2016, March 15). Pancasila Economic and the Challenges of Globalization and Free Market In Indonesia. Retrieved March 2020, from https://mpra.ub.uni-muenchen.de/; https://mpra.ub.uni-muenchen.de/70279/

Kartasasmita, G., Prabowo, A., Kesowo, B., Suherly, T., Martoredjo, W., Supardi, R., & Kale, A. (1980a). *30 Tahun Indonesia Merdeka: 1945–1949*. Jakarta: PT Tira Pustaka.

Kartasasmita, G., Prabowo, A., Kesowo, B., Suherly, T., Martoredjo, W., Supardi, R., & Kale, A. (1980b). *30 Tahun Indonesia Merdeka: 1950–1964*. Jakarta: PT Tira Pustaka.

Kartasasmita, G., Prabowo, A., Kesowo, B., Suherly, T., Martoredjo, W., Supardi, R., & Kale, A. (1980c). *30 Tahun Indonesia Merdeka: 1965–1973*. Jakarta: PT Tira Pustaka.

Kawai, M., & Inoue, M. (2011). The possibility and challenge of achieving sustainable rural finance by a credit union of the Dayak people: The case of the middle-upper Mahakam region in East Kalimantan, Indonesia. *Topics, 19*(4), 157–178.

Kementerian Koperasi. (2019). *Data Koperasi*. Retrieved April 2020, from http://www.depkop.go.id/data-koperasi; http://www.depkop.go.id/uploads/laporan/1580298872_Data%20Koperasi%2031%20Desember%202019-1.pdf

Kencana, M. R. (2018, July). Retrieved March 2020, from https://www.liputan6.com/; https://www.liputan6.com/bisnis/read/3584274/smi-terbitkan-obligasi-hijau-pertama-dan-sukuk-senilai-rp-3-triliun

Kujana, G. (2018, August 3). 8 Wirausaha Sosial Indonesia Masuk 100 Social Venture Challenge Asia Artikel ini telah tayang di Investor.id dengan judul "8 Wirausaha Sosial Indonesia Masuk 100 Social Venture Challenge Asia" Penulis: Gora Kunjana Read more at: https://investor.id/busin. Retrieved April 2020, from www.investor.id; https://investor.id/archive/8-wirausaha-sosial-indonesia-masuk-100-social-venture-challenge-asia

Kunjana, G. (2018, November 21). *Adaro Gelontorkan Rp 1,1 Triliun untuk CSR Pendidikan*. Retrieved April 2020, from www.investor.id; https://investor.id/market-and-corporate/adaro-gelontorkan-rp-11-triliun-untuk-csr-pendidikan

Liger, Q., Stefan, M., & Britton, J. (2016). *Social Economy*. Retrieved January 2020, from https://www.europarl.europa.eu/; https://www.europarl.europa.eu/RegData/etudes/STUD/2016/578969/IPOL_STU(2016)578969_EN.pdf

Mahita, D., Rifa, D., & Taruli, H. (2015). Sustainable Agribusiness For Indonesia's Farmers' economic Well-Being: Case Study of Javara Indonesia. *15th Indonesian Scholars International Convention*, (p. 130). London.

Maskur, F. (2019, Maret 12). Politeknik Petrokimia di Banten, Ini Sistem Pendidikan dan Program Studinya. Retrieved April 2020, from ww.ekonomi.bisnis.com; https://ekonomi.bisnis.com/read/20190312/257/898565/politeknik-petrokimia-di-banten-ini-sistem-pendidikan-dan-program-studinya

Mishra, P., & Sharma, R. (2014). A hybrid framework based on SIPOC and six sigma DMAIC for improving process dimensions in supply chain network. *The International Journal of Quality & Reliability Management, 31*(5), 522–546.

Mubyarto. (2002). Peran Ilmu Ekonomi Dalam Pemberdayaan Ekonomi Rakyat. *Jurnal Ekonomi dan Bisnis Indonesia, 17*(3), 233–242.

Nizar, M. (2017). Teknologi Keuangan (Fintech): Konteks dan Implementasinya di Indonesia. *Warta Fiskal, 5*, 6–13.

Noventari, W. (2016). Harmonisasi Nilai-Nilai Pancasila Dalam Sistem Among Sesuai Dengan Alam Pemikiran Pendidikan Ki Hajar Dewantara. *JPK (Jurnal Pancasila dan Kewarganegaraan), 1*(1), 50–59.

Pandit, V., & Tamhane, T. (2018, February). A closer look at impact investing. Retrieved from www.mckinsey.com; https://www.mckinsey.com/industries/private-equity-and-principal-investors/our-insights/a-closer-look-at-impact-investing#

Poesponegoro, M., & Notosusanto, N. (1984). *Sejarah Nasional Indonesia IV*. Jakarta: Balai Pustaka.

Kartu Pra-Kerja. (2020, April). Kementerian Koordinator Bidang Perekonomian Republik Indonesia. Retrieved April 2020, from www.prakerja.go.id; https://www.prakerja.go.id/tentang-kami

Pratono, A., Pramudija, P., & Sutanti, A. (2016). Social enterprise in Indonesia: Emerging models under transition government. *ICSEM Working Paper.*

Pulungan, S. M. (2019). Konsepsi Bangun Perusahaan Koperasi: Kerangka Pemikiran Badan Usaha Yang Ideal Menurut Pasal 33 Ayat (1) UUD 1945. *Jurnal Hukum & Pembangunan, 49*(2), 241–264.

Pusponegoro, M., & Notosusanto, N. (1984). *Sejarah Nasional Indonesia V* (Vol. 5). Jakarta: PN Balai Pustaka.

Radyati, M. (2019). *Interview with the Founder of a Communiy Enterprise "punyabersama.id" [Recorded by I. Noviansyah].* Jakarta, Indonesia: CECT Trisakti University.

Radyati, M., & Simmonds, T. (2018b). *Case Study of TELAPAK - Indonesia.* Retrieved April 2020, from www.fabmove.eu; https://fabmove.eu/case_study/case-study-of-telapak-indonesia/

Radyati, M. R. (2008). Third Sector Organisation Governance in Indonesia: Regulations, Initiatives and Models. In S. Hasan & J. Onyx (Eds.), *Comparative Third Sector Governance in Asia: Structure, Process, and Political Economy* (pp. 253–275). New York: Springer.

Radyati, M. R. (2010). *Governance and performance of third sector organisations: Credit unions in Indonesia.* Sydney: University of Technology, Sydney.

Radyati, M. R. (2014). *Corporate Social Responsibility dan Sustainable Business.* Jakarta: CECT Trisakti University.

Radyati, M. R., & Simmonds, T. (2018a). *Social Enterprises in Indonesia - Country Report.* Retrieved April 2020, from www.fabmove.eu; https://fabmove.eu/country_report/social-enterprises-in-indonesia/

Rahayu, N. (2019, August 16). Sebut Koperasi di Indonesia Semakin Berkualitas, LPDB-KUMKM Berikan Bimtek Dana Bergulir. Retrieved April 2020, from www.wartaekonomi.co.id; https://www.wartaekonomi.co.id/read241777/sebut-koperasi-di-indonesia-semakin-berkualitas-lpdb-kumkm-berikan-bimtek-dana-bergulir.html

Redaksi. (2019, October 12). *Bank Kalbar Dinilai Kalah dengan CU.* Retrieved May 2020, from www.kalimantantoday.com; https://kalimantantoday.com/2019/10/23/bank-kalbar-dinilai-kalah-dengan-cu/

Rolindrawan, D. (2015). The impact of BPJS health implementation for the poor and near poor on the use of health facility. *Procedia-Social and Behavioral Sciences, 211*, 550–559.

Rubiyanto, P., & Darmawan, I. (2006). Warisan Koperasi Rochdale dalam Gerakan Koperasi di Indonesia Menurut UU No. 25 Tahun 1992. In Y. Harsoyo, P. Rubiyanto, Y. Purbocahyono, M. Suwarni, K. C. Astuti, Y. Mudayen, & I. Darmawan (Eds.), *Ideologi koperasi menatap masa depan* (pp. 22–47). Yogyakarta: Universitas Sanata Dharma and Pustaka Widyatama.

Rymsza, M. (2015). The role of social enterprises in shaping social bonds. *International Journal of Social Economics, 42*(9), 830–840.

Santika, D. (2017). Analisis Persepsi Masyarakat Kota Pontianak Tentang Keberadaan Dan Peranan Credit Union Di Kota Pontianak. *MABIS, 7*(2), 74–80.

Setiawan, S. (2015). Financial depth and financial access in Indonesia. *Journal of Indonesian Economy and Business : JIEB, 30*(2), 139–158.

Simani, W. (2020). Together we can do great things an inclusive business model. *Journal of the International Academy for Case Studies, 26*(1), 1–20.

Siregar, B. (2019, July 3). *Pacu Vokasi, Industri Butuh 600 Ribu Tenaga Kerja per Tahun.* Retrieved April 2020, from www.wartaekonomi.co.id; https://www.wartaekonomi.co.id/read234859/pacu-vokasi-industri-butuh-600-ribu-tenaga-kerja-per-tahun.html

Suhendra. (2016, July 12). *Bapak Koperasi Indonesia.* Retrieved May 2020, from www.tirto.id; https://tirto.id/bapak-koperasi-indonesia-bsRQ

Sulistyowati, R. (2003, August 4) Pemerintah Diminta Ubah Status Kementerian Negara Koperasi dan UKM. Retrieved April 2020, from: https://bisnis.tempo.co/read/7238/pemerintah-diminta-ubah-status-kementerian-negarakoperasi-dan-ukm

Sunaryo, A. (2019, February 7). *2019, BUMN Naikkan Dana Kemitraan untuk UMKM Menjadi Rp 3,2 T.* Retrieved March 2020, from www.merdeka.com; https://www.merdeka.com/uang/2019-bumn-naikkan-dana-kemitraan-untuk-umkm-menjadi-rp-32-t.html

Suparman, E., Supriyatni, R., Ratnasari, D., & Sofianto, K. (2018). Alternative dispute resolution mechanisms (Adrm) in land cultivation profit-sharing in Kuta, West Java. *Journal of Legal, Ethical and Regulatory, 4*(21), 1–7.

Susilowati, K. (2018). Creating economic value through multi-stakeholder partnership (case study on the black soybean farmers development programme of Unilever Indonesia). *International Journal of Monetary Economics and Finance, 11*(3), 289–297.

Tutwiler, A. (2016). Access to seeds - why seed companies need to bridge the gap to reach small-holder farmers. *Appropriate Technology, 43*(2), 27–28.

UN. (2015, September). *Sustainable Development Goals.* Retrieved April 2020, from https://sustainabledevelopment.un.org/; https://sustainabledevelopment.un.org/?menu=1300

UNDP. (2019, October 9). *Ministry of Development Planning (BAPPENAS) joins forces with UNDP and Tanoto Foundation to launch SDGs Academy Indonesia.* Retrieved May 2020, from www.id.undp.org; https://www.id.undp.org/content/indonesia/en/home/presscenter/pressreleases/2019/SDGs-Academy-Indonesia.html

Wahyono, B., & Margono, S. (2001). *Hukum Yayasan: Antara Fungsi Karitatif atau Komersial.* Jakarta: CV. Novindo Pustaka Mandiri.

Walfajri, M. (2017, October 30). *Berikut 13 Koperasi Unggulan Indonesia.* Retrieved May 2020, from https://keuangan.kontan.co.id/; https://keuangan.kontan.co.id/news/berikut-13-koperasi-unggulan-indonesia

World Culture Forum. (2016, Oct 12). Water, the source of life. ACN Newswire.

Wuryaningrat, N. F., & Kumajas, L. I. (2017). Examining an endangered knowledge transfer practice known as "mapalus" in an Indonesian village: implications for entrepreneurial activities and economic development. *International Journal of Business and Society, 18*, 309–322.

Chapter 5
The New Social Economy in Israel: From the *Kibbutz* Ideal to *Social-Tech Entrepreneurship*

Ronny Manos and Benjamin Gidron

Introduction

When one is asked to give an example of social economy in Israel, the first thing that comes to mind is usually the Kibbutz—an agriculturally based community that follows a collectivistic way of life.

Specifically, the traditional Kibbutz is a worker-controlled, agricultural production cooperative (Rosenthal & Eiges, 2013). It is organised as a collective community that is based on socialist values, egalitarian principles and equal sharing of all means of production and labour. It certainly answers the description of a social economy, even if there is still no universally accepted definition for that term (Liger, Stefan, & Britton, 2016). Indeed, Liger et al. (2016) identify four distinctive features of social economy which the *traditional* Kibbutz model undoubtedly fulfils.[1]

First, it emphasises the primacy of the individual. Indeed, one of the first principles of the Kibbutz is that each member should work according to his/her ability, and be provided for by the Kibbutz, in accordance with his/her needs (Rosenthal & Eiges, 2013). **Second, the overall aim of the Kibbutz is not the pursuit of profit, but rather to achieve sustainable growth**. Accordingly, wealth created by

---

[1] Note that our discussion of the Kibbutz relates to the *communal Kibbutz*, that is, the traditional Kibbutz before the wave of privatisation that has occurred in the Kibbutz movement since the late 1990s, resulting in a new model called 'renewing Kibbutz'.

R. Manos (✉)
School of Business Administration, College of Management Academic Studies, Rishon Le Zion, Israel
e-mail: rmanos@colman.ac.il

B. Gidron
Professor Emeritus, Business Administration, Ben-Gurion University of the Negev, Beer-Sheva, Israel

© Springer Nature Switzerland AG 2021
B. Gidron, A. Domaradzka (eds.), *The New Social and Impact Economy*, Nonprofit and Civil Society Studies, https://doi.org/10.1007/978-3-030-68295-8_5

the commune goes into a common pool while members hold no private property (Kislev, 2015). The pooled wealth is then used to provide for all the needs of members as well as to guarantee mutual and reciprocal aid. **Third, the Kibbutz balances social and economic activity.** Specifically, the Kibbutz is a cooperative in terms of labour and production of goods, but also in terms of consumer services (e.g. accommodation, education, childcare, medicine) and social life (Rosenthal & Eiges, 2013). Moreover, key in Kibbutz's ideology is the good of the collective and of the country. For example, during periods of mass immigration to Israel, the Kibbutz movement was heavily involved in this process, providing accommodation, language learning programmes and other essential services. **Fourth, the Kibbutz is based on democratic governance**. It is an egalitarian society in which members collaborate on a voluntary basis and the governance and decision-making process are by way of direct participatory democracy. Each member can directly influence issues and events in the community by taking part in regular Kibbutz meetings and voting on subject matters. In addition, the Kibbutz differs from regular cooperative (producer, consumer) in that it follows the form of a commune, sharing not only assets and ideology but also where members live and raise children together.

However, even though the Kibbutz fulfils the four social economy conditions as articulated by Liger et al. (2016), it would be incorrect to interpret the development of the Israeli society and its social orientation, solely based on the Kibbutz model. In fact, Kibbutz population never accounted for more than 6.5% of total population, and in most years less than 5% (CBS, 2008). Moreover, most immigrants that arrived in the land of Israel after World War I—and especially during the 1930s and 1940s—settled in towns, cities and non-Kibbutz rural settlements. Some of those newcomers had capital and resources allowing them to establish free-market industrial and business endeavours.

Moreover, although by 1950 5.6% of the population were living in Kibbutz communities, this figure—as well as the growth rates in the number of Kibbutz communities and members—had been declining throughout the 1950s. There are several demographic reasons for this declining trend, as well as an ideologic dispute relating to the affiliation of the Kibbutz movement with the Soviet Union. The Kibbutz, however, was not dead by the end of the 1950s. In fact, the number of Kibbutz communities and members had been increasing throughout the 1960s, 1970s and 1980s—despite a major social and economic crisis which the Kibbutz movement endured during the 1980s. That crisis resulted in a process of soul-searching during the 1990s, by many Kibbutz communities and members. Subsequently, the Kibbutz—as a collective cooperative—transformed itself in such a way that by the end of the process it became less obvious that it was still a classic collectivistic entity.

Parallel to the demise of the Kibbutz in its classical form, Israel was undergoing political, social and economic shifts during the 1980s and 1990s that saw the country turning into a neoliberal, individualistic society with a flourishing high-technology sector. Indeed, Israel became to be known as the *start-up* nation (Senor & Singer, 2011), a term used to indicate its innovative and entrepreneurial spirit. It was therefore only natural that following the global and local socio-economic tremors of 2008 and 2011, new type of social economy has developed in Israel, namely the social-tech enterprise. This new social economy is markedly different from the Kibbutz collectivistic ideal.

That, in short, is the story we are going to unveil in detail in this chapter, which is structured as follows. In section "The Kibbutz Ideal and the Welfare State" we review the Kibbutz ideal, including the ecopolitical and financial context within which it flourished and dwindled. Section "The Start-Up Nation and Growing Inequalities" describes neoliberal Israel and its emergence as a start-up nation alongside growing inequalities and social discontent which came to a boil in the summer of 2011. This provides the backdrop to renewed interest in social economy. Thus, we continue to describe the emergence of the new social economy in Israel, one that draws from Israel's strength as a start-up nation, oriented towards technological entrepreneurship. We also review the financial ecosystem that has developed around it. The section "Concluding Remarks" offers insights and conclusions.

The Kibbutz Ideal and the Welfare State

Quasi-Socialism and the Kibbutz

To understand the Kibbutz as an early form of social economy in Israel, we need to go back to 1882, when the first immigrants arrived at Ottoman-ruled Palestine seeking to settle down (Silber & Rosenhek, 1999).[2] This formation was in response to antisemitism, and on the backdrop of pogroms and discrimination against Jews. It was driven by Zionist ideology, which emerged in Europe at the turn of the nineteenth century, advocating the return of the Jewish people to their historical homeland *and the resumption of Jewish sovereignty thereof.*

The Zionist ideology coincided with the expansion of the socialist and communist ideologies in Europe, and the events leading to the creation of the USSR. The combination of Zionism and socialism streams of thought influenced many young Jews from Eastern Europe—primarily Russia. Driven by those nationalist-socialist ideas, many decided to immigrate to the land of Israel (Palestine) with the vision of building there a Zionist-socialist state. Indeed, the nature of the institutions that the newcomers established in Palestine reflected the Zionist-socialist ideology that guided them. The best-known example of those institutions—as we noted in the introduction above—is the Kibbutz collaborative cooperative. It was not the only one.

Nonetheless, the Kibbutz model certainly proposed a way out of trade and moneylending, the traditional occupations of Jews in Eastern Europe, and into communes where members worked as farmers and settled the land. The first

---

[2] Prior to the establishment of the State of Israel in 1948, during the Ottoman rule and the British Mandate, the land of Israel was known as Palestine. After WWI it included the geographical area that today covers the State of Israel, the West Bank and the Gaza Strip.

Kibbutz—*Degania*—was established in 1910 as a close social cooperative, sharing all property and means of production and labour, while providing for all the needs of its members. *Degania* illustrated not only total transformation from traditional Jewish life in Eastern Europe, but also the assimilation of Zionist ideas *alongside* socialist principles. Throughout the proceeding four decades, Degania became a model for many more Kibbutz communities, which spread all over the country.

The formation and spreading of Kibbutz communities all over the country were supported by the Zionist movement through a set of organisations which it established. Those organisations (national institutions) were well functioning, ideology driven and non-profit (see Katz & Greenspan, 2015). They included the World Zionist Organization, the Jewish Agency for Israel, Jewish National Fund and Keren Hayesod.[3] As well as collecting funds to support the establishment of a state, the four national institutions also engaged in diverse activities including settling migrants, strengthening Jewish diaspora, combatting antisemitism and furthering education. By 1948, following a long and costly war of independence, the Zionist movement's political goal to create a Jewish state succeeded. Before and following independence, millions of immigrants were flocking into Israel, for whom accommodation and jobs had to be found.[4] In order to survive these difficulties while building a state, Israel adopted a welfare state approach and a nationalistic collectivistic rhetoric (Sternhell, 1998).

Thus, upon independence and continuing well into the 1970s, Israel was governed by a socialist-nationalist-interventionist government which was involved in every facet of the economy and society.[5] Foreign trade, exchange rate and bank credit were all centrally controlled. Likewise, laws were legislated to make the state responsible for the delivery of education, healthcare and welfare services. The government founded development towns, and was involved in the construction of

---

[3] First, **the World Zionist Organization** (*HaHistadrut HaTzionit Ha'Olamit* in Hebrew) is a non-governmental organisation that promotes Zionism. It was established in 1897 at the First Zionist Congress in Basel, Switzerland (https://www.wzo.org.il/). Second, **the Jewish Agency for Israel** (*HaSochnut HaYehudit* in Hebrew) is a non-profit organisation that was established in 1929 to look after the interests of the Jewish people. It played a key role in the development of the State of Israel and the absorption of Jewish diaspora into Israel (see https://www.jewishagency.org/aliyah/). Third, the **Jewish National Fund** (*Keren Kayemeth LeIsrael* in Hebrew) was established at the fifth Zionist Congress in 1901, as a non-profit organisation, wholly owned by the World Zionist Organization. Its original aim was to purchase land for the Jewish people (https://www.kkl-jnf.org/). Lastly, **United Israel Appeal** (*Keren Hayesod* in Hebrew) was established in London in 1920, to serve as the fundraising arm of the Jewish people and the Zionist movement. It is recognised today as a national institution (public benefit company), operating under a special law that was passed by the Israeli Parliament in 1956 and which grants it fundraising status (https://www.kh-uia.org.il/about-us/).

[4] According to Kislev (2015) 700,000 Jewish immigrants entered Israel within the first 4 years following independence, doubling the number of Jews in the country. Others followed thereafter, tripling the number within 15 years.

[5] All governments until 1977 were led by the Labour Party, generally considered socialist. However, Strenhell (1998) notes that the founders of the Labour Party were not committed to the socialist ethos. Certainly, the economy could not be described as pure socialism.

massive infrastructure projects such as ports (in Haifa, Ashdod and Eilat) and national water carrier (Peretz, 2018).

The combination of a socialist-nationalist-interventionist government with an evolving state that was facing varied socio-economic challenges created the conditions under which cooperatives flourished (Russell & Hanneman, 1992). Specifically, various types of cooperatives had developed which were based on socialist ideas, and arguably made economic sense given the socio-economic and geopolitical conditions prevailing at the time. For example, the Moshav, similar in spirit to the Kibbutz, developed as an agricultural community cooperative, comprising a collection of individually owned farms (Rosenthal & Eiges, 2013).

Particularly, while the Kibbutz is essentially a worker-controlled, agricultural production cooperative, the Moshav is a service cooperative (Rosenthal & Eiges, 2013). Thus, on a Moshav the marketing and purchasing of farm input are done cooperatively, but families work in their own farms, relying on the cooperative to provide labour assistance only when needed (Kislev, 2015). The first Moshav, named Nahalal, was established in 1921, and—like the Kibbutz—the Moshav model was well established by the time Israel gained independence in 1948.

The Kibbutz and the Moshav, as two alternative forms of agricultural community cooperatives, were proven to be an effective way to sustain economic stability. Moreover, they were perceived as pioneers that fulfilled a crucial role in settling and working the land, defining the country's borders, absorbing immigration and bringing about industrial development (Halamish, 2009). Consequently, the Kibbutz and the Moshav were promoted by the Labour Party-led political leadership as ideal institutions for settling the land and building a just society. Considerable funds were invested in those agricultural cooperatives, facilitating their fast growth and the accumulation of considerable political influence and monopoly power within the agricultural market (Rosenthal & Eiges, 2013). Correspondingly, the agricultural community cooperatives grew in numbers. By 1947—one year before independence—there were 127 Kibbutz communities and 87 Moshav communities spread around the country. By 2011 these figures stood at 266 and 433, respectively (Kislev, 2015).

Still, even at the height of Kibbutz days, most people were living in cities and towns. Moreover, Sternhell (1998) argues that the Kibbutz was mainly used as a propaganda tool, to promote nationalistic collectivism. Notwithstanding this criticism, the Kibbutz and Moshav were not the only form of social economy prevalent in Israel during its early years. Specifically, other cooperatives, often linked to the Kibbutz and Moshav, also played a role in the Israeli economy during its first three decades.

In particular, the Kibbutz and the Moshav were themselves members of regional associations, established to carry out activities such as water provision, transportation, labour and machinery, marketing, or communal purchasing of farm inputs on wholesale terms. The latter later developed additional services such as slaughterhouses and cold storage. Moreover, the cooperative concept was prevalent not only in rural areas, but also in the consumer market in the form of cooperative supermarkets and banks in the cities. These cooperatives served their members by enhancing their economic power and protecting their rights. They later became the basis for workers' rights legislation (Levi, 2004).[6]

To sum, the establishment of cooperatives reflected the socialist tradition and collectivist orientation of the Zionist movement. However, given the large fraction of privately owned enterprises, it would be imprecise to describe Israel as a purely socialist state. Instead, the deep government intervention in all aspects of daily life could alternatively be explained in terms of nationhood (Wolfsfeld, 1988) or patriotism (Eisenstadt, 1967). Indeed, the government intervened in monetary, fiscal and exchange rate policies, as well as using discriminating interest rates to influence business activity (Aharoni, 2014). Given heterogenous mass immigration, wars and economic hardship, nurturing nationhood and patriotism provided the needed legitimacy for subordinating sectoral interests to the national interest. The big challenge was how to finance this interventionist policy.

Welfare State and Finance

It is often argued that the economic model of interference that characterised Israel in its first three decades was necessary to achieve certain national goals (Krampf, 2018). Accordingly, building a country is a public good that justifies such an approach (Gross & Metzer, 1999; Krampf, 2018; Metzer, 1979). Levi-Faur (1998) refers to this idea as developmental state (see also Krampf, 2018). Certainly, the policy of government interference came against a backdrop of heterogenous mass immigration, wars and economic hardships. To cope with these challenges, an ideology that emphasised nationhood had to be adopted (Wolfsfeld, 1988). This came in the form of *nationhood* (or *statism—Mamlchtiut*) ideology which stressed the subordination of sectional interest to the interests of the state.

Nationhood was adopted as an overriding ideology, coupled with high value which was placed on patriotism (Eisenstadt, 1967). This ideological stance was personified by the first Prime Minister, David Ben-Gurion, who enjoyed the broad support of many, for whom the establishment of a Jewish state was the culmination of a dream. The *nationhood* ideology also provided legitimacy for Israel to undertake a *welfare state* approach, turning the sectorial system of social services in the pre-state era into a statutory system. It was a process similar to that experienced by many other countries in the aftermath of World War II.

Upon establishment, Israel had to recover from the War of Independence while simultaneously absorbing Jewish immigrants, Holocaust survivors and refugees from all over the world. The country went into deep economic crisis, including high unemployment, food shortages, absence of housing and lack of foreign currency.

---

[6] Large and well-established cooperatives include *Tnuva*, for dairy and food production; *Koor*, in the business of heavy industry; and *Egged* for transportation.

This situation forced the government to declare and implement a policy of austerity and rationing that lasted from 1949 to 1959.

Parallel to the austerity measures, Israel was seeking financial aid in the form of donations, grants and loans. The first port of call was Jewish diaspora. For example, up until the 1980s, the United Jewish Appeal collected at least 80% of donations from American Jewry, which were subsequently passed to the Jewish Agency in Israel (Fleisch, 2014).[7] In addition, Israel's first Prime Minister, David Ben-Gurion, conceived the idea of sourcing funds from Diaspora Jewry directly rather than through the Jewish Agency for Israel, by raising loans from private US Jewish citizens. Thus, in 1951, Israel embarked on the Bond Program, floating State of Israel Bonds, which turned up to be very successful (Fleisch, 2014). This, clearly, was not philanthropy. Indeed, as Fleisch (2014) points out, although these bonds were promoted as a tool to assist in the development of Israel, they came with a promise for financial returns and high redemption rates.[8]

Another promising source of funds was compensations from West Germany, in line with the claim that it should reimburse Israel for absorbing Holocaust survivors. In 1952, following internal debate and morally based opposition, Israel signed the Reparations Agreement.[9] Ben-Gurion maintained that the agreement was based on moral grounds to compensate Jews and Israel for the Holocaust as well as to ease the financial strain of absorbing and rehabilitating Holocaust survivors (Auerbach, 1991). Some of the money from the Reparations Agreement was channelled to government-owned companies, to the Histadrut labour union and to the Jewish Agency.[10] It is estimated that during the 12 years that the Reparations Agreement was active, it accounted for approximately 15% of Israel's GNP growth and contributed to the creation of 45,000 jobs (Segev, 1993).

The financial support provided by the Reparations Agreement, Diaspora Jewry and Israel Bonds, together with the government's commitment to development, led to impressive economic growth rates over the first two decades of Israel's existence (Aharoni, 2014). Helpman (2003) notes that Israel's growth rate was relatively high in the 1960s but fell sharply in the 1970s and 1980s. For example, between 1960

---

[7]The United Jewish Appeal was set up in 1939 as the United Jewish Appeal for Refugees and Overseas Needs and is now known as the Jewish Federations of North America. It is a Jewish philanthropic umbrella organisation that represents over 100 Jewish non-profit organisations across North America (https://jewishfederations.org/).

[8]Excluding two periods of crisis when redemption rates dropped below 30%. These two periods include the years 1951–1957, immediately following independence, and the years 1967–1973, covering the 6-Day War, the War of Attrition and the Yom Kippur War (see Fleisch, 2014).

[9]The Reparations Agreement (*Heskem HaShillumim* in Hebrew) specified that West Germany would pay Israel for the costs associated with resettling Jewish survivors as well as compensate individuals for losses resulting from Nazi persecution (see Honig, 1954, and Auerbach, 1991).

[10]Two clarifications are in order. First it is important to note that some of the Reparations Agreement was paid to individual survivors and to families of victims. Second, it is relevant to our discussion to explain that the **Histadrut,** the national labour union, was created in 1920 as the General Organization of Workers in Israel, to represent Jewish workers. It became a very powerful organization, the owner of key businesses and the employer of many people.

and 1973 annual growth rate in GNP was 8.5%, dropping to 2.6% between 1973 and 1977 (Fischer, 1987). The turning point was the 1973 Yom Kippur War, and the winds of change that followed.

Collapse of the Kibbutz Ideal and Transformation of the Welfare State

The 1973 Yom Kippur War and the ensuing global oil crisis led Israel into an economic crisis. Peretz (2018) describes the period from 1973 until the mid-1980s as the lost years of the Israeli economy. Defence costs were climbing to 30% of gross domestic product while government expenditure was expanding too. At the same time the budget deficit was deepening, government borrowing was increasing and inflation was rising in steps from 2% in 1967 to 500% in 1984 (Fischer, 1987).

The economic challenges that followed Yom Kippur War (1973) were further accompanied by a political change marking a shift in the predominant ideology under which Israel had been governed since inception in 1948 (Lebel, Fuksman-Sha'al, & Orkibi, 2018). Specifically, the general elections of May 1977 resulted in the right-wing liberal-nationalist Likud party taking over, after about 30 years of Labour-led governments.[11] A protective, socialist and collectivistic thought—or at least quasi-socialist thought as described by Ram (2008)—was replaced with one based on free market, capitalism and individualism. In line with the new political approach, economic reforms were enacted to transform the economy and the institutional structure along capitalist ideology. For example, by the end of 1977, liberalisation in the form of greater access to foreign exchange and to foreign exchange-linked accounts was introduced, sending inflation rates to triple-digit figures (Fischer, 1987).

To add to the challenging situation, a storm was brewing in the banking sector as banks were manipulating their shares. The bubble burst in 1983 when those shares collapsed, and the Tel Aviv Stock Exchange was shut down for about 3 weeks. Subsequently, the government nationalised Israel's four major banks (Blass & Grossman, 1996). In the meantime, the country was still suffering from growing inflation and continuing outflows of reserves. By 1985 the US Government was providing military and economic aid to Israel on an annual basis to the tune of $3 billion. It also indicated that it would provide additional emergency aid if Israel was to make a serious attempt to improve its economic situation (Fischer, 1987).

And so, in 1985 Israel initiated an economic stabilisation plan. It included price controls, reduction in government expenditure and external debt, privatisation programmes, wage controls, devaluation of the local currency and a move to a fixed foreign exchange policy. The stabilisation programme proved to be successful in

---

[11] Lebel et al. (2018) describe the results of the 1977 general elections in Israel as 'political upheaval' and 'one of the most dramatic moments in Israeli political history' (pg. 939). It is noted that the Labour Party was leading Israel not only since independence in 1948, but actually since 1933, in its pre-state status as the Zionist movement.

controlling the inflation and was thus proceeded by market-oriented structural reforms. In particular, restrictions on imports were cancelled, privatisation programmes of state-owned enterprises were undertaken, the government pooled out of the capital market, price controls were lifted, subsidies were removed and the currency market was liberalised (Peretz, 2018).[12]

Parallel to these shifts, the Kibbutz, which had been the most prominent realisation of the socialist facet of the Israeli economy, was experiencing strong shockwaves too. Specifically, up until the 1970s, the Kibbutz movement continued to grow and expand, diversifying away from agriculture into industry and services. It was also expanding in terms of size, as new members joined. However, on a backdrop of a general shift from collectivism to individualism, pressures were mounting, calling for changes to the underlying socialist-based rules. A classic example is the pressure to end communal sleeping for children.

Thus, starting from the 1970s and continuing in earnest during the 1980s, Kibbutz-born young people who were not as ideological as their parents about the Kibbutz and its role in building and defending the state were leaving to the cities (Shapira, 2005). Moreover, with the political change from the socialist-collectivistic Labour Party to a liberal-national Likud party in 1977, socially and economically deprived groups arose to challenge the Kibbutz privileges, demanding equal opportunities. Consequently, the Kibbutz lost the government's ideological support, guarantees and financial backing which it was relying on during years of debt accumulation.

Jointly, these social, demographic and economic strains led to reforms of the Kibbutz movement and to the birth of the privatised/renewing Kibbutz. The new structure maintained communal ownership of the means of production, but began the process of privatisation of some property, principally members' homes. Likewise, many of the Kibbutz services, such as health, food and education, have been privatised. In addition, in many Kibbutz communities, members were permitted to work outside of the Kibbutz and salaries were shifted from equal allocation based on family size and needs to a differential salary system based on occupation.

In the arena of the welfare state—like in many other Western countries and following changing ideology during the 1980s—a process of privatisation of public services had been taking place. Among privatised public services were health, welfare, education and immigrants' absorption, which were traditionally funded primarily by public money and provided within statutory services. Many of these services were funded and delivered by for-profit and non-profit organisations and a complex system of contracts and tenders. These changes gave a major boost to Israel's non-profit/third sector (Gidron, Bar, & Katz, 2004).

---

[12] As part of the 1985 economic stabilisation plan, the Israeli Shekel was replaced by the New Israeli Shekel, and a fixed exchange rate regime was imposed. But in 1989 the currency market was liberalised by introducing a fluctuation band policy with the New Israeli Shekel allowing to fluctuate within predetermined upper and lower borders. The fluctuation band was expanded over the years until it was cancelled in 2005, moving the New Israeli Shekel into a floating exchange rate regime (Israel Central Bureau of Statistics, 2008).

To sum, the tremors of the period 1973–1985 included a war, an economic crisis, a fundamental political change, a shift from socialist-collectivistic thought to liberal-nationalism and weakening of the Kibbutz movement. Subsequently, by the end of this period, Israel has transformed itself from a welfare state with socialist-collectivistic tendencies into a neoliberal economy with an individualistic society. This shift, as noted by Gidron et al. (2004), was due to changes in the demographic, political, technological, economic and social characteristics of the rapidly developing country. The economic and ideological facelift, which Israel had undergone, revived its economy, leading to high rates of growth in the 1990s.

The economic revival, however, came with increased social inequality, more instances of poverty and growing concern over social justice (Peretz, 2018). These events and evolutions led to a new expression of social activism and involvement, one that is based on unorganised, individual entrepreneurship. But for this to develop, Israel had to undergo another transformation, into entrepreneurship and innovative nation, also known as *the start-up nation* (Senor & Singer, 2011).

The Start-Up Nation and Growing Inequalities

Neoliberalism and the Rise of the Start-Up Nation

Following the stabilisation programme of the mid-1980s, and throughout the remaining of the 1980s and the 1990s, additional liberalisation measures were taken, transforming the state from developmental to a neoliberal model (Mandelkern & Shalev, 2018). It is often argued that up until the late 1970s, Israel was a socialist economy, and refer to the change following the stabilisation programme in 1985 as transformation from a socialist to a capitalist economy (see Aharoni, 2014; Ben-Basaṭ, 2002; Peretz, 2018).[13] Another view, however, is that Israel was never a classic socialist economy. Ram (2008) describes the early Israeli economy as quasi-socialist, while Krampf (2018) maintains that it was socialist mainly in rhetoric. Krampf (2018) further argues that government intervention in the early days of the state was aimed mainly to achieve national objectives, and that in fact Israel transformation was from one type of capitalism to another.

---

[13] Peretz (2018) describes the transformation of Israel from a socialist to a capitalist economy in 1985 as no less than the biggest event in its economic history. While this may overstate the situation, the Israeli Government certainly reduced its intervention following the events of the 1970s and 1980s. For example, government expenditure on education was reduced from 86% of total expenditure in 1980 to 74% in 1987, while its expenditure on health was reduced from 51% of total expenditure in 1985 to 45% in 1990 (Shapira, 2010). Similarly, welfare services were privatised, forcing those providers to adopt business strategies and become more efficient, thereby establishing the moral legitimacy and positive public perception of the association between business and society (Dart, 2004).

Regardless of semantics, Israel emerged from the 1980s as a more capitalist society, with severe implications for socio-economic inequality (Mandelkern & Shalev, 2018). It also underwent industrial shifts, which subsequently facilitated its development into a start-up nation. For example, the share of agriculture in GDP dropped from 12% in 1953 to 4.5% by the 1990s, while over the same period services rose from 25% to 40% and manufacturing from 21% to 30% of GDP (Helpman, 2003). The industrial structure has also changed, moving from traditional, labour-intensive industries (e.g. textiles) to human capital-intensive industries, such as electronics (Helpman, 2003).

In the meantime, while Israel was liberalising its economy and opening to the world, the technological revolution was gathering pace globally. Indeed, between 1986 and 2007, the world's technological capacity to receive information through one-way broadcast networks, to exchange information through two-way telecommunication networks and to store information grew at an annual growth rate of 7%, 30% and 25%, respectively (Hilbert & López, 2011). These developments penetrated the Israeli business sector, driven by initiatives within the Israeli military forces (e.g. the establishment of high-tech R&D units), investment by the defence and aerospace industries and government deliberate policy (Offenhauer, 2008).

In fact, since the late 1960s, Israel has been pursuing an industrial policy aiming to encourage innovation through private entrepreneurship and without central targeting for support of specific sectors or technologies (Trajtenberg, 2000). This is best articulated by a 1984 Law for the Encouragement of R&D, and reflected in the establishment—in 1969—of the Office of the Chief Scientist (now known as the *Israel Innovation Authority, IIA*) at the Ministry of Economy.[14] The IIA was assigned the role of implementing the 1984 R&D Law, which it did by initiating a set of programmes (Offenhauer, 2008; Prainsack & Firestine, 2006). First, it established grants to kickstart technological entrepreneurship (Trajtenberg, 2000). Second, in the early 1990s, the IIA set up technology incubators to assist newly immigrating entrepreneurs (Avnimelech, Schwartz, & Bar-El, 2007). Third, the IIA sought to promote the development of a venture capital (VC) industry by creating, in 1993, a government-run VC fund, called Yozma.

Thus, starting in the 1990s, substantial diffusion of R&D and innovation capabilities occurred throughout the Israeli business sector. This facilitated the transformation of technological opportunities into business opportunities (Avnimelech, 2009). Offenhauer (2008) notes that while initially the high-tech sector focused mainly on information and communication technology, it has since diversified. For example, the biotechnology sector has been gaining increasing attention and has also been declared a national priority (Offenhauer, 2008). Another emerging field

---

[14] The **Encouragement of Industrial Research and Development Law 5744–1984** was amended a number of times and is also referred to as the 'R&D Law'. The **Office of the Chief Scientist** was replaced in 2016 by the National Authority for Technological Innovation, also known as the Israel Innovation Authority, IIA. The **Ministry of Economy** changed its name several times to reflect changes in its responsibilities. It has been known as the Ministry of Economy since 2013, but until 1978 it was called the Ministry of Commerce and Industry.

within the Israeli high-technology sector is cleantech, including in the areas of resource preservation, environmental protection, renewable energy and water technologies.

To conclude, deliberate government actions as well as development of a comprehensive venture capital industry to invest in start-ups resulted in the Israeli high-tech sector becoming one of the best-known centres of innovation in the world. The sector features many—typically small—firms, is heavily export oriented and spans a broad range of science and technology fields, including cleantech (Offenhauer, 2008).

However, notwithstanding the fact that it is often described as the engine of growth of the Israeli economy, the high-tech industry accounts for a small fraction of the overall economy.[15] Furthermore, Srivastava (2018) notes that while the Israeli high-tech industry has doubled its share of GDP from about 6% in 1995 to about 12% in 2018, it has also contributed to income inequality and social discontent. Indeed, while the average wage in the industry stood at about $10,000 a month in 2018, the national average was $2800, while 15% of the workforce were below the poverty line (Srivastava, 2018).

Inequality Leading to the 2011 Outburst and the Ensuing Creative Stage

The expansion of the high-tech sector during the 1990s has contributed to the rapid economic growth which Israel has experienced since. This economic growth was further reinforced by the great wave of immigration from the former USSR including highly educated scientists and engineers (Sherwood, 2011). The solid economic trends continued into the twenty-first century, including the period of the global financial meltdown of the late 2000s.[16]

However, the period from the late 1980s onwards has also seen increasing inequality within the Israeli society. Cornfeld and Danieli (2015) compare Israel with other developed countries and find not only that it had one of the highest levels of inequality, but also that those gaps were widening. The authors report that during the period 1987–2011, there had been a decline in the wage of the middle-wage earners, as well as an increase in the prevalence of part-time jobs at the lower end of the labour market. Their data also show that people with secondary-level education or less did not benefit from the economic growth Israel was experiencing.

---

[15] For example, according to Israel Ministry of Foreign Affairs, as of 2018, the high-tech sector accounts for less than 9% of employees (https://mfa.gov.il/mfa/aboutisrael/economy/pages/econ-omy-%20sectors%20of%20the%20economy.aspx).

[16] This excludes an economic downturn in the early 2000s, brought about by the global dot-com bubble and the Palestinian uprising against Israel (the Second Intifada) which broke out in 2000 (de Boer & Missaglia, 2007).

In response to growing inequalities alongside social services' privatisation that have characterised neoliberal Israel since the 1990s, the Israeli business sector started to explore the concept of Corporate Social Responsibility (CSR). This phenomenon was not unique to the Israeli business sector but saw the emergence of new initiatives and programmes, for example, for-profit organisations guiding and cooperating with non-profit organisations, or executives and staff of for-profit organisations volunteering to contribute to various community projects. Indeed, during the two decades around the turn of the twenty-first century, trends such as company executives volunteering to sit on the boards of charities, or businesses and staff thereof taking part in direct fundraising activities for various social causes, had become the *bon ton* in the business sector (Katz & Greenspan, 2015). The increasing involvement of the business sector in the social arena contributed to the acceptance and adoption of business values and practices by the non-profit sector. An illustration is provided by many philanthropic foundations which started to demand that organisations receiving their grants use reliable measures and evaluation methods to demonstrate the outcome of their activities (Gidron, Schlanger, & Alon, 2008).

Brewing social discontent came to a boil in the summer of 2011 in the form of widespread demonstrations, nicknamed 'the tent protest'. It was started by a group of young people in Tel Aviv who set out tents in public parks and boulevards protesting against the lack of adequate housing, high cost of living, growing inequality and poor public services. The protest soon expanded to other perceived ills of the Israeli sociopolitical and economic reality including the power structure, crony capitalism and concentration of the financial sector (see also OECD, 2011). They spread across the cities and towns of Israel, taking place mainly during weekends and drawing crowds of hundreds of thousands!

One noteworthy outcome of the widespread demonstrations was the formation of a *social university* whereby caucuses of activists and intellectuals, including university faculty members, used to gather in the parks and boulevards where otherwise protests took place.[17] These gatherings were used to discuss the grievances, plan for further protests and propose possible ideas to remedy society from its ills of inequality. Reasons and answers were sought for the government's inappropriate handling of the plight of (mostly) young people, unable to plan their future. In fact, it would not be an overstatement to claim that it was these gatherings that gave birth to the new social economy in Israel.

Indeed, the *social university* was where ideas surfaced relating to the relationship between economic ideologies and structures and the ills of the Israeli society. The cooperative model, a distant historical remnant of pre-neoliberal Israel, had featured prominently during the discussions, as well as other forms of hybrid structures combining business and social objectives. Several initiatives along those ideas, which were subsequently implemented, can be traced back to the social university of the summer of 2011. Those initiatives include various forms of social enterprises as well as socially oriented financial innovations such as a cooperative bank.

---

[17] https://www.themarker.com/news/protest/1.680645

In the years following the social unrest of the summer of 2011, many social initiatives, led mostly by young people, popped up across Israel, without the assistance or support of the public sector. Instead, those initiatives were often backed by certain business persons. Moreover, having no specific legal framework to fit their goal of combining social and business objectives, the new social enterprises took the form of existing legal frameworks, namely, businesses, non-profit organisations and cooperatives, and later also as part of the public sector (Abbou et al., 2017).

Some examples of such endeavours include the Liliyot restaurant in Tel Aviv, which trains youth in distress (mostly school dropouts) to become chefs[18]; the Call Yachol call centre, which employs persons with disabilities as telephone operators[19]; and AndJoy[20] and Rebook,[21] which employ people with mental or physical disabilities. AndJoy sells gifts and flowers, while Rebook sells second-hand books.

An analysis of these social enterprises over the past decade yields two insights. First, these enterprises target mostly disenfranchised populations (e.g. persons with disabilities, former prisoners or Arab and ultra-orthodox women) with employment solutions. Second, these enterprises are limited in scope, often communal in nature, employ at best several dozen individuals and have little prospects for growth. As no public policy to support them exists to date, the danger of mission drift looms constantly over these enterprises.

Yet social enterprises in the WISE (Work Integration Social Enterprise) domain were not the only creative outcome of the 2011 social protest. Parallel developments initiated by high-tech entrepreneurs generated another form of social entrepreneurship, often referred to as 'social tech' or 'social techpreneurship'. This new form evolves around seeking technological solutions to social problems. It focuses on specific populations (such as elderly persons or people on the spectrum of autism) and attempts to develop a device or a mobile application that helps the target clientele to overcome a specific common problem they face. Interestingly, often the involvement of a social-tech enterprise with a particular social problem or clientele is driven by the founders' personal familiarity with the problem or clientele and their desire to help.

An example of such enterprises is *Eyecontrol*,[22] which provides a communication solution for 'locked-in' patients. The device recognises eye movements and transmits alerts and messages to the desired location by using the eye as a joystick. It can be used by those who are verbally or physically limited in their ability to communicate or express themselves, such as people with ALS. Another example is *Ninispeech*,[23] a start-up that provides an app to assist people maintaining daily training. It is essentially a social media platform for people who stutter, aimed to mobilise

---

[18] https://dualis.techmarketing.co.il/

[19] https://callyachol.co.il/en/home-2/

[20] www.andjoy.co.il/

[21] Rebook.org.il

[22] https://www.eyecontrol.co.il/

[23] https://www.talknsave.net/blog/startup-nation/solution-to-stuttering/

community support in order to motivate individuals to stick to their practice regime. For instance, children often prefer to work with the app than with their parents, due to the comfort the community affords. Finally, *Givingway*[24] utilises the most popular trend in international travel, 'voluntourism', to support social and environmental causes across the globe. It is an online marketplace which enables travellers seeking to volunteer their time and skills to simply and reliably connect with impactful non-profit organisations worldwide.

In some respects, the social-tech enterprises differ from social enterprises in the WISE domain. For example, the former aim to serve not merely a local target clientele, but rather a *global* clientele. If the product of the social-tech enterprise is successful, it can have a global impact and a global market, much in the same way as the product of the classic high-tech enterprise businesses. In other respects, however, the social-tech enterprise is similar to the WISE. In particular, both types of social enterprises had generally emerged during the second decade of the twenty-first century, receiving little support from the public sector. In both cases the founders typically receive guidance and support through incubators and accelerators although there is yet to develop a more formal infrastructure for that particular type of activity.

To sum, the development of the new social enterprise in Israel was quite dramatic, emerging out of a real demand as reflected by the tent protest of the summer of 2011. But the development of the financial ecosystem to support the new type of social economy was not less dramatic. The tent protest of the summer of 2011 targeted, among other social ills, the financial sector and the concentrated banking system which were perceived as lacking in competition.[25] In December of 2011, the Trajtenberg Committee, appointed to examine these issues, published its recommendations.[26] It confirmed that the traditionally concentrated banking sector had severe implications for the supply of credit to households and small businesses. For example, while large borrowers in Israel enjoyed easy access to credit from a range of institutional bodies, small borrowers typically depended on the banking system. Another committee, the Zaken Committee, was convened which concluded that the highly concentrated banking structure resulted in increased banking-related costs, at the tune of about 8 billion shekels per year.[27]

In July 2012, the Zaken Committee published an interim report including the recommendation to expand the number of local financial actors by encouraging foreign banks to enter the Israeli market and by establishing an Internet bank and a

---

[24] https://www.givingway.com/

[25] The Israeli protest over economic inequality and against the financial sector preceded **Occupy Wall Street**, a similar protest which took place on September 17, 2011, at the financial district, New York City. It soon spread around the world and marked the initiation of the **Occupy Movement**.

[26] The **Trajtenberg Committee** was appointed by the Israeli Prime Minister on August 8, 2011, to examine Israel's socio-economic problems.

[27] The Zaken Committee was set up in December 2011 named after its chairperson. It estimated the additional costs relating to lack of competition in the banking sector at about 2.3 billion dollars (see https://www.boi.org.il/en/NewsAndPublications/PressReleases/Pages/19032012e.aspx).

credit union. Consequently, in 2012, the cooperative Ofek was set up in order to provide financial services to its members. However, social developments within the Israeli financial sector did not stop with Ofek, the cooperative bank. Indeed, a whole financial ecosystem, to support the emerging new social economy, has developed. It is referred to as impact investment.

The Impact Investment Scene

The impact investment ecosystem in Israel is still in its early development stages.[28] This new approach to financing social businesses emphasises the need for private investment alongside public funds and philanthropy in order to create social value in a manner that ensures sustainability and growth. The idea is that social value is created not only by third sector actors—as was originally the case in Israel—but also by profit-oriented private business activities. Moreover, this value should be financed using measurable market solutions alongside philanthropy and state support. In other words, the impact investment ecosystem should facilitate the channelling of private capital to finance activities that address global as well as local social and environmental challenges while creating measurable financial and social returns to investors.

Although still young, the impact investment ecosystem in Israel is showing impressive growth. For example, it has doubled in size from $130 M in 2016 to more than $260 M in 2018 (OurCrowd, 2019).[29] Currently, it includes three Social Investment Bonds (SIBs) and various actors. A recent report by OurCrowd (2019) maps out the industry, identifying key actors including social investment funds, the government, incubators and accelerators, financial institutions and intermediaries.

Starting with **social investment funds**, these are private funds that **aim to achieve impact by investing in social businesses.** Edmond de Rothschild Foundation (2019) identifies 14 private impact funds of various sizes and types in Israel. One example is Zora Ventures[30] which invests in Israeli social-tech companies that address the UN Sustainable Development Goals (SDGs) in areas such as the environment, health and hunger. According to the report by Edmond de

---

[28] The Global Impact Investing Network (GIIN) defines impact investments as *investments made into companies, organisations and funds with the intention to generate social and environmental impact alongside a financial return (see* https://thegiin.org/).

[29] Moreover, traditional third sector organisations, such as charitable foundations, have also been changing and adapting their strategies in line with new thinking about charity and charitable giving. For example, while in the past donors used to provide funds and let the charitable organisation decide to what use those funds would be put, today they are much more involved. In particular, not only do the younger generation of contributors want to know exactly where their funds are going, but they also want to track the impact of their philanthropic giving (see Impact Investing Meets Social Welfare by Alex Traiman, August 28, 2019, *Jewish News Syndicate* at https://www.jns.org/impact-investing-meets-social-welfare-how-a-99-year-old-israeli-institution-stays-relevant/).

[30] http://www.zora.vc/

Rothschild Foundation (2019) the aggregate asset under management of impact funds in Israel is between $250 million and $622 million. **Another well-known social investment fund is** Yozma. The fund was set up in 2015 by the non-profit association, IVN, which was awarded a government tender to establish a fund for investing in social businesses in the areas of youth employment, youth at risk and people with special needs.[31] The Yozma project is based on cooperation between the National Insurance Institute, the Finance Ministry and the National Economic Council. It pools capital from **private and philanthropic sources,** but also from the **government which,** by investing in the fund, reduces the risk borne by the other capital providers, thereby attracting investments.

Indeed, the **government** plays an important part in the Israeli impact investment ecosystem. For example, from 2019, institutional investors have been required by the Ministry of Finance[32] to include a statement in their financial reports concerning their Environmental, Social and Governance (ESG) strategy and impact investment policies. Moreover, the government also influences the local impact investment ecosystem through the IAA (Israel Innovation Authority), a unit of Israel's Ministry of Economy. The unit was set up to support technological development and to encourage innovation, entrepreneurship and economic growth, and for that purpose it runs a number of incentive programmes. One worth mentioning is the Grand Challenges Israel Incentive Program which provides support for R&D into humanitarian health, water and agriculture challenges prevailing in developing countries. The aim is to encourage Israeli companies to seek solutions to global challenges by developing products that also have commercial potential in developed countries. The Grand Challenges Israel Incentive Program offers participants support of up to 90% of approved budget (subject to a predetermined maximum). It also offers an exemption from the repayment of royalties on the revenues received from target countries, as well as **exposure to new markets and potential partners.**[33]

---

[31] IVN was established in 2001 and today it **manages three key social funds, among them Yozma.** The other two include **Tandem** and **Seed**. Tandem was launched in 2013 to provide loans, working capital, mentoring and relevant networks to businesses that seek solutions to social challenges in the areas of economic development, employment and education. **Seed** was established in 2014 in collaboration with Bank Mizrahi-Tefahot to support young, socially minded entrepreneurs by providing funding in the form of grants as well as mentoring (see http://ivn.org.il/the-program).

[32] More specifically, by the Capital Market, Insurance and Savings Authority which is part of the Ministry of Finance.

[33] We mentioned the IIA in section "Neoliberalism and the Rise of the Start-Up Nation" above (see also https://innovationisrael.org.il/en/contentpage/israel-innovation-authority). The authority has six divisions, among them the Societal Challenges Division which focuses on inspiring technological innovation to improve social welfare. There are several incentive programmes under the Societal Challenges Division, each focusing on a different aspect of impact. The Grand Challenges Israel Incentive Program which we discussed above is one example. Other examples include the Assistive Technology for the Disabled Incentive Program and the Incentive Programs for Ultra-Orthodox and Minorities. The latter target entrepreneurs from sectors of the Israeli society that are under-represented in the local innovation ecosystem (e.g. Israeli Arabs, the ultra-orthodox and women).

Moreover, in line with the view of entrepreneurship and innovation as catalysts for economic growth, the IIA also operates several **incubator programmes** across Israel to provide start-ups with required infrastructure. These incubator programmes are normally formed in partnership with well-established companies and provide start-ups with conditional grants, office space, technical mentoring and business guidance. Some of these incubators specialise in specific impact fields, such as clean technology, while some target specific start-ups (e.g. peripheral). An example is **Terralab, a peripheral incubator managed by** Terra Venture Partners **which specialises in cleantech.**[34]

Incubators are similar to **accelerators**, another key actor in the Israeli impact investment ecosystem. According to Invest in Israel (2018) there are two key differences between accelerators and incubators. First, unlike incubators which normally focus on innovation, accelerators focus on the growth of an existing business. Second, while incubators enjoy the IIA's funding and usually operate under a flexible time schedule, accelerators are managed by local and foreign companies/NGOs which provide services for a relatively short time of about 4 months. The typical accelerator invests a small amount of between $5 and 25 K, in exchange for ownership stake in the business. There are several Israeli accelerators that are associated specifically with social businesses and impact investment. For example, the 8200 Social Program is a non-profit accelerator for social-tech enterprises.[35] Founded in 2013 by the 8200 Alumni Association, the aim is to harness the human capital of 8200 alumni for the benefit of society by supporting businesses in clean technology, education and healthcare for a period of 5 months. Hackaveret is another social entrepreneurship accelerator. It was established by JDC Israel and the National Insurance Institute Funds, two organisations concerned with developing social services in Israel.[36] The Hackaveret accelerator supports entrepreneurship that seeks solutions to the social challenges faced by populations at risk (e.g. elderly, people with disabilities). It does so by providing mentoring, establishing networks and more.

Our next key actor in the Israeli impact investment scene is the **financial community**, perhaps responding to the public anger directed at it during the tent protest and beyond. Accordingly, some Israeli investment houses offer responsible investment portfolio to clients (e.g. IBI) or ESG mutual funds. For example, Meitav Dash, one of the leading and largest investment houses in Israel, has developed a mutual fund (Meitav ESG) that invests in companies which take a stakeholder rather than a limited shareholder view on their business, endeavouring to balance between the needs of *all* their stakeholders. Likewise, the two leading Israeli banks (Leumi and Hapoalim) have invested in Israel's early SIBs, while the rest of the industry, including local banks and pension funds, is also increasingly involved in the impact

---

[34] http://www.terravp.com/

[35] 8200 is the elite intelligence and cybersecurity unit of the Israeli Defense Forces. The Internet site of the 8200 Social Program is https://www.8200impact.com/

[36] https://www.hackaveret.org/

investment market. Even the Tel Aviv Stock Exchange (TASE) has joined the bandwagon, offering solutions to investors interested in socially responsible investment. An example is the TA-Maala SRI (Socially Responsible Investing) Index which includes shares ranked by Maala for social responsibility.[37]

In addition, there are a number of **intermediaries and advisory bodies**, which play an important role in the Israeli impact investment scene, but Social Finance Israel (SFI) is undoubtedly the leading one.[38] SFI endeavours to promote the Israeli impact investment ecosystem by developing impact measurement tools, steering the Israeli investment community towards impact investment, spreading best practices locally and structuring innovative investment instruments, such as SIBs. Indeed, to date, it has launched three **SIBs**.

The first of these three SIBs is an 8-year programme launched in 2015 which aims to reduce the dropout rate among computer science students in higher education. The second is a 7.5-year programme, launched in 2016, and is concerned with preventing the onset of type 2 diabetes among prediabetics. The third is a 6-year programme launched in 2017 to improve the educational attainments in mathematics of Bedouin students in the Negev. Other SIBs are still under development including for early detection of cancer, poverty alleviation among single mothers, reducing loneliness among the elderly and preventing childhood obesity.

To sum, Israel impact investment ecosystem has expanded in recent years, although it still has some way to go. Sir Ronald Cohen, Chairman of Social Finance Israel and of the Global Steering Group for Impact Investing, asserts that "Israel is already on the world stage as the start-up nation but is swiftly developing its position as the impact nation" (OurCrowd, 2019, pg. 5). Cohen further explains that Israel's lead in technology gives it an edge in addressing global social and environmental challenges. Israel, however, also faces grave inequalities that threaten the cohesion of its society and—as noted by Cohen—impact investing could assist in narrowing this gap by empowering those left behind. We summarise these conflicting dynamics and conclude this chapter in the next section.

Concluding Remarks

The evolution of the social economy and the new social economy in Israel reflects the predominant values, beliefs and ideologies that have prevailed and governed the local society. In that respect, Israel is no different to other countries.

The Kibbutz ideal has traditionally reflected the Israeli social economy. In addition, the socialist leadership of the Zionist movement encouraged the formation of

---

[37] Maala is the non-profit Corporate Social Responsibility (CSR) standard-setting organisation in Israel. The TA-Maala SRI Index was launched in 2005 and was initially limited to 20 shares. It was later expanded to all shares that meet the index criteria.

[38] SFI was established in 2013 and its story can be found at http://www.social-finance.org.il/category/Our-Story

cooperatives, including in urban and non-Kibbutz rural areas. Moreover, the economy was tilted towards socialist and protective philosophy, with many workers protected by a strong workers' union, and provided for with a set of social, health and educational services. Given the socialist ideology of the leadership of the Zionist movement—as well as economic pressures—this attitude made a lot of sense during the pre-state era and the first three decades of the State of Israel.

Still, the socio-economic reality of the Jewish community in Israel during its transformation into a state could not be described as a purely socialist one. Indeed, alongside many collectivistic oriented economic entities, privately owned enterprises existed too. When Israel gained independence in 1948, the socialist leadership of the Zionist movement became the leadership of the state and attempted to pursue the same models, albeit in the new context of statehood and against a backdrop of heterogenous mass immigration, wars and economic hardships. To cope with these challenges, a different ideology—emphasising nationhood—had to be adopted (Wolfsfeld, 1988). The *nationhood* ideology provided legitimacy for Israel to undertake a *welfare state* approach. During the 1950s and 1960s an infrastructure of statutory services in health, education and welfare was built, replacing the nongovernmental entities that provided these services in the pre-state era.

However, the *welfare state* faced severe economic challenges during the 1970s and 1980s, and had to undergo radical economic reforms, transforming Israel into a neoliberal economy. The neoliberal reforms alongside the development of government policy and infrastructure (e.g. relating to military technology and R&D) facilitated the emergence of Israel as a start-up nation, highly innovative and with considerable entrepreneurship activity. This, in turn, made the Israeli response to the social unrest of the first and second decades of the twenty-first century quite specific and very characteristic of a technology-driven, so-called *start-up nation*. In particular, the local response to these social upheavals was the advent of two types of social enterprises and a corresponding impact investment ecosystem to support them. Specifically, the two forms of social enterprises include WISE type which is limited in scope and local in focus and the social-tech type which is technology oriented and global in scope.

Studying the evolution of these three pillars of the new social economy in Israel, there are three insights that emerge. The first relates to the idea of hybridity combining business and social objectives in organisations and finances. The debate on the purpose of the organisation and the balance between accountability to shareholders versus society (or contracts versus communities) is at least 150 years old (Sundaram & Inkpen, 2004). Indeed, those authors show that the pendulum on this debate swings in accordance with the socio-economic and political ecosystem in which organisations operate. For example, following the Great Depression of the 1930s, the emphasis on profit maximisation was revalued, as articulated by Dodd (1932) who argued that the corporation—as a separate entity—has citizenship responsibilities. The 1980s and 1990s, with the fall of communism and Reagan and Thatcher-style capitalism that underlined the success of the high-technology revolution, had seen the pendulum swinging again towards emphasising profit maximisation. Then came the global financial crisis of 2008, followed by social unrest around the globe and growing concerns over poverty and the environment as reflected in the UN Sustainable Development Goals (SDGs) of 2015. These events drove the creation of the new social economy which has not yet taken a uniform format or even definition. In Israel, as in the rest of the world, the social economy has emerged in response to these events. It has, however, taken its own unique touch in line with the local ecosystem, and particularly the Israeli high-technology entrepreneurship spirit.

The second insight relates to the importance of an appropriate infrastructure and ecosystem for new social economy endeavours to succeed. For instance, the success of the Israeli high-technology sector, and the emergence of Israel as a start-up nation with a dynamic and innovative entrepreneurship, is no doubt partly due to supportive industrial policy. Likewise, for the new social economy to thrive, perhaps becoming an 'impact nation', it needs the support and vision of policymakers.

Lastly, as this chapter was written, Israel and the rest of the world had been coping with an unprecedented health, social and economic crisis brought about by the Covid-19 pandemic. Many businesses and organisations—ranging from schools to service and entertainment providers—had to close, reduce their activities or lay off staff. Indeed, in its September 2020 report on Israel, the OECD warns that the Covid-19 pandemic could undo many of Israel's recent economic achievements which included halving its employment rate, raising its standard of living and reducing public debt. With growing uncertainty relating to the pandemic and the feasibility of a vaccine, the report forecasts that unemployment would reach 6.1% in 2020, rising to 6.5% in 2021. A rise in bankruptcies was also expected to weigh heavily on the Israeli economy, the gross domestic product of which was predicted by the OECD report to contract by 6% in 2020.[39]

The Covid-19 pandemic has broken out at a time of a major political crisis in Israel. Between April 2019 and March 2020, Israel had three general elections which ended with a fragile government, led by Prime Minister Netanyahu who at the time was awaiting trial and facing accusations of corruption. A national unity government was finally and reluctantly formed on the pretext that it had to deal with the Covid-19 pandemic. Low public trust, emanating from Netanyahu's legal proceedings and the government's perceived inability to effectively deal with the pandemic due to pressure groups constantly influencing policy decisions, translated into almost daily demonstrations spreading all over the country. Thus, Israel's conduct during the Covid-19 pandemic can serve as a case illustrating the importance of trust in a country's leadership for effectively coping with crises.

Certainly, the health crisis resulting from the spreading of coronavirus in Israel was still at a critical stage, when attention had turned to the ensuing economic crisis. At the time this chapter was written, the government was dealing with the immediate economic and social impacts of the crisis on unemployment, small businesses, major industries such as the airline sector, educational system and *third sector*

---

[39] The report by the OECD (Organization for Economic Cooperation and Development) is entitled *September 2020 Economic Survey of Israel* and is available at http://www.oecd.org/economy/israel-economic-snapshot/. Note also that the unemployment figures exclude workers on unpaid leave.

services, to name a few. While special budgets were allocated to deal with these acute issues, no discussions were taking place concerning the fundamental economic and structural changes required to prepare the country for the long-term impact of ongoing and future crises, namely the climate crisis. Such long-term planning is obviously difficult under enduring political and governance instability.

Notwithstanding the political challenges, social unrest and Israel's health system crisis exposed by the Covid-19 pandemic, one cannot afford to ignore the need to engage in long-term planning. Actions taken to reduce the unemployment rate and recover the economy should consider what needs to fundamentally change. A visionary leadership is required to deal with the looming climate crisis by establishing policies that promote sustainability, pooling the country's technological knowhow and creating investment opportunities, all of which could contribute to transforming the local economy into a green and sustainable one. This should involve, for example, transforming conventional energy sources and the infrastructure based upon them, as well as other economic processes (e.g. construction).

It is our belief that the Covid-19 pandemic and its enunciation in the Israeli context will have a profound impact on the development of the local social economy. It could parallel the influence that the political shift and economic crisis of the 1980s had on the development of Israel as a *start-up nation* and subsequently on the evolution of its *new social economy* as a hybrid system combining business and social objectives and based on individual, social-tech entrepreneurship. Specifically, the Covid-19 crisis and the ensuing realisation that we need to learn to cope with social distancing and with global-wide natural disasters could be a catalyst for a search for creative solutions to engage the *start-up nation* in the coming years. We learned from similar junctures in history that a visionary and creative leadership is needed to support and facilitate these desired developments.

References

Abbou, I., Gidron, B., Buber-Ben David, N., Greenberg, Y., Monnickendam- Givon, Y., & Navon, A. (2017). Social enterprise in Israel: The swinging pendulum between collectivism and individualism. *Social Enterprise Journal, 13*(4), 329–344.

Aharoni, Y. (2014). *The Israeli economy (Routledge Revivals): Dreams and realities*. London: Routledge.

Auerbach, Y. (1991). Ben-Gurion and reparations from Germany. In R. W. Zweig (Ed.), *David Ben-Gurion: Politics and Leadership in Israel* (pp. 274–292). London: Frank Cass Publishers.

Avnimelech, G. (2009). *VC policy: Yozma program 15-years perspective*. Available at SSRN 2758195.

Avnimelech, G., Schwartz, D., & Bar-El, R. (2007). Entrepreneurial high-tech cluster development: Israel's Experience with venture capital and technological incubators. *European Planning Studies, 15*(9), 1181–1198.

Ben-Basaṭ, A. (Ed.). (2002). *The Israeli Economy, 1985–1998: From Government Intervention to Market Economics*. Cambridge, MA: MIT Press.

Blass, A. A. & Grossman, R. S. (1996). *A harmful guarantee? The 1983 Israel Bank Shares Crisis Revisited*. Discussion Paper 96.03, Research Department, Bank of Israel.

Cornfeld, O., & Danieli, O. (2015). The origins of income inequality in Israel-trends and policy. *Israel Economic Review, 12*(2), 51–95.

Dart, R. (2004). The legitimacy of social enterprise. *Nonprofit Management and Leadership, 14*(4), 411–424.

De Boer, P. & Missaglia, M. (2007). Economic consequences of intifada: A Sequel (No. EI 2007–39).

Dodd, E. (1932). For whom are corporate managers trustees? *Harvard Law Review, 45*(7), 1145–1163.

Edmond De Rothschild Foundation. (2019). *Impact innovation in Israel: Ecosystem overview*.

Eisenstadt, S. N. (1967). Israeli identity: Problems in the development of the collective identity of an ideological society. *The Annals of the American Academy of Political and Social Science, 370*(1), 116–123.

Fischer, S. (1987). The Israeli stabilization program, 1985–86. *The American Economic Review, 77*(2), 275–278.

Fleisch, E. (2014). *Israeli NGOs and American Jewish Donors: The Structures and Dynamics of Power Sharing in A New Philanthropic Era*. Doctoral Dissertation, Brandeis University.

Gidron, B., Bar, M., & Katz, H. (2004). *The Israeli third sector*. New York: Kluwer/Plenum.

Gidron, B., Schlanger, A., & Alon, Y. (2008). The contribution of foreign foundations to Israeli society. *Civil Society and the Third Sector in Israel, 2*(1), 11–32.

Gross, N. T., & Metzer, J. (1999). Palestine during the second world war. In N. T. Gross (Ed.), *Not by spirit alone: Studies in the economic history of modern Palestine and Israel* (pp. 300–324). Jerusalem: The Hebrew University Magnes Press and Yad Izhak Ben-Zvi Press. (Hebrew).

Halamish, A. (2009). The Yishuv: The Jewish Community in Mandatory Palestine. *Jewish Virtual Library*.

Helpman, E. (2003). Israel's economic growth: An international comparison. *Israel Economic Review, 1*(1).

Hilbert, M., & López, P. (2011). The World's technological capacity to store, communicate, and compute information. *Science, 332*(6025), 60–65.

Israel Central Bureau of Statistics (CBS), 2008. The Kibbutzim and their population, publication number 1327 (in Hebrew)

Invest in Israel. (2018). Doing business in Israel 2018, *Ministry of Economy and Industry, State of Israel*. Retrieved from Https://Investinisrael.Gov.Il/Howwehelp/Downloads/Doing_Business. Pdf

Katz, H., & Greenspan, I. (2015). Giving in Israel: From old religious traditions to an emerging culture of philanthropy. In *The Palgrave handbook of global philanthropy* (pp. 316–337). London: Palgrave Macmillan.

Kislev, Y. (2015). Agricultural cooperatives in Israel: Past and present. *St-Soviet Eu, 281*.

Krampf, A. (2018). *The Israeli path to neoliberalism: The state, continuity and change*. Routledge, (Abingdon, Oxon and New York)..

Lebel, U., Fuksman-Sha'al, M., & Orkibi, E. (2018). 'Mahapach!': The Israeli 1977 political upheaval–implications and aftermath. *Israel Affairs, 24*(6), 939–943.

Levi, Y. (2004). *Yesh Kalkala Aheret, Yesh Hevra Aheret: Kalkala Hevratit Vemigzar Shlishi Beidan Haglobalizatzia (There is a different Economy, there is a different Society: The Social Economy and the Third Sector in the Age of Globalization)*. Yad Tabenkin. (Hebrew).

Levi-Faur, D. (1998). The developmental state: Israel, South Korea, and Taiwan compared. *Studies in Comparative International Development, 33*(1), 65–93.

Liger, Q., Stefan, M. & Britton, J. (2016). Social economy. *European Union, European Parliament*.

Mandelkern, R., & Shalev, M. (2018). The political economy of Israeli neoliberalism. In R. Y. Hazan, A. Dowty, M. Hofnung, & G. Rahat (Eds.), *The Oxford handbook of Israeli politics and society*. New York, NY: Oxford University Press.

Metzer, J. (1979). *National capital to national home, 1919–1921*. Yad Itzhak Ben-Zvi, Jerusalem, (Hebrew).

OECD. (2011). *Israel: Review of the private pensions system*, OECD Working Party on Private Pensions. Retrieved from Http://Www.Oecd.Org/Finance/Private-Pensions/49498122.Pdf

Offenhauer, P. (2008). *Israel's Technology Sector*. Library of Congress Washington DC Federal Research Division. Retrieved from Https://Apps.Dtic.Mil/Dtic/Tr/Fulltext/U2/A513983.Pdf

OurCrowd. (2019). *Impact Investing in Israel: Status of the Market*. Retrieved from Https://Info.Ourcrowd.Com/Impact-Report-A/

Peretz, S. (2018, April 18). 70 years on: Thoughts on Israel's imperfect capitalism. *Haaretz.* Retrieved from Https://Www.Haaretz.Com/Israel-News/Business/70-Years-On-Thoughts-On-Israel-S-Imperfect-Capitalism-1.6011475

Prainsack, B., & Firestine, O. (2006). 'Science for survival': Biotechnology regulation in Israel. *Science and Public Policy, 33*(1), 33–46.

Ram, U. (2008). *The globalization of Israel: Mcworld in Tel Aviv*. Jihad in Jerusalem: Routledge.

Rosenthal, G., & Eiges, H. (2013). Agricultural cooperatives in Israel. *Journal of Rural Cooperation, 42*(886–2016-64707), 1–29.

Russell, R., & Hanneman, R. (1992). Cooperatives and the business cycle: The Israeli case. *Journal of Comparative Economics, 16*(4), 701–715.

Segev, T. (1993). *The seventh million: The Israelis and the Holocaust*. New York: Henry Holt & Co.

Senor, D., & Singer, S. (2011). *Start-up nation: The story of Israel's economic miracle*. New York: Random House Digital, Inc.

Shapira, A. (2010). *Tahalichey Hafrata Merkaziyim Be'Israel (major privatization processes in Israel)*, Parliament (64), The Israel Democracy Institute. (Hebrew). Retrieved from Https://www.Idi.org.Il/Parliaments/11097/11143

Shapira, R. (2005). Academic capital or scientific progress? A critique of studies of kibbutz stratification. *Journal of Anthropological Research, 61*(3), 357–380.

Sherwood, H. (2011, August 17). Israel's former soviet immigrants transform adopted country. *The Guardian*. Retrieved from Https://Www.Theguardian.Com/World/2011/Aug/17/Israel-Soviet-Immigrants-Transform-Country

Silber, I., & Rosenhek, Z. (1999). *The historical development of the Israeli third sector*. Beer-Sheva, Israel: Ben-Gurion University of The Negev Press.

Srivastava, M. (2018, December 10). Israel's Tech Expansion Stokes Glaring Inequality in Tel Aviv. *Financial Times*. Retrieved from Https://Www.Ft.Com/Content/9836aa92-F235-11e8-Ae55-Df4bf40f9d0d

Sternhell, Z. (1998). *The Founding Myths of Israel: Nationalism, Socialism, and the Making of The Jewish State*. Princeton, NJ: Princeton University Press.

Sundaram, A. K., & Inkpen, A. C. (2004). The corporate objective revisited. *Organization Science, 15*(3), 350–363.

Trajtenberg, M. (2000). *R&D policy in Israel: An overview and reassessment*. Science, Technology and the Economy Program Working Papers Series, Samuel Neaman Institute, Technion.

Wolfsfeld, G. (1988). *The politics of provocation: participation and protest in Israel*. New York: State University of New York Press, Albany.

Chapter 6
The New Social Economy in Poland: The Crisis-Led Innovation

Anna Domaradzka

Introduction

Despite the long tradition of mutual associations and cooperative movement, social economy in Poland is not as deeply rooted as one could expect in the European context. Mainly because of its non-linear history, marked with wars and lack of independence, the sector faces relative impairment nowadays. The First and the Second World War and the subsequent communist period (1945–1989) caused significant breaks in the social economy development. Later, the character of the capitalist transition and a new socio-economic system introduced after the 1989 was in itself a barrier for the (re)development of the sector.

Till the recent 2008 economic crisis, the evolution of social economy in Poland was often described in terms of three main phases: (1) traditional social economy (before World War II); (2) old social economy (communist period); and (3) new social economy (after 1989) (Kaźmierczak, 2007: 102). However, as this chapter illustrates, in the last decade we could observe the development of a new post-crisis social economy, emerging alongside its more traditional forms. During that period, both the digital revolution and EU membership (since 2004) created important impulses shaping social economy in Poland. Most recently, the COVID-19 crisis brought new development in the social economy sector, highlighting its potential for fast response and local aid.

This chapter addresses the validity of this new post-crisis social economy concept in the context of Poland, analysing its development and new directions based

A. Domaradzka (✉)
Robert Zajonc Institute for Social Studies, University of Warsaw, Warsaw, Poland
e-mail: anna.domaradzka@uw.edu.pl

© Springer Nature Switzerland AG 2021
B. Gidron, A. Domaradzka (eds.), *The New Social and Impact Economy*,
Nonprofit and Civil Society Studies, https://doi.org/10.1007/978-3-030-68295-8_6

on the literature review and case studies conducted during the FAB-MOVE project.[1] The first part offers reflection on the main changes in the area of social economy in Poland, focusing on the topic of cooperatives and social enterprises, their historical evolution, dominant legal forms and fields of activity, as well as the political and economic environment of the sector's development. The recent changes in the forms of activity as well as financing, including the impact investment, are described in a second part, concluding with description of the newest developments.

What makes the Polish case different to western EU countries is that it has to overcome the negative stigma of social economy, resulting from the forced coopera-tivization and collectivization under the communism. On the other hand, Poland did not suffer radical losses during the 2008 economic crisis, compared to other EU countries. As a result, the new social economy has been developing in a more grad-ual way, inspired by the revival of the pre-war cooperative traditions, new societal challenges and technological opportunities.

This chapter is written in the midst of the COVID-19 pandemic, which has already resulted in a global economic breakdown. In the concluding part, I will hypothesise what type of impact the current crisis may have on the social economy sector in Poland.

Main Definitions of Social Economy

The contemporary social economy model in Poland is a mix of an older cooperative movement with EU-supported forms of social entrepreneurship buffering the impact of market economy on the socially marginalized people. Among typical forms of social economy developing in the last 20 years, we can therefore distinguish social enterprises, social cooperatives and non-government organizations that engage in economic activities (Rymsza, 2008). Most discussed in Polish literature are social enterprises defined as profit-oriented organization with the goal to distribute profit among the communities rather than owners (Praszkier, Zabłocka-Bursa, & Jóźwik, 2014) and usually a local scope of interest (Bohdziewicz-Lulewicz, 2013). Another comprehensive definition of a social enterprise was introduced by Wygnański and Frączak. (2007), who describe social enterprise as "a private, autonomous organiza-tion delivering products or services for the broadly understood community, which is founded by a group of citizens and which profit is limited. The social enterprise attaches importance to its autonomy and is ready to face an economic risk related to its continuous socio-economic activity" (Wygnański 2007: 18).

---

[1] The article is based on information and data gathered through literature review and desk research on the topic of social entrepreneurship and the welfare system in Poland. It also summarizes the experience of FAB-MOVE team members and our discussions within the hosting institutions, which helped to sharpen my understanding of the specificity of Polish social enterprise sector. Scientific work was financed from Polish Ministry of Science and Higher Education funds for sci-ence 2016–2018, allocated for the implementation of an international cofinanced project.

Rymsza (2008) describes one of the key characteristics of modern social economy as cohesive grassroots-based activities (often initiated by civil society organizations) with the active support of the state (which is often called an active social policy, see also Rymsza & Kaźmierczak, 2009). As such, the model of the social economy in Poland used to be based on the principle of filling the market niches that are unattractive to other commercial enterprises and creating employment for marginalized groups. In this model, voluntary leaders and social activists have a key role in initiating and promoting social economy activities, and most of the initiatives are locally based and financially unstable.

Recently, we could observe the growing interest in new forms of sharing economy, social investments and communal economic activities, which challenge the conventional model of "doing social economy". What gives the social economy its new dynamic are mainly the activities of non-governmental organizations, social cooperatives and not-for-profit enterprises. As Rymsza points out, the significant shift was the emergence of institutions that are on the border between civil society and the private sector, bracketing the traditional social institutions from both sides (Rymsza, 2008: 5). On the one side, we can observe the associations and foundations that engage in economic activities and create jobs or products in order to support their statutory goals. On the other side, there is a multitude of organizations linking social and economic goals and closely resembling the business sector as well as engaging in the open competition within the commercial sector.

As a result, new institutional and legal forms have emerged constituting the social economy that transcends the traditional division between the private and the voluntary sector. Many are hybrid institutions linking the characteristics of civil society with those of enterprises. Rymsza observes that the social cooperative can be viewed as an institution that is "3/4 non-government organization", while the local community enterprise could be described as "3/4 business" (Rymsza, 2008: 6).

As Kwaśnicki (2005) emphasizes, all current definitions of the social economy recognize that it is the role of social economy to deal with the needs and social expectations that other sectors cannot meet. It is all about generating social cohesion and creating jobs, encouraging entrepreneurship and building a pluralist, participative, democratic society based on solidarity (Kwaśnicki, 2005: 16). Thus, "in the ordinary sense, the social economy deals with social activity not belonging to the market and the state" (Kwaśnicki, 2005: 11). Therefore, it is not a social economy understood as a branch of economics (a scientific discipline), but a sector of the economy distinguished by its specificity, in which economic activity is associated with social purposes in a unique way (Rymsza, 2005: 4).

To summarize, in the Polish context, mainstream forms of social economy fulfil both economic criteria, such as employing staff, taking economic risks and carrying out business activities, and social criteria, such as grassroots-based participative governance, acting for the common good and working with both employed staff and volunteers (Rymsza, 2008: 7). However, alongside the development of new information and communication technologies and a changing culture of consumption, we could observe innovative approaches to defining social needs, offering services and producing goods, among social economy actors.

History of Social Economy Sector in Poland

The old social economy has a rich tradition developed during the period between 1772 and 1918 when Polish territories were partitioned between three neighbouring countries of Russia, Prussia and Austria. Social economy activities developed during that time in order to maintain the economic potential of the nation under the foreign occupation. Social economy was associated mainly with French thought and referred to entities conducting economic activity, which main goal was not to maximize profit, but to achieve specific social goals. Social economy in this traditional meaning was, therefore, an expression of criticism of the classical political economy and competition, as the causes of poverty and exploitation of the workers.

Looking back at the first phase of Polish social economy development, we should note that during the interwar period, the cooperative movement in Poland was one of the most dynamic in Europe (Majdzińska, 2014). At that time, two main forms of social economy evolved and developed, and to this day are considered to be its classical mechanisms: mutual insurance companies and cooperatives. This period was abruptly stopped by the Second World War, which led to disappearance or weakening of most of the social economy activities.

The next stage took place during the Polish People's Republic period (1952–1989), when social economy was appropriated by the communistic system, which resulted in the absorption of the cooperative movement into the government sector. This included the confiscation of cooperative assets, control by state administration bodies, transfer of state policy tasks to cooperative areas like housing construction (housing cooperatives), production of dairy products (dairy cooperatives), labour activation (worker cooperatives) or modernization of agriculture (agricultural cooperatives). These reforms resulted in the complete lack of autonomy or initiative to take over the state tasks, as well as total reliance on financing from the state budget (Broniszewski, Goleński, & Mesjasz, 2013).

The main difference between the pre-war and the communist concept of social economy was a departure from the democratic, internal social structures of these entities for central (institutional) control. While the original idea created before Second World War was based on the self-defence and self-help movement that referred to the values of cooperation and solidarity (Okraska, 2012), during the socialist period the idea and foundations on which the social economy was based were nationalized and became state controlled (Broniszewski, 2016). The communist ideology censured all forms of enterprises that were not directly linked to party's political goals, favouring the state-controlled cooperative forms of production and distribution.

As a result, the centralized economic system destroyed most types of traditional economic activity and deformed the cooperative idea. This led to a negative perception of the social economy in Polish society and a rather unfavourable climate for its development after the 1989 transformation. As Rymsza points out, "in the 1990s, cooperatives and other forms of collective economic activity were looked upon as remnants of communism from which the country was in the process of emerging, and were considered suspicious" (Rymsza, 2008: 6).

After 1989, there were some unsuccessful attempts to revive the mutual insurance companies, highly popular before the Second World War and based on the idea of free association and solidarity. However, most of the reform efforts went into the creation of individual commercial savings schemes subsidizing the pension system, instead of supporting the mutual insurance solutions. The result was the full commercialization of the insurance sector and a complete marginalization of its mutual forms based on solidarity. Similarly, the workers' cooperatives that were functioning during the communist period did not survive the process of economic restructuring and only some remained on the margins of the market. The only success in the revival of the traditional social economy model was the restoration of cooperative savings unions (SKOK). However, soon enough the management of these quasi-banks was also commercialized, resulting in serious doubts whether they should be considered a part of the social economy.

In the context of the centrally planned economy the cooperative movement was also subject to a specific form of degeneration. The negative consequences of politization and cooptation are still visible in some of the cooperative sectors—especially in housing and agriculture, where power structures did not necessarily renew after the 1989.

However, in the years following the democratization, we could observe the shy renaissance of some of the social economy ideas and institutions. The transition to liberal democracy revived both civic engagement and entrepreneurial spirit in the society constrained for over 40 years by the communistic regime. New cooperative banks, mutual insurance companies, cooperatives, guarantee funds, social enterprises, regional development agencies, associations or foundations emerged (Grewiński & Wronka, 2012; Pieńkowska, 2004). Along classical civil society organizations, we observed a rapid increase in hybrid forms of civic activism, including social economy initiatives. The main impulse to create them came as a response to negative side effects of the transformation, including the welfare gap and unemployment leading to growing inequality and poverty (Siemieńska & Domaradzka, 2009, 2016).

At the beginning of the 1990s Poland favourized the Anglo-Saxon model of economic transformation, resulting in the commercialization of the welfare regimes, hindering the institutionalization of the partnership between social enterprises and public sector in shaping and realizing public policies. However, the availability of EU funds and the growing popularity of CSR in the recent years reignited the interest in this form of creating employment and solving social problems. In the subsequent shift from the welfare state to welfare society, the social economy took on a new meaning and became a space where active social policy programmes (often financed by EU funds) could be implemented. As a result, social economy became a tool to increase both social and economic participation of members of neglected local communities and people marginalized on the labour market.

The most important push within the social economy sector in Poland was the introduction of the EQUAL programme (2001–2007)—part of the EU strategy for more and better jobs, testing the new ways of tackling discrimination and inequality on the labour market. After Polish accession to EU in 2004, the European Social

Fund programmes were introduced to enable the transnational cooperation and promote new means of combating all forms of discrimination and inequalities in connection with the labour market. Both EQUAL and the follow-up Structural Funds underlined the importance of grassroots activity and building human capital through civil and entrepreneurial efforts. This led to a growing popularity of social economy concept, which became recognized by both policymakers interested in effective EU fund allocation and practitioners that seized it as a new funding opportunity (Ciepielewska-Kowalik et al., 2015).

As a result of both EU policies and grassroots pressure, in the recent years, the managers started to have the most significant role in terms of developing and leading the social economy initiatives. Also, the state is more engaged as an establisher and promoter of social economy, offering legal advantages to its institutions and subsidizing the workplaces for certain groups of employees (disabled, long unemployed, single mothers, etc.). As Brandeleer (2013) remarked, the recent evolution of the social economy sector in Poland proves that it has now the capacity to play a significant role in the Polish society. It also indicates the new stage of social enterprises and investment development, where new actors, new logics and values are entering the field.

Legal Framework and Welfare System Context

Thirty years after transformation, there is still no legal act specifying the definition or regulating the sector (Pazderski, 2013). In Polish literature, the social economy, also called the economy of solidarity, solidarity economy or civic economy, remains a rather fuzzy conceptual category (Leś, 2013), which makes it difficult to measure its size and impact.

Inspired by Polish traditions as well as the European view of social economy, social enterprises are understood as new, proactive part of the third sector, with high potential to solve social problems. The idea of doing good through business activity resonated with local leaders and entrepreneurs alike. However, for many years this form remained underdeveloped due to lack of systemic regulations and incentives. The existing legal forms of social enterprises (like cooperatives) were perceived as less flexible than other forms of civil society organizations, which led to their relative unpopularity. This is one of the reasons why the reported numbers of social enterprises do not reflect the real scope of entrepreneurial engagement among CSOs in Poland (Domaradzka, 2015).

During the last 15 years, one part of social economy—social entrepreneurship—underwent a number of legal regulations. Among the most important were the Act on Public Benefit and Volunteer Work (2003) and the first Law on Social Employment (2003). Other relevant regulations include the Law on Associations and Funds, the Law on Professional Activation Centers and the Law on Social Cooperatives (2006) with subsequent amendments. In August 2014, the Polish Government accepted the National Programme for Social Economy Development, which describes in detail the government strategy to be implemented during the 2014–2020 period. Representatives of the social economy sector, trade unions, academia, employers' organizations as well as local and central government developed the document together. The programme was also the subject of extensive consultations with various stakeholders. Its main objective was to create conditions for the social economy entities to become an important element of activation of vulnerable people on the labour market and a provider of social services commissioned by local government. The document presents an extensive list of tasks to be performed in order to achieve this goal by 2020. It treats social enterprises as an important element of social policy, used to employ the unemployed as well as other people in difficult life situation, e.g. due to disability or poverty.

As part of the effort to create a National Programme for the Social Economy a definition was constructed, but not written in a law (National Programme, 2014). The programme defined social enterprises as entities that do not distribute profit or financial surplus among investors, employees nor members, but only use it to increase the enterprise capital and provide social and employment integration or public benefit services for the community. According to the definition, SEs would also have to be democratically governed or at least secure the consultative role of employees, members and other stakeholders. The programme also assumed salary limits for managerial staff and restriction that the profit from economic activity (sales of goods and services) can be the only source of income.

In practical terms, the most binding definition is the one written in the European Social Fund guidelines for the implementation of projects in the area of social inclusion and combating poverty. Most recent guidelines of July 8, 2019, state that the social enterprise (1) is a social economy entity that conducts business activities registered in the National Court Register or payable public benefit activities, or educational or cultural activities; (2) employs at least 30% of people in difficult situation; (3) does not distribute profit among shareholders or employees, but allocates it for the development of the company or for professional and social reintegration; (4) is managed on a democratic basis; (5) has a limit on the amount of remuneration so that its amount is not contrary to the idea of a social enterprise; (6) employs on the basis of an employment contract, a cooperative employment contract or a civil law contract at least three persons with a working time of at least ¼ full time, and in the case of civil law contracts for a period of not less than 3 months and covering not less than 120 h of work in total; and (7) conducts the reintegration process agreed with the employed persons, aimed at obtaining or regaining professional qualifications or key competences (Ekielski, 2019).

The advantage of existing regulations is that they offer a diversity of organizational and legal forms to people interested in establishing a social enterprise. This is regarded by many as a strong side of the Polish legal system as it guarantees flexibility and allows to choose an organizational frame that best suits the needs of the social entrepreneurs (Andrukiewicz, 2012). However, social economy representatives expressed the need for a more unified approach, which would result in one general law on social enterprises, determining the necessary conditions for the company to be considered a social enterprise and leading to certain privileges

(Praszkier et al., 2014). Apart from the already existing acts of law, there are some other regulations, which aim to stimulate social enterprises. One of the most relevant is a social clause that allows local governments to outsource certain public tasks to social enterprises without putting a project out to tender (Schimanek, 2006). As highlighted in the recent EFESEIIS report (Praszkier et al., 2014) the majority of changes in the legislative system have been carried out thanks to insistence of social leaders and the social entrepreneurship environment.

According to the existing research, despite the abundant stream of EU funds and the efforts of legislators at the EU, state and local government levels, social entrepreneurship remains perceived as "a hybrid on the border between charity and volunteering". This image not only is a harmful stereotype, but also severely limits social entrepreneurs striving to show that social products and services are something better, and more valuable than classic business (ekonomiaspoleczna.pl, 2014). However, the number of social enterprises that are able to translate their activity in the public benefit sphere to strengthening their brand and building relations with their social environment is growing.

To summarize, while social economy is deeply rooted in Polish tradition and history, its legal context itself remains unstructured and controversial. However, in response to the failures of the neoliberal economy framework, many authors point to the growing need for labour market solidarity and development of alternative forms of economic activity. Already in 2008, the Polish Social Economy Manifesto underlined solidarity as one of the binding agents specific for the area. This puts an emphasis on the importance of solidarity among people, but also as the constitutionally defined foundation of the Polish welfare regime.

Size of Social Economy Sector

Because of the diversity of organizational forms and types of activity it is hard to distinguish leading traits characterizing the whole Polish social economy sector. The sector includes cooperatives, foundations, associations, professional activity centres, vocational integration centres and clubs, and mutual insurance companies, with specific goals and styles of action.

In case of some SEs (cooperatives and mutual societies), their dominant function is to run a business and implement the social goals using the obtained financial surplus. There are also SEs in which economic activity is a condition for the implementation of the social goal. Some entities do not run business at all and are maintained through contributions and subsidies, such as foundations and some associations (Izdebski & Małek, 2007). The main areas of activities carried out by social economy entities include education, social services, local development, healthcare, environmental protection, tourism and civic initiatives. For these reasons, it is difficult to establish uniform rules for raising capital and create appropriate regulations relevant for the whole sector (Hausner, 2008).

As Leś and Ciepielewska-Kowalik (2014) estimate, in 2012 there were around 85,000 third-sector entities in Poland, including associations, foundations and cooperatives (Central Statistical Office, 2013). Depending on the applied definition, the number of social enterprises would range from about 3000 (draft law definition) to over 5000 (the operational definition), or even 20,000 social enterprises (modified EMES criteria, see also Defourny & Nyssens, 2012).

In 2016, Central Statistical Office (2019) estimated that the social economy sector comprised 90,900 non-governmental (civic) organizations and 1500 active cooperatives, among which the majority (60%) were social cooperatives.[2] In addition, this population included about 100 non-profit companies. Social economy entities (in the segment of CSOs) constituted 133,400 full-time jobs and 50,000 employed under civil law contracts, which represented 1.4% of the average employment in the national economy in 2016. Characteristic patterns of employment in the sector include the feminization of employment (nearly 2/3 of employees are women), employment of people with disabilities twice as high as in the whole economy (6.5%) and employment of people of retirement age (6.4%) almost three times higher than in the national economy. This indicates the potential of the social economy sector as an organizer of jobs for people with difficulties in the labour market.

In the cooperative segment, social cooperatives, labour cooperatives as well as invalids and blind co-ops employed over 33,500 people in 2017. In total, in 2017, 11,900 people at risk of social exclusion worked in cooperatives, including people with disabilities (10,100) and the long-term unemployed (1400). This means that in the cooperative sector the employment of people at risk is significantly higher than in the economy or in non-governmental organizations. It is worth noting, however, that while the number of social cooperatives is growing dynamically, the group of cooperatives of the disabled and the blind decreases. From 2009 to 2017, their number decreased by 120 entities. During this period, the number of people employed in cooperatives of the disabled and the blind also decreased by 27,500.

Institutional and Financial Support for Social Economy

As our FAB-MOVE analysis pointed out (Domaradzka, Matysiak, Jasińska, Siemieńska, & Żbikowska, 2016), the existing institutional support system in Poland is highly dependent on EU funds, as well as third-sector umbrella organizations like the Foundation for Social and Economic Activities (FISE). Among FISE achievements is launching of the Internet portal on social economy serving as a knowledge base and the organization of several nationwide projects supporting SE development in Poland (ekonomiaspoleczna.pl).

An analysis presented by Schimanek (2015) shows that most social enterprises in Poland generate very low incomes, barely sufficient to finance current activities.

---

[2] In the first quarter of 2019 already over 1840 social cooperatives were registered.

Only a few social enterprises are financed by business entities; most of them remain dependent on public funds, and do not have the capacity for further financing development, especially in terms of investments. The situation may be improved through consistent implementation of activities planned in the National Programme for Social Economy Development, but only if public funds will be used to strengthen the financial sustainability of social enterprises (Schimanek, 2015).

Initially channelled through EQUAL programme and later through European Social Fund and several regional and central Structural Funds programmes, EU policies continue to have an important impact on shaping social economy ecosystem. The cooperatives that are set up by previously unemployed people are also eligible for public start-up funding from Labour Offices operating at the district level. For CSOs, an additional source of funding is the 1% mechanism introduced in 2004, enabling Poles to allocate 1% of their taxable income to a social cause of choice (Cahalane, 2011).

For many years there were no special banking products for the social entrepreneurship sector in Poland. However, there are two commercial loan funds dedicated to supporting social economy entities: PAFPIO financing non-governmental organizations and TISE financing all social economy entities, including social enterprises. The PAFPIO fund was established in 1999 by the Polish-American Enterprise Fund in order to support the young Polish democracy and the market economy; currently PAFPIO belongs to the Polish-American Freedom Foundation, supporting the development of civil society in Poland. TISE, the Socio-Economic Investment Society, was established in 1991 by the BISE Bank, the Foundation for Social and Economic Initiatives and the French investment fund SIDI. Today, its owner is the French bank Crédit Coopératif, which has been financing the needs of social economy entities for over 120 years. A unique regional initiative is Malopolska Social Economy Fund, a foundation established to support the development of non-governmental organizations and social enterprises by providing loans and guarantees. During 3 years of the operation it has provided over 70 guarantees to the social economy entities.

Recent changes in terms of institutionalization of support for social economy include the establishment of the national network of local advisory centres. Within the frames of an ESF-funded project "Integrated system of social economy support" (ZWES, 2009–2014), a sustainable network of institutions offering standardized and comprehensive support for the social economy sector was created. New local Social Economy Support Centres (OWES) were expected to provide a wide range of advisory and consulting services, supporting entrepreneurs, advising on existing sources of financing and assisting in fundraising and formalization of SE initiatives (Bogacz-Wojtanowska, Przybysz & Lendzion, 2014). However, due to the project-nature system of funding, the centres had limited impact in terms of the number of beneficiaries as well as period of activity. Apart from the ESF-funded OWES centres, there are some projects funded by Civic Initiatives Fund (FIO), granted mostly to CSOs and social cooperatives, which aim at creating and promoting the new social cooperatives.

The important element of existing institutionalized support for SEs in Poland is Annual Polish Social Economy Meetings (OSES) organized for representatives of social economy institutions, academic experts, strategic partner institutions from other sectors and decision makers. This several-day event offers participants the opportunity to network, reflect on the current condition of the sector and consider its future perspectives.

Initiated in 2014, the implementation of the National Programme for Social Economy Development translates into a strong emphasis on achieving results. According to the National Programme, in 2020 the sector should employ 35,000 people, with help of 50 Social Economy Support Centres (OWES) involved in the implementation. To reach these goals certain funds were made available at the regional and national levels. For example, more than PLN 35 million has been reserved in the Regional Operational Program of the Mazowieckie Voivodeship for the period 2014–2020. As a result of cooperation between the social entrepreneurs and OWES a business plan is created, and the initiatives are eligible to receive the start-up grants of an average of PLN 15,000 to create one workplace.

In addition to subsidies, the support for social entrepreneurship includes repayable instruments, such as loans and sureties. In 2016, National Economy Bank (Bank Gospodarstwa Krajowego, BGK) launched loans up to PLN 100,000 for start-ups, while for entities operating over 12 months up to PLN 500,000. These financial instruments will target, among others, social enterprises, social cooperatives, foundations and associations. Importantly, interest rates on loans are more preferential in case of job creation, which emphasizes the importance of SEs' labour market effectiveness.

Impact Investment and Socially Responsible Investing Market

According to the latest JRC report on impact investment (Maduro, Pasi, Misuraca, 2018) Poland belongs to the group of EU member states with "infant social impact investment markets" including also Belgium, Croatia, Finland, Ireland, Lithuania, Luxembourg, Malta, Slovenia and Sweden. These infant markets found in Central and Eastern parts of the European Union seem to be driven by demand and market infrastructure rather than supply (Maduro, Pasi, Misuraca, 2018: 45). While we can observe the exponential growth of impact investment in the region, there is still a lack of patient early-stage capital.

The pioneer in creating ethical funds in Poland was the Towarzystwo Funduszy Inwestycyjnych Spółdzielczych Kas Oszczędnościowo-Kredytowych S.A., which as one of the first financial institutions in Poland decided to introduce SRI principles into the investment policy of the products they offer (Ostrowska, 2011). The first ethical fund—SKOK Etyczny 1 SFIO—was registered in the register of investment funds on December 9, 2008 (Krawiec, 2015).

However, despite the development of the Polish capital market, the socially responsible investing market is still in a very early stage of growth. According to the

2012 Eurosif report, the assets of Polish funds classified as SRI funds amounted to PLN 5 billion (Eurosif, 2012). The net asset value of all investment funds in Poland. The share of net assets of the SRI funds in the net asset value of all funds was 2.89% in 2016, which is very low (Sulik-Górecka & Rubik, 2017).

The socially responsible investing concept took off with the debut on the Warsaw Stock Exchange of the first in Central and Eastern Europe index of companies applying the principles of responsible business—the RESPECT Index—in 2009. The index name is an acronym of words that define the pillars of social impact: responsibility, ecology, sustainability, participation, environment, community and transparency (Paszkiewicz, 2013: 185).

Market analyses and a few scientific studies on the socially responsible funds in 2012 (Krupa, 2012) anticipated rapid development of the SRI funds in the future. However, in the Eurosif report of 2016, a less optimistic vision is presented. According to the report, the main reason for the low popularity of social impact funds is a low demand for such investments resulting from a lack of knowledge and high distrust among involved actors. Therefore, it is not possible to determine which of the funds (if any) can shape a more stable sector of SRI funds in the future (Eurosif, 2016). According to Sulik-Górecka and Rubik (2017), the reason for the SRI underdevelopment is the low awareness of Polish investors regarding the idea of social responsibility. The lack of trust and knowledge among investors, along with its low expected effectiveness, makes impact investment unpopular (Sulik-Górecka and Rubik, 2017).

The recent development of new impact investment instruments brings some hope for the more dynamic growth of new social economy. Established in 2017, Simpact is the first investment fund in Poland, in which the key criterion for investing and engaging in technology projects will be their positive impact on society and the environment. The fund was created as part of the Bridge Alfa programme coordinated by the National Centre for Research and Development. Start-ups interested in raising capital can receive up to PLN 3 million.

The Simpact Fund is a venture capital fund that is the first in Poland and one of the first in Central and Eastern Europe with innovative investment strategy, linking the conscious use of capital in projects that, apart from financial results, also generate social or environmental profits. The fund focuses on the search for technological solutions "to make the world better" in areas like improving the daily lives of residents, protecting health, improving the state of the environment and living conditions, reducing pollution and other.

Another interesting development concerns the Social Venture Capital method of financing using a venture capital strategy model and instruments known from the capital market to finance civil society organizations and social enterprises that generate a social impact. While the traditional financing model is mainly based on loans or guarantees, thanks to SVC, social economy entities can use the equity or quasi-equity instruments. To this end, TISE signed an agreement with BGK regarding the preferential loan fund for social economy entities managed by TISE. TISE has established a company—Fundusz Kapitałowych Inwestycji Społecznych (FKIS Fund), which will carry out such investments using 11 million PLN allocated under the project. The funding comes from the EU's POWER Programme and TISE's own funds. The project offers financial support in the form of the capital and subordinated loans (facilitating the acquisition of funds from other sources) and consultancy for investors. The Fund supports social economy by investing in social enterprises that pursue projects in the areas of care services, creating jobs for people at risk of social exclusion, assistance in achieving or maintaining independence and ecology. The investments are long-term, up to 10 years.

Another novelty on Polish financial market was the issuing of government environmental bonds. Green bonds were issued in December 2016, and will be bought back in December 2021 for 750 million EUR. It was the first type of such issue carried out by a government. As such, the Polish Government contributed to the introduction of a new segment in the green bond market.

Social Economy 2.0?

Since the idea of social economy has become popular in many EU countries, some authors started to talk about the social economy movement. Initiatives of this kind—in contrast to the old social economy—are oriented not only in favour of members (reciprocity principle), but also for external benefits, especially concerning local communities and marginalized groups (Leś, 2013; Rymsza, 2005). In addition, while the old social economy was created from the bottom up, public institutions or policies often support the social economy movement from above. However, in recent years, the idea of corporate social responsibility, impact investment and crowdfunding emerged in Poland, and started to shape the social economy sector in new ways. In my further analysis, I will refer to this phase of widening the social economy ecosystem as new social economy. In contrast to some of the cited works, I will mainly refer to the changes resulting from the global economic crisis of 2008 and the social economy response to new socioeconomic threats and opportunities.

Common feature that distinguishes new wave of social economy actors from classic ones is the ability to build a community around the brand and selling the idea rather than the product. This idea is often based on the vision of a better, smarter world in which a specific social problem is solved, environment is respected and employees are well treated. This strategy assumes that members of the community for whom a certain idea is important and who feel emotionally connected to it will not only choose related products, but also become brand ambassadors. However, the commitment of clients very much depends on how sincere and attractive are the value and change it propagates.

More importantly, the new social economy actors not only produce and sell but are also very active in promoting the idea of cooperation and educating their clients. It is not uncommon that clients undergo an evolution from a consumer to an engaged member of a certain community. Physical places (coop shops, cafes, restaurants, co-working spaces) and virtual spaces created by social economy agents are designed to engage, fuel curiosity and enable learning. For example, in case of gastronomy, clients often have a chance to learn about the values and ideas behind a cooperative movement or a social enterprise and may become inspired to to actively involve in social economy. This type of activity is therefore presented as something more than a service or product, but rather as a key part of a certain lifestyle (cruelty free, pro-equality, pro-democratic, sustainable, ecological, circular, anti-exploitation, etc.).

The main role of SEs, as defined by the current policies, is to make up for the deficiencies of social welfare system providing goods and services that are better suited to the needs of citizens "falling through the welfare gaps". To this effect, in the past few years, SEs have been extending their activity into some new areas including circular economy, alternative food distribution, social and economical revitalization and sustainable technologies. The popularity of these areas has been growing due to new EU policies and funds, prioritizing the sustainable development, revitalization of degraded urban areas and community development through economic empowerment. Social enterprises filled these new niches, offering innovative approach to community development and creating innovative solutions to urban poverty and lack of cohesion. Their impact was mainly visible on the local level, where they developed and focused their efforts.

According to Hausner (2012), a particularly promising area for the social economy is currently various types of personal services, the demand for which is growing rapidly along with the intensification of demographic changes characteristic of developed societies. These needs concern in particular the elderly, the disabled and the children. The demand grows strongly due to changes in the family model and spread of the single lifestyle. Recognizing a developmental opportunity in this area, social economy entities more and more often show an intense orientation towards a specific client and his/her specific needs.

Other types of structural socio-economic changes also contribute to the growing demand for specific services in which new social economy plays an important role. It relates to cultural needs concerning leisure as well as ecology, new lifestyle and sustainable consumption. The services that meet these new needs can be labelled "relational services" as they are provided in direct personal contact between the user and the provider, often with the user's active involvement. These types of services are not subject to standardization as in the case of many mass-rendered services— they are tailored to a specific individual need. Therefore, their provision requires relatively high qualifications, flexibility and a lot of effort and may prove unprofitable for market entities. This creates the competitive advantage for social economy entities, especially if they were able to involve consumers to some extent in the production of these services (Hausner, 2012).

Emphasizing the importance of the social economy in offering goods that meet new needs does not mean disregarding the possibilities of social economy entities in offering additional or new ways to meet the already identified needs. This is particularly visible during the current COVID-19 crisis, where some of the SEs focus more on responding to the basic need of the local vulnerable population, and then on developing new products or approaches. The possibilities of advancement and innovation seem endless, especially if one accepts the legitimate concept of a comprehensive system of supplying goods and does not see the social economy as a separate economic silo, but one of the necessary segments of a modern and dynamic economy.

While its input is obvious in the fields of employment, care or food-related services, the new social economy can also play a significant role in culture and education. The development of social enterprises conducting different cultural, craft-related and educational activities creates a lively and innovative social environment by involving residents in such ventures. Often, such initiatives use modern media technologies, finding innovative applications for them and at the same time caring for the natural environment (using so-called green technologies) (Mendell, Pestoff, Noya, & Clarence, 2009).

The new social economy focuses not only on the excluded and helpless people, but also on the provision of services that meet the needs of wide circles of society, which underlies the growing role of stakeholders. Social economy entities are particularly predisposed to this, as in their case the role of the owner is limited, and the importance of stakeholders is crucial. In the case of social economy entities developing services considered here, the point is to look at their potential consumers as stakeholders of the demand side, but to also include them from the supply side (Laville, 2009). As Izdebski (2012) writes, social economy entities are clearly more outwardly oriented today, while their pedigree binds them strongly to inward orientation in relation to their founding members. Therefore, we can talk about a dual orientation of the new type of social economy entities.

Social Economy in the Face of a COVID-19 Crisis

At the beginning of 2020, the COVID-19 virus outbreak has hit the global economy and society in an unprecedented way. Thousands of workplaces, production lines and supply chains began to rapidly disintegrate, and the basic principles of economics and finance suddenly ceased to apply. They were replaced by new reality of social isolation and quarantine, which soon resulted in the economic recession. For social economy these circumstances are both a great threat and—in a perspective—an unexpected and unique opportunity for development.

While worldwide turnover in many industries fell to almost zero, all data indicate that the economic paralysis caused by the virus will almost certainly turn into a longer recession. Mass quarantines, closed workplaces, massive layoffs and increasing uncertainty directly translate into sudden decrease of expenses for both companies and consumers. A decline in turnover affects producers and suppliers of all goods and services except for the basic ones (such as food, telecommunications services or some medicines and medical services) or those that are not affected by the crisis for some reason (e.g. digital entertainment platforms). All companies and organizations that do not have large savings or a stable, long-term (usually public or local government) source of financing found themselves in a very difficult place overnight.

The epidemiological emergency and the economic crisis translate directly into the negative situation of enterprises and households, and also affect companies and organizations providing services or acting for the benefit of the social good. In Poland, where there is at least 1.3 million people who are self-employed or employed for a definite period, the COVID-19 crisis will likely cause a wave of social problems resulting from individual bankruptcies, including depressions, suicides and increase in domestic violence.

As Konopczyński (2020) points out, the scale of needs that cannot be met due to the epidemics is difficult to estimate. It is certain that the shock caused by the coronavirus not only multiplies existing problems (unemployment, care for vulnerable or excluded people, poverty, dependence), but also generates new ones (such as lack of sanitary materials, medical equipment or transport opportunities). From the point of view of some industries (e.g. hotels and hostels, restaurants, cafes), quarantine means immediate closures. In case of schools or kindergartens new forms of education had to be established overnight, with many glitches and shortcomings involved. For other industries, they experience significant difficulties in continuing work (switching to home office and online forms of communication, changes in production lines or supply chains, etc.) or additional expenses connected with ensuring protection for employees and covering for their absences.

There is no doubt that many micro, small and medium enterprises found themselves in an unprecedented difficult situation, which—without a financial cushion for difficult times—can easily turn into insolvency and bankruptcy. These risks very much affect the social economy sector that is losing support from both public institutions (already overburdened with additional costs of crisis response) and private investors (focused on survival rather than social impact or CSR).

The new report from March 2020 prepared by the Association for Social Cooperatives and the Wielkopolska Centre of Social Economy (research in the context of the crisis of social enterprises caused by the SARS-CoV-2 virus epidemic) indicates that the situation of the social business sector in Poland was dramatic from the first days of the quarantine. Almost all studied social enterprises immediately felt the negative effects of the epidemic. Closed enterprises have lost the opportunity to earn and retain employees. Financial liquidity was shaken, and the future of enterprises was very uncertain. Those who have not stopped operations were struggling to reduce the number of orders or a timely settlement of all obligations. Majority of social enterprises also declared that they are waiting for support addressed specifically to them, to enable their survival. Due to the existing grant system for financing CSOs and contracts with a central or local government institutions, the situation of some of the associations and foundations was initially more stable. This, however, changes with time, meaning that also third-sector part of social economy may lose the ability to continue paying salaries and sustain their activities. The part of social economy activities that is based on direct involvement with clients (e.g. care services) was harmed most severely, while digital services and ICT-based production could hope for survival or even development.

In the context of a global crisis, some of the social economy actors remain beacons of solidarity, through direct involvement in fight with the epidemic (carers, therapists, volunteers) or donating crucial medical supplies (swabs, masks, medical equipment). The activities of thousands of volunteers, CSOs and social enterprises, which were on the front line of the fight against the epidemic, show the importance of this value-driven sector in a crisis situation where the logic of profit needs to be suspended. Because of the requirement for social isolation, people who work with people at risk (elderly, disabled, addicted, homeless) had to take special precautions and were more likely to be infected, which illustrates the size of social responsibility that lies on the sector focused on care and social support.

Quarantine caused the majority to change their daily routines and ways of spending time and money. This creates a new opening and promotes perhaps long-lasting changes in some sectors of employment and production. In a crisis situation, people also tend to ask themselves more often how to help others, especially those in a more difficult situation.While the physical economy is largely paralyzed, the digital economy is quickly developing and instantly filling some of the niches. Due to the coronavirus outbreak, the process of digitization of socio-economic relations was fast-tracked all over the globe. More areas of life migrated to the Internet: from office work, through education, to everyday shopping and socializing. If we consider social interactions mediated via the Internet as a market, then we are observing a moment of radical improvement in the economic opportunities in this sector. In a situation of social isolation, the attention of customers/viewers became an even more valuable resource. Almost all industries attempted to move businesses to the Internet at the same time, competing for a limited time that the customers can spend browsing the web. Some social enterprises and civic organizations followed the same path. However, this change was not about digitization understood as running a website or social media profile, but also developing new, flexible forms of self-organization that enable self-help, services or charity functions free of charge.

According to Konopczyński (2020), in Poland, the most famous example of this form of spontaneous mobilization is the Facebook Group "Visible Hand". Its activity was based on free exchange of knowledge, information, contacts and coordination to solve problems arising in connection with the COVID-19 pandemic. The original group gathered over 100,000 users within couple of days, and soon continued to develop local branches at the provincial or city levels. Another initiative called "Psychologists for Society" grouped over 200 specialists who offered free remote psychological help to people having emotional problems in a pandemic situation. Several initiatives based in the Internet focused on sawing protective gear for people at risk or networking and pairing people who can help each other.

We expect that this new wave of Internet activity and services will be key for shaping the perspective development of the social economy sector. Paradoxically, the fact that the majority of enterprises struggle with serious financial problems can improve the situation of social economy organizations, especially those working in social assistance or focused on satisfying important human needs. The crisis situation creates a more levelled playfield, which at least theoretically enables the development of new solidarity-based strategies and alliances.

Many of the social economy actors reacted to pandemic by sewing face masks and distributing them free of charge among seniors, people in hospices and social assistance personnel (e.g. Activisation and Integration Foundation in Nowe, Zielona Dolina Foundation, Makowo Foundation, Social Cooperative Mammamija). Others joined the action "Meal for the medic" that offered free meals to medical doctors, nurses and paramedics (e.g. Victus) or created an offer of Easter meals for people in quarantine (e.g. Social Cooperative Zbójeński Kredens). Many social enterprises moved their business to the Internet, by focusing on online sales or services. Their educational workshops were moved online, food produce were home-delivered and additional cleaning and sanitation services were offered.

Some media and regional governments invested in advertising the activities of the social enterprises during the pandemic.[3] Some municipalities channelled regional development and EU funds to special COVID-19 grant programmes that allowed to support the elderly and staff providing social services in the field of counteracting the spread of COVID-19, mitigating its effects on the regional level.[4]

In the face of an epidemiological disaster, we could also observe a growing respect for individuals and institutions that care for the broadly understood common good. Solidarity, care and commitment to the local community took on a new, tangible meaning. If these emotions transform into permanent attitudes, then public pressure could also increase to support people and the environments that make them happen on a daily basis. A crisis-induced change in thinking about society and economy is therefore a chance for deeper integration and cooperation between public institutions and organizations working for the common good: companies, foundations, associations or informal groups. The task of the social economy sector is to actively lobby for the governments to recognize the importance of its broadly understood services and give priority to their development.

Conclusion

In Poland, recent years allowed for re-establishing the importance of social economy and revival of certain forms of social entrepreneurship, but with a modern twist. The contemporary social economy turns to the non-state sector, and to the original roots that shaped its traditional initiatives. However, the current development differs fundamentally from the previous phases, because both the historical context and the types of problems are different. The reason for the re-emergence of SE in public discourse in Poland is the contemporary problem of decent employment opportunities, deeply connected with the phenomenon of social exclusion and

---

[3] See for example the YouTube clips advertising the social economy initiative responses to COVID-19 in Warminsko-Mazurskie Voivodeship: http://www.mediagroupinfo.pl/przedsiebiorczosc-spoleczna-na-warmii-i-mazurach-w-walce-z-covid-19/ or OWES Tłok summary of the inspirational practices of social enterprises during pandemic: https://www.rops.torun.pl/1206-jak-przetrwac-koronawirusa-pomysly-przedsiebiorcow-spolecznych.

[4] SE, e.g. https://www.rops.torun.pl/granty-covid-19/doplaty-do-wynagrodzen/ogloszenie-o-naborze.

the nation state's inability to effectively regulate the problems caused by market mechanisms. This notion is reflected in the National Programme of Social Economy Development, adopted in August 2014; however, there is a discussion on the definition criteria of the sector of social economy entities.

Despite its growing popularity, the activity of social enterprises faces many limitations in Poland, especially the barriers related to raising capital. Restrictions in access to financing sources constitute one of the basic barriers to the development of social enterprises. The factors determining the barriers in accessing capital by social enterprises include the diversity of organizational and legal forms of SE, the difficulty with the assessment of their financial credibility, high risk level and low income stability. Therefore, the organizational form and the degree of economization strongly influence the possibilities of SE development.

Economic weakness of the SEs also results from the fact that financial resources are allocated primarily to the current implementation of statutory objectives, and not to multiply assets and maximize profits. Therefore, social enterprises in order to determine the financing possibilities require a different measurement of effectiveness, in comparison with traditional enterprises. As a standard, profitability and financial liquidity criteria are used as measures to assess business ventures. The application of these criteria to social enterprises means that the possibilities of obtaining support in the form of market financial instruments are limited. In particular, this applies to debt financing in the form of loans and credits.

The evolution of the SE concept in Poland is primarily a response to specific threats and socio-economic-political problems that have been going on for centuries. The key examples of great projects include Społem Cooperative or the Warsaw Housing Cooperative that were the answer to social problems of their time, enacting innovative social solutions. The concept was fostered by different opportunities and influenced the evolution of social organizations currently belonging to the social economy sector.

Existing forms and funding possibilities involve both bureaucratic and financial constraints that hinder the innovative capacity of social economy. That is why many of the SE activities are realized through classical CSOs rather than dedicated legal forms. The local focus of social entrepreneurs is sometimes hindered by the general distrust of local communities towards organizations that try to create social impact through profit-generating activities. Also, the relationship with local municipality as well as other important institutions is the key to success (Bogacz-Wojtanowska, Przybysz & Lendzion, 2014).

Unfortunately, the understanding of the social economy concept is not widespread among municipalities. As there is no specific programme that would create the incentives to support social enterprises by the municipality they are often perceived as suspicious. For example, when the food cooperative "Dobrze" wanted to rent the communal premises for a grocery store, the municipality was highly reluctant to offer preferential rates to the non-profit shop (Domaradzka, Matysiak, Jasińska, & Żbikowska, 2018). A certain level of stubbornness and stamina is therefore required to break the barriers and implement the social economy ideas in the neoliberal context of Polish society.

One of the important challenges for the years to come is for the local authorities to accept and support the role of social economy sector in complementing other market entities and assisting the provision of high-quality and stable employment opportunities. As Kaźmierczak (2007) points out, in view of the exhaustion of the possibilities of old concepts it is necessary to create a new institutional order, an order that would establish foundations for social economy development, reaching beyond the current period of EU-financed growth.

As Karwińska (2008) underlines, the significance of social economy lies in showing alternative ways to "become an entrepreneur" or to "become an employee", assuming proactive attitudes in searching for solutions instead of waiting for help. The implementation of these values calls for the cooperation between local authorities with the third-sector organizations, proper legal regulations and strengthening of the role of social enterprises as a partner in economic relationships (Karwińska, 2008: 35). Importantly, social economy entities must build their competitive advantage not only by upholding important social values—like solidarity, integration, trust, psychological comfort, acceptance and sense of belonging—but also by offering goods and services that are in demand.

References

Andrukiewicz, M. (2012). Ekonomia społeczna i rola samorządów w ich rozwoju, http://fundacjabycrazem.blox.pl/2012/07/Ekonomia-spoleczna-i-rola-samorzadow-w-jej-rozwoju.html
Bogacz-Wojtanowska, E., Przybysz, I., Lendzion, M. (2014). Sukces i trwałość ekonomii społecznej w warunkach polskich, Instytut Spraw Publicznych, Warszawa 2014—http://www.isp.org.pl/publikacje,25,833.html [access: 20.04.2020].
Bohdziewicz-Lulewicz, M. (2013). Ekonomia społeczna w dokumentach strategicznych Małopolsk. *Ekonomia Społeczna, 1*(6), 83–88.
Brandeleer, C. (2013). Social economy in Poland. Working Paper, Pour la Solidarite, Bruxelles.
Broniszewski, M. (2016). Rozwój podmiotów ekonomii społecznej w Polsce ze szczególnym uwzględnieniem regionu opolskiego—uwarunkowania instytucjonalno-organizacyjne, Ekonomia Społeczna, no 2/2016, 38–47.
Broniszewski, M., Goleński, W., & Mesjasz, K. (2013). Trzy formy kapitału w podmiotach ekonomii społecznej województwa opolskiego. In A. Zagórowska (Ed.), *Problemy Śląska ze szczególnym uwzględnieniem województwa opolskiego wyzwaniem dla ekonomii społecznej* (pp. 140–148). Opole: ROPS w Opolu.
Cahalane, C. (2011). The state of the social enterprise sector in Poland. *Guardian, 10*(02), 2011. https://www.theguardian.com/social-enterprise-network/2011/feb/10/social-enterprise-poland-sector.
Central Statistical Office (2013). Podstawowe dane o wybranych organizacjach trzeciego sektora w 2012 r. Warsaw: Central Statistical Office.
Central Statistical Office (2019). Spółdzielnie jako podmioty ekonomii społecznej w 2017 r., Warsaw: Central Statistical Office.
Ciepielewska-Kowalik, A., Pieliński, B., Starnawska, M. and Szymańska, A. (2015). Social enterprise in Poland: Institutional and historical context. ICSEM Working Papers No. 11.
Defourny, J. Nyssens, M. (2012). The EMES approach of social enterprise in a comparative perspective. Working Paper no. 12/03, Belgium: EMES European Research Network.

Domaradzka, A. (2015). State of civil society in Poland. In C. Schreier (Ed.), *Mapping civil society in the Visegrád countries* (pp. 109–142). Berlin: Maecenata Institute.

Domaradzka, A., Matysiak, I., Jasińska, J., Siemieńska, R., Żbikowska, A. (2016). Social enterprises in Poland. FAB-MOVE National report.

Domaradzka, A., Matysiak, I., Jasińska, J., Żbikowska, A. (2018). Food cooperative "Well". FAB-MOVE Case study report.

Ekielski, W. (2019). Co to jest przedsiębiorstwo społeczne. Retrieved from: https://przedsiebiorstwospoleczne.pl/dlaczego-i-kiedy-przedsiebiorstwo-jest-spoleczne/

ekonomiaspoleczna.pl (2014). Jak mogłaby wyglądać współpraca biznesu z ekonomią społeczną i czemu tak nie wygląda. 22.0.2014. Retrieved from: https://publicystyka.ngo.pl/jak-moglaby-wygladac-wspolpraca-biznesu-z-ekonomia-spoleczna-i-czemu-tak-nie-wyglada

Eurosif (2012). European SRI Study 2016. Brussels. Retrieved from http://www.eurosif.org/sri-study-2012/

Eurosif (2016). European SRI Study 2016. Brussels. Retrieved from http://www.eurosif.org/sri-study-2016/

Grewiński, M., & Wronka, M. (2012). Gospodarka społeczna w UE i w Polsce—między przedsiębiorczością społeczną i CSR. In A. Frączkiewicz-Wronka & M. Grewiński (Eds.), *Przedsiębiorczość w Polsce—bariery i perspektywy rozwoju*. Warszawa: WSP.

GUS. (2019). *Spółdzielnie jako podmioty ekonomii społecznej w 2017 r.* Warszawa: GUS.

Hausner, J. (2008). *Ekonomia społeczna i rozwój. Ekonomia społeczna. Teksty nr 12*. Warszawa: FISE.

Hausner, J. (2012). Ekonomia społeczna a państwo. In M. Frączek, J. Hausner, & S. Mazur (Eds.), *Wokół ekonomii społecznej* (pp. 111–123). Kraków: MSAP, Uniwersytet Ekonomiczny w Krakowie.

Izdebski, H., & Małek, M. (2007). Formy prawne przedsiębiorczości społecznej w Polsce. In T. Kaźmierczak & M. Rymsza (Eds.), *Kapitał społeczny. Ekonomia społeczna*. Warszawa: Instytut Spraw Publicznych.

Izdebski, H. (2012). Prawo. In M. Frączek, J. Hausner, & S. Mazur (Eds.), Wokół ekonomii społecznej (pp. 211–226). Kraków: MSAP, Uniwersytet Ekonomiczny w Krakowie.

Karwińska, A. (2008). Social economy to deal with social exclusion in Poland, Ekonomski Horizonti, Univerzitet u Kragujevcu, Ekonomski Fakultet, godina IX, broj 1-2.

Kaźmierczak, T. (2007). Zrozumieć ekonomię społeczną. In T. Kaźmierczak & M. Rymsza (Eds.), *Ekonomia społeczna. Kapitał społeczny*. Warszawa: Instytut Spraw Publicznych.

Konopczyński, F. (2020). Niedobór środków, inflacja potrzeb. Przedsiębiorstwa społeczne pod kwarantanną, ekonomiaspołeczna.pl - https://ekonomiaspoleczna.pl/niedobor-srodkow-inflacja-potrzeb-przedsiebiorstwa-i-organizacje-spoleczne-pod-kwarantanna/ [access: 20.04.2020].

Krupa, D. (2012). Fundusze inwestycyjne odpowiedzialne społecznie. Annales Universitatis Mariae Curie-Skłodowska, 46(1), 307–316.

Krawiec, W. (2015). Impact investment–istota i otoczenie rynku. Annales Universitatis Mariae Curie-Skłodowska, Sectio H Oeconomia, 49(4), 279–289.

Kwaśnicki, W. (2005). Gospodarka społeczna z perspektywy ekonomii liberalnej, Trzeci Sektor, 2005, no. 2.

Laville J.-L. (2009). Supporting the Social and Solidarity Economy in the European Union, In A. Amin, The Social Economy. International Perspective on Economic Solidarity, Zed Books, London, New York.

Leś, E. (2013). *Organizacje non-profit w nowej polityce społecznej w Polsce na tle europejskim*. Warsaw: Publishing House ASPRA.

Leś, E., Ciepielewska-Kowalik, A. (2014). Social enterprises in Poland: Competitive advantages, challenges, obstacles and innovative ways forward. A case of early childhood education and care services, Paper for 54th ERSA Congress, 26–29 August, 2014.

Maduro, M., Pasi, G., Misuraca, G. (2018). Social impact investment in the EU. Financing strategies and outcome oriented approaches for social policy innovation: narratives, experiences, and recommendations, Publications Office of the European Union, Luxembourg.

Majdzińska, K. (2014). Aid and support for the social economy in Poland—The Case of Social Cooperatives, CIRIEC No. 2014/11, http://www.ciriec.ulg.ac.be/fr/telechargements/ WORKING_PAPERS/WP14-11.pdf, 2014.

Mendell, M., Pestoff, V., Noya, A. and Clarence, E. (2009). Improving social inclusion at the local level through the social economy: Report for Poland, OECD Local Economic and Employment Development (LEED) Working Papers, 2009/01, OECD.

National Programme (2014). Krajowy Program Rozwoju Ekonomii Społecznej. Ministerstwo Pracy i Polityki Społecznej. Retrieved form: https://www.ekonomiaspoleczna.gov.pl/download/files/EKONOMIA_SPOLECZNA/KPRES_2014.pdf

Okraska, R. (2012). *Edward Abramowski. Braterstwo, solidarnoŚć, współdziałanie. Pisma spółdzielcze i stowarzyszeniowe.* Łódź: Stowarzyszenie Obywatele—Obywatelom.

Paszkiewicz, A. (2013). RESPECT Index GPW w Warszawie jako giełdowy indeks społecznej odpowiedzialności biznesu. Prace Naukowe Uniwersytetu Ekonomicznego we Wrocławiu, (311), 182–191.

Pazderski, F (2013). Alternatywne mechanizmy finansowania przedsiębiorstw społecznych w Europie, [in:] Podsumowanie monitoringu prawa przedsiębiorczości społecznej, ed. T. Schimanek, Instytut Spraw Publicznych, Warszawa 2013—http:// www.isp.org.pl/publikacje,1,655.html [access: 20.04.2020].

Pieńkowska, D.. (2004). Ekonomia społeczna—podstawowe informacje, http://www.ngo.pl/x/ 29348

Praszkier, R., Zabłocka-Bursa, A., and Jóźwik, E. (2014). Social Enterprise, Social Innovation and Social Entrepreneurship in Poland: A National Report. EFESEIIS project report Warsaw: University of Warsaw.

Rymsza A. (2005). Partnerzy służby publicznej? Wyzwania współpracy sektora pozarządowego a administracją publiczną w świetle doświadczeń amerykańskich, Trzeci sector, no 3.

Rymsza, M. (2008). The Social Economy and the Third Sector. Poland Compared to European Experiences, Trzeci Sektor, Special Edition 2008, 4-10.

Rymsza, M., & Kaźmierczak, T. (Eds.). (2009). *Social economy in Poland, past and present.* Warsaw: Institute of Social Affairs.

Schimanek, T. (2006). Wpływ zewnętrznych źródeł finansowania na zatrudnienie w organizacjach pozarządowych, Trzeci Sektor, no. 4.

Schimanek, T. (2015). Finansowanie przedsiębiorstw społecznych w Polsce. Ekonomia Społeczna, (2), 7–20.

Siemieńska, R., & Domaradzka, A. (2009). The welfare system in Poland: Transformation with difficulties. In K. Schubert, S. Hegelich, & U. Bazant (Eds.), *The handbook of European welfare systems* (pp. 378–397). New York: Routledge.

Siemieńska, R., & Domaradzka, A. (2016). Between constrained opportunities and social expectations: Social policy in contemporary Poland. In K. Schubert, P. de Villota, & J. Kuhlmann (Eds.), *Challenges of European welfare systems.* Springer.

Sulik-Górecka, A. & Rubik, J. (2017). Development trends of socially responsible investment funds. View from Poland. Global Journal of Business, Economics and Management: Current Issues. 7(3), 275–284.

Wygnański, J. J. (2007). Social Economy in Poland: definitions, application, expectations and uncertainties. Warsaw: Foundation for Social and Economic Initiatives.

Chapter 7
The Social and Solidarity Economy in France Faced with the Challenges of Social Entrepreneurship

Didier Chabanet and Laurence Lemoine

Over the past 15 years or so, the theme of social entrepreneurship has gradually taken hold in France, both in the public space and at the political agenda. While this observation may be trivial, research on the way in which this phenomenon operates remains scarce. This chapter aims precisely to understand how social entrepreneurship emerged and competes with the notion of the social and solidarity economy. The change of direction and meaning is profound. The social and solidarity economy is traditionally defined by its statutes and includes all cooperatives, unions, foundations, and employers' associations, while the social entrepreneurship "covers all economic initiatives whose main purpose is social or environmental and which reinvest the majority of their profits into developing their mission" (Barthélémy & Slitine, 2012: 28). The law of July 31, 2014, pertaining to the social and solidarity economy legitimizes these two definitions as it provides commercial companies pursuing an aim of "social utility" with the possibility to integrate the field of the social and solidarity economy. This recent legislation presents the opportunity to review the different sequences that have first enabled social entrepreneurship to become socially conceivable, and then to be formalized and supported by a number of stakeholders before being recognized in legislation.

This study employs traditional public policy analysis tools, which generally distinguish three main phases (Mény & Thoenig, 1989). The first is that of the general context which makes a question collectively conceivable at a given time. The second is that of the positioning of different actors who will make proposals about the issue in question. Often little known to the public, these actors are also the most

D. Chabanet (✉)
IDRAC Business School and Triangle (Ecole Normale Supérieure de Lyon), Lyon, France
e-mail: didier.chabanet@idraclyon.com

L. Lemoine
IDRAC Business School, Montpellier, France
e-mail: laurence.lemoine@idracmontpellier.com

involved in the preparation of the decision. The third is the emergence of the issue at the political agenda. The job of "political entrepreneurs" is thus to take advantage of the "windows of opportunity" that have been created, and even if possible to generate such windows (Kingdon, 1984), to ensure that the decision made best fits their interests. We will see in this regard how people who support social entrepreneurship are able to take advantage of a situation combining three levels of negotiations: the French law of July 2014 on the social and solidarity economy, the Social Business Initiative launched by the European Commission in 2011, and the G8 Taskforce dedicated to the impact of social investments in 2013. These three different sequences can be considered as the elements of a global configuration confirming the new balance of power which today crosses the field of social and solidarity economy in France.

This chapter draws on a large body of primary data collected from 2013 to 2018 via two EU-funded projects—EFESEIIS[1] and FAB-MOVE.[2] A sociohistorical theoretical framework which incorporates recent sociopolitical evolutions developed from past events (Noiriel, 2008) was adopted for this research in order to understand how current policy initiatives strengthen and institutionalize specific aspects of the social and solidarity economy. Therefore, the first two sections of this chapter discuss the historical evolution of the social and solidarity economy, while the third section deals more specifically with policy issues which have arisen since the 2008 economic crisis. This approach enables a portrayal of the long-term effects of the historical and social aspects which underpin current social and policy changes. The fourth section presents a table illustrating the social and solidarity economy today, identifying its main issues.

From a methodological perspective, a qualitative approach was adopted. First of all, an analysis of the specialized literature focusing on the social and solidarity economy in France was undertaken, looking particularly at the context of the preparation of the social and solidarity economy law, which was finally passed in July 2014. Following this, between April 2014 and May 2015, ten social and solidarity economy actors were interviewed, grouped into three categories: academics specialized in the social and solidarity economy, social entrepreneurs, and policy makers involved in the social and solidarity economy regulation processes on national, European, and international levels. Although sample representativity is beyond the scope of this qualitative approach, the various conceptualizations and viewpoints which exist surrounding the social and solidarity economy were successfully addressed over the course of the interviews. These interviews, which lasted for 1 h on average, were recorded and transcribed, thus providing the empirical basis of the considerations expressed throughout this chapter.

---

[1] http://www.fp7-efeseiis.eu/

[2] https://www.uni-muenster.de/IfPol/FAB-MOVE/

Institutionalization of the Social and Solidarity Economy

The social economy is the result of a long and eventful history, which in France has its roots in the second half of the nineteenth century when the first mutual aid structures for craftspeople and workers became widespread in order to fight against the impoverishment which had accompanied the country's industrialization (Gueslin, 1987). Workers' cooperatives were thus created underground, before the law authorized their constitution in 1867. For example, consumer cooperatives emerged and developed as an expression of collective efforts to find answers to certain essential needs: obtaining basic products (food, clothing, etc.) at the best possible prices because money was very scarce at the time. Workers' production cooperatives have reflected the response of workers, especially craftsmen, who, in the face of capitalist industrialization, sought to defend their trade, remain in control of their work, and not allow themselves to be locked into a wage system synonymous with deprivation. Not to mention those who were simply thrown into unemployment by nascent capitalism and were trying to fight back by joining with others to set up their own businesses (Demoustier, 2001, p.20–33).

Mutual organizations experienced the same evolution simultaneously. While the risks of accidents at work and illness were very high, families from working-class backgrounds joined forces to provide modest but regular contributions to the emergency funds which then helped them in the event of misfortune. This system of collective assistance made it possible to cope with unexpected events. The law of 1898, which led to the creation of the mutual insurance charter, ratified and legitimized this situation. Three years later, the 1901 law authorized freedom of association, which was a far-reaching republican freedom, given that it granted every citizen the right to associate, following submission of a simple administrative declaration. In barely 30 years, the three main legal forms of the social and solidarity economy have been both recognized and encouraged by the French State[3] and this laid the groundwork for the contemporary social protection system established at the end of the Second World War. At that time, the main political forces—Gaullism and Communism—agreed to build a strong and interventionist social state, which would largely rely on the social and solidarity economy throughout the period known as "*Les Trente Glorieuses*." Since the country was undergoing an extensive process of reconstruction, two important economic sectors were specifically targeted: banking and insurance. Cooperative banks made accessing credit easier and contributed to the large-scale financing of agriculture, which still employed about half the workforce in 1945 (Draperi, 2012). Mutual insurance companies were formed slightly later, in the 1960s, mainly in the automotive and the residential construction industries. They also played a key role in the health sector by complementing the basic protection offered by the social security system (Dreyfus and Gibaud 2000). Finally, associations also played an important part since they worked

---

[3] The birth of foundations, as a specific form of association, is much more recent and dates from July 1987.

alongside the state in a key number of areas. They ran the overwhelming majority of services for the disabled, as well as numerous home care and home support services (Archambault, 1996). The state heavily regulates mutual organizations and cooperatives, which are exempt from some of the rules governing private businesses. Associations operate in even closer cooperation with the state, to such an extent that their services can, in effect if not in theory, be considered as an extension of the state's public services. "Tutelary regulations bring associations and administrations into close contact, in order to encourage them to form large, nationwide, secular or Catholic federations. A close examination of the relationship between associations and public authorities reveals the quantitative importance of the social services they provide, but also the system's reliance on a heavily centralized structure, with associations depending on the central state for funding and regulation" (Chanial and Laville 2014, p. 18).

Following the first oil crisis in 1974, the social and solidarity economy underwent a new phase of institutionalization and found in the subsequent economic crisis yet more reasons to assert its legitimacy. The National Liaison Committee for Mutual, Cooperative and Associative Activities (CNLAMCA—*Comité national de liaison des activités mutualistes, coopératives et associatives*) was the first to be established, and presented itself as a bastion against the mass unemployment which was beginning to grow (Duverger, 2016a). In the aftermath of the election of François Mitterrand as President of France, the left in power strongly supported the development of the social and solidarity economy. This recognition resulted from the merging of two schools of thought which are both complementary and competing: the social economy and the solidarity economy. The first obtained strong political support was in 1981 with the creation of the Interministerial Delegation for Innovation, Social Experimentation and the Social Economy (DIIESES)— *Délégation Interministérielle à l'innovation, à l'expérimentation sociale et à l'Économie Sociale*. Originally placed under the authority of the Prime Minister, the social economy has since generally been overseen by the ministries of social affairs, youth, and/or sports. The solidarity economy appears for the first and only time in a government organigram in 2000, in the form of a State Secretariat for the solidarity economy, before disappearing 2 years later. In reality, however, this tradition remains alive and stands out for its strength of opposition. It demonstrated a strong will for political change and in particular the desire to fight against inequalities. The solidarity economy can thus be defined as "all economic activities motivated by a desire to act democratically wherein social relationships and solidarity take precedence over individual interest or material profit; it thus contributes towards a democratization of the economy through the social engagement of citizens" (Eme & Laville, 2006: 302). Today, the terms "social economy" and "solidarity economy" are often used in conjunction, even in official texts, thus forming the term "social and solidarity economy."

As the product of a very French tradition, the State largely protects the actors of the social and solidarity economy, in the "public interest," of which it claims to be the guarantor. Social entrepreneurship tends to question this logic, by asserting that the statutes of the social and solidarity economy alone are not sufficient to define the social utility of an organization, and that the state can no longer govern society alone. The neoliberal turning point (Jobert, 1994), experienced by most industrialized countries following the election of Margaret Thatcher in Great Britain in 1979 and Ronald Reagan in the United States in 1980, also affected France, although to a lesser extent. The paradox here is that the development and popularity of the private company rose soon after the election of François Mitterrand in 1981, at the very moment when the socialist party converted—without really saying so—to economic liberalism. However, the country refused to sacrifice its welfare state. While on the one hand, in key sectors of social security (pensions and health in particular), one austerity reform follows the next in order to make savings, the number of support structures established to help the growing number of needy people is increasing (solidarity allowance, minimum income benefit, universal healthcare coverage, etc.), in such a way that the costs of combating exclusion increase structurally. The French welfare state now redistributes almost 32% of GDP, which is the highest rate of all OECD countries, ten points above the average.[4]

The fall of the Berlin Wall in 1989 followed by the collapse of the Communist Bloc meant, for some political analysts, the end of history (Fukuyama, 1992) and the definitive advent of capitalism. It was in this context that social entrepreneurship was born, considered by its promoters as a means of reconciling economic efficiency and social utility. The movement emerged from the United States, with the creation of Ashoka International in 1980 by Bill Drayton, the programs of which developed throughout the decade. The most prestigious American business schools followed the same path, such as *Harvard Business School* which created its own *Social Initiative* in 1993, or the *Schwab Foundation for Social Entrepreneurship* which was opened in 1998. But Europe did not drag its feet. In 1991, Italy created a specific statute for social solidarity cooperatives which made explicit reference to social entrepreneurship, while in 1995 Belgium passed a law on commercial companies with social objectives. Furthermore, the United Kingdom has been a champion of social entrepreneurship, patronage, and social philanthropy, notably through the *Coalition for Social Enterprise* in 2002, followed by the *Big Society* project in 2010.

The 2004 expansion of the EU to include ten new member states, almost all of which were former communist countries very often wary of a government-driven economy, has also positively influenced the promotion of social entrepreneurship. The defenders of the traditional French historical model of the social and solidarity economy suddenly found themselves more isolated within the EU, at the same time as the European Commission launched "the European Alliance for Corporate Social Responsibility," a forum open to all European companies, with the aim of encouraging social initiatives.

The Commission is also interested in the status of social economy enterprises nationwide in order to ensure that their activity does not violate the principle of free and undistorted competition. Supported financially by the European Commission,

---

[4] https://stats.oecd.org/Index.aspx?DataSetCode=SOCX_AGG&Lang=fr

the Emergence of Social Enterprises in Europe (EMES) network helps to develop the concept of social enterprise based on several indexes. A definition was therefore developed, based on a list of nine indicators which has been widely diffused in France and elsewhere, not only in academic circles but also within decision-making spheres. Four are predominantly economic indicators: (1) a continuous activity of production of goods and services; (2) a high degree of autonomy; (3) a significant level of economic risk-taking; and (4) a minimum level of paid employment. The remaining five indicators reflect the social character of the organization: (1) an explicit objective to serve the community; (2) an initiative emanating from a group of citizens; (3) a decision-making power not based on capital ownership; (4) a participatory dynamic, involving different stakeholders of the activity; and (5) limits placed on the distribution of profits (Defourny, 2004). Although it does not, strictly speaking, relate to social entrepreneurship, such reflection nevertheless contributes to its development as it conceptualizes social enterprise without considering the statutes. In all their diversity, all social organizations therefore constitute a vast field made up of relatively specific domains and traditions, which follow their own paths, but which are also somewhat complementary (Gianfaldoni, 2015).

Chronologically, the development of the statutory social and solidarity economy and other social enterprises—which constitute all social organizations—can be summarized as follows:

– From the end of the nineteenth century, agricultural cooperatives participated in the effort to modernize the agriculture and food industries.
– Banking cooperatives occupied an increasing share of the banking market, both in the agricultural and other sectors.
– Health and contingency insurance companies were pioneers in the field of social protection between 1880 and 1945 and had to redefine their role when the system of universal social security was established in 1945.
– Insurance companies developed in the 1960s, especially in car and home insurance.
– After 1945, associations for the defense of rights of handicapped people, created between the two world wars, managed virtually all institutions and services for people with disabilities.
– Social tourism emerged with the introduction of paid holiday in 1936, but it really boomed after the war, through public education movements and cultural centers.
– Ecology, feminism, defense of human rights, Third-Worldism, and antiracism all characterized the wave of associations created before and after 1968.
– Marked by an increase in unemployment, the 1980s and 1990s were defined by the fight against exclusion and integration through economic activity.
– During the 2000s, the ageing of the population engendered an increase in the number of at-home services under labels often combining cooperatives, insurance companies, and associations.[5]

---

[5] This summarizes the work of Archambault (2007).

The Structure of Social Entrepreneurship in France

The French State itself is torn between plural conceptions of organizations with a social purpose. Thus, while in 1980 the CNLAMCA developed a Charter to try to put pressure on public authorities and defend a social economy based on its statutes, different networks close to circles of power sought to thwart this initiative. The Liaison Agency for the Development of Alternative Enterprises was created for this purpose on February 1, 1981. Its founders—including Patrice Sauvage, a senior civil servant who worked for a long time at the Ministry of the Economy, Industry and Employment—define themselves as "internal mutants, i.e., agents of change within institutions" (Duverger, 2016b: 3). They advocate opening up the social and solidarity economy to all forms of socially useful initiatives taken by economic actors. In an even more official stance, almost two decades later, in 2000, Alain Lipietz was commissioned by Martine Aubry, the then Minister of Employment in Jospin's government, to publish a report on the social economy, in which he supported the creation of a "social enterprise label" for organizations which uphold a certain number of principles (Lipietz, 2001). Tensions arise between a proposal of this kind and the mission of the DIIESES, which seeks to defend the traditional boundary of the social and solidarity economy. The idea of implementing a label was taken up by MP Vercamer (2010), asked by Prime Minister François Fillon to write a report on the social and solidarity economy. The aim was already to go beyond the statutory approach to better take the multiple forms of organizations into account, in other words, to include capital companies which combine an entrepreneurial approach and a wider societal purpose under the umbrella of social and solidarity economy. At the same time, the French State partially reconsidered the regulatory protections and regimes which derogated from the competitive system which benefited social and solidarity economy organizations (Demoustier & Colletis, 2012). In unions and cooperatives in particular, the statutes have gradually adapted in order to widen membership and offer an increasingly significant place to financiers who do not participate in the business, which increases the profitability imperative (Bidet, 2003). The privileged access of cooperatives to public markets was also restricted. As a result, they found themselves increasingly in competition with traditional commercial enterprises and, consequently, having to adopt their way of functioning. This was also true for associations. The competitive regulation established over them—notably through the spread of calls for tender, reduction of subsidies, and development of management forms borrowed from the private sector—accentuated their entrepreneurial nature.[6] Decentralization reinforced this phenomenon even further. The emergence of local authorities, which gained a large number of powers in the field of social action from the mid-1980s onwards, "was accompanied by the spread of commodification of a series of goods and services, the development of public-private partnerships to entrust often lucrative public interest projects to private companies, and the predominance of a performative

---

[6] Interview with Mrs. J, April 9, 2015.

conception of the productive efficiency of companies" (Richez-Battesti, Petrella, & Vallade, 2012). Gradually, the capacity of the central government to steer the social and solidarity economy has declined.[7]

For their part, traditional social and solidarity economy actors are finding it increasingly difficult to make themselves heard and to rally themselves together. Weakened by the rise of economic liberalism, the "families" of the social and solidarity economy tend to adopt a strategy based on defending their status, when it is obviously no longer sufficient to guarantee the social or participatory nature of their activity.[8] They are also penalized for their difficulty in speaking with one voice and their difficulty therefore in effectively lobbying public authorities. From this perspective, the Higher Council for the Social Economy—supposed, as its name suggests, to represent all of its constituent units—has above all defended the interests of cooperatives rather than those of foundations, unions, and associations (Archambault & Bloch-Lainé, 2016). Divided, the social and solidarity economy has failed to take advantage of the opportunities that arise, as in 2011 when it missed the opportunity to impose on the state a framework law on the social and solidarity economy, however desired and "advocated" by Roselyne Bachelot, the then Minister of Solidarity and Social Cohesion.[9]

As the influence of the state and the statutory social and solidarity economy declined, other collective actors emerged from the early 2000s, carrying the social entrepreneurship banner. The agency for the promotion of socioeconomic initiatives (AVISE—*Agence de valorisation des initiatives socio-économiques*) was therefore created in 2002 and attempted to raise awareness of the traditional social and solidarity economy on new forms of social entrepreneurship. Ashoka France was founded soon after, in 2004, and the Collective for the Development of Social Entrepreneurship (CODES—*Collectif pour le Développement de l'Entrepreneuriat Social*) was created in 2006 and in 2009 a white paper was published containing the main proposals made by social entrepreneurs. Finally, the movement of social entrepreneurs (MOUVES—Mouvement des Entrepreneurs Sociaux) was born in 2010 and undoubtedly today constitutes the main force of representation of this movement. Over these years, many other leading public or private structures have promoted social entrepreneurship, including MACIF and the Fondation de France who, with the Caisse des Dépôts et Consignation, support the Chair of Social Entrepreneurship ESSEC, created in 2003, and certain other large French companies which have joined the Social Business Chair created by HEC in 2008. All of these organizations constitute a "reform nebula" (Topalov, 1999) characterized by an effervescence of ideas, experiences, and proposals, which emanate from different actors, acting in a more or less coordinated way—including within the state—to try to change the situation. They play a decisive role in improving social entrepreneurship,

---

[7] Interview with Mr. I, April 23, 2014.

[8] Interview with Mr. G, June 18, 2014.

[9] Interview with Mrs. B, February 17, 2015.

not only because they provide cognitive resources, but above all because they are effective structures of influence.[10]

The 2008 Crisis, a Window of Political Opportunity for Social Entrepreneurship

The economic crisis of 2008 propelled social entrepreneurship to the core of the political agenda not only in France but also EU-wide and internationally. In every scenario, the primary objective of political decision makers is the same: the main issue is to develop the social and solidarity economy in order to fight unemployment, since its capacity to create jobs is clearly superior to that of the traditional economy. It was along these lines that the Commission created the Social Business Initiative at the end of 2011. In order to operate, an expert group on social economy and social enterprises (GECES) was created in February 2012, comprising a representative of each member state and actors drawn from the social economy. This group focuses particularly on the question of measuring social impact, while the Commission defined new mechanisms to finance social enterprises, in particular through European structural funds. Although the work it undertakes is not binding, the GECES nevertheless constitutes an epistemic community, which is "a network of professionals with recognized expertise and skills in a particular domain and an authoritative claim to knowledge pertaining to policies within that domain" (Haas, 1992: 3). As such, it contributes towards guiding public debate, if only by blurring the lines between the concepts of social entrepreneurship and social economy, which it uses in an undifferentiated manner as if they were synonymous.[11] Even if a plurality of opinion was able to express itself within the organization, the GECES has created a sounding board which has, in France, rather served those who defended the fact of opening the field of social and solidarity economy to commercial enterprises. The European arena has somehow prepared for the adoption of the French law of July 2014, giving arguments proposed by MOUVES, the vice president of which was a member of the GECES and who has constantly supported the approach taken by the Commission.[12] Conversely, Jean-François Draperi, qualified as "a brilliant academic spokesperson for his resistance to social entrepreneurship" (Sibille, 2016:3) and more generally a whole stream of thought and action structured in particular around the International Social Economy Review (*Revue internationale de l'économie sociale*), was kept out of the way. French political decision makers in charge of preparing the law were very sensitive to these debates. On January 16–17, 2014, the European Commission organized a large gathering in Strasbourg of nearly 2000 social entrepreneurs, adopting a joint declaration to demonstrate their

---

[10] Interview with Mr. F, June 11, 2015.

[11] Interview with Mr. G, June 18, 2014.

[12] Interview with Mr. A, May 20, 2014.

determination, at which Benoît Hamon, minister in charge of the law on social and solidarity economy, was present. "He measured the dynamics of renewing social entrepreneurship and the desire of most European countries to promote an inclusive vision between a social economy and the social and solidarity economy. The law he was preparing will bear the mark of this" (Ibid.: 9).

A few months later, the French legislator effectively presented commercial enterprises with the opportunity to join the social and solidarity economy field, on the condition that they pursue a goal of "social utility" and that they adopt participative governance. Social entrepreneurship automatically integrates the field of social and solidarity economy, which was one of the main demands of its promoters.[13] From the offset of consultations, Benoît Hamon and his entourage had indicated that "this change was nonnegotiable."[14] Some of the traditional social and solidarity economy supporters find this regrettable. Large organizations such as the National Federation of Services for Homeless People (FNARS—*Fédération nationale des associations d'accueil et de réinsertion sociale*), which brings together nearly 9000 social and solidarity economy stakeholders, or Emmaüs France, thus officially opposed this measure, and the law itself more generally.[15] Three issues account for most of the grievances expressed:

– The law favors job-creating approaches, to the detriment of those which are perhaps more socially innovative, or which are underpinned by alternative models of society. Social and solidarity economy organizations would all tend to be part of a market—the activity of which is moreover almost always measured using quantitative indicators, generally growth indicators—leaving aside all activities with a social purpose which challenge the concept of the market, often called the "nonmarket spheres of the economy." For those who favor a militant and political approach to the social and solidarity economy, the issue is to think about an alternative model of society. The main goal is not to create jobs, especially if they are unstable and precarious, but rather to provide a change or a break in the capitalist paradigm (variously called degrowth, socialism, or a revisited version of solidarity).[16]
– The promotion of social entrepreneurship is an opportunity to legitimize the withdrawal of public action, and in particular that of the state in the management of educational, social, and solidarity services. Several phenomena support the idea of leaning in this direction. Some observers first point out that the development of social entrepreneurship has contributed to calling into question the idea that the state has to be the guarantor of public interest. The state would, in a way, relinquish its historical missions, by subcontracting and developing quasi-markets for certain services which were previously considered public. The usefulness of the social and solidarity economy would then no longer be assessed in

---

[13] Interview with Mr. C, May 20, 2014.
[14] Interview with Mrs. B, May 10, 2015.
[15] Interview with Mr. D, February 11, 2015.
[16] Interview with Mr. E, June 16, 2014.

terms of the services provided to the community, but rather in terms of their profitability and their ability to compete, with the consequence of accentuating their managerial functioning, bringing them closer to conventional companies (Bode, 2000). This development would result in the reduction of public funding for associations (Tchernonog & Prouteau, 2019).

– The social entrepreneurship would hardly be compatible with the requirement of a democratic and participative functioning, which is at the very heart of the social and solidarity economy and which meets specific requirements. As Benoît Hamon, in charge of the social and solidarity economy in 2014, points out: "shared management of the structure equally among stakeholders, and not according to the share of capital held" (Duverger, 2016a: 7). Indeed, if, in a traditional company, the power of decision-making is linked to the share of the capital held, in social and solidarity economy organizations, it is the "one person = one voice" principle which prevails for all the members. The question is therefore that of citizen participation, which is particularly central to the solidarity economy (Hillenkamp & Laville, 2013), or, to put it another way, of the democratic nature of the governance systems implemented within organizations. For some specialists, social entrepreneurship and social and solidarity economy irreducibly differ from this point of view: "While the historic social and solidarity economy more or less equates to social entrepreneurship, social entrepreneurship however does not integrate the democratic issue of the social and solidarity economy. This is characteristic of large capital companies: once regulation by democracy has been ruled out, the market takes back its rights" (Draperi, 2017: 5). Here we thus find the traditional opposition between social entrepreneurship, which promotes the figure of the entrepreneur—applied here to a social activity—and social and solidarity economy much more sensitive to the collective dimension of its project (Richez-Battesti, 2016).

Whether we regret it or celebrate it, social entrepreneurship has been legitimized by French legislation and has the wind in its sails internationally, the two phenomena being sometimes linked. Hugues Sibille has an impressive background: a banker by training from the cooperative movement, former interministerial delegate for the social economy in 1998, founder of AVISE, vice president of MOUVES, member of GECES, and a tireless activist for the recognition of social entrepreneurship. He was one of the two official representatives of France to the Taskforce dedicated to social impact investment, formed in June 2013 by the G8, then chaired by the United Kingdom under David Cameron's leadership. In this context, he directed a report entitled *How to promote social impact investments and why: how to innovate financially in order to innovate socially*, which was delivered in September 2014 to the Secretary of State for the social and solidarity economy.[17] The document aims to make social and solidarity economy more profitable so that it is more attractive to private investors. Noting the scarcity of public funds, it proposes to organize a social protection market by generalizing evaluation protocols which enable management

---

[17] http://www.economie.gouv.fr/files/files/PDF/RapportSIIFce_vdef_28082014.pdf

of the social and solidarity economy based on the tools and values of the private sector. These funding logics can be seen as a better system of allocation of resources, but they induce a profound change in the functioning of organizations.

Between Institutionalization and Diversion: The Social and Solidarity Economy at the Crossroads

The developments occurring in the field of the social and solidarity economy are both complex and recent, so much so that it is difficult to measure and assess their effects. Following the Law of July 2014, four models of social organizations can nevertheless be defined according to four essential dimensions: the degree of individual redistribution of profits, nature of governance, mobilized resources, and values.[18]

Today, these social organizations manage 90% of establishments for people with disabilities, 45% of retirement homes, and more than 60% of services to individuals.[19] They also play an important role in household services (health or social sector), or in tourism. Present across a large number of sectors, these organizations are particularly anchored in the banking and insurance sector. Cooperative banks therefore collect more than 50% of all deposits and mutual insurance companies dominate the property and damages insurance sector. In percentage terms, associations account for 82.5% of employment in the social and solidarity economy, cooperatives 13%, mutual insurance companies 3.7%, and foundations 0.8% of employment in the social economy. Taken as a whole, the SSE represents about 10.5% of all salaried employment in France.[20]

It is in the last two lines of Table 7.1 that we find the famous "commercial companies of the social and solidarity economy," as this is now their official name since the Law of July 2014. From a strictly quantitative point of view, the change is minor, since there were only 236 of these in April 2017 (CNCRESS, 2017, p. 3). Experts estimate that in the future, at most 5000 commercial enterprises will enter the field of the social and solidarity economy,[21] which is a very low number given the total number of organizations in existence (Table 7.2).

---

[18] Here we are inspired by two typologies set out by other researchers, which we partially combine. See on the one hand "Tableau - Les organisations porteuses d'innovation sociale" developed by Richez-Battesti (Nadine), Petrella (Francesca), and Vallade (Delphine), 2012, L'innovation sociale, une notion aux usages pluriels: quels enjeux et défis pour l'analyse. *Innovations*, n°38, p. 33. On the other hand, "Tableau - Renouveau des modèles d'ESS et typologie d'entrepreneurs," by Richez-Battesti (Nadine), 2016, Diversification des modèles d'entreprises d'économie sociale et solidaire: quelle place pour l'entrepreneur? *Revue de l'entrepreneuriat*, n°3, p. 139.

[19] CNCRES, ESS Atlas, Paris, Dalloz, 2017.

[20] https://recherches-solidarites.org/media/uploads/economie_sociale_28-06-2017.pdf

[21] Interview with Mrs. B, February 17, 2015.

Table 7.1 Typology of models of social organizations

	Degree of individual redistribution of profits	Nature of governance	Mobilized resources	Values
Social economy	Nonprofit or limited profit	Collective property. Decision-making principle: One person = one voice	Market and nonmarket; donations and volunteering	Prosocial/economic
Solidarity economy	Nonprofit or limited profit	Collective property. Decision-making principle: One person = one voice	Market and nonmarket; donations and volunteering	Prosocial/political
Social enterprises	Limited profitability	Variable, often multi-stakeholder ownership. Decision-making principle: Undefined, but not based on capital ownership	Market and nonmarket with a high level of risk	Prosocial/economic
Social entrepreneurship	Limited profitability	Property held by investors. Decision-making principles: Based on ownership of capital. Importance of the leadership	Private capital (financial autonomy)	Prosocial/economic

Table 7.2 Number of social and solidarity economy organizations according to their status

Cooperatives	Mutual insurance companies	Associations	Foundations	Commercial companies
27,250	8368	185,145	1568	236

Source: CNCRESS, 2017

Beyond the figures, which remain modest, the arrival of commercial companies within the social and solidarity economy, and the legitimacy with which they can now claim to speak "on behalf" of this sector—in the same way as do other organizations—is indicative of a change in discourse and people. As Mr. A states, "a new generation is emerging, which is seeking both professional success and personal fulfilment by making themselves useful. Previous generations, with ingrained ideologies, dreamed of transforming society. Since the 1990s, the youth has invented pragmatic solutions for the here and now ... by creating businesses" (Gérome, 2015, p. 54). The gamble made by these social entrepreneurs is that economic efficiency can benefit everyone. In other words, they seek to reconcile the principles of the market economy, or capitalism, to which they adhere, with the virtues of solidarity and social action, which they feel are necessary in the fight against inequalities and to guarantee minimal social cohesion. Wishing to be pragmatic, they more or less implicitly refer the advocates of a historic social and solidarity economy to their old-fashioned ideas, a vision of the social economy which they consider to be both ideological and ineffective (Duverger, 2019).

Social entrepreneurship has been able to assert legitimacy which is essentially based on its capacity to obtain concrete results, in the field of employment, for instance. It also assumes the profitability of its activity—even if this is limited—and pragmatically adapts to the new modes of financing available, particularly private means. With the recognition of social entrepreneurship, the social and solidarity economy field is richer than ever in differentiated models, traditions, and practices. The 2014 law chose an inclusive definition which does not impose a single model. On the contrary, it assumes a cross-fertilization between approaches and conceptions under debate—and sometimes in conflict—but which are also in constant interaction.[22] Social and solidarity economy actors today have the option of seizing opportunities offered by the legislation, which effectively establishes competition, but also possible dynamic cooperation, between stakeholders. In the mind of the legislator, there is no doubt that the desired isomorphic effect—understood as a "constraining process that forces one unit in a population to resemble other units that face the same set of environmental conditions" (Di Maggio & Powell, 1983, p. 150)—must lead traditional social and solidarity economy organizations to draw inspiration from private sector commercial and management companies.

Within this perspective, Social Impact Bonds are one mechanism implemented by the legislation to dynamize the sector, finance it, and also incite it to adopt assessment criteria and return on investment which are the rule in a market economy founded on the search for profit. These tools are all the more interesting to analyze given that they are not in-keeping with French tradition and were implemented immediately after the Law of July 2014. They can therefore be considered as elements of a single public policy. The main principle is as follows: a private investor finances a social project, proposed by a social and solidarity organization, and which assumes the financial risk, therefore avoiding the use of public funds. At the end of the project, an independent assessment mechanism must make it possible to establish—in an objective and opposable way—the achievement of the program objectives and, depending on the success of the project and its social impact, sets out the repayment, with interest, of the investment made by the public authority. If the objectives set when the social impact contract was drawn up are not achieved, the investor will not obtain any reimbursement from public authorities (Dermine, 2019). Several calls for tender have been disseminated by the French State since 2016 and have enabled the funding of around ten projects for amounts of up to 1.7 M€ each. Open to all actors of the social and solidarity economy, these mechanisms remain relatively modest on the scale of needs within the sector (according to the Office of the High Commissioner to the Social and Solidarity Economy and Social Innovation), but these are in addition to the many other existing financial means, whether they are regional, national, or even European. The French Government is evidently determined to continue in the same vein, as it decided in

---

[22] Interview with Mrs. H: April 9, 2015.

September 2019 to create a "French payout fund" of 30 million euros, exclusively reserved for social and solidarity economy organizations. While those within the sector are pleased that funding has increased over recent years, criticisms of Social Impact Bonds remain vociferous. Some have reported that files are needlessly complex, time consuming, and therefore inaccessible to most small organizations, especially associations. Others highlight the very notion of social impact, as it is understood by public authorities, often leading to a focus on certain actions, the effects of which are easily quantifiable and felt in the short term, while some measures that are not easily quantifiable are often more effective in the long term (Hély, 2017). Finally, and even more crucially, one must wonder whether social action should necessarily be subject to principles of profitability.

These questions occupy, and divide to a certain extent, the social and solidarity sector, and are asked with even more acuity—animosity even—since the Law of July 2014. The relatively large incidence of "greenwashing" or "social washing" with which certain commercial companies of the social and solidarity economy are familiar can "lead us to believe that social entrepreneurs are the 'useful idiots' of large companies wishing to improve their image" (Gérome, 2015, p. 59). The recurrent controversies surrounding the SOS group—one of the most well-known commercial companies of the social and solidarity economy, which employs more than 12,000 people working in nearly 350 organizations established all over France and overseas—provide an excellent illustration of these debates. The group takes the form of organizations with various activities (ranging from support for professional reinsertion to business consulting and real estate management, etc.), the legal statutes of which are very diverse (associations, commercial companies, cooperatives, etc.) and which are placed under the authority of three associations: SOS-Drogues, SOS-Habitat et Soins, and SOS-Insertion. This structure promotes the constitution of equity and enables organizations to take out significant loans with extremely low rates of interest. One of the objectives of the group is therefore to raise capital from banks or investment funds to finance the social activities of its companies. The profitability of these companies is a requirement fixed at, on average, 5% (Gérome, 2015, p. 58). Rarely have the logic and instruments of the world of finance been as intertwined with those of the social and solidarity economy as they are today. Management of the group and its charismatic founder—Jean-Marc Borello—has been highlighted many times by public authorities which applaud a "concentration of decision-making authority" not usually compatible with the democratic ideal of the social and solidarity economy, as well as the importance of precarious contracts and a particularly high turnover. There are also reports of aggressive, exhausting managerial practices which are little supported by some staff (Hély, 2012). In light of these elements, some prefer to stress the success of a group whose volume of business is constantly increasing, and which is developing innovative and ambitious mechanisms for insertion and social aid, while others denounce the ambiguity of communications and practices, or even the divergence of making social vocations a business like any other.

In France, the social and solidarity economy is in a crucial phase of its existence. On the one hand, it is now recognized by public authorities more than ever before.

On the other hand, its specific features and ambitious aims for reform mean it risks receding and diminishing. For many observers, the two phenomena are linked (Duverger, 2016b). In this context, one of the questions raised is how the most fragile fringes of society will be protected. To take just one example: How can we properly care for elderly dependents, the number of which we know will increase in the coming years, if the care facilities of the social and solidarity economy are subjected to profitability requirements? The Covid-19 crisis has incited many commentators on French public life, as well as political leaders, to reconsider the idea that the social economy is a sector like any other, which should be subjected to market laws.

Part of the social and solidarity economy has been severely shaken by the recent sanitary crisis. Many small structures, particularly in the sectors of culture, sport, and social integration, have thus been weakened by the period of lockdown. Some stopped their activity, with significant uncertainties as to the conditions of their resumption. National and local authorities have set up several financial support mechanisms to try to help those in severe difficulty, which proves their attachment to the sector. However, other social and solidarity economy organizations have benefited from the Covid-19 crisis. This is the case for market gardening, dairy products, and meat, which have seen their direct sales to the public increase. The almost total stoppage of transport for several months has indeed had globally positive effects on short circuits and local production, which constitute one of the main axes of development of the social and solidarity economy.

In a way, the sanitary crisis has also had the merit of bringing jobs that are too often overlooked or underestimated to the forefront. Many social and solidarity economy actors have been on the front line to deal with emergencies in retirement homes, nurseries, home help, school support, and, more generally, social and solidarity actions. In this exceptional and extreme context, the social and solidarity economy has demonstrated its creativity and its ability to adapt, by enabling poor people to access goods or services from which they have been excluded for a long time (such as housing, food, or health); by creating new methods of remote support (for example within retirement homes, when visits were prohibited); by encouraging public authorities to develop new practices of collective solidarity (particularly by generalizing service vouchers or support for integration enterprises); and by encouraging companies to develop their social responsibility. A famous French insurance company thus redistributed more than 100 million euros in contributions to its members and to nonprofit associations, arguing that the decrease in car traffic generated by the health crisis had enabled it to make substantial profits. This decision inspired an interesting public debate on how economic actors could contribute to the emergence of a more equal, united, and fraternal society (Ibanda Kabaka, 2020).

More broadly, social and solidarity economy actors have contributed to the debate on the "world after," which many citizens are demanding. Even if the debate has been unchecked, abundant, and inconsistent in quality, the cognitive contribution of the social and solidarity economy has been decisive. The sanitary crisis has indeed highlighted the limits of an economic model based on exponential and limitless productivity growth. We now know that the growing destruction of ecosystems and the strong pressures exerted on biodiversity have been increasing zoonoses, which are one of the causes of the current pandemic. The economies of developed countries have been able to ensure an incredibly high standard of living for a proportion of humanity, but it has also resulted in the uncontrolled exploitation of natural resources, waste, and pollution, without even mentioning the deleterious effects on the psychological state, physical health, and well-being of an increasingly important proportion of the world population. On all of these issues, social and solidarity economy actors are proactive and are able to design a more equitable, sustainable, and human world. The future remains open, but in the light of the current tragic sanitary episode, the evolution of the social and solidarity economy has led us to rethink what makes our society cohesive and, in a certain way, to also rethink the values upon which our social contract is founded.

Interviews

Mr. A: Secretary of MOUVES
Mrs. B: Academic, social, and solidarity economy specialist
Mr. C: AVISE
Mr. D: FNARS, Member of the GECES
Mr. E: Association Rencontres sociales
Mr. F: Social entrepreneur, Director of Envie Rhône
Mr. G: European Commission
Mrs. H: Academic, social, and solidarity economy specialist
Mr. I: Vice President of Crédit Coopératif, member of the GECES
Mrs. J: Academic, French associations specialist

References

Archambault, E. (1996). *Le secteur sans but lucratif. Associations et Fondations en France. Paris*: Economica.
Archambault, E. (2007). L'économie sociale en France dans une perspective européenne, First International CIRIEC Research Conference on the Social Economy, Victoria, BC, Canada, October 22–25, https://halshs.archives-ouvertes.fr/halshs-00178635/file/_Victoria.pdf
Archambault, E., & Bloch-Lainé, J.-M. (2016). Associations et économie sociale et solidaire, ancrage ou dilution? In R. Lafore (Ed.), *Refonder la solidarité. Les associations au cœur de la protection sociale* (pp. 119–136). Paris: Dalloz.
Barthélémy, A., & Slitine, R. (2012). *Entrepreneuriat social, innover au service de l'intérêt général*. Paris: Vuibert.
Bidet, É. (2003). L'insoutenable grand écart de l'économie sociale: isomorphisme institutionnel et économie solidaire. *Revue du MAUSS, 21*, 162–178.
Bode, I. (2000). De la solidarité au marché? En France et en Allemagne, nouveaux défis pour les organismes d'assurance maladie à but non lucratif. *Revue Internationale de l'économie Sociale, 278*, 67–79.

Chanial, P., & Laville, J.-L. (2014). L'économie sociale et solidaire en France. In J.-L. Laville, J.-P. Magnen, G. Carvalho de Franca Filho & A. Medeiros (eds.), Action publique et économie solidaire. Paris: Erès.

CNCRESS (2017). Sociétés commerciales de l'économie sociale et solidaire : premiers éléments d'analyse. Montreuil: Observatoire national de l'ESS.

Defourny, J. (2004). L'émergence du concept d'entreprise sociale. Reflets et perspectives, 3(XLIII), 9–23.

Demoustier, D. (2001). L'économie sociale et solidaire. Paris: Syros.

Demoustier, D., & Colletis, G. (2012). L'économie sociale et solidaire face à la crise: simple résistance ou participation au changement. Revue internationale de l'économie sociale, 325, 21–33.

Dermine, T. (2019). Contrat à impact social : une opportunité pour le financement de l'action sociale ? Informations sociales, 199(1), 116–123.

Di Maggio, P. J., & Powell, W. W. (1983). The iron cage revisited. Institutional isomorphism and collective rationality in organizational fields. American Sociological Review, 48, 147–160.

Draperi, J.-F. (2012). La République coopérative. Paris: Larcier.

Draperi, J.-F. (2017). L'ESS entre démocratie et commerce. Revue Internationale de l'économie Sociale, 346(4), 4–6.

Dreyfus, M., & Gibaud, B. (2000). La mutualité dans le siècle (1900-2000). Paris: Mutualité Française.

Duverger, T. (2016a). L'économie sociale et solidaire Une histoire de la société civile en France et en Europe de 1968 à nos jours. Lormont: Le Bord de l'eau.

Duverger, T. (2016b). Les transformations institutionnelles de l'économie sociale et solidaire en France des années 1960 à nos jours. Revue Interventions Économiques, 54. https://journals.openedition.org/interventionseconomiques/2711#quotation.

Duverger, T. (2019). L'institutionnalisation de l'économie sociale et solidaire : État et société civile organisée en France de 1981 à 2017. Informations Sociales, 199(1), 28–35.

Eme, B., & Laville, J.-L. (2006). Economie solidaire (2). In J.-L. Laville & A. D. Cattani (Eds.), Dictionnaire de l'autre économie. Paris: Gallimard.

Fukuyama, F. (1992). La fin de l'histoire et le dernier homme. Paris: Flammarion.

Gérome, C. (2015). Les entrepreneurs sociaux à l'assaut du monde associatif. Mouvements, 81(1), 51–59.

Gianfaldoni, P. (2015). Les enjeux identitaires des entreprises sociales françaises. Entreprendre & Innover, 27, 51–59.

Gueslin, A. (1987). L'invention de l'économie sociale. Le 19e siècle français. Paris: Economica.

Haas, P. (1992). Epistemic communities and international policy coordination. International Organization, 46(1), 1–35.

Haut-Commissariat à l'Economie sociale et solidaire et à l'innovation sociale (2019). Pour un développement du Contrat à impact social au service des politiques publiques, Ministère de la transition écologique et solidaire, https://www.ecologique-solidaire.gouv.fr/sites/default/files/Rapport%20-%20Pour%20un%20d%C3%A9veloppement%20du%20contrat%20%C3%A0%20impact%20social%20au%20service%20des%20politiques%20publiques.pdf

Hély, M. (2012). Le travail salarié associatif est-il une variable d'ajustement des politiques publiques ? Informations sociales, 172(4), 34–42.

Hély, M. (2017). De l'économie sociale « historique » à « l'économie sociale et solidaire » : une nouvelle configuration des relations entre monde associatif et collectivités publiques. Revue Française d'administration Publique, 163(3), 543–556.

Hillenkamp, I., & Laville, J.-L. (2013). Socioéconomie et démocratie: L'actualité de Karl Polanyi. Érès: Toulouse.

Ibanda Kabaka, P. (2020). La pandémie du coronavirus COVID 19 en Europe. Leçons tirées de l'option de défaire l'économique en vue de reconstruire le capital humain, https://hal.archives-ouvertes.fr/hal-02681607/document

Jobert, B. (Ed.). (1994). Le tournant néo-libéral en Europe. Paris: L'Harmattan.

Kingdon, J. (1984). Agendas, alternatives, and public policies. New York: Harper Colins.

Lipietz, A. (2001). *Pour le tiers secteur*. Paris: La Documentation Française.

Mény, Y., & Thoenig, J.-C. (1989). *Politiques publiques*. Paris: Presses Universitaires de France.

Noiriel, G. (2008). *Introduction à la Socio-Histoire*. Paris: La Découverte.

Richez-Battesti, N. (2016). Diversification des modèles d'entreprises d'économie sociale et solidaire : quelle place pour l'entrepreneur? *Revue de l'entrepreneuriat, 3*, 129–142.

Richez-Battesti, N., Petrella, F., & Vallade, D. (2012). L'innovation sociale, une notion aux usages pluriels : quels enjeux et défis pour l'analyse? *Innovations, 38*, 15–36.

Sibille, H. (2016). D'où vient, où va l'entrepreneuriat social en France ? Pour un dialogue France—Québec sur l'entrepreneuriat social. *Revue Interventions Économiques, 54*. https://journals.openedition.org/interventionseconomiques/2784#quotation.

Tchernonog, V., & Prouteau, L. (2019). *Le paysage associative français. Mesures et évolutions (third edition)*. Paris: Dalloz. https://www.associatheque.fr/fr/fichiers/etudes/paysage-associatif-francais.pdf.

Topalov, C. (Ed.). (1999). *Laboratoires du nouveau siècle : la nébuleuse réformatrice et ses réseaux en France. 1880–1914*. Paris: EHESS.

Vercamer, F. (2010). *Rapport sur l'Economie Sociale et Solidaire. L'économie sociale et solidaire. Entreprendre autrement pour la croissance et l'emploi*, http://www.vercamer.fr/pdf/2010/04/rapport-ess-f-vercamer.pdf

Chapter 8
Social Economy in Spain: Economic Crisis and Society

Millán Díaz-Foncea and Carmen Marcuello

Introduction

The social economy in Spain has a long tradition and a great capacity to adapt and create new models of organisations. Among its different actors we find some organisations of more than 100 years old and others very recent that have emerged to respond to the new challenges in a context of globalisation and uncertainty.

The social economy sector has a heterogeneous and diverse group of institutional participants that share internationally recognised principles and values in their genesis, development and management, among them, the primacy of social object over the capital, seeking after a common interest by means of economic activity and democratic governance. In the case of Spain, we define the social economy sector through the Spanish Law 5/2011 (Anon, n.d.-b). Spain was one of the pioneer countries to develop a general law about social economy in Europe[1].

During the last decades, and especially since the outbreak of the last economic crisis, the social economy has received a new portion of attention from the civil, academic and political fields. From the social point of view, it is evident that civil society continues to organise itself through the social economy in order to face new social challenges and satisfy needs that are not addressed by the states or capitalist private sector. In this way, new social economy practices continue to emerge in areas as diverse as social and labour integration, health and social care, migration,

---

[1] See Monzón and Chaves (2017). At this moment, Denmark, France, Greece and Portugal have their own social economy law. Countries with law drafts about social economy in Europe are Bulgaria and Italy.

M. Díaz-Foncea (✉) · C. Marcuello
GESES Research Group, Zaragoza University, Zaragoza, Spain
e-mail: millan@unizar.es; cmarcue@unizar.es

© Springer Nature Switzerland AG 2021
B. Gidron, A. Domaradzka (eds.), *The New Social and Impact Economy*,
Nonprofit and Civil Society Studies, https://doi.org/10.1007/978-3-030-68295-8_8

social finance, renewable energies, recycling and food distribution. For example, in December 2015, the Council of the European Commission published a report "Council conclusions on the promotion of the social economy as a key driver of economic and social development in Europe". This text stresses that the social economy "plays an important role in the transformation and evolution of contemporary societies, social welfare systems and economies and thus contributes substantially to the economic, social and human development of Europe, and is complementary to the social welfare systems existing in many Member States" (p. 1). In addition, this document underlines that, for several years, the European Commission has been paying a special attention to providing support to the social economy organisations.

The study published by the European Economic and Social Committee in 2017 and carried out by CIRIEC International on the dimensions of the social economy sector in Spain found the following figures concerning 2015: 1.4 million jobs, equivalent to 7.7% of employment; 190,000 organisations and companies; more than 8 million members; and nearly 1.3 million volunteers.

The social economy in Spain is defined by the Law 5/2011 on social economy approved by common consent of all political parties. Article 2 says that social economy is "all economic and business activities carried out in the private sphere by entities which, in accordance with the principles set out in the article 4, pursue either the collective interest of their members, or common economic or social interest, or both, are referred to as social economy". That is, the law itself states that there are principles and values that distinguish the social economy organisations and reflect their model of behaviour.

Article 4 of this law describes principles and values of the social economy in the following way: "These entities are governed by some guiding principles, among which the primacy of people and social purpose over capital; application of the results obtained from the economic activity employing the available resources; promotion of internal solidarity and solidarity with society that favours commitment to local development, equal opportunities, social cohesion, social integration of people at risk of social exclusion, creation of stable and quality employment and sustainability; independence from public authorities".

Likewise, Article 5 of the same law lists organisations that participate in the social economy: "cooperatives, mutual societies, foundations and associations that carry out economic activity, 'sociedades laborales',[2] Work Integration Social Enterprises, Special Employment Centres (CEE), fishermen's guilds, agricultural transformation companies and singular entities created by specific rules and principles established earlier in the article 2. Likewise, the entities which carry out economic and business activity, whose functioning rules are based on the principles listed in the previous article, and which are included in the catalogue of entities established in the article 6 of this Law, may form part of the social economy".

---

[2] "Sociedades laborales" are commercial companies whose shares belong mainly to the workers with permanent labour contracts, and to the capitalist partners whose share cannot exceed 33%.

During the COVID-19 pandemic in 2020, which was particularly harsh in the case of Spain, all these types of organisation have faced the effects of the health, economic and social crisis by redirecting and transforming their activity to keep companies and jobs active, as well as to continue offering their products and services, which are essential in many cases. This has been coupled with actions with a high level of commitment, solidarity and intercooperation that demonstrate the capacity of this business model focused on people.[3]

In recognition of the importance of the social economy in contributing to the remaining of the welfare system, in 2020 the Ministry of Labour and Social Economy was promoted with the arriving of the new Left Government. This Ministry, as previously, since 1997, the General Directorate for Self-Employment, Social Economy and Corporate Social Responsibility, has assumed, among other functions, the annually announcing grants for activities to promote the social economy and to cover the transaction costs of some organisations.

Another important initiative in this field is the Spanish Social Economy Strategy 2017–2020. It defines different actions that will contribute to the development of different initiatives at national and regional levels. However, at this moment the present document has not yet introduced a change in current policies and is awaiting development at national and regional levels with a new strategy for the period 2021–2024.

In this chapter the objective is to analyse the evolution in the last 20 years of the social economy in Spain and the new emerging forms. The structure of the chapter is the following: in the next section we present the historical evolution and the social economy framework; in the second section we analyse the impact of the 2008 crisis; in the third section we examine the evolution of the new social economy experiences; and in the fourth section we present the final conclusions.

National Context

Historical Evolution of the Social Economy Concept in Spain

In Spain, the emergence of the concept of social economy is linked to the previous cooperative, associative and foundational movements. The first cooperative practices date back to the nineteenth century. In the same period in the UK, Germany and Italy first cooperatives were emerging and gave rise to the modern cooperative movement. According to Salinas (2003), "from the 1930s onwards, cooperatives of all kinds (production, consumption, agriculture …) emerged in different parts of

---

[3] CEPES (2020) collects information on the actions and initiatives developed by social economy companies in all territories and from a wide range of economic sectors before the COVID-19. The report includes experiences from sectors such as industry, banking, health, insurance, hotels, electricity, food and agriculture, livestock, distribution, education, dependency, technology, construction, culture and leisure.

Spain, and even the subsequent developments of the 1812 Cadiz Constitution recognised the establishment of industries, including cooperatives"[4].

Furthermore, the associative, foundation and mutualism movements in Spain and internationally were the fundaments for the development of social economy concept. In the nineteenth century in Spain and in most of the countries emerged the experience of the first mutuals, associations and foundations and the laws that regulated this new phenomenon. Some previous legal references of the associations are found in the Constitution of 1869, in the Constitution of 1876 and in the Constitution of 1931, as well as in the Fuero de los Españoles, 1945, the first Law of Associations was approved in 1887. On the other hand the old Law of 20 June 1849, General of Charity, is undoubtedly one of the oldest provisions still formally in force in the Spanish system. It constitutes the starting point of the regulation on foundations. Finally, at the beginning of the nineteenth century, the Sociedades de Socorros Mutuos, friendly societies, have been an important mechanism for organising the world of work in contemporary societies, where expressions of solidarity, reciprocity, independence and democracy were beginning to emerge.

Thus, when Article 129.2 on the promotion of cooperativism was included in the Constitution in 1978, a fundamental historical phenomenon was recognised in order to explain the economic, political, social and cultural development in Spain. We can affirm that Article 129.2 of the Constitution has been the source of inspiration for the creation of a regulatory framework on cooperatives and social economy that is constantly being revised and adapted to the evolution of the Spanish society and economy. Furthermore, the promotion of the associations and foundations was included in the Constitution of 1978, art.: 9–2°, 22 y 48 and art. 34, respectively.

On the other hand, the Law 5/2011, of 29 of March, on the Social Economy in Spain also refers to this and other articles of the Constitution as the ones that inspired one of the pioneering laws at international level in which a reference to the social economy is made for the first time. Thus, in the explanatory statement of this law, it is expressly stated, "in Spain, it is of interest to highlight the legal substratum on which the entities of the social economy are based and which obtained the highest rank deriving from the articles of the Spanish Constitution". This is the case of several articles that refer, generically or specifically, to some of the social economy institutions, such as Article 1.1, Article 129.2 or the social equality clause itself in Article 9.2, and other specific articles such as 40, 41 and 47 of the constitutional text, which reflect strong roots of these organisations in Spain.

---

[4] According to Reventos (1960) and Chaves and Monzón (2008) the first production cooperative in Spain named Compañía Fabril de Tejedores was created in 1842, in Barcelona. In Valencia, in 1856, a production cooperative, La Proletaria, and the railway consumer cooperative, El Compañerismo (Herrero, 2015), were created, while in Andalusia, in 1870, the Association of Agricultural and Industrial Workers in Morón de la Frontera (Seville) emerged, and another one, Sociedad Cooperativa de Agricultores del Campo de la Verdad, was constituted in Cadiz in 1870. In Aragon, Casa de Ganaderos is a currently active livestock cooperative and one of the oldest companies in Spain dating back to the thirteenth century. However, the INE's Historical Yearbooks contain information on the Spanish cooperatives only starting from 1932 onwards, counting 592 cooperatives (all types included) registered in that year.

Finally, in the consolidated text of the Law 5/2011 on the social economy, it is noted, in the preamble, that "the historical framework of birth of the modern concept of Social Economy is built through the first cooperative, associative and mutualist practices that arise from the end of the 18th century and develop throughout the 19th century in several European countries (England, Italy, France and Spain). Based on this traditional concept of 19th century that encompasses cooperatives, mutual companies, foundations and associations, in different European states during the 1970s and 1980s one after another followed the declarations that characterise the identification of the social economy around different principles".

Legal Forms in Spanish Social Economy

The legal forms in Spanish social economy are defined in the Law 5/2011 on Social Economy, as well as on the conceptualisation and classification of the social economy by CIRIEC (International Centre for Research and Information on the Public, Social and Cooperative Economy); the following classification in the social economy sector in Spain has been proposed (Table 8.1):

The concept and characteristic of cooperatives, associations, foundations and mutual in Spain are very similar to those in other European countries. However, Sociedades Laborales, Special Employment Centres, Work Integration Social Enterprises and the Fishermen's Guilds (Cofradías de Pescadores) have special requirements:

"Sociedades Laborales": This type of organisations have shown a high potential for generating new companies. In them, the capital is owned mainly by the workers. The fact that the workers are partners favours self-motivation when facing projects. The minimum of workers required is three and the incorporation procedures are similar to those of any other company.

The Special Employment Centres (CEE): These are companies that combine economic viability and participation in the market with a social commitment towards groups with fewer opportunities in the labour market. Its workforce consists of the greatest proportion of people with disabilities (it cannot be less than 70% of the total number of workers). They develop a productive and competitive capacity that allows them to introduce their products on the market.

Work Integration Social Enterprises: These are defined as "learning structures, in commercial form, whose purpose is to enable access to employment for disadvantaged groups, through the development of a productive activity, for which a process of inclusion is designed, and at the same time through establishing conventional employment relationships". Its staff must have a percentage of workers in a situation of social inclusion, which depending on each autonomous community will range between 30% and 60%. 80% of the profit is reinvested in the company.

Table 8.1 Social economy operators by ESA 2010 institutional sector

ESA 2010 institutional sector			SE Enterprises and Microeconomic Organisations		
Market producers	Non-financial corporations (S11)		Cooperatives (workers, agri-food, consumers, education, transport, housing, healthcare, social, etc.) Social enterprises Other association-based enterprises Other private market producers (some associations and other legal persons) Non-profit institutions serving the social economy non-financial organisations Non-financial corporations controlled by the social economy		
	Financial corporations (S12)		Credit cooperatives Mutual insurance companies[a] and mutual provident societies Insurance cooperatives Non-profit institutions serving the social economy non-financial organisations		
	General government (S13)				
Non-market producers	Households (S14)[b]		Non-profit institutions serving households that are not large		
	Non-profit institutions serving households (S15)	Serving	Social action associations[c] Social action foundations[c] Other non-profit organisations (cultural, sports, etc.)	Serving	Households

[a]Excluding social security management organisations and, in general, mutual societies of which membership is obligatory and those controlled by non-social economy companies
[b]The household sector (S14) includes individual traders and general partnerships without legal personality that are market producers and belong to the social economy. It also includes non-profit organisations of limited size ("not very important") that are non-market producers and do form part of the social economy
[c]Non-profit organisations that are private non-market producers, with voluntary membership and participation, and strategic and functional autonomy, and whose purpose consists of achieving social welfare objectives through supplying or providing goods and social or merit services, free of charge or at prices which are not economically significant, to people or groups of people that are vulnerable, socially excluded or at risk of exclusion. These organisations form part of the Social Action Third Sector, which, obviously, forms part of the SE

The Fishermen's Guilds (Cofradías de Pescadores) are non-profit public corporations that represent economic interests of the owners of fishing vessels and of the workers in the extractive sector, acting as consultative and collaborative bodies of the competent administrations in matters of sea fishing and fishing sector management. Such guilds aim at satisfying needs and protecting interests of its members, with a commitment to contribute to the local development, social cohesion and sustainability.

The main organisations of the social economy sector in Spain are members of the CEPES-Spain (Confederación Empresarial de la Economía Social)[5] which is a general institution representing the entire sector. There are also sectorial confederations and platforms. Thus, the capacity of the SE to articulate its own support structure in order to promote itself at national and regional levels and to collaborate with the university and researchers should be especially highlighted. This capacity is probably the reason of the scale that the institutional recognition of the social economy reached in Spain.

On the other hand, the development of the research and training in the social economy field should be highlighted. Furthermore, CIRIEC-Spain, the International Centre for Research and Information on the Public, Social and Cooperative Economy created in 1985, is one of the more active research networks in the country joined with RedEnuies network. On the teaching side as well, master courses in the social economy have emerged in recent years at well-established university centres, most of which are linked to these networks, within the framework of the European Higher Education Area. An official doctorate programme on social economy (cooperatives and non-profits) exists at the University of Valencia (Spain).

Regarding the funding instruments for social economy organisations, Chaves and Monzón (2018a, 2018b) indicate that "since 2015, it has been the first country to have an Operative Programme co-financed by the European Social Fund, which specifically defines priorities for the promotion and development of the social economy in Spain during the period 2014–2020. This Operative Programme is called 'Social Inclusion and Social Economy' (POISES) and is one of the instruments in the European structural and investment funds (IEE Funds) which the Spanish state has designed to help reach the targets set by the Europe 2020 strategy. The Government of Spain has decided to prioritize the social economy in this Operative Programme and implement it in partnership with social economy and third sector platforms to increase its effectiveness". The POISES programme has a budget of EUR 800 million for the period 2014–2020. The Spanish Social Economy Employers' Confederation (CEPES), as top umbrella representative organisation of the Spanish social economy, has been declared by the government as an intermediate body responsible for managing and funding some of the measures and objectives set out in the POISES programme to support the social economy.

Finally, Chaves and Monzón (2018a, 2018b) point out that Spain, as well as other European countries, has a "percentage tax designation mechanism" as a financial support tool for non-profit/non-governmental organisations. The percentage designation mechanism allocates state resources—a percentage of income tax—to public benefit purposes in a decentralised manner: taxpayers designate a part of their paid income tax to public benefit purposes (mainly to civil society organisations). This mechanism should not be considered a "percentage philanthropy" and the allocated resources are not donations, as it is not compulsory, altruistic giving;

---

[5] CEPES-España https://www.cepes.es/principal/socios_miembros y https://www.ciriec.es

instead the resources used are not private resources and it is only available to taxpayers".[6]

The Welfare System and Its Link to the Social Economy

Social economy entities play a key role in social cohesion, local and territorial development, innovation and employment in Spain (Chaves & Monzón, 2008; Urra, 2010; Vázquez, Albarrán, & Salinas Ramos, 2013; among others). According to Monzón and Chaves (2012) "the main efforts made by the Social Economy as a provider of social welfare goods and services have been concentrated mainly in the areas of labour and social integration, social services and community care".

There are many different services offered by the social economy in Spain, but the most relevant are the following (Vázquez et al., 2013):

Firstly, social and healthcare services for the elderly and people with disabilities: From the quantitative point of view and according to Martínez et al. (2013) the specialisation of social economy entities in the provision of services related to the area of care for dependency (old age and disability) is relatively significant, representing 10% of the total number of companies offering this type of services in 2010, and observing a significant growth trend.

Secondly, child and youth care and protection services, with special attention to people whose socio-family environment is characterised by a high social risk: These services include residential or non-residential care centres, prevention, assistance and reintegration centres for young people who are maladjusted or at risk of social exclusion, counselling programmes, prevention and child protection, etc.

Thirdly, healthcare and educational services: The generalisation of concert systems and the expansion of the delegated management of public centres in the educational and health fields have given rise to new opportunities for the social economy to participate in the production of these preferential goods. In 2010, social economy entities represented around 9% of all companies whose economic activity is linked to education, with a particularly notable presence in infant education (14%) and primary education (13%) (Martínez et al., 2013).

Finally, other services of social interest, such as prevention and attention to drug addiction; social reintegration of prisoners, drug addicts, etc.; and promotion of the social integration of marginal groups (ethnic minorities, refugees, etc.).

---

[6] One special case in Spain is the case of National Organisation of Spanish Blind People (ONCE). Part of the public lottery monopoly has been given to the ONCE, one of the biggest social economy entities in the country. A state regulation authorised it to sell lottery tickets for the blind so that its members could earn a living. The profits obtained must be used for integrating disadvantaged people into the labour market and offering them social services. Over the last three decades, ONCE has created a large business group, Ilunion, following mergers. In 2016, ONCE had 72,256 members, most of them blind people. In 2016, a total of 68,500 workers were employed by all of the entities linked to ONCE, 57% of which were people with disabilities. ONCE earmarks more than EUR 230 million a year for social activities (Chaves and Monzón, 2018).

It should be noted that during the confinement experienced in Spain between March and June 2020, other services emerged such as the provision of food to the population, which in Spain depends to a large extent on the agricultural cooperatives, as well as a multitude of other solidarity initiatives like donations, volunteer work and other social action activities (CEPES, 2020), which demonstrated the importance of social economy entities to enable an adequate level of well-being for society.

New Social Economy in Spain

Impact of the 2008 Crisis on Spanish Economy and Society

The effects of economic crisis of 2008 had a relevant influence in the society and the general economy. However, 10 years prior to the crisis a polarised society had been created and there had already been a structural exclusion within the so-called society of success in Spain. More than 16% of the population were experiencing a deep social exclusion.[7]

The onset of the crisis revealed weaknesses in the public protection mechanisms while dealing with the consequences of the crisis. A significant number of households were facing job loss, reduced income, accumulation of debts and inability to meet the most basic needs. These effects were multiplied due to the cuts in public policies. According to the FOESSA (2019) report, in just 6 years from 2007 to 2013, the number of socially excluded people in Spain went from 7.4 million to 11.8 million.

The crisis produced an immediate destructive impact on the job market. The highest unemployment rate was 26.09% in 2013 and in the case of young people (age 20–24) was 51.78%.[8] The inertia of Mr. Zapatero's government aggravated the situation and the PP government led by Mr. Rajoy, along with the enforcements coming from the European Union, created a moment of great negative impact, uncertainty and despair in the Spanish society. It was not only an economic and financial crisis, but everything that provided a minimum of security to the people was disappearing.

However, the recovery that began in 2014 has revealed, according to FOESSA (2019), clear but sustained improvements on weak bases and worrying worsening among the poorest which only encourage us to redouble our efforts. The number of people and households in a situation of social integration at the end of this cycle has increased. However, the conditions of a considerable group of them are characterised by such precariousness that the probability of an upcoming crisis affecting them quickly is high. There is also a large group of socially excluded people that

---

[7] VI FOESSA Report of 2008
[8] INE Instituto Nacional de Estadística

confirms the countercyclical nature of poverty and social exclusion. There are currently 8.6 million people in the situation of social exclusion, 1.2 million more than in 2007. There is a 12% increase in the global social exclusion with respect to the beginning of the cycle and a 40% increase in the severe social exclusion, in which 4.1 million people live in 1.5 million households. The recovery continues not reaching people and households in the situation of exclusion and, moreover, the most critical cases of exclusion are constantly increasing.

The situation caused by the multidimensional effects of the crisis has led to the delegitimisation of corporations and other economic institutions by being perceived as the cause and beneficiaries of the crisis: for example, an important contrast was observed between the rescue of Spanish banks and the abandonment of people affected by the crisis through evictions, energy poverty, etc.

As a response, on May 15, 2011, the so-called 15-M Movement or Movement of the Indignants emerged in Spain. Against the economic crisis, a series of peaceful protests began throughout the country appealing to a more participatory democracy and measures aimed at an improvement of the political system. The movement was born on social networks and Internet proving to have an unexpected convening power. In most of Spanish cities and abroad, camps were organised in squares where debates were held, and popular assemblies and various acts of protest were open to anyone who wanted to participate. The image of the Puerta del Sol campsite in Madrid, which became the symbol of protest, went around the world. The movement gave rise to various platforms and collectives that continue their work of protest until now.

Various waves and social movements of people affected by different policies and crisis effects originated from the 15-M. An important moment in February 2013 was when up to ten different tides took place, among which White Wave: in defence of public health and against privatisation; Multicolour Wave: a coordinator of tides, 15-M assemblies and social collectives that have emerged in some locations; Orange Wave: in defence of social services; and Green Wave: for public education. The 15-M Movement ended up being institutionalised and founding the party PODEMOS. We can see that it is the result of the integration of different waves, left-wing political parties and other social movements. One of the most powerful was the Platform of the Affected by the Mortgages (Plataforma de Afectados por las Hipotecas: https://afectadosporlahipoteca.com/). Furthermore, the REAS Network and social and solidarity network of organisations were very active in this period. All these movements and social and solidarity organisations share some ideas and values: strengthening the democracy system, protecting the welfare system and taking care of the vulnerable population.

On the other hand, the situation of corruption, especially in the PP, discontent with the traditional parties[9] and uncertainty about socio-economic situation have been making the party CIUDADANOS more and more prominent in the political

---

[9] Another new party which emerges against the discontent with PP right traditional party is VOX, with an ultra-right profile and tendency to gather more and more supporters for the 2019 national elections.

agenda. It proposes a liberal right-wing perspective promoting rights of individual and market relationships as key issues.

To sum up, we can affirm that the development of Spanish society, since the crisis has started, as well as the structural problems in economic, social, cultural and political life, has fragmented and polarised the society providing more extreme identities for part of the population, both to the left and to the right of the political spectrum. Meanwhile, the living conditions of the population as reported by FOESSA, 2019, continue to embed greater problems of exclusion and deterioration than before the crisis. This situation has been increased during the COVID-19 pandemic Spain experiences in 2020.

New Forms of Social Economy

During the first decades of the twenty-first century, the social economy in Spain has undergone an unprecedented process of consolidation and institutionalisation. Some organisations of the social economy, like REAS, the Work Integration Social Enterprises (FAEDEEI), the platforms of handicapped people, CEPES and new platforms, were very active in order to deal with the serious problems of social exclusion and deterioration that were emerging and increased during the crisis. Background trends of these developing activities have emerged along with new arising social economy practices.

Firstly, there is an observable evolution in the traditional market producers of the social economy (cooperatives, mutual societies, employee-owned companies, social enterprises, among others), mainly in cooperatives, to the point where they become a motor for social innovation in sustaining the employment and substituting the public services (FAECTA, 2014).

In this sense, new legal forms of cooperatives have been developed. These have a very broad sectoral approach, and in all of them there is a hybridisation, either between the cooperative sphere and that of social action (social initiative co-op), between the public and collective spheres (public service co-op), as collective support to autonomous work (business impulse co-op) or between the educational sphere and business world (co-op June). The more relevant examples are the following[10]:

Social Initiative Cooperatives: They are non-profit cooperatives whose social purpose is (1) health, educational, cultural or other activities of social nature, or (2) any economic activity aiming at integrating socially excluded people into the labour market and, in general, satisfying social needs not met by the market (Art. 106, Law on Cooperatives). They emerged in social and health services, education

---

[10] Business Cases of Business Impulse Coop. (FAECTA, 2014). Junior Cooperatives (Gizartelan, 2016).

mainly, but also professional activities, food, etc. (TIEBEL, S. Coop. de Iniciativa Social[11], ECO-QUEREMOS S. Coop. de Iniciativa Social[12]).

Public Service Cooperatives: They are a special type of cooperatives that enable local and regional administrations to participate and aim at providing quality public services (Art. 101 of Decree 123/2014 of the Junta de Andalucía). They are specialised in activities of common interest, and management of public patrimony or communal services. Currently, they are present only in Andalusia and Valencian Community.

Business Impulse Cooperatives: This type of cooperative works as an umbrella organisation channelling the entrepreneurial initiative of its members and allowing pilot projects to develop (Art. 81 of Decree 123/2014 of the Regional Government of Andalusia). They appear in the fields of entrepreneurship, cultural projects and journalism. Examples are Smart-Ibérica, S. Coop. de Impulso Empresarial,[13] that focuses on creative and cultural projects and Se buscan periodistas-Comunicadores Asociados SBP-CA, S. Coop. de Impulso Empresarial,[14] that focuses on communication and journalism.

Junior Cooperatives: These cooperatives are promoted by students, and work towards the application of skills and knowledge acquired in the educational centres in which they are enrolled, by developing economic activities aimed at producing goods or providing services (Art. 132, Basque Cooperatives Act). They are present only in the Basque Country.

Likewise, throughout the twenty-first century, business structures that were covering social and labour necessities since the 1980s have been consolidated. This is the case of the Work Integration Social Enterprises, commercial organisations with a special qualification when incorporating the management itineraries of social and labour inclusion to the productive process of the enterprise. In 2007, the Law 44/2007 was enacted to regulate the system of these organisations, creating this same year the Federation of Business Associations of Work Integration Social Enterprises (FAEDEI), which comprises regional associations of these organisations. Since then, these organisations have been expanding throughout the economic sectors, mainly in waste treatment, food and beverage services, retail trade, professional gardening and cleaning services.

Secondly, among non-market producers (social initiative associations and foundations), there has been a rapprochement of these third-sector entities towards the market. The disability sector has undergone a process similar to that of the Work Integration Social Enterprises, with a rapid development linked to the support of the public administration that addressed the promotion of the employability of disabled people. This process has led to the creation of "Groups of Social Enterprises" that bring together Special Employment Centres. The latter have been created around a

---

[11] https://tiebelcooperativa.com/

[12] http://www.ecoqueremos.com/

[13] https://smart-ib.coop/

[14] http://sebuscanperiodistas.com/

foundation or association dedicated to social insertion and have reached a size of a large company (more than 250 employees).

A paradigmatic case in this sense is the ILUNION Business Group (https://www. ilunion.com/es), a business project of the ONCE and its Foundation, born as a representative organisation of blind people in Spain and which has extended its work to the rest of disabled people in the country. It is made up of five divisions that develop more than 50 business lines: business services, healthcare, tourism, marketing and consultancy, serving clients in the hotel, retail, energy, transport, logistics, hospitality, industrial, pharmaceutical, education, banking, insurance and telecommunications sectors. In 2017, 35,000 people were employed, 40% of whom were disabled, against a turnover of 850 million euros.

These forms of social economy that emerged in the first decades of the twenty-first century have been accepted by the traditional social economy approach without any dissonance. However, there are other forms of social economy that have raised a revisionist approach to this sector in two ways: on the one hand, deepening the values and principles of the social economy as do the movements of solidarity economy, and on the other hand, through the development of the concept of social enterprises and social entrepreneurship, beyond the traditional forms.

As to the solidarity economy movements, they introduce an impulse towards social transformation provided by social economy institutions if its governing values and principles are respected. To this end, they are organised into broad networks that bring together various stakeholders whose objective is a conscious search of the principles and values of the social economy. One of the most representative networks is the alternative and solidarity economy network—REAS Network of Networks (https://www.economiasolidaria.org/). It brings together 14 territorial networks (all the autonomous communities, except Asturias, Cantabria and Castilla-La Mancha) and four sectorial networks (Unión Renovables—renewable energy cooperatives; the Spanish Association of Social and Solidarity Economy Recyclers—recycling; the State Fair Trade Coordinator—development cooperation; and the Ethical Finance Table—ethical credit cooperatives and cooperative banks), which seek to respond to the dehumanisation of the economy, deterioration of the environment and loss of social values.

Thus, these organisations go beyond the recognition of the positive externalities of the social economy as a consequence of its institutional structure and the daily activity carried out by these actors. Solidarity economy is producing a positive impact (socially just and ecologically sustainable) on the economic sectors and tends to imply traditional legal forms of social economy (mainly associations and cooperatives). However, they also incorporate others, such as autonomous individuals, capitalist commercial societies and even informal models of organisation, as long as their work is based on the principles and values of the social economy and participation in networks together with other organisations.

As a result of collaboration in networks innovative collective projects arise such as social markets, renewable energy cooperatives, promotion of ethical finance, collective housing or cooperative supermarkets. Table 8.2 presents these activity projects.

Table 8.2 Innovative collective projects related to the solidarity-based economy

Projects	Description	Solidarity-based economy cases
Social markets	Network of production, distribution and consumption of goods and services with ethical, democratic, ecological and solidarity criteria, constituted by companies and entities of the social and solidarity economy together with individual and collective consumers Its objective is to interconnect different economic initiatives that we promote in a single economic circuit consistent with the values we share, and to decouple as much as possible the solidarity economy from the capitalist economy	Commission of Social Market Networks of the Alternative and Solidarity Economy Association REAS brings together territorial associations, representatives of strategic sectors (Fiare Banca Ética, Ethical and Solidarity Insurance CAES, Unión Renovables—Energy—and Coop57 Ethical Financing Services) and relevant entities in the field of responsible consumption (Ecologistas en Acción and Periódico El Salto) https://www.mercadosocial.net/ Cooperativa de Mercado Social MESCoop Aragón: https://mercadosocialaragon.net/
Renewable energy cooperatives	A business model where citizens jointly own renewable energy or participate in energy efficiency projects: community energy initiatives	SOM ENERGIA: National https://www.somenergia.coop/ GOIENER: Basque Country https://www.goiener.com/
Ethical finances	Projects that make economic profitability compatible with human rights and environment, exclusively investing in projects with an added value for society from a social, environmental, cultural, educational and other points of view, making it easier for clients to know where their savings are invested Include banking sector tools, insurance and alternatives to banking services	COOP57, Cooperativa de Servicios Financieros Éticos: National http://coop57.coop/ FIARE, Banco Ético Cooperativo: National https://www.fiarebancaetica.coop/ CAES, cooperación para el aseguramiento ético y solidario: National http://caes.coop/
Collective housing cooperatives	Form of housing where a person becomes a member of an association and receives the right to use an apartment owned by the association. Therefore you do not buy the property itself, but you buy the right to use a part of the property Blocking the possibility of speculation is the main virtue of the model, as well as the creation of community around it.	It has a long tradition in Denmark and Uruguay. In Spain, it is currently emerging. Some of the cases are: LA BORDA: Barcelona http://www.laborda.coop/es/ SOSTRECIVIC: Barcelona https://sostrecivic.coop/ ENTREPATIOS: Madrid https://www.entrepatios.org/

(continued)

Table 8.2 (continued)

Projects	Description	Solidarity-based economy cases
Cooperative supermarkets	A model that combines the traditional supermarket with the developing agroecological consumer cooperatives. On the one hand, it works as a supermarket with an extensive range of items (not only food), long opening hours and affordable prices. On the other hand, it is cooperative and social, offering products of proximity, sustainability and health, with a direct, fair and trusting relationship with suppliers, without profit motive, and with a democratic, participative and transparent management The shareholders must dedicate working hours along with their main job	LANDARE: Navarra https://www.landare.org/ BIO ALAI: Vitoria http://www.bioalai.org/ Som Alimentació: Valencia https://somalimentacio.com/

Source: Own Elaboration

These innovative projects, mainly the Social Market project and other solidarity economy initiatives, use the sieve of social economy principles in their economic activity. For this purpose, they developed an instrument for evaluating and measuring quality and ethical behaviour known as the "Social Balance".[15]

On the other hand, there has been advancement in the concept of social enterprises. This evolution has been guided by a blackout experienced during a long period of the last decades in the European Commission's political agenda on the legal forms of the social economy and its reduction to the narrow scope of social enterprises, related to the anti-poverty initiatives and social and labour inclusion, on which various legislative acts were elaborated and transferred to the Spanish national level. Likewise, the Anglo-Saxon approach to view social enterprise as a company with a social mindset has been introduced in Spain, focusing on the organisations of social innovation and on the spheres of the traditional entrepreneurship, which addresses social sector and social entrepreneurship. These revisionist proposals of the social economy model give emphasis to the social mission of companies, ignoring the sense that their business values and principles provide, as well as the models of participatory and collective governance proposed by the social economy.

---

[15] More information about "Social Balance" can be found on the following websites: https://mercadosocialaragon.net/balancesocial/, https://madrid.mercadosocial.net/que-es-el-balance-social/, or http://xes.cat/es/comisiones/balance-social/

Development of New Frameworks Combining Business with Social Orientations

Combination of business with social orientations is an international process that had an impact in Spain as well. The development of these new frameworks delves in different dynamics related with the phenomena of social enterprises, social entrepreneurship and social entrepreneurs. Defourny and Nyssens (2008, 2014, 2015) compare the different schools of thought about the emergence of social enterprises in various contexts, especially in the USA and Europe. They distinguished between "earned income" school of thought, "social innovation" school of thought mostly developed in the USA and Anglo-Saxon countries and social economy school mostly developed in European countries. Regarding the proposal of Defourny and Nyssens in the previous section we presented the new forms based on social economy and in this section we describe the new business with social orientations that emerged in Spain.

Firstly, we identify the rapprochement of the commercial and market organisations with the social sphere that has taken place, both through the discovery of "the social" as a new business niche and through the attention paid to the sectors left uncovered or abandoned by the state.

Traditional capitalism projects have been discovered in areas such as social inclusion, education, social services or dependence, among others, as market niches. This is the case of the development of the Special Employment Centres (CEE), which were born as a scope of aiming at labour inclusion of people with disabilities, by means of any business activity, and therefore obtaining significant tax advantages. In the light of these tax advantages, for many traditional capitalist companies the employment of people with disabilities started to become equal to benefits. This led to the emergence of the Social Initiative CEE, non-profit and managed by foundations or associations, and explicitly involved in the social economy, by differentiating themselves from for-profit CEE, managed by capitalist companies. One of such examples is an organisation of both CEE models around the Spanish Business Federation of Associations of Special Employment Centres, FEACEM (non-profit CEE),[16] and the National Confederation of Special Employment Centres, CONACEE (CEE in general, mainly including those for profit).[17]

Secondly, likewise the reduction of the state's social security programme allowed the traditional companies to step in and meet these unaddressed social needs. In this way, some of the frameworks of new generation in Spain are "social entrepreneurship" and "social innovation", emerged in 2005 along with the establishment of the Ashoka Foundation, and subsequently developed with other actors such as the B-Corp movement and the socialenterprise.es website. These actors played a role of a reference of an imaginary collective imagination of the community created around this vision on social enterprises in Spain. This community arises informally from

---

[16] More info about FEACEM is available at http://www.feacem.es/

[17] More info about CONACEE is available at http://conacee.org/

the local and separate initiatives, but with its own work agenda and discourses related to the relationship between social motivations and business. This differs from the traditional social economy communities that have a sharper focus on an individual, social mission of businesses and without considering the governance.

The third dynamics would be the process of bringing the social sphere closer to the market, reflected in the search of new sources of income and funding for social organisations. During the last decades, new entities have emerged enabling impact investments and other arising niches of responsible investment. These entities have a financial capacity to influence social organisations, adapting them to their own mechanisms, but in the end they rarely succeed in transforming business models of true social economy nature. The organisations that stand out in this field are La Caixa Foundation,[18] one of the largest donors to the social initiative organisations, or La Bolsa Social,[19] involved in the equity crowdfunding of social entrepreneurship.

The rapprochement between the social sphere and the market is also promoted by the initiatives of the high education sector, which reinforce the symbols and concepts of the "social entrepreneurship" and "social innovation". Some examples in this sense are BBVA Momentum[20] and ESADE's Institute for Social Innovation.[21]

These organisations that come from the specific field of social entrepreneurship and social innovation, which use the term "social enterprise", are still evolving and do not have commonly recognised organisational structures. This lack of institutionalisation occurs at least formally, since at the informal level there are websites[22] and organisations (Ashoka Spain, BBVA, ESADE …) that serve as a pole of attraction for this type of community. In this sense, it should be noted that these poles of attraction are more linked to some financially empowered superstructures that propose as a framework of action the attention to the accomplishment of the social mission and an arrangement than on a set of entities with intrinsic social economy principles and values, coordinated between them to strengthen and extend their impact in this area. The agents involved in the field of social entrepreneurship emanate from a culture of business efficiency, search of business and funding opportunities and attainment of economic objectives rather than from the traditional social field. This implies less incentives to the coordination between the organisations in

---

[18] More info is available at https://obrasociallacaixa.org/es/

[19] More info is available at https://www.bolsasocial.com/

[20] BBVA Momentum is a 5-month programme that includes training, strategic accompaniment, financing, collaboration, networking, visibility … which enables social businesses to grow and have a positive impact on a higher number of lives. More information at https://www.momentum.bbva.com/

[21] The Institute for Social Innovation is one of the knowledge units of the ESADE Business School whose mission is to develop the capacities of individuals and organisations in business and non-profit sectors, and to strengthen their activities and their contribution to a more sustainable and fairer world. More information at https://www.esade.edu/es/profesorado-investigacion/investigacion/unidades-conocimiento/instituto-innovacion-social.

[22] Some references are https://www.corresponsables.com/, https://socialenterprise.es/ and https://emprendedorsocial.org/.

this field and to the maintenance of their activity. The latter can switch the focus if another more appealing pole of attraction appears with no attention to the social mission of enterprises. One of such examples of lack of interest accompanied by the shortage of economic support observed between 2008 and 2014 during the period of economic crisis regards corporate social responsibility.

New Hybrid Funding Instruments

According to Díaz-Foncea and Marcuello (2016) in Spain different new actors appear related to the new social economy and social enterprises. There are different funding instruments promoted by public and private organisations: (1) Social economy sector: some of these new instruments are undertaken mainly by the social and solidarity economy sector (Coop57 and Fiare), and ethical banking sector (Triodos Bank). (2) Social and impact investing: other private initiatives are the Creas Foundation or the Isis Foundation focused on social investment or impact investment, and traditional banks like CAIXA Bank and BBVA Bank.

In the first case, social economy sector, we observe two main trends. One is the traditional social economy banks. They have a long-standing tradition or are associated with other social economy organisations. Social economy traditional banks are focused on social projects and initiatives from social enterprises, mainly in the local area. The banking conditions of social economy banks are sometimes better than those of private banks because they understand better the characteristics and dynamics of the social sector. Furthermore, in the social and solidarity economy sector two main organisations, Coop57 and Fiare, more related with the new social economy got promoted and spread in the last years.

In the second case, the new initiatives of social investment and impact investment, Díaz-Foncea and Marcuello (2016) consider that "the recent developments observed in the field of finance for social enterprises, the current economic situation in Spain has led to a shift in the attitude of Spanish social impact investors and private providers of financing (CREAS, ISIS, Caixa and BBVA). There is a change in their interest from social enterprises acting in the fields of international cooperation and environmental issues towards social enterprises focusing on groups at risk, such as the unemployed or disabled. Despite being an incipient field, impact investments have seen increasing interest in recent years. This is illustrated in the rising popularity of cases where: (1) investment funds provide seed capital for social and environmental activities; (2) clients of private banks seek investment with a return in social or environmental terms; (3) private foundations seek to contribute to the mission through investment rather than philanthropy".

Regarding the philanthropy sector, there are few traditions in Spain. Some years ago, the Spanish Government was studying the promotion of a Law of Donors and Sponsors to make it more attractive to donate to foundations and non-profit organisations by providing tax incentives. The Law is also designed to help social enterprises secure better financial resources. However, the Law has suffered several delays, and there is currently no concrete date for it to be brought into force.

Finally, there are different initiatives to create tools for measuring the social impact of activities of social economy organisations. The objective is to increase the investing attractiveness of social economy organisations to the potential. For example, the Cluster of Social Impact of Forética was created in 2018 with the leadership of Endesa, Grupo Cooperativo Cajamar, Ibercaja and ILUNION together with 56 other large companies committed to the development and improvement of social impact. Furthermore, social impact is also being integrated into public procurement and the concession and financing of large investment projects. The public administration is thus trying to have greater traceability of its projects, promote their social value and contribute to the improvement of impacts. The companies subject to this type of operation are the ones that, for the time being, are leading the efforts to develop increasingly advanced measurement models and metrics.

Conclusions

The social economy in the first two decades of the twenty-first century has undergone a notable evolution in Spain, either because of the growth of organisations, which have consolidated the existing coordination and collaboration structures; or because of the long-lasting institutional processes in the area of social needs coverage (such as Work Integration Social Enterprises); or because of the new forms that were created to cover other nascent needs (new types of cooperatives).

In this context, the revisionist trends within the social economy have arisen and expanded its traditional framework, incorporating new discourse nuances and behaviours of the traditional social economy organisations. The solidarity economy has been based on deepening the application of the principles and values that are presumed to pertain to social organisations and on emphasising social transformation and construction of viable economic alternatives to the capitalist market. On the other hand, social entrepreneurship and social innovation suggest that companies can be a tool for addressing social and environmental problems, balancing their social and economic missions. Thus, they expand the frontiers of the social economy, incorporating a hybrid enterprise model using market mechanisms to change the world and paying less attention to the legal form which is important for the traditional social economy framework.

Such development and consolidation of social economy organisations, taken in a broad sense, have led to the creation of coordination structures such as CEPES-Spain and the Third Sector Platform as well as organisational tools for meetings such as the 2020 World Social Forum of Transforming Economies. The strategy developed by CEPES-Spain[23] from the social economy sector moves towards an intensified collaboration between these dimensions, as there are multiple niches that

---

[23] https://www.cepes.es/noticias/581_oit-ministerio-trabajo-espana-cepes-refuerzan-papel-central-economia-social-futuro-trabajo

can be covered by exploiting strengths of the corresponding actors. Such niches include social challenges such as depopulation in rural areas, development of digital economy initiatives (new for all social economy organisations), business areas in need of large investments or aggregation of demand like in telecommunications or others. Another new area of development of the sector is the commitment with the Sustainable Development Goals.

Furthermore, CEPES-Spain is working on increasing social visibility of the sector and its recognition as a political mediator in order to reach more favourable public policies for social and solidarity economy organisations as a whole. A key area in case of public policies must derive from the development of a responsible public procurement that must consolidate the progress already made with the enactment of the new Public Sector Contracts Act in 2017. The latter incorporates social and environmental criteria in the contract documents, surpassing the minimum price criterion that until now made it difficult to use this consumption capacity of the public administration (which represents about 20% of GDP in Spain) to advance in the consolidation of the social economy. This will be a key field to define organisational models of the new social economy enabling more opportunities for development and mediating by the political parties of national, regional and local governments that will have to specify the opportunities of the social economy in public procurement.

Summing up, there is a certainty that the social economy, new and traditional, is working especially in the areas of social exclusion, rural development and care and is emerging in new fields in urban context. On the one hand, as explained in the chapter, social needs in Spain have continued to grow during this period, more during the COVID-19 pandemic; on the other hand, the transformation of society to solve the root causes of these social needs is a long-standing process and requires innovative projects that might provide the alternatives. The new social economy is deepening the values and principles of the social economy as do the movements of social and solidarity economy: democracy, solidarity, cooperation, mutual support and non-profit objectives.

References

Anon   (n.d.-a).   https://orbi.uliege.be/bitstream/2268/180666/1/EMES%20WP%2012_03%20 JD%20MN.pdf

Anon (n.d.-b). Law 5/2011, on March 29, Social Economy. from https://www.boe.es/boe/ dias/2011/03/30/pdfs/BOE-A-2011-5708.pdf

CEPES (2020). Actuaciones e Iniciativas de las Empresas de las Empresas de Economía Social ante el COVID-19. from https://www.cepes.es/documentacion/559

Chaves and Monzón (2018b). Best practices in public policies regarding the European Social Economy post the economic crisis, European Economic and Social Committee, https://www. eesc.europa.eu/sites/default/files/files/qe-04-18-002-en-n.pdf

Chaves, R. and Monzón, J. L. (2008): The Social Economy in the European Union. Informe elaborado para el Comité Económico y Social Europeo. Centro Internacional de Investigación e

Información sobre la Economía Pública, Social y Cooperativa (CIRIEC). from https://www.eesc.europa.eu/resources/docs/qe-30-12-790-es-c.pdf

Chaves, R., y Monzón, J. L. (2018a). La economía social ante los paradigmas económicos emergentes: innovación social, economía colaborativa, economía circular, responsabilidad social empresarial, economía del bien común, empresa social y economía solidaria. CIRIEC-España Revista de Economía Pública, Social y Cooperativa, 93: 5–50.

CIRIEC-International. (2000). *The enterprises and organizations of the third system: A strategic challenge for employment.* Liege: CIRIEC – Directorate General V of the European Union.

CIRIEC (2017), Recent evolutions of the Social Economy in the European Union, European Economic and Social Committee, European Union, http://www.ciriec.uliege.be/wp-content/uploads/2017/10/RecentEvolutionsSEinEU_Study2017.pdf

Clemente, S., García, A. and Salobral, N. (2012). Estrategias y Políticas de Conciliación en las Empresas de Economía Social, favorecedoras de la igualdad de oportunidades laborales entre mujeres y hombres. Diagnóstico participativo. from https://www.economiasolidaria.org/reas-red-de-redes-de-economia-alternativa-y-solidaria/biblioteca/sostevidavilidad-una-guia-para-el

Colaborabora (2018). Soste[vida]vilidad: una guía para el emprendimiento con la vida en el centro. from https://www.economiasolidaria.org/biblioteca/estrategias-de-corresponsabilidad-en-las-cooperativas-para-no-dejarnos-la-piel

Comisión Europea (2016). Social enterprises and the social economy going forward. Expert Group on Social Entrepreneurship. https://ec.europa.eu/growth/content/social-enterprises-and-social-economy-going-forward-0_en.

Defourny, J., Nyssens, M. (2008). Social enterprise in Europe: recent trends and developments. EMES European Research Network Working Paper, Brussels WP no. 08/01 https://orbi.uliege.be/bitstream/2268/11568/1/WP_08_01_SE_WEB.pdf

Defourny, J., & Nyssens, M. (2014). The EMES approach of social enterprise in a comparative perspective. EMES European Research Network Working Paper, Brussels WP WP no. 12/03 https://orbi.uliege.be/bitstream/2268/180666/1/EMES%20WP%2012_03%20JD%20MN.pdf

Defourny, J., & Nyssens, M. (2015). Fundamentals for an International Typology of Social Enterprise Models, ICSEM Working Paper no. 33 Series: Comparing Social Enterprise Models Worldwide. http://www.iap-socent.be/sites/default/files/Typology%20-%20Defourny%20%26%20Nyssens_0.pdf

Díaz Foncea, M., (Coord). (2017). Social Enterprise in Spain: A Diversity of Roots and a Proposal of Models ICSEM Working Papers 29, 105496 (2017), [53 pp.]

Díaz-Foncea, M., & Marcuello, C. (2012). Social enterprises and social markets: Models and new trends. *Service Business, 6*(1), 61–83.

Díaz-Foncea, M. and Marcuello, C. (2016). Social enterprises and their eco-systems: A European mapping report. Updated country report: Spain. European Commission, Directorate-General for Employment, Social Affairs and Inclusion, 2016.

FAECTA (2014). La innovación social y las cooperativas: el impacto social de las cooperativas y experiencias innovadoras socialmente. Federación Andaluza de Cooperativas de Trabajo Asociado. from https://www.faecta.coop/doc/faecta_informe_innovacion_social_cooperativismo.pdf

FOESSA (2019). VIII Informe FOESSA: La exclusión social se enquista en una sociedad cada vez más desvinculada. Cáritas Española. from https://www.foessa.es/blog/viii-informe-foessa-presentacion/

Gizartelan (2016). Junio Cooperativas. Programa de Reactivación de Empleo 2013–2016. from http://www.gizartelan.ejgv.euskadi.eus/contenidos/noticia/junior_cooperativas/es_jun_coop/adjuntos/JUNIOR%20COOP%2020130704%20cas.pdf

Herrero, M. (2015). Las empresas sociales: un grupo en expansión en el ámbito de la Economía Social. Identificación y análisis de las características identitarias de la empresa social europea y su aplicación a la realidad de los Centros Especiales de Empleo de la economía española. Doctoral Dissertation at the Universidad de Valencia (Spain). from http://roderic.uv.es/handle/10550/52971

Martínez, M. I., et al. (2013). *El impacto socioeconómico de las entidades de economía social.* Madrid: Fundación Escuela de Organización Industrial.

Monzón, J. L. (2003). El cooperativismo en la historia de la literatura económica. *CIRIEC-España, Revista de Economía Pública, Social y Cooperativa, 44,* 9–32.

Monzón, J. L. and Chaves, R. (2012). The Social Economy in the European Union, European Economic and Social Committee, and CIRIEC-International.

Monzón, J. L. y Chaves, R. (2017). Recent evolutions of the social economy in the European Union. European Economic and Social Committee, European Union, Brussels. https://www.eesc.europa.eu/sites/default/files/files/qe-04-17-875-en-n.pdf.

REAS Euskadi (2018). Manual de cultivo de los cuidados. from https://www.economiasolidaria.org/reas-red-de-redes-de-economia-alternativa-y-solidaria/biblioteca/manual-de-cultivo-de-los-cuidados

Reventos, J. (1960). *El movimiento cooperativo en España.* Barcelona: Editorial Ariel.

Salinas Ramos, F. (2003): Economía Social una forma diferente de hacer empresa, Sociedad y utopía: *Revista de ciencias sociales 22,* pp. 95–116.

Urra, M. (2010). El papel de la Economía Social en los regímenes del bienestar. *Revista Miscelánea Comillas, 68*(133), 791–816.

Vázquez, J. J., Albarrán, C., & Salinas Ramos, F. (2013). La Economía Social ante el nuevo paradigma de Bienestar social. *CIRIEC-España, Revista de Economía Pública, Social y Cooperativa, 79,* 5–34.

Chapter 9
The Evolving Field of Social Economy in Italy: Continuity and Change

Mara Benadusi, Giulio Citroni, Teresa Consoli, Deborah De Felice, Irene Falconieri, Francesco Mazzeo, and Carlo Pennisi

Introduction

The organizational, political, institutional, and legal landscape of social enterprises in Italy is rather complex and slippery. Indeed, historical national peculiarities have jeopardized its institutionalization process, as well as social enterprise's developments over time. This is why a high number of different traditions and work practices converge under the general category of "social economy" in the country: mutualistic organizations, NPOs and professional charity bodies, cooperatives and social cooperatives, social start-ups, and benefit companies, each with different statuses and different organizational and political cultures, entailing different tax exemptions, employment conditions, and access to public tenders. This makes the production and discussion of statistics very complex, and the debate on current trends even more ambiguous. This ambiguity is also reinforced by the uneven use of the concept of "social economy" in the country. If in Europe the expression social economy has long been used to describe organizations operating in the no-profit sector, in Italy this category is only recently emerging. Definitions such as "third sector" or, more recently, "civil economy" have been much more used than social economy in the country (Zamagni, 2002).

For this reason, the chapter refers mainly to the concept of social enterprise that has a crucial role in current debates on the so-called third sector in Italy. Social enterprise also includes new hybrid forms of organization (profit-non-profit):

M. Benadusi (✉) · T. Consoli · D. De Felice · F. Mazzeo · C. Pennisi
University of Catania, Catania, Italy
e-mail: mara.benadusi@unict.it

G. Citroni
University of Calabria, Rende, Italy

I. Falconieri
University of Messina, Messina, Italy

© Springer Nature Switzerland AG 2021
B. Gidron, A. Domaradzka (eds.), *The New Social and Impact Economy*,
Nonprofit and Civil Society Studies, https://doi.org/10.1007/978-3-030-68295-8_9

organizations of public interest that share economy platforms/applications or multi-company utilities, as well as foundations that carry out a business activity of general interest, for civic, solidarity, and social purposes. Where the expression "social economy" is used in this chapter, the concept indicates a set of socio-economic subjects whose activities are not oriented to profit and distribution of income, but to the supply of goods and services according to principles of mutual reciprocity; this definition is consistent with definitions proposed by the European Commission and Parliament, and taken from the Italian Ministry of Labour and Social Policies (https://www.lavoro.gov.it/temi-e-priorita/Terzo-settore-e-responsabilita-sociale-imprese/focus-on/Economia-sociale/Pagine/default.aspx).

According to Istat data updated to 31 December 2017, the vast social economy system in Italy includes more than 350,000 organizations, which employ 844,775 employees. The sector expands with average annual growth rates higher than those relating to market-oriented companies, in terms of both the number of companies and the number of employees. As a result, the importance of non-profit institutions increases compared to the overall Italian production system, from 5.8% in 2001 to 8.0% in 2017 (per units) and from 4.8% in 2001 to 7.0% in 2017 (per employees) (https://www.istat.it/it/files/2019/10/Struttura-e-profili-settore-non-profit-2017.pdf).

When the economic crisis hit Italy and public spending in 2008, the national government gradually curtailed investments in social and labour policies. Despite this institutional disengagement, however, the world of Italian social economy seems to have been growing (Carini & Borzaga, 2015; Carini & Carpita, 2013; Carini, Costa, Carpita, & Andreaus, 2013), particularly in the areas of social agriculture and environmental sustainability. Indeed, protection of the environment has become one of the main values for the new social economy ecosystem and, at the same time, one of the areas of higher intervention for social enterprises, thanks also to specific funding lines by national and European institutions.

The data collected by public and private research institutes denies the dominant perception of Italian social economy as lacking entrepreneurial skills and economic capacity, as well as the image of its complete dependency on public administrations (Borzaga, 2014). At the opposite, especially Italian social enterprises have developed remarkable vitality and resilience in response to crisis, as shown by the increase of work opportunities in this sector (Carini & Costa, 2014). They have also expanded their activity: whereas the classic social cooperative form only provided social, healthcare, educational, and work integration services, new-generation social enterprises include the provision of other innovative services such as environmental, cultural, sport, and recreational activities, the promotion of economic development, etc. (Borzaga, Poledrini, & Galera, 2017).

The coronavirus crisis has recently put to the test the resilience and effectiveness of social economy and social enterprises in coping with social and economic challenges; while it is too early—and beyond the scope of this chapter—to provide an overall assessment, it is important to stress some points that are directly or indirectly important to the following discussion. First of all, the impact of Covid and of prevention measures has been massive on some of the most pressing issues in Italian society and welfare: migrant labourers in agriculture and other fields, the elderly, prisoners, and (women in) low-income families are just the most prominent examples; this is likely to have long-lasting consequences on levels of inequality. Secondly, the capacity of the civil and social economy to set up an emergency network to support families and people in need appears to have been significant in the early months of the Covid crisis: food distribution, home help, conversion of production to strategic health equipment, telephone helplines, and all kinds of emergency services have been set up by networks of local government, civic and social organizations, and volunteers. Thirdly, the role of the social and civic economy is strikingly absent in the debate on the plans for social and economic recovery; outside the epistemic communities most connected to the social innovation and social enterprise milieus, very little or nothing at all is discussed in the media or in government documents about the role of the social sector in reconstruction. Suffice it to say that the urgent economic decrees of spring 2020 provided virtually no specific support for the third sector and social economy, and that the early guidelines for Italy's "next-generation EU" spending of over 200 billion euros make no mention of them.

In this chapter we describe the complex trajectory of social enterprises in Italy through three main steps. First, we illustrate the historical background determining the emergence of a social enterprise's ecosystem at national level, and its main transformations over time. Then, in the second part of the chapter we analyse the impact of the 2008/2009 economic crisis on the country's welfare system, and other national events responsible of opening a space of new generation for social entrepreneurship in Italy. Finally, the third part of the chapter presents a specific case study, L'Arcolaio Società Cooperativa Sociale in Sicily, in order to explore the concrete modes through which social enterprises are actually reacting to enabling and disabling factors produced by the changing economic and political environment in Italy. Our conclusive remarks try to capture some specificities of the current situation, and trace possible future developments.

The Italian Welfare System

The Italian welfare system reveals specific limits derived from the implementation of "social rights" at the beginning of the twentieth century. At the time of its foundation, it was of "corporatist" type, with the state progressively granting interest groups specific privileges and setting up a national fund (later INPS) to provide retired and disabled people with public social transfers. This approach to social questions, known as the Bismarckian model after the Prussian chancellor's system of social insurance, strongly influenced the Italian welfare system, particularly the scenarios in which social questions have come to emerge, and the modes used for their treatment. In the 1970s, Italy experimented for the first time a growing rift between new, emerging needs and the ability to cope of the public welfare system. The public or semi-public structures that provided a few social services, i.e. the so-called welfare and charity institutions (Istituzioni di Assistenza e Beneficienza, or

IPABs), were not only unprepared to face the new needs, but also tended to segregate—rather than integrate—those who turned to them. In fact, at the time, the Italian welfare system was still somehow "incomplete" (the healthcare reform was only carried out in 1978), and this system was primarily redistributive in nature, with a tendency to respond to social needs by providing monetary compensation rather than services. Moreover, in contrast to other countries, the non-profit sector was also poorly developed (Borzaga et al., 2017, 4).

Fragmentation of welfare entitlements and organizations, a narrow scope of universalism (notably limited to healthcare), low penetration of the state and collusion between public and private sectors, and clientelism are the characteristics that most distinctively differentiate Italy—and the "Southern model" of welfare from the Bismarckian imprint according to the classic study by Ferrera (1996). This model also reproduces the typical administrative and territorial architecture of the Italian state developed in the second half of the twentieth century. Three aspects of the political environment appear to be relevant to the discussion on welfare and the social enterprise phenomenon in Italy: first, the decentralization-recentralization pattern, which defines the autonomy and differentiation of local welfare and governance models; second, the territorially diverse political culture and legacy; third, the subsequent structure of diversity (and inequality) in economic status and welfare provision standards in the country. This third factor directly depends on the previous two, in combination with the strong economic divide which separates the North from the South.

In order to solve these limits, since the 1970s, the provision of social services has been entrusted to regional and local administrations. In the absence of a definition of national standards, this choice has favoured the emergence of small regional welfare systems and a municipal differentiation of social services. This trend was reinforced by the constitutional reform of 2001, which increased the power of regions in the definition of welfare models, and by Act 328 of 2000 with which territorial autonomy was established in the design of polymorph combinations of welfare, or communities of welfare. In a national context characterized by strong differences in local economic structures, the welfare federalization (Di Pietra, 2002) has strengthened inequalities in the availability and access to services. Furthermore, starting from 2005 the contraction of public resources, exacerbated with the "spending review" programme in 2011, has further influenced local administrations and in particular social services for the poor.

Current national social expenditures are around 30% of GDP, in line with the European average of the wealthiest countries (Eurostat.eu). However, they differ by type of investment. In Italy, in fact, over 50% is still spent on pensions, 25% on health, and a smaller percentage on family support, housing, and social exclusion (Istat, 2015). The data provided by Istat outline a contemporary welfare framework characterized by inequality in the provision of social services. Social rights indeed are granted only to specific groups. The post-crisis (and, presumably, post-Covid) economic conditions have emphasized the propensity in favour of "insiders" who are less and less but still well protected, while the unemployed or recently employed workers are "unrelated" and have almost no service available.

The Social Economy Puzzle

Italian Catholic Church as well as the socialist political tradition have played a relevant role in the whole evolution of the Italian welfare system, and consequently in the foundation of the cooperative movement first, and in the development of the national social economy framework later on. Cooperatives and NPOs in Italy have a long-standing history, indeed. Since the mid-nineteenth century, they have grown in numbers and in scope of activities, originating partly from religious initiatives, partly from political and trade union associations, and partly from social movements of the 1960s and 1970s.

This sector is characterized by the effort to promote a vision of the market different from the capitalist model, a vision that is both competitive and supportive, mutualistic, and community based. The effort to transform the economic system by using the best existing skills (such as new technologies) but channelling them for the benefit of the community is becoming crucial in the third sector. Economy and social life are intertwined within a shared framework of values. These include (1) a humanism based on civil, political, economic, cultural, and environmental rights, as recognized in national and international regulations and agreements; (2) the promotion of a democracy based on the recognition of people's ability to contribute to public decisions, decisions related to what is produced, how it is produced, and how surpluses are redistributed or invested; (3) the strengthening of a form of sustainable development attentive to environment and biodiversity, and based on the common use of resources and ecosystems; and (4) the adoption of novel, sustainable technologies to respond to specific needs and contexts of intervention.

Literature on the Italian social economy sector revolves around the idea that the diverse array of social enterprises developed at national level can be distinguished by an organizational structure capable of rendering demand independent of supply, and by the fact that these entities' welfare services are used in a "relational" manner (Becchetti, 2014; Bruni, 2009; Bruni & Zamagni, 2004, 2005; Venturi & Rago, 2011). For this reason, Zamagni (2002) prefers the term "civil economy" over "social economy", on the grounds that it is more effective in capturing the propulsive capacity and non-residual autonomy of this economic sphere which, thanks to the creation of inter-organizational networks and relational contracts, is able to deter opportunistic behaviours (ibid.). The varied organizations that have traditionally sought to combine entrepreneurship and solidarity, to meet the needs of people and communities by producing specific goods and services in Italy, are also characterized by the following factors: the redefinition of forms of partnership between public and private entities, the emergence of a communitarian focus (Bandini, Medei, & Travaglini, 2015; Bodini et al., 2016; Borzaga & Zandonai, 2015), and more recently the principles of vertical and horizontal subsidiarity (Musella, 2013; Musella & Santoro, 2012), specific strategies of governance and human resource management (Borzaga & Depedri, 2003; Cesarini & Locatelli, 2007), and new rules of accountability (Mari & Poledrini, 2014). Furthermore, relational sociology has contributed to developing the analysis of social capital (Degli Antoni & Portale,

2007; Ferrucci, 2010; Rossi & Boccacin, 2011) and so-called added social value (Bassi, 2011; Manelli, 2004) as indicators that can be used to define the impact and performances of social enterprises in Italy, in their past and current trends.

If we look at the existing picture, depending on the definition of the term "social economy" or "civil economy" we adopt, the boundaries of the organizations involved will change, but they certainly include entities from at least four main fields, distinguished in terms of their legal structure, their historical origin, and the content of their activities: (1) non-profit organizations (NPOs), many of which have an entrepreneurial style and a market orientation which may qualify them as social enterprises; (2) traditional cooperatives; (3) "social cooperatives", a legal form which was created in the early 1990s and soon became very relevant and influential—located somewhere in between the first two types; and (4) the more recent social-innovation start-up companies. None of these types, however, covers exactly what the Italian law defines as "social enterprises", since this is a qualification that any type of organization can acquire. In addition, the boundaries between these four types are not always clear, either in legislation or in the public debate, as signalled by Sapelli (2015) and Moro (2014).

As far as NPOs are concerned, Istat (Venturi & Zandonai, 2014) reports almost 290,000 entities; of these, over 82,000 are market oriented—towards either private or public clients. In the last decades, in this latter population there has been a tendency towards professionalization, increase in size and employment, and specialization in sectors where revenue is more appealing (health, assistance), although voluntary work and networking remain strategic resources for many Italian NPOs (ibid.).

Since the mid-nineteenth century, traditional cooperatives have also grown in numbers and in scope of activities, in particular consumer cooperatives and agricultural cooperatives. In 2008 (Borzaga, Carini, Costa, Carpita, & Andreaus, 2012), over 71,000 cooperatives were active in the fields of services (33,600) and construction (13,700), as well as agriculture, commerce and catering, and industry (5000–7000 each). In the services and agriculture sectors, they employ over 7% of all labour in the respective fields (ibid.).

However, the most illustrative sample of the social economy sector in Italy is represented by social cooperatives. In their original formulation, that appeared in Italy in 1991 (Disciplina delle cooperative sociali), social cooperatives were identified as those third sector organizations intervening in active labour policies aimed at tackling social exclusion of the unemployed and other vulnerable groups (Defourny & Nyssens, 2006). They either employ underprivileged workers or supply services for underprivileged people, and benefit from advantages in tax legislation. The law n. 381/1991 had defined as social those cooperatives that aim to pursue the community general interest with regard to human support and social integration by means of (a) managing healthcare, social, and educational services and (b) developing several activities—agricultural, industrial, and commercial ones—directed to the inclusion of unprivileged people in the job market. In practice, social cooperatives have taken on a business model—largely overlapping with what is internationally known as WISE (Work Integration Social Enterprises)—which was not included in the original understanding of a traditional cooperative, and thus they were meant to be the typical form of social enterprises in Italy. In 2011 there were 12,570 social cooperatives, employing over half a million people (Venturi & Zandonai, 2014). More than half of them operated in health and assistance services; almost three-quarters had a turnover of under 500,000€.

The last category of organizations mentioned above has a shorter and more difficult life, still to be monitored in its development and effective social impact. The status of "innovative start-ups with social goals", indeed, was introduced in Italy only in 2012, and that of "benefit companies" in 2015, with financial and organizational features that are still under scrutiny. Specific analysis on a phenomenon of "social innovation start-ups" is also small scale and emergent in Italy (Osservatorio Startup Hi-tech, 2014; Michelini & Iasevoli, 2015; Caroli, 2015). The literature finds that these companies' socially useful orientation gives them a significant advantage, potentially impacting their ability to raise and increase share capital. Scholars have also underlined the role played by the social entrepreneurship ecosystem as a driving force of local development and social innovation initiatives, and the contribution coming from foundations, urban institutions, incubators, coworking spaces, and new forms of philanthropy and social financing.

The different organizations that make up the framework of the social economy in Italy show how this composite model contributes today to the solution of new social problems and has become necessary to give stability and sustainability to economic growth. At the same time, it must be underlined that in Italy those forms of investment based on the assumption that private capital can intentionally contribute to creating positive social impacts and, at the same time, economic returns (impact investing) are still underdeveloped. There is more: compared to the Anglo-Saxon countries, the tool of the social impact bond, or "pay for success bond", an agreement through which the public sector collects private investments to pay the suppliers of welfare services, is still underdeveloped. A first experiment was carried out in Turin (Piemonte) and has as its objective the social and work reintegration of prisoners. The national project was promoted by the CRT Development and Growth Foundation and the Human Foundation with the cooperation of the Ministry of Justice, and will be carried out inside the "Lorusso e Cutugno" district house, a large prison on the outskirts of Turin.

While confirming the lack of dynamism in this sector, the 2019 report of the UBI BANCA Observatory on Finance and Third Sector (https://www.aiccon.it/pubblicazione/osservatorio-su-finanza-e-terzo-settore/) notes an increase in the spread of social impact finance instruments, and a positive trend in expectations on financial needs for social investments. The recent Italian third sector reform mentions new forms of financing for social enterprises, such as crowdfunding (donations, prizes, loans …), mini bonds, and social impact funds. In addition, the interest of "profit-making banks" among new suppliers is beginning to provide tailor-made products for the ESS, as well as that of private citizens, who provide direct financing for projects thanks to new technological platforms. For social entrepreneurship, the encounter with impact investments could represent an opportunity to strengthen and refine their business model, and stimulate the growth of a new generation of investors. However, there are also several critical aspects deriving from the adoption of similar financial models that should be better analysed in the future.

Changing Legal Frameworks for Social Enterprises

If these are the four main categories that can be possibly counted under the label of social enterprises, the actual legal form of social enterprise was introduced in Italy only in the last decade, with the legislative decree of March 24, 2006, n. 155, and is now specifically regulated by the legislative decree of 3 July 2017, n. 1121, implementing the delegation law of 6 June 2016, n. 106 (Fici, 2017). Ex lege social enterprises are non-profit private organizations that either (1) mainly and constantly perform economic activities aiming at the production and exchange of socially useful goods and services or (2) promote entrepreneurial activities aiming to the inclusion of disabled or unprivileged individuals into society.

Limited numbers, however, testify to limited interest or understanding of the advantages of these forms. The data analysed by the Iris Network and Euricse shows that SEs legally recognized as such by Law 118/05 are a minority in relation to the sector as a whole. According to Chamber of Commerce figures, by the end of 2013 a total of 774 private organizations had taken on the role of social enterprise, although there were more than 574 additional organizations whose official company names included the phrase "social enterprise", despite the fact that they had only registered as general companies.

Among the 774 registered SEs, the prevailing legal form is the cooperative (38% of the total), with social cooperatives playing a dominant role (86%). There is also a significant number of limited companies (30%), most of which are limited liability companies, plus only four joint-stock companies. Partnerships occupy a more marginal position (11% of the total, 70% of which are limited partnerships) along with non-profit entities that are not cooperatives (2%, half of which are associations). This means that, while there is a vast world of de facto social enterprises, at this point only a small percentage have chosen to adopt the legal categorization of a social enterprise. Furthermore, as far as organization is concerned, there is a high degree of internal "biodiversity" especially in terms of entrepreneurial type corporate models.

As for the types of activity being carried out, the Chamber of Commerce figures show that 60% of registered social enterprises are condensed into two specific fields, namely education and healthcare/welfare. Other activities related mainly to the services sector represent a much more marginal group (see Table 9.1). According to the rules established by Legislative Decree no. 155/2006, social entrepreneurship is mainly broken down into education, training, and research (with an incidence of 32.4%), social/welfare services (accounting for 23.6%), and job placement activities (representing 15%).

In parallel to these legislative developments, there has been a process of institutionalization of the larger field of voluntary work in Italy that has also contributed

Table 9.1 Social spending by policy areas: Italy-Europe comparison (% of total social spending)

	Italy	EU 25
Social security	61.8	45.7
Health	25.7	28.3
Disability	6.4	8.0
Family/childhood	4.1	8.0
Unemployment	1.8	6.6
Housing/social exclusion	0.2	3.5

Source: Eurostat-ESSPROS

to renovating our social economy system. The Legge Quadro (Framework Law) n. 266 on voluntary work associations, non-profit associations, and social support associations dates back to 1991. With this law the Parliament tried to institutionalize these entities through a comprehensive legal frame, although it did not want to grant them unnecessary fiscal or economic advantages. This law defines (Art. 3) as voluntary work the activities occurring when a member of any freely constituted entity works mainly and consistently on a voluntary basis (for free), to pursue the entity's solidarity aims. In addition, the DL n. 460/1997 has introduced the definition of non-profit organizations of social utility (ONLUS) that encompasses associations, committees, cooperatives, and other private entities pursuing social solidarity aims in specific areas. Finally, the law L. N. 383/2000 defines APSs (social support associations) as movements, groups, and federations engaged in non-profit and socially useful activities, performed in favour of associates and third parties, and fully respecting their freedom and dignity (Art. 2).

This legislative evolution displays how difficult it is to categorize social enterprises according to the types of activity that, increasingly, challenge the distinction between state and market, as well as between profit and non-profit. The blurring borders of these categories led practitioners and academicians to label social enterprises in Italy as "the third sector". Some norms have lately been dedicated to this development, which pledge to redesign both the market and the state. The most important steps are the Law n. 208/2015 Legge di stabilità per il 2016, which introduces the benefit societies, and the recent launch of the reform of the third sector. According to Art. 1 cc 376–384 of Law 208, a "benefit society" aims to share the earnings among the associates while performing a given economic activity, and is also characterized by having one or more shared benefits as aim, behaving in a responsibly sustainable way, being clear towards people, communities, territories, and environment, towards social and cultural activities, associations, and other stakeholders. The DDL C. 2617 Delega al Governo per la riforma del Terzo settore, dell'impresa sociale e per la disciplina del servizio civile universale introduces the first institutional definition of third sector: private groups which gather to pursue non-profit, civil, and socially useful aims, and which support and realize general interest activities through free voluntary actions, or through mutual exchange of goods and services in compliance with the principle of subsidiarity and in accordance with their regulations and statutes.

Impact of the Economic Crisis

In Italy the demand for social services has grown significantly in the last decade. The causes can be attributed, in particular, to the ageing of the population as well as to the impact of the global financial crisis on poverty and income distribution. The increased demand for social services is not balanced by an increase in the corresponding supply, in terms of neither quality nor quantity.

In the past years, indeed, one of the main goals of the Italian economic policies has been to reduce the effects of the financial crisis on national accounts. In order to decrease the country's public debt and to meet the stability rules coming from the participation in the EMU, Italian governments reduced the social policy budget, decreasing the funds allocated to public social services. Between 2009 and 2013, the Italian Government cut almost entirely the National Fund for Social Policies (FNPS). The FNSP, as provided by the Law 328/2001, is intended to finance precisely the social services system. As a result, the main source of funding comes from municipalities' own resources, which finance more than 67% of the total expenditure on local welfare policies (year 2012: Istat, 2015). In 2013, the resources allocated by the municipalities to the social services system amounted to about 6.8€ billion, a reduction of 4% compared to 2010 (year 2013: Istat, 2016).

Municipalities spend on average 117€ per capita per year for assistance and social services with significant territorial variability. Social expenditures per capita range from about 51€ in the South to 159€ in the Northeast. At regional level, variability in social per capita spending increases even further, ranging from 25€ in Calabria to 259€ in Trentino-Alto Adige (Istat, 2015). As a result, in the South, people have fewer social services than their fellow citizens in the North. The "willingness to contribute" in terms of user's financial contribution to the cost of social service depicts a remarkable cleavage between regions (e.g. Puglia and Campania are below 3%, Trentino-Alto Adige is about 24%, and Valle d'Aosta is at 26%) (Istat, 2015). Once again, the divides between North (13%) and South (3.7%) emerge.

Due to recent political tensions between municipalities and the central government, as well as cuts to public service spending, in the near future we cannot expect any expansion of municipal social services in Italy. Given that both the number and range of public services provided by local authorities are likely to keep decreasing, some of these voids represent interesting market areas for social enterprises, especially for new generation of SEs that can be regarded as being a viable alternative, not only to the public provision system, but also to the for-profit sector which cannot—or is unable to—attract several target groups. This is why, despite the contraction in public spending in social and labour policies, both at national and local levels, the more consolidated world of social economy in Italy continues to expand (Carini & Borzaga, 2015).

This trend must be absolutely remarked. The financial crisis indeed has allowed proper business initiatives to pursue general interests tangibly, by means of productive solutions that are sustainable and efficient, and involve stakeholders directly, also thanks to the new norms dedicated to this development, which pledge to redesign both the market and the state. An analysis of innovation trends in this sector reveals the following developments:

- The reorganization of new services associated with previously overlooked sectors (i.e. social agriculture and environmental sustainability).
- Reusing goods seized from criminal organizations for social ends.
- Producing member services independently and at controlled prices.
- Increase in community cooperatives offering personal services—welfare and social services, and education—as well as so-called neighbourhood services (Mori, 2015).
- Social cooperatives aimed at locating employment for disadvantaged individuals also have enjoyed continuous growth despite the general decline in national employment rates, thus displaying a remarkable degree of resilience (Depedri, 2015).

And yet, despite encouraging developments, social entrepreneurship in Italy still has considerable room for improvement in the way it relates to the recipients of its services and activities, which has hampered growth and innovation. As Zandonai and Rensi highlight (2015), public administrations together with service providers developed tools for need and demand analysis in a top-down manner. This situation is exacerbated by the limited role played by genuine practices of user co-production, and their limited involvement in decision-making and governing bodies (ibid.). The assessment tools and certification currently in use, drawn from the customer satisfaction surveys (and therefore not well suited to assessing the services offered by social enterprises), represent an additional problem (ibid.).

Opportunities and Challenges in Times of Troubles

On the national level another important challenge for Italian social enterprises is to counter the negative image of the sector held by a part of the Italian public opinion following scandals related to tenders for the management of services aimed mostly at asylum seekers, migrants, and people held in national prisons. The judicial inquiries that followed "Mafia Capitale" (2014) have tarnished the reputation of the world of active social cooperation in job placement programmes. In particular, in 2014–2015 mass medias and part of the political world began to express scepticism towards the decision of public institutions to outsource services to social cooperatives, going so far as to draft a proposal to amend the law of stability—not approved by the government—which introduced the ban on public administrations to resort to direct negotiation for social cooperatives only (Borzaga, 2014: 8).

Further criticalities may affect social enterprises in the near future. On the one hand, their development depends on how the question of impact and impact assessment will be framed in legislative and political debates. The bill passed in the Italian Parliament poses new organizational challenges, but how they will be implemented into legislative decrees and which administrative/bureaucratic conditions will be adopted are not yet clear. On the other hand, social entrepreneurship's future depends on its ability to locate and respond to a profitable demand for goods and services. Another emergent area of debate revolves around technological innovation and co-working. In particular, new technologies offer additional opportunities to the world of the social economy in general, and to the different organizations that make it up. Technological innovation—from artificial intelligence to big data, from automated guided vehicles to robotics—can help improve processes, products, and production methods of goods and services, and also allow the automation of routine tasks (Borzaga et al., 2017). If this phenomenon has the potential effect of increasing the risk of a decrease in job opportunities and the quality of work relations within the social economy, based on social and relational skills that cannot be performed by a machine, the use of new technologies would probably allow to respond with more effectiveness to the new needs that emerge from changes in society. However, technological innovation cannot develop unless business owners/shareholders are aware of the special nature of their businesses; there is a consolidated, pre-existing social network responsive to these measures; and the country's policy and regulatory environment develop in a way that fosters and facilitates this kind of innovations (Borzaga & Fazzi, 2011, 104).

Among current trends in the sector, there is also the progressive overlapping of the concept of social innovation with the concept of social enterprise, with a propulsive ongoing debate over the boundaries between one and the other, and how to concretely differentiate the two notions (Bassi & Ecchia, 2015; Borzaga, 2013; Calò & Fiorentini, 2013). The fact that social innovation is gradually being affirmed as a "matrix for redefining social protection systems" (Rensi & Zandonai, 2015: 4) is helping to grant new significance to "the dimension of social justice that is at the origin of many non-profit and cooperative ventures" in Italy (ibid.). However, despite the fact that scholars perceive the current reforms of the third sector as a first step in this direction, social enterprises do not yet display the characteristics of a truly innovative model, and indeed the results of current reforms will only be visible in the long term. In addition, the Italian model is characterized by a "path-specific and place-specific" implementation of social innovation, in which each new instance depends on the sociocultural background as well as the historical features of the specific context where the innovation takes place (Bassi & Moro, 2015; Guida & Maiolini, 2013; Picciotti, 2013; Venturi & Zandonai, 2014; Zamagni, 2005).

Most studies (Caulier-Grice, Davies, Patrick, & Norman, 2012) agree that, in order for social innovation processes to not only emerge, but also develop, there must be a market capable of absorbing the supply of goods and services that social enterprises produce. The context must also offer both founders and suppliers who are able to provide specialist resources or the "core" necessary to get the initiative up and running. A third prerequisite for the emergence of social innovation is a physical (or even virtual) space in which stakeholders can truly interact with each other (Caroli, 2015). Another feasible option is implementing a strategy of diversification or positioning within a market niche (Caroli, 2015; Rago & Venturi, 2014).

Alongside the diffusion of new tools of philanthropy and social financing (Bengo & Ratti, 2014) including crowdfunding campaigns (Balboni, Kocollari, & Pais, 2015), one of the most interesting trends in Italy is the almost exponential growth of incubators, co-working spaces, and centres for fuelling social entrepreneurship (Caroli, 2015; Carrera, Meneguzzo, & Messina, 2008; Venturi & Zandonai, 2014). These spaces meet the needs of the multiple actors working in the field by giving them opportunities to synchronize their efforts and, as such, they also attract new generation of social entrepreneurs. They usually develop practices of informal socialization, horizontal exchange, and collaborative technologies that encourage cooperation between public and private actors, and profit and non-profit organizations. This allows for creation of communities of practice and project-oriented communities, with the potential to foster knowledge spillover. In addition to offering physical spaces and opportunities for networking, these work environments also provide technical assistance and coaching, a fact which allows them to incubate and accelerate start-up processes, and to "more easily bring innovative content to light" (Venturi & Zandonai, 2014). Of course, "the economic, cultural and especially political context shapes the very nature of the incubator and its degree of effectiveness in revitalizing or rethinking the economic and social landscape and relations of the territory in which it operates" (ibid.: 16). Another key element is the incubator's specific target, which may range from social cooperatives or "economically significant" associations (market oriented) to other non-profit organizations or socially oriented start-ups (ibid.).

Over the last decade, sociological inquiry (Donati & Colozzi, 2004; Stanzani, 1997) has also shown an increasing interest in the idea of entrepreneurship and self-entrepreneurship, particularly in conjunction with the EU policy agenda. Indeed, the literature has begun to dedicate considerable space to studies of foundations and productive organizations, which are the forms of non-profit entities most likely to have entrepreneurial objectives, and to investigations of the boundaries between for-profit and non-profit organizations (Moro, 2014).

Another important feature of current trends in social entrepreneurship is related to the concept of hybridization. "The concept of hybridization (the linkage of profit and no-profit sector's objectives, without losing their own identity) has arisen from the strategic alliance between social enterprises and conventional entrepreneurs. It could represent a starting point to implement the concept of circular subsidiarity, which is the systemic partnership between public bodies, for profit enterprises and social enterprises to the realization of shared projects and purposes based on protocols signed by the parties" (Venturi & Zandonai, 2014) (Biggeri, Testi, Bellucci, Franchi, & Manetti, 2014, 31).

New-Generation Social Entrepreneurship: A Transitional Ground

The identification of a new generation of social enterprises (NGSEs) in Europe, its features, needs, and constraints as well as its contribution to social innovation was one of the main objectives of the European Commission-funded project EFESEIIS (Enabling the Flourishing and Evolution of Social Enterprises in Europe). Most of all, the EFESEIIS project activity WP5 "New Generation of Social Enterprises" was devoted to the question of whether or not this new generation can be legitimately identified as such, with different behaviours and different needs from previous conceptualizations. On the basis of the analysis of the 55 case studies carried out in Italy, Sweden, England, Poland, Scotland, Serbia, Albania, France, Germany, the Netherlands, and Austria—on SEs established specifically during the economic crisis, from 2006 and 2012 (Benadusi & Sapienza, 2017)—NGSEs' most innovative aspects encompass governance and decision-making processes, gender or age balance, use of ICT and social media, coping mechanisms, and collaborative work styles. Social innovation also appears to be an essential ingredient of NGSEs, which particularly translates into the tendency to turn problems into opportunities. Despite these positive outcomes, however, the possibility to exploit the social economy and incorporate it in conservative rather than transformative ways is also present as a potential risk. By facilitating the transfer of services out from the state, indeed, NGSEs may contribute to the state of affairs in which local communities are obliged to increasingly manage their own welfare (ibid.).

One of the main results of the EFESEIIS project demonstrates that, more than a new phenomenon independent from previous forms of social entrepreneurship, a "transition space" of new generation exists, where traditional and emerging features converge, hybridizing each other. This feature contradicts the common belief according to which new-generation social enterprises, invariably characterized by the age factor, are naturally inclined to adopt "new" expressive codes, attitudes, and work styles that are typical of the world of start-ups.

Starting from these findings, in order to give a glimpse on the Italian context, we have selected for this chapter a case study that clearly occupies a space of transition: a Work Integration Social Enterprise (WISE) that began its life in the classical third sector/non-profit sphere and is now in search of a new internal structure and equilibrium, moving towards a "proto-social" enterprise, which means a "social business" operating for the common good rather than seeking only to make a profit.

The selected organization is based in the city of Syracuse, in Sicily, the largest Italian region in terms of territory (2,583,239 km^2) and the fourth in number of residents (5,074,261). The regional economy is characterized by a dramatic condition of the labour market, characterized by a constant increase in the unemployment rate especially among the most underprivileged social groups, women, and young people (Asso, 2010). The crisis and the decline in employment have exacerbated the economic situation of many families that increasingly live below the relative poverty line (Azevedo, 2015, 16). Indeed, in Sicily, as in the rest of southern Italy, social enterprises operate in a particularly complex environment due to the greater burden of bureaucracy, the pervasiveness of corruption, and the poorer quality of public and social services (De Blasio & Sestito, 2011). Social enterprises therefore play a fundamental socio-economic role, assisting numerous categories of underprivileged people, although their work does not benefit from proper followings from the regional institutions and local authorities.

The inclusion in this chapter of a brief account of the case study is deemed useful to exemplify effectively some of the issues raised in the previous sections (legal forms, relationship to the welfare system and to the public sector, response to crisis and changing environment), and to illustrate the mechanisms of path dependence, innovation, response, and change that operate in an organization and that are the building blocks of wider societal and economic change. Contextual and organizational features of the case make it rather representative of the "new-generation social enterprises" with all their contradictions and potential for innovation.

L'Arcolaio Società Cooperativa Sociale

L'Arcolaio Società Cooperativa Sociale—hereafter L'Arcolaio—is a type B social cooperative formally established in 2003 with the aim of providing work training programmes for social and work integration to the inmates of the Cavadonna Penitentiary in Siracusa (Sicily). The cooperative manufactures and markets high-quality typical Sicilian confectionery products under the brand "Dolci Evasioni", nowadays sold in the national and European circuits of fair-trade and organic markets. L'Arcolaio exclusively uses local organic crops, such as almonds of Avola, lemons of Siracusa, and Sicilian carob. In line with this production activity, in 2015, the cooperative also founded a social and organic agriculture start-up, "Frutti degli Iblei", which comprises a processing plant for drying and packaging herbs, medicinal plants, and vegetables, an activity that allows L'Arcolaio to follow the people under custody also on their exit from prison, supporting them in job placement and accommodation.

Initially L'Arcolaio was founded under the legal status of Small Social Cooperative—Onlus with limited liability. On May 25, 2004, however, its social base grew from three to nine members and the organization adopted a new legal status as an ordinary cooperative, allowing an increase in employed members. Currently, L'Arcolaio employs 22 people, divided in descending order between the bakery, herb processing plant, administrative office, and agricultural work. In its different phases of growth and internal transformation, as well as during the moment of crisis and economic contraction, the skills and the relational work of L'Arcolaio's founder, Giovanni Romano, were decisive both to bear the financial burdens and to transform negative challenges into opportunities. A first moment of severe difficulty occurred in 2008. Almost 3 years after its inception, with the economic crisis scaling up, the resignation of its founding members shattered the social base and the economic capital of L'Arcolaio. Giovanni Romano then endeavoured to constitute a new, highly motivated group, with the gradual inclusion of the current members of the Board of Directors. Thanks to these organizational and financial changes, between 2008 and 2014 the cooperative expanded and diversified both its social and business activities, through the purchase of new equipment and the implementation of projects parallel to the activity of confectionery manufacture. At this time, the ability to build networks and attract partners willing to invest their resources in the SE's activities proved also to be crucial. This period is remembered by members as a successful phase in which the cooperative managed to transform and achieve good business and social results. The management of the prison's kitchen in particular increased the capacity for job placement of the detainees.

2015 was another decisive year in L'Arcolaio's history. The management of the prison cafeteria and the beginning of social agriculture projects increased its business capacity, as well as social impact. In fact, in 2015 L'Arcolaio closed with a positive balance of €1195.00. However, the simultaneous occurrence of at least three events, listed below, led again to a sharp reversal of this positive trend, and jeopardized its financial sustainability.

1. The Department of Prison Administration suddenly revoked the assignment of the management of prisons' kitchens to social cooperatives, stopping the initial prospect of extending this experience to all national prisons.
2. The sudden increase in the price of almonds, the main raw material and flagship product of the confectionery production of the social cooperative, led to a substantial increase in production costs and a consequent reduction in profits.
3. The "Frutti degli Iblei" social agriculture project, based on the production, processing, and marketing of spices and herbs, was unable to carve out a commensurate market share to sustain production costs, thereby reducing the cooperative's strength and ability to intervene in prison exit strategies.

Due to these problems, L'Arcolaio went through a particularly complex period, which in 2016 resulted in a budget deficit of €171,572.00. The judicial inquiry called "Mafia Capitale" (2014) constitutes a crucial disabling factor in this phase. Indeed, by weakening the reputation of the social economy system in Sicily, the scandal was responsible of the public decision to cut funds in the management of prisons' kitchens. As pointed out by L'Arcolaio's founder:

> All that period, let's say, of Mafia Capitale […] has created the idea that cooperatives were made up of people who profited, who speculated. Particularly, the idea that the prisons could increasingly interact with social cooperatives to entrust them with services was strongly curbed. And we stumbled upon the decision to brutally crush the allocation of kitchen management to social cooperatives. We invested in the kitchens in Syracuse for 5 years. And then came that decision to withdraw, instead of, as it seemed, to develop that project and have all the kitchens of the penitentiary system run by social cooperatives (Giovanni Romano, interview).

However, as in 2008, bolstered by the mutual understanding and dedication of the management team, the cooperative strived to turn difficulties into opportunities for reflection and growth, developing useful strategies to offset the losses. In order to counterbalance the abovementioned problems, for instance, L'Arcolaio created the

"Sapori Cult" project in collaboration with other third sector companies, and funded by UniCredit under the fourth national edition of the "Social cohesion strategies for young people" competition, with a donation of €68,000. This project launched a new line of high-end Sicilian foods and wines, based on a concept of food as a metaphor for the encounter of cultures, and as an opportunity for economic development and social inclusion. In addition, while lacking a sustainability plan, L'Arcolaio has engaged two Banca Intesa consultants to analyse and assess internal critical issues, and overcome this lengthy period of financial instability. Last but not least, it also envisages the strengthening of its public communication strategy by hiring website and social media professionals.

In synthesis, since its foundation (2003) the history of this social cooperative has been punctuated by moments of crisis that strained its financial stability. Over the years, its survival has been guaranteed chiefly by the dedication of its founder and members of the board, both in terms of time and financial resources, and by the support of the wide network of local and national partners who share the same values and principles. Despite the success achieved in terms of longevity and impact, however, L'Arcolaio is still undergoing a phase of economic instability that makes the introduction of new organizational and strategical changes even more necessary. This is why L'Arcolaio has reformed its organizational structure in recent years, changing its economic model to adopt a more explicitly entrepreneurial approach.

Especially if viewed from a temporal perspective, L'Arcolaio is not a typical NGSE, but rather a product of the evolutionary development of voluntary organizations, cooperatives, and mutual aid organizations in Italy: a company in transition that has been able to call into question and revise its own structure and values in view of the transformations taking place in today's welfare system. This transition involved changes that affect the level of governance, as well as the system of values and corporate structure, with increased degrees of professionalization in the services offered as well as its organizational model, the composition of employees, and programme lines being pursued. There was also a progressive diversification of the business' financial basis and the scaling up of operational project-oriented divisions.

Conclusions

As L'Arcolaio case study clearly shows, new-generation social enterprises in Italy appear to address both the classical needs traditionally covered by the welfare system through public/private forms and emerging needs that are not covered by the welfare state, even when it does manage to respond to specific needs in the local area. L'Arcolaio's life trajectory is a classic example indeed of that intermediate, hybrid space where new ways to solving social problems already being addressed by the national system (such as social inclusion and work reintegration of inmates in penitentiaries) intersect with the capacity of meeting emerging needs and problems that usually remain unmet or only partially met by public social policies (such as environmental sustainability, biodiversity, and new styles of food consumption).

This feature makes it possible to identify L'Arcolaio with both a "WISE" (work integration social enterprise) approach and a "proto-social" orientation more focused on exploring new forms of social business.

As we already explained in the first part of this chapter, Work Integration SEs appear to be so dominant at national level as to be considered synonymous with social enterprises tout court, offering a fundamental contribution to labour market policies directed at the reintegration of at-risk populations. NGSE, in contrast, is a blurrier category in Italy. Social start-ups indeed are often defined as cases in which "profit comes first" and innovation represents a strategic asset, while social impact ideals remain peripherical, although present. However, apart from these two extremes, there are several examples in Italy of hybrid organizations: organizations that, like L'Arcolaio does, in the current state of affairs seek to minimize environmental impact and utilize natural resources more effectively, operating in the intermediate space between the WISE and proto-social entrepreneurship models.

Another important question regarding NGSEs is whether or not they can be considered a product of the crisis, that is to say, the macroeconomic situation that has resulted in a progressive decline in public spending on social policies, and a weakening of the national and local welfare systems (Benadusi & Sapienza, 2018). From this point of view, NGSEs gain their energy, whether symbolic or economic, from the progressive withdrawal of the state and the consequent increase in social needs, needs that are both growing in intensity and diversifying in type. L'Arcolaio cooperative represents a good example of this trend, given the impressive increase and differentiation of its activities after the rise of the financial crisis. The two main periods of difficulty experienced in 2008 and 2015, indeed, were an occasion for the cooperative to better identify market opportunities and review its previous organizational patterns, and thus develop a more aware business and revenue model.

At the same time, however, a more critical perspective questions "whether social enterprise could really be seen as the logical result of scarce economic resources and challenged the seemingly unproblematic combination of market-based approaches and the pursuit of social goals" (Dey & Teasdale, 2013, 250). Current trends in the social economy systems at European level indeed may also reflect the dynamics of neoliberal governmentality, which have a stronger hold on this sector in moments of crisis. As in other European countries, in Italy too there is a risk that this emergent space of new-generation social entrepreneurship provides vaguely defined communities with the assets to increasingly manage their own welfare, thus exploiting the social economy and incorporating it according to neoliberal logics.

As L'Arcolaio case demonstrates, this risk that a drift into commercial logics might challenge social rights by emphasizing market solutions and privatizing social services is especially evident in organizations that have survived a delicate phase of transition and are currently obliged to adapt to the forces that are blurring the boundaries between the market and the welfare state. However, our case study also shows a "counter-narrative" or at least signs that SEs are hesitant to embrace the dominant discourse surrounding the role social business ought to play in times of crisis. This suggests that NGSEs cannot be reduced to an image that casts them in the role of docile subjects engaged in endorsing the inherent norms and principles of neoliberalism. Often, in fact, founders and members (especially if coming from the traditional voluntary and cooperative sector, such as Giovanni Romano) display a critical reflexivity capable of eroding dominant logics and values from within. As Giovanni Romano and other enterprise's members remarked,

> We seek to be a cooperative for the community of our territory, we try to be a cooperative of the prison community [...] one born inside with the friendship of all, with the support of all. And so, there is a sense of bonding, even if always undergoing the usual controls ... (Giovanni Romano, interview: 5.12.207).

> I do not feel like defining us as a successful business, absolutely. Indeed, it is a company that risks bankruptcy. It risked it very recently. It is a business, however, that has tried to become part of the territory's community (Giovanni Romano, interview 5.12.2015).

> On another level, the social one, we fly quite high. We are also an example at national level [...]. In the prison context in Italy we are truly an example. But this example comes with a high price, it means effort, goodwill. It would be easier to abandon ship at this point (Valentina D'Amico, interview, 23.01.2018).

References

Asso, P. F. (2010). La crisi e i problemi dell'economia siciliana. In *StrumentiRes - Rivista online della Fondazione Res, II*, 6. http://www.strumentires.com/index.php?option=com_content&view=article&id=243:lacrisi-e-i-problemi-delleconomia-siciliana&catid=4:economia-siciliana&Itemid=12

Azevedo, F. (2015). Situazione economica, sociale e territoriale della Sicilia. In *Analisi Approfondita, Dipartimento tematico B: Politiche strutturali e di coesione*. Bruxelles: Unione europea. http://www.europarl.europa.eu/RegData/etudes/IDAN/2015/540372/IPOL_IDA(2015)540372_IT.pdf.

Balboni, B., Kocollari, U., & Pais, I., (2015). I segreti del successo delle campagne di crowdfunding delle imprese sociali italiane. *Impresa Sociale, 6*, http://www.rivistaimpresasociale.it/component/k2/item/134-crowdfunding-impresesociali.html

Bandini, F., Medei, R., & Travaglini, C. (2015). Territorio e persone come risorse: le cooperative di comunità, in La morfogenesi dell'impresa di comunità. Processi generativi, forme organizzative e percorsi di institution building, numero monografico. *Impresa sociale, 5*, http://www.rivistaimpresasociale.it/rivista/item/117-cooperative-comunita.html

Bassi, A. (2011). Il valore sociale aggiunto delle organizzazioni di terzo settore che erogano servizi alla persona. Verso un sistema di indicatori (VSA) per la misurazione della performance delle imprese sociali, in Donati P., Colozzi I. (a cura di), Il valore aggiunto delle relazioni sociali. *Sociologia e Politiche Sociali, XIV*, 1.

Bassi, A., & Ecchia, G. (2015). La sfida dell'innovazione sociale: dall'Italia a Vienna (e ritorno). *Impresa sociale, 6*, http://www.rivistaimpresasociale.it/component/k2/item/122-sfidainnovazione-sociale.html

Bassi, A., & Moro, G. (2015). *Politiche sociali innovative e diritti di cittadinanza*. Milano: Franco Angeli.

Becchetti, L. (2014). *Wikieconomia*. Bologna, Il Mulino: Manifesto dell'economia civile.

Benadusi, M., & Sapienza, R. (2017). *New generation of social entrepreneurs*. Explanatory case studies series. EFESEIIS, Enabling the Flourishing and Evolution of Social

Entrepreneurship for Innovative and Inclusive Societies. http://www.fp7-efeseiis.eu/new-generation-of-socialenterprises/

Benadusi, M., & Sapienza, R. (2018). The in-between space of new generation social enterprises. In M. Biggeri, E. Testi, M. Bellucci, R. During, & T. Person (Eds.), *Social entrepreneurship and social innovation: Ecosystems for inclusion in Europe* (pp. 164–178). London: Routledge.

Bengo, I., & Ratti, M. (2014). Datemi una leva... Nuovi strumenti di filantropia e finanza per il sociale. *Impresa Sociale, 4,* http://www.rivistaimpresasociale.it/component/k2/item/98-datemiuna-leva-nuovi-strumenti-di-filantropia-e-finanza-per-il-sociale/98-datemi-una-leva-nuovistrumenti-di-filantropia-e-finanza-per-il-sociale.html?limitstart=0

Biggeri, M., Testi, E., Bellucci, M., Franchi, S., & Manetti, G. (2014). *Social enterprise, social innovation and social entrepreneurship in Italy: A national report,* EFESEIIS, Enabling the Fourishing and Evolution of Social Entrepreneurship for Innovative and Inclusive Societies, http://www.fp7-efeseiis.eu/national-report-italy/

Bodini, R., Borzaga, C., Mori, P., Salvatori, G., Sforzi, J., & Zandonai, F. (2016). *Libro bianco. La cooperazione di comunità: Azioni e politiche per consolidare le pratiche e sbloccare il potenziale di imprenditoria comunitaria.* Euricse, http://www.euricse.eu/wpcontent/uploads/2016/05/Libro-Bianco.pdf

Borzaga, C. (2013). Innovazione sociale e impresa sociale: un legame da sciogliere. *Impresa Sociale, 1,* http://www.rivistaimpresasociale.it/component/k2/item/28-innovazionesociale-e-impresa-sociale-un-legame-da-sciogliere.html

Borzaga, C. (2014). Prefazione. In Venturi, Z. (a cura di). *L'impresa sociale in Italia. Identità e sviluppo in un quadro di riforma. Rapporto Iris Network.* Trento: Iris Network.

Borzaga, C., Carini, C., Costa, E., Carpita, M., & Andreaus, M. (2012). Cooperation in Italy in 2008. In *Euricse Working Paper 26, 12.* Trento: Euricse.

Borzaga, C., & Depedri, S. (2003). *La cooperazione sociale italiana al microscopio: I punti di forza e di debolezza Dei modelli organizzativi e della gestione delle risorse umane.* Franco Angeli: Milano.

Borzaga, C., & Fazzi, L. (2011). *Le imprese sociali.* Carocci: Roma.

Borzaga, C., Poledrini, S., & Galera, G. (2017). Social enterprise in Italy: Typology, diffusion and characteristics. In *Euricse Working Papers, 96.*

Borzaga, C., & Zandonai, F. (2015). Oltre la narrazione, fuori dagli schemi: i processi generativi delle imprese di comunità, in La morfogenesi dell'impresa di comunità. Processi generativi, forme organizzative e percorsi di institution building, numero monografico. *Impresa Sociale, 5,* 1–7.

Bruni, L. (2009). L'impresa civile. In *Una via italiana all'economia di mercato.* Milano: Università Bocconi editore.

Bruni, L., & Zamagni, S. (2004). Economia civile. In *Efficienza, equità, felicità pubblica.* Bologna: Il Mulino.

Bruni, L., & Zamagni, S. (2005). *L'economia civile.* Bologna: Il Mulino.

Calò, F., & Fiorentini, G. (2013). *Impresa sociale & innovazione sociale. Imprenditorialità nel terzo settore e nell'economia sociale: il modello IS&IS.* Milano: Franco Angeli.

Carini, C., & Borzaga, C. (2015). La cooperazione sociale: dinamica economica ed occupazionale tra il 2008 e il 2013. In F. Zandonai (a cura di), *Economia cooperativa. Rilevanza, evoluzione e nuove frontiere della cooperazione italiana. Terzo Rapporto Euricse,* http://www.euricse.eu/wpcontent/uploads/2015/09/09-Carini-Borzaga.pdf

Carini, C., & Carpita M. (2013). L'evoluzione delle cooperative tra il 2008 e il 2011: gli aspetti occupazionali. In *La cooperazione italiana negli anni della crisi. Secondo Rapporto Euricse* (pp. 25–36). Trento: Euricse Edizioni.

Carini, C., & Costa, E. (2014). La resilienza delle cooperative sociali. In Venturi, Z. (a cura di) *L'impresa sociale in Italia. Identità e sviluppo in un quadro di riforma. Rapporto Iris Network* (37–52). Trento: Iris Network.

Carini, C., Costa, E., Carpita, M., & Andreaus, M. (2013). L'evoluzione delle cooperative tra il 2008 e il 2011: gli aspetti economici e patrimoniali. In *La cooperazione italiana negli anni della crisi. Secondo Rapporto Euricse* (pp. 11–24). Trento: Euricse Edizioni.

Caroli, M. G. (Ed.). (2015). *Modelli ed esperienze di innovazione sociale in Italia, Secondo Rapporto sull'innovazione sociale*. Roma, Luiss: CeRIIS International Center for Research on Social Innovation.

Carrera, D., Meneguzzo, M., & Messina M. (2008). Incubatori di impresa sociale, volano di sviluppo locale. *Impresa Sociale, 1*, 1–24, http://desmacerata.it/wpcontent/uploads/2011/06/CarreraMeneguzzoMessina_2008__Incubatori-di-impresa-socialevolano-di-sviluppo-locale1.pdf

Caulier-Grice, J., Davies, A., Patrick, R., & Norman, W. (2012). Defining social innovation. In *A deliverable of the project: The theoretical, empirical and policy foundations for building social innovation in Europe? (TEPSIE), European Commission, 7th Framework Programme*. Brussels: European Commission, DG Research.

Cesarini, F., & Locatelli, R. (2007). *Le imprese sociali. Modelli di governance e problemi gestionali*. Milano: FrancoAngeli.

De Blasio, G., & Sestito, P. (Eds.). (2011). *Che cos'è il capitale sociale*. Roma: Donzelli Editore.

Defourny, J., & Nyssens, M. (2006). Defining social Enterprise. In M. Nyssens (Ed.), *Social Enterprise at the Crossroads of market, public policies and civil society* (pp. 1–28). London: Routledge.

Degli Antoni, G., & Portale, E. (2007). *Organizzazioni del terzo settore e creazione di capitale sociale: il caso delle cooperative sociali e il ruolo della responsabilità sociale d'impresa, working paper n. 47*, http://www.aiccon.it/file/convdoc/47.pdf

Depedri, S. (2015). *Costi e benefici delle cooperative di inserimento lavorativo*. In F. Zandonai (a cura di), *Economia cooperativa. Rilevanza, evoluzione e nuove frontiere della cooperazione italiana. Terzo Rapporto Euricse*, http://www.euricse.eu/wp-content/uploads/2015/09/15-Depedri.pdf

Dey, P., & Teasdale, S. (2013). Social enterprise and dis/identification. *Administrative Theory & Praxis, 35*(2), 248–270. https://doi.org/10.2753/ATP1084-1806350204.

Di Pietra, L. (2002). "Welfare community": programmazione e federalismo, dai LEA ai Piani di zona. *Tendenze Nuove, 4–5*, 397–430.

Donati, P., & Colozzi, I. (Eds.). (2004). *Il terzo settore in Italia: culture e pratiche*. Milano: Franco Angeli.

Ferrera, M. (1996). *The 'Southern model' of welfare in social Europe. Journal of European social policy, 6*(1), 17–37.

Ferrucci, F. (2010). *Capitale sociale e partnership tra pubblico, privato e terzo settore. Vol. 2 Il caso delle fondazioni di comunità*. Milano: Franco Angeli.

Fici, A. (2017). La nuova disciplina dell'impresa sociale. Una prima lettura sistematica. *Impresa sociale, 9*, http://www.rivistaimpresasociale.it/archivio/item/183-nuova-disciplinaimpresa-sociale-prima-lettura-sistematica.html

Guida, M. F., & Maiolini, R. (2013). *Il Fattore C per l'Innovazione Sociale*. Rubbettino: Soveria Mannelli.

Istat (2015). *Interventi e servizi sociali dei comuni singoli o associati*, Roma, http://www.istat.it/it/archivio/166482

Istat (2016). *Disegno di legge C. 3594 Governo. Delega recante norme relative al contrasto della povertà, al riordino delle prestazioni e al sistema degli interventi e dei servizi sociali,* Audizione del Direttore centrale delle statistiche socio-economiche dell'Istituto nazionale di statistica Cristina Freguja, Roma, 14 marzo 2016, http://www.istat.it/it/archivio/182848

Manelli, A. (2004). La creazione di valore nell'impresa sociale. Il valore aggiunto sociale secondo il modello Cosis. *Quaderni Monografici Rirea, 25*.

Mari, L. M., & Poledrini, S. (2014). *L'accountability nelle organizzazioni non profit. Il caso della cooperativa sociale Cadiai*, paper presentato in occasione di Colloquio scientifico sull'impresa sociale, 23–34 maggio 2014, Dipartimento di Economia, Università degli Studi di Perugia, http://irisnetwork.it/wp-content/uploads/2015/02/colloquio14-mari-poledrini.pdf

Michelini, L., & Iasevoli, G. (2015). *Le start up innovative a vocazione sociale: il ruolo dell'enterpreneurship ecosystem e l'impatto sul capitale sociale*, paper presentato in occasione del Colloquio scientifico sull'impresa sociale, 22–23 maggio 2015, Dipartimento PAU (Patrimonio, Architettura, Urbanistica), Università degli Studi Mediterranea di Reggio Calabria, http://irisnetwork.it/wp-content/uploads/2015/06/colloquio15-michelini-iasevoli.pdf

Mori, P. A. (2015). Le cooperative di comunità. In F. Zandonai (a cura di), *Economia cooperativa. Rilevanza, evoluzione e nuove frontiere della cooperazione italiana. Terzo Rapporto Euricse*, http://www.euricse.eu/it/publications/2887/

Moro, G. (2014). *Contro il non profit*. Bari: Laterza.

Musella, M. (Ed.). (2013). *La sussidiarietà orizzontale. Economia, politica, esperienze territoriali in Campania*. Roma: Carocci.

Musella, M., & Santoro, M. (2012). *L'economia sociale nell'era della sussidiarietà orizzontale*. Giappichelli: Torino.

Osservatorio Startup Hi-tech (2014). The Italian Startup Ecosystem: Who's Who. Research Report, https://www.coopstartup.it/wp-content/uploads/2015/04/ItaliaStartup_Report_WhoIsWho.pdf

Picciotti, A. (2013). *L'impresa sociale per l'innovazione sociale. Un approccio di management*. Milano: Franco Angeli.

Rago, S., & Venturi, P. (2014). *Teoria e modelli di organizzazioni ibride presenti all'interno dell'imprenditorialità sociale*. In Venturi P., Zandonai F. (a cura di), *Ibridi organizzativi. L'innovazione sociale generata dal gruppo cooperativo Cgm*. Bologna: Il Mulino.

Rensi, S., & Zandonai, F. (2015). *Per chi e per quanti opera la cooperazione sociale?* In F. Zandonai (a cura di), *Economia cooperativa. Rilevanza, evoluzione e nuove frontiere della cooperazione italiana. Terzo Rapporto Euricse*, http://www.euricse.eu/wp-content/uploads/2015/09/16-Rensi-Zandonai.pdf

Rossi, G., & Boccacin, L. (2011). *Riflettere e agire relazionalmente. Terzo settore, partnership e buone pratiche nell'Italia che cambia*. Santarcangelo di Romagna: Maggioli Editore.

Sapelli, G. (2015). *La cooperazione: impresa e movimento sociale*. Firenze: goWare.

Stanzani, S. (1997). *La specificità relazionale del terzo settore*. Franco Angeli: Milano.

Venturi, P., & Rago, S. (2011). Verso l'Economia del Ben-Essere. In *Atti de "Le Giornate di Bertinoro per l'Economia Civile 2010 – X ed."*. AICCON: Forlì.

Venturi, P., & Zandonai, F. (2014). Rapporto IRIS network. In *L'impresa sociale in Italia: identità e sviluppo in un quadro di riforma*. Trento: IRIS Network.

Zamagni, S. (2002). *Dell'identità delle imprese sociali e civili: perché prendere la relazionalità sul serio*, in S. In *Zamagni (a cura di), Il nonprofit italiano al bivio*. Milano: Egea.

Zamagni, S. (2005). *Per una teoria civile dell'impresa cooperativa*. In E. Mazzoli, S. Zamagni (a cura di), *Verso una nuova teoria economica della cooperazione* (pp. 15–56). Bologna: Il Mulino.

Chapter 10
The (New) Social Economy in Austria

Hanna Schneider and Ruth Simsa

Introduction

It has only been within the last 10 years or so that the discourse on the NSE or SE (we use these two terms synonymously here) has gradually gained traction in Austria. While the discourse is rather new, aspects associated with the NSE such as the generation of sales revenue or the innovative approach to problem-solving are not new at all. The main aim of this chapter is to map the various understandings and paths of the NSE in Austria.

Up until now, the new social economy has been a blurry concept in Austria. Broadly defined, three different, but not necessarily mutually exclusive, approaches can be distinguished. While all three understandings share the focus on a social/societal mission, they differ in the way they put emphasis on additional factors, such as innovation or importance of an inspirational founder (for an overview of this debate see Vandor, Millner, Moder, Schneider, & Meyer, 2015). Within the first perspective the focus lies on the **generation of commercial income**; thus, social enterprises are understood as organizations, which fulfill public purposes and try to generate substantial parts of their income from sales revenues. The devil is in the details. In practice, questions like what share of the total income needs to come from sales revenues or whether performance-based contracts with the government are seen as sales revenue emerge. Other perspectives put more focus on **innovation**; thus the innovative capacity of social enterprises and the individual social entrepreneur is highlighted, while in many cases it remains vague what innovation actually

H. Schneider (✉)
Wu Wien, Vienna University of Economics and Business, Wien, Austria
e-mail: hanna.schneider@wu.ac.at

R. Simsa
University of Economics and Business, Vienna, Austria
e-mail: ruth.simsa@wu.ac.at

© Springer Nature Switzerland AG 2021
B. Gidron, A. Domaradzka (eds.), *The New Social and Impact Economy*,
Nonprofit and Civil Society Studies, https://doi.org/10.1007/978-3-030-68295-8_10

means. Often innovation is linked to digital approaches, such as providing a specific app or digital platform to solve societal problems. A third understanding which is more country specific confines social enterprises to **work integration social enterprises** (Mathis, Heckl, & Senarclens de Gracy, 2014). Across the different perspectives, the importance of the founder also differs. While some understandings put strong emphasis on an inspirational leader or founder, others focus on collective action. Considering the goal to map the full scope of the phenomenon in Austria, all three definitions are taken into consideration, when it comes to compiling and synthetizing secondary literature on the topic.

Chapter 2 builds on desk research on the new social economy and the sociohistoric context in Austria. We will first trace the historical paths of the social economy in Austria and in doing so relativize the often-made claim that the social economy is a new phenomenon. We will then contextualize the phenomenon against the Austrian political, economic, and welfare situation. In Chap. 3, we summarize existing literature and data sources on the social economy in Austria and line out how the social economy positions itself vis-à-vis the nonprofit, market, and state sectors. In Chap. 4, we conclude with an outline of trends and suggestions for further research.

National Context of the Social Economy in Austria

In this section we describe the welfare and legal context against which the social economy developed and set forth how the social economy evolved in Austria.

The Austrian Context: Size, National Welfare System, and Public Social Services System

In 2018, Austria had around 8.8 million inhabitants, and by 2030 the population is expected to rise to more than 9 million (Statistik Austria 2018[1]). Austria is a developed social market economy, and in terms of GDP per capita, it is among the richest countries in the world. The average GDP per capita at PPP amounted to €38,700 in 2018. It is thus significantly higher than the average GDP per capita at PPP of €30,400 for the EU28 (Eurostat 2018[2]). In 2018, GDP per capita growth rates amounted to 1.9% in real terms, compared to 1.8% within the EU28 (Statistik

---

[1] https://www.statistik.at/web_de/statistiken/menschen_und_gesellschaft/bevoelkerung/index.html

[2] https://ec.europa.eu/eurostat/tgm/table.do?tab=table&init=1&language=en&pcode=sdg_10_10&plugin=1

Austria 2018[3]). The unemployment rate is still rather low with 4.9 in 2018, compared to 6.8% within the EU28 (Statistik Austria 2018). In Austria, the risk of poverty rate (after social transfers) amounts to 14% of the population (Statistik Austria 2015).

99.6% of all enterprises are small- and medium-sized enterprises (SMEs), each employing less than 250 employees (BMWFW, 2014). Until the 1980s, a huge part of Austria's large industrialized companies were nationalized. Since then, many have been privatized, and state holdings are on a comparative level with other European countries.

In the comparative welfare state literature, Austria is variously referred to as continental, corporatist, or conservative welfare state (Esping-Andersen, 1990). Characteristic for this type of welfare state is a **strong, mandatory social insurance system** (Österle & Heitzmann, 2009). In Austria it covers health, pension, accident, and unemployment insurance and depends heavily on contributions from both employees and employers (with cross-substitutions from general tax payments). Further, **universal benefits** specifically related to family issues and long-term care policies complement the social insurance-based system. As a third pillar, **means-tested benefits** exist with regard to poverty relief, but they amount to a miniscule part of overall welfare expenditures. The welfare state is thus dominated by insurance benefits based on either employment or family nexus, with universal and means-tested benefits as complementary instruments.

In Austria, social service provision is to a strong extent done by nonprofit organizations. The nonprofit sector receives the majority of funds from public institutions: in total 50% of NPO income stems from contracts with public institutions and 17% from direct subsidies. Another 22% come from sales revenues, a relatively small share of 9% from private donations, 2% from membership fees, and 1% from sponsoring (Pennerstorfer, Schneider, & Reitzinger, 2015).[4] As a legacy of the strong power of the two major parties, this **political duality** still manifests itself within the **nonprofit sector** (Pennerstorfer, Schneider, & Badelt, 2013). In many thematic fields (e.g., sports, social services, automotive clubs) there are often large nonprofit organizations closely related to the two large political parties (Pennerstorfer et al., 2013). Even now, it can be difficult for nonprofits without close political ties to receive public support for their missions. Another peculiarity of the Austrian political system is the system of "**social partnerships**," referring to the involvement of unions and professional associations in political decision-making processes. These institutions are closely linked to the two major parties (Pelinka & Rosenberger, 2007). The underlying goal of social partnerships is the achievement of consensus in economic and social matters, through an institutionalized form of negotiation between employers' associations, workers' associations, and political parties. Large and established nonprofit organizations are also especially involved in such a politi-

---

[3] http://www.statistik.at/web_en/press/122046.html

[4] These figures concern the nonprofit sector as a whole and thus do not only include social services.

cal negotiation process, and thus can exert political power (Neumayr, Schneider, Meyer, & Haider, 2007). Because of these characteristics, political scientists often categorize Austria as a **concordance democracy**, where consensus decisions are made, sometimes at the price of reinforcing already existing political structures and providing few incentives for political change (Pelinka & Rosenberger, 2007).

In terms of development of the social protection system, **neoliberal elements have been introduced** since the 1990s (e.g., stricter compliance requirements in return for unemployment benefits, shifts of government funding from lump-sum subsidies to performance-based service contracts), but to a much lesser degree than in other OECD countries (Obinger & Tálos, 2010; Pape et al., 2019). This is in no small part due to EU regulations, which led to new obligations for procurement where nonprofit and profit actors have to compete with each other and with a strong pressure to offer services for low prices. While the share of for-profit providers is still comparatively low, there are a couple of areas, such as in the field of shelters for asylum seekers and retirement and nursing homes, in which for-profit social service providers have gained contracts (More-Hollerweger et al., 2014). The competition between nonprofit and profit institutions brings up questions about the quality of social services (Neumayr & Meichenitsch, 2011). Cost cutting in social services has become a continuous challenge for social service providers, whether from the public, nonprofit, or for-profit sector. They are often of subtle nature (e.g., rates that are not raised for many years, more services are demanded for the same rates) (Simsa et al., 2016, Simsa & Schober, 2012).

Taken together, these peculiarities of the Austrian welfare system led to high-quality social services, however with clearly established and cemented power structures, making it difficult for new entrants, such as social entrepreneurs, to get a say on the political floor and receive public funds (Anastasiadis & Lang, 2016). At the same time, neoliberal reforms have promoted the idea of SE, bringing together actors that are not dependent on government money.

Country-Specific Forms and Development Paths

It was only after 2006 when Muhammad Yunus won the Nobel Peace Prize that the English term "social entrepreneurship" gained traction in the Austrian discourse, and various national and global actors began to promote this new notion. In the following years, a set of institutions emerged (here referred to as the ecosystem of SE), specifically dedicated to foster social entrepreneurship and the new social economy. This ecosystem includes awards dedicated to SE; intermediaries, organizing specialized trainings and support infrastructure for social entrepreneurs; universities, offering courses on SE; and financial support institutions, providing funds or special loans for social entrepreneurs. Moreover, government institutions launched initiatives such as a stakeholder dialogue for social entrepreneurs or a special impact bond (see Millner & Vandor, 2014; Schneider & Maier, 2013).

The first support institutions that entered the scene were national actors, such as the Erste foundation, founding *good.bee*,[5] that provides special loans to social entrepreneurs or a university course and a closely linked student award (the *Social Impact Award*[6]) for social entrepreneurial projects and ideas was initiated. Soon afterwards, in 2010, the first global players came to Austria, such as the *Impact Hub Vienna*,[7] an international intermediary, that offers a network and community space for SE or *Ashoka*,[8] an international fellowship program for SE.

Additionally, a small number of foundations began to offer investments specifically dedicated to social entrepreneurs. Among them were Austrian-based foundations such as the *Turnauer*[9] or *Essl*[10] *foundation*. Interestingly, also established intermediaries such as *Arbeit Plus*,[11] an umbrella organization for work integration social enterprises, started to take part in the social entrepreneurship discussion and repositioned their organization. Also formerly created awards, such as the *Trigos Award*,[12] added an award category that particularly focused on social entrepreneurship.

Moreover, media attention for social entrepreneurship rose. A media analysis shows that between 2006 and 2012 newspaper articles focusing on "social entrepreneurship" and synonymous terms increased sixfold (Schneider & Maier, 2013).

Gradually also impact investors, who see social enterprises as par excellence organizations to be supported, have entered the Austrian stage. However the topic is still in its infancy and fragmented. A couple of banks, such as *Gutman Bank* (in cooperation with the Austrian Development Bank)[13] and *Erste Bank*,[14] as well as private foundations offer tailor-made impact-oriented products. Additionally a special fund supporting social entrepreneurs with measurable impact (*Social Entrepreneurship Venture Capital Fund*)[15] was set up. Crowd investment platforms like *Green Rocket*[16] and an impact bond called *PERSPEKTIVE:ARBEIT*,[17] launched by the government in cooperation with private investors, can be seen as initiatives going in the same impact-oriented direction. A common denominator of all actors involved in impact-related investments is that these investments should somehow

---

[5] http://www.erstestiftung.org/project/good-bee/

[6] https://austria.socialimpactaward.net/

[7] https://vienna.impacthub.net/

[8] https://ashoka-cee.org/austria/

[9] http://sinn-stifter.org/katharina-turnauer-privatstiftung/

[10] https://zeroproject.org/uber-die-essl-foundation/

[11] https://arbeitplus.at/

[12] http://www.trigos.at/

[13] https://www.oe-eb.at/news-presse/news/2019/gutmann-oeeb-impact-fund.html

[14] https://www.sparkasse.at/erstebank/wir-ueber-uns/social-banking

[15] https://senat.at/sef/sef-info/

[16] https://www.greenrocket.com/

[17] https://www.sozialministerium.at/Themen/Soziales/Soziale-Themen/Soziale-Innovation/Social-Impact-Bond.html

achieve a social or ecological impact, and that the money lent is seen as an investment that should be paid back. However, in practice their investment strategies and behavior are very diverse and a common identity and understanding about impact investment are still missing. In terms of financial return, some foundations do not require the social entrepreneurs to pay back the money, while others want to achieve a financial return. In terms of social or ecological impact, some require clear impact indicators to be measured, while others only have very vague impact expectations and do not formally measure the social impact. This is to a large part due to the fact that standardized impact measurement instruments are rare. More so, large international impact investors normally invest in rather established and large initiatives, which are rare in Austria, with many social enterprises not being investment ready (Millner, Scholda, & Vandor, forthcoming).

Figure 10.1 summarizes the ecosystem of social entrepreneurs, dividing it into actors that directly provide financial, social, or intellectual capital to SE and those that provide the context and the framework conditions, such as the media, government, and universities. In the figure examples of organizations operating in each category are provided.

Notwithstanding the late emergence of the NSE or SE discourse in Austria, ideational elements of it have far-reaching roots. The oldest ones lie in the traditions of cooperative businesses and philanthropically minded entrepreneurs. Cooperative businesses had their peak in Austria in the nineteenth century, when German social reformers such as Friedrich Wilhelm Raiffeisen and Hermann Schulze-Delitzsch and less known reformers in Austria, such as Franz Michael Felder (Bertolini, 2012), propagated them as means to alleviate the social problems triggered by industrialization. For instance the Erste Foundation and its social banking branch *good.bee*, which are involved in the support of SE, can be traced back to cooperative roots. The collective generation of commercial income, self-autonomy, and

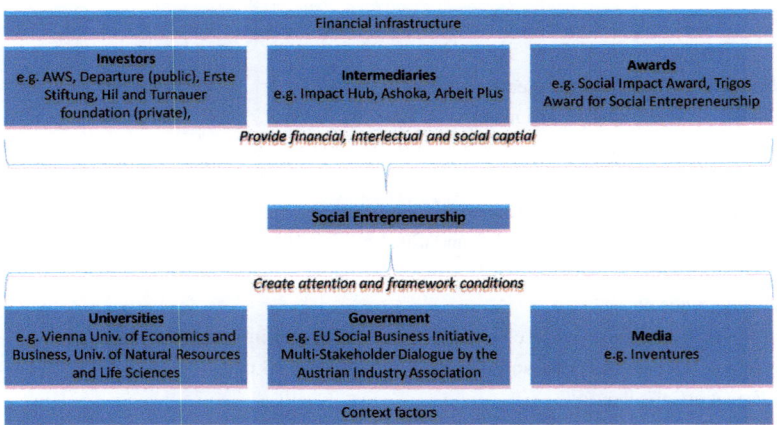

Fig. 10.1 The ecosystem of social entrepreneurship in Austria (adapted from Millner & Vandor, 2014)

solidarity is an important principle in cooperative businesses. While cooperatives played an important role historically, they have lost relevance with time (Pennerstorfer et al., 2013). Some argue that there is a recent renaissance of cooperatives active in areas like regional development or consumer cooperatives (Bertolini, 2012).

Further, some of the nineteenth-century businesses were founded by philan-thropically or religiously inclined entrepreneurs and families, such as the Mautner-Markhof family (Mentschl, 1990). They provided improved employment conditions and community infrastructure, such as schools and hospitals, to avoid depravation of workers. They forged an early link between entrepreneurial behavior and social purposes. One support organization active today, the Essl Foundation, roots in this tradition.

At the end of the 1960s, ideological currents emerged, which criticized the main-stream focus on economic growth and capitalism. They focused on ecological sus-tainability, social cohesion, and personal self-actualization. New parties and social movements (e.g., ecological, green, and student movements) were established, along with new economic activities that were less focused on profit and more on social change. The intermediary Pioneers of Change[18] that offers a fellowship pro-gram and special educational programs for pioneers of social change shares ele-ments of these roots.

Another influence relates back to labor market reforms in the 1980s, a decade marked by massive structural change and growing unemployment in Austria. Under the guidance of Alfred Dallinger, the Social Democratic Minister of Social Affairs at the time, a program was implemented to reintegrate long-term unemployed work-ers into the labor market (Leichsenring, 2001). It comprised measures to subsidize the employment of such workers in charitable organizations and to create new enter-prises for work integration. These initiatives were given much freedom in experi-menting with different measurements and creating innovative approaches to fight long-term unemployment (Anastasiadis, 2016). Work integration social enterprises managed by professional staff such as social workers and managers originated from this movement. These projects receive substantial public funds, but are required to generate part of their revenues through sales revenue (Gschöpf, 2010). Often, work integration social enterprises are branches of one of the large nonprofit organiza-tions, such as *Caritas* or *Volkshilfe*. In Austria, *ArbeitPlus* acts as an umbrella orga-nization for work integration social enterprises and is related to ENSIE[19] (European Network of Social Integration Enterprises) on the EU level.

Looking at the status quo, one could argue that SE or NSE as a label, and as a field with a specialized support infrastructure, is a rather new development in Austria, only gaining prominence within the last 10–15 years, while having its roots in developments that date back much earlier. This manifests itself on the level of support institutions: the majority has been founded within the last 10 years. In paral-lel many new organizations emerged that have adopted the social entrepreneurship

[18] http://pioneersofchange.at/

[19] http://www.ensie.org/

label and are closely linked to the newly founded support institutions, offering them a common identity and community (Schneider, 2017). However many of these organizations also adopted the SE label instrumentally, as it brought them fame and attention of important stakeholders (Dey, Schneider, & Maier 2016).

A study that looked at those social entrepreneurial projects affiliated with major support institutions in Austria found that the typical social entrepreneurial project in Austria is founded by people with a business background, is young (75% are younger than 4 years), has an average annual budget of €30.000 (including all private means put in the organization), and employs two full-time and two part-time employees (Schneider & Maier, 2013).

Legal Framework

Within the Austrian legal framework, there is no specific legal form for nonprofit organizations in general, not to mention the NSE or SE. A social enterprise could theoretically select any legal form. In practice, three different legal forms are most relevant: associations, private limited companies, and sole proprietorships. Other legal forms such as cooperatives or philanthropic foundations, which would theoretically be relevant to set up a nonprofit organization or a social enterprise, are not used frequently in practice (see Nowotny, 2013).

Looking at the most comprehensive study that quantitatively mapped social enterprises, associations (37% of all interviewed social enterprises) are the most prevalent legal form for a social enterprise, followed by private limited companies (23%) and organizations incorporated as sole proprietorships (17%) (Schneider & Maier, 2013). Given the young age of many of the surveyed organizations, 18% did not have a legal form at the time of the study. As no legal form perfectly fits social enterprises, different legal forms are often combined and intertwined (Schneider & Maier, 2013).

Associations are the most prevalent form of social enterprise. This can be due to the easy establishment of an association and the low entry barriers. Regulations for annual reporting and financial accounting are not very strict, and no minimum capital stock is required (Nowotny, 2013). The association law dates back to 1867 and has been used extensively since then. Overall, more than 116,000 associations exist in Austria (Pennerstorfer et al., 2013). In fact, when looking at the overall nonprofit sector, associations are even more important: more than 90% of all nonprofit organizations are incorporated as associations (Pennerstorfer et al., 2013).

Private limited companies (*Gesellschaft mit beschränkter Haftung*) are the second most important legal form for social enterprises. The shareholders, in general, are not personally liable for the liabilities of the corporations and there is a minimum share capital of €35,000. Every individual or legal entity might be a shareholder of the corporation. Whether they receive specific tax reliefs is not dependent on the legal form, but is awarded by fiscal authorities based on the fulfillment of specific criteria (see *Bundesabgabenordnung §§34–38*).

Sole proprietorship is the third most common form selected by social enterprises. It is represented by one person, the sole proprietor, and mostly used for small enterprises. Accounting is simple and no minimum capital requirements are necessary. The sole proprietor is legally responsible and financially liable with all his/her money and property. As a minimum requirement, one needs to have a trade license.

In Austria, no matter which legal form is chosen, organizations which primarily follow charitable, public benefits or religious purposes can get a **tax-related public benefit status** (*steuerlicher Gemeinnützigkeitsstatus*), allowing for tax alleviations (*§§ 34–38 Bundesabgabenordnung*). Tax exemptions refer to corporate income tax, value-added tax, municipal tax, and capital transfer tax. To get such a status, an organization needs to comply with specific principles: the stipulated public benefit is directed towards the general public and purposes are exclusively for public benefit. Until recently it was also necessary that benefits would directly benefit public purposes (e.g., not through intermediaries). In this regard a very recent change in the tax law was made, especially with the purpose to strengthen Austrian grant-making foundations, which do not directly give money to the target group.[20]

When it comes to incentives to financially support social enterprises and non-profits in general, laws regulating the **deductibility of charitable donations** are relevant. Introduced in 2009, these regulations allow individuals and organizations to deduct donations of up to 10% of their revenue as a special expense.[21] It refers to donations in the areas of public good, emergency relief, development aid, or animal and environmental protection.[22]

During a multi-stakeholder dialogue involving the most important stakeholders in the field of SE in Austria in 2015, a catalogue of claims[23] was developed to strengthen social enterprises in Austria. With regard to legal matters, the following propositions were made:

- A specific legal form for SE that better captures their combination of social and commercial goals.
- The broadening of existing support instruments for new start-ups, such as the law for the establishment of new organizations (*Neugründungsförderungsgesetz*), so that social enterprises can use them as well.
- Improving the legal environment for specific types of private funding institutions such as impact investors or foundations.

---

[20] https://www.parlament.gv.at/PAKT/VHG/XXV/ME/ME_00153/index.shtml

[21] https://www.bmf.gv.at/steuern/selbststaendige-unternehmer/einkommensteuer/absetzbarkeit-spenden.html

[22] In some specific cases it also refers to arts and culture. In 2016 a new law on charities has been installed. Donations to art and culture organizations are only tax deductible if they are given to organizations which parallely receive money from government funds.

[23] http://ashoka-cee.org/austria/wp-content/uploads/sites/2/2015/03/Arbeitspapiere_Multistakeholder-AGs_-fu%CC%88r-mehr-gesellschaftliche-Innovation-und-Sozialunternehmertum-in-O%CC%88sterreich_Stand24.06.2014.pdf

The New Social Economy in Austria

In this section, we summarize the current state of research and literature on the NSE or SE, give an overview of the political discourse on the NSE, summarize in what types of activities social enterprises on the ground are involved, and discuss the different connections the NSE has with the government, NPO, and market sector.

Existing Literature and Data

Literature on SE in Austria remains relatively rare. This is mainly due to the fact that research on SE coincides with the emergence of the new breed of social enterprises and related support institutions, which were established only within the last 10–15 years. Before, social enterprises were mostly reduced to work integration social enterprises (Mathis et al., 2014).

Since 2008, a couple of studies have emerged that try to capture the broader landscape of social enterprises in Austria.

The two most comprehensive **empirical (mapping) studies** specifically focusing on SE were conducted by Vandor et al. (2015) and Schneider and Maier (2013). Both focused on mapping SE actors in Austria. The study by Schneider and Maier (2013) is based on those organizations/people who are affiliated with crucial support organizations, described in section "Country-Specific Forms and Development Paths". For the purpose of the study, self-definition of actors as social entrepreneurs/social enterprises was chosen as a criterion. Out of 273 organizations/people, which could be identified due to their affiliation with a support organization, 105 were phone-interviewed. Of the interviewed sample, 80 used SE (at least partly) as a professional self-definition. Besides questions concerning areas of activities, funding, legal form, and age, more qualitative questions concerning different discourses and understanding of SE were also asked.

The second study by Vandor et al. (2015) used three existing databases, but reanalyzed using a test-based definition. These three databases comprised the above-mentioned study by Schneider and Maier (2013); another study, based specifically on members of the support organization Impact Hub Vienna (Vandor, 2014); and a database on more traditional nonprofit organizations (Pennerstorfer et al., 2015). The test-based definition stipulated that social enterprises needed to generate at least half of their income from commercial activity. Revenue stemming from performance-based contracts was categorized as commercial income. According to this study, and based on all three databases, the number of social enterprises is estimated to be between 1200 and 2000.

Another scholarly paper by Dey, Schneider, and Maier (2016) looked specifically at support organizations of SE in Austria and tried to capture different understandings of SE and why the concept of SE is so attractive these days. Vandor, Hansen, and Millner (2012) are conducting ongoing research on the support needs of social entrepreneurs in Austria and other countries, focusing on members of the international Impact Hub network.

Additionally, a couple of broader **literature review articles** on SE and social enterprise have been written by Millner and Vandor (2014), who try to capture the broader discourse on SE.

In the realm of larger **comparative projects on EU level**, two reports on the landscape of SE have emerged recently. One report (Mathis et al., 2014) issued by the European Commission, called "A map of social enterprises and their eco-systems in Europe,"[24] focuses on the definition of social enterprises in Austria, the ecosystem evolving around it, and the mapping of SE. The other one, equally commissioned by the European Commission (Benadusi, Schetelig, & Sapienza, 2014) as part of the EFESEIIS[25] project ("Enabling the flourishing and evolution of social entrepreneurship for innovation and inclusive societies"), looks at the historical background of SE and key institutions involved in SE in Austria. Both study groups conducted interviews with experts, but in terms of databases, they relied on the above-described mapping studies.

On a more specific level, a couple of national reports within larger EU projects exist that specifically look at the phenomenon of **work integration enterprises** in Austria (BDV Austria, 2008; Gschöpf, 2010). Moreover, there are official statistics on work integration social enterprises. According to statistics, 189 work integration social enterprises were active in 2010 (BMASK, 2013).[26]

Political Debate on Social Enterprise

Until recently, social enterprises did not appear as a crucial topic on the agenda of political decision makers. A study (Mathis et al., 2014) in which a variety of different stakeholders in the field of SE were interviewed shows that there is no pronounced understanding and consideration of SE by public authorities or by any public institution responsible for SE matters. For the abovementioned studies, only a single representative from a public ministry was able to contribute content-wise to the topic.

Within another study, the researchers drew the conclusion that social enterprises in the public discourse are still mainly associated with work integration social enterprises (Benadusi et al., 2014).

However, recently, some concrete policy-related measures and instruments have been established to specifically support SE:

---

[24] http://ec.europa.eu/social/main.jsp?langId=en&catId=89&newsId=2149

[25] http://www.fp7-efeseiis.eu/

[26] Work integration social enterprises can be set up either as SÖBs (social economic enterprise) or GDPs (non-profit employment projects). For further details on the distinction see Leichsenring (2001).

- AWS, the *Austrian Wirtschaftsservice Gesellschaft*,[27] the Austrian federal development and financing bank, launched the AWS Social Business Initiative to improve the know-how on SE, and foster knowledge transfer and the development of cross-regional networks.
- The *Austrian Development Agency* (ADA)[28] has created the first "social entrepreneurship challenge," a prize issued for social innovations in the field of international aid and development. €1 million will be distributed in total.
- The Vienna Business Agency (*Wirtschaftsagentur Wien*),[29] an institution set up by the city of Vienna, issues financial support for social entrepreneurs in the field of creative economy.
- While not directly catering to SE, the first social impact bond has been launched by the *Federal Ministry of Labor, Social Affairs and Consumer Protection* (BMASK). In an international context, social impact bonds often foster social enterprises.[30]
- Improvements on the foundation law and new incentives for crowdsourcing can be indirectly seen as strengthening the position of SE.
- The matching platform "*Social City Vienna*,"[31] connected to the municipality of Vienna, is an agency to promote SE, and to foster learning and exchange of knowledge.

Typical Fields of Activities and Business Models

Concerning the fields of activities, old and new organizations within the social economy show great differences.

Work integration social enterprises, classified here as part of the "old" social economy, are mostly active in catering, recycling, repairing, relocations, green space management, home services, second-hand shops, and copy shops. In this case, the production of low-threshold products and services takes center stage (BDV Austria, 2008). If we look at the social enterprises founded in the last decade, often associated with the NSE, education and research, social inclusion, and environment/sustainability are among the most prominent topics (Schneider & Maier, 2013; Vandor et al., 2015). Other important topics are support for other social enterprises, work integration, as well as foreign aid. These organizations often state that they try to support topics that have not yet received much attention, thus assuming a complementary instead of a substituting role, emerging in niches left open by traditional

---

[27] http://www.awsg.at/Content.Node/foerderungen_alle/nationale-finanzierung/4067.de.php

[28] http://www.entwicklung.at/socialentrepreneurship/

[29] https://wirtschaftsagentur.at/foerderungen/programme/call-social-entrepreneurship-47/

[30] https://www.sozialministerium.at/cms/site/attachments/1/2/2/CH3434/CMS1454342099172/projektu_bersicht_sib_oesterreich_aktuell_mp.pdf

[31] http://www.socialcity.at/

nonprofits. Moreover, their approaches often involve digital tools and platforms, such as apps or online learning platforms. For instance, the social enterprise Three Coins[32] has developed an app called CureRunners, with the aim of playfully familiarizing young people with different financial topics, such as saving money, indebtedness, or coping with financial resources.

In a meta-study on social enterprise (Vandor et al., 2015), another set of actors come into focus: established nonprofit organizations that generate at least half of their income from market income (including performance-related contracts). Thus, if we define the new social economy as a set of organizations that generate their own income, such nonprofit organizations would fall within the definition. These organizations support a totally different set of activities; more classical welfare state activities like the provision of social services (e.g., elder- or childcare facilities) or health-related services (e.g., hospitals or rescue services) play a dominant role. Much of the income of these organizations stems from performance-related contracts with the government, which in some definitions is seen as market income. By using such a broad definition of the social economy, in fact many established nonprofit organizations could be seen as part of this movement (for a discussion of this debate see Vandor et al., 2015). While some of them have always generated large parts of their income from sales revenues, we have observed a general trend that sales revenues have become more relevant for all types of nonprofit organizations (Pennerstorfer et al., 2015). Pennerstorfer et al., (2015) found out that between 2006 and 2014, the percentage of sales revenues has increased by eight percentage points, whereas the level of government subsidies and grants has fallen by almost six percentage points.

No matter what activities social entrepreneurs are involved in, most of them try to implement strategies, allowing them to generate their own income. Vandor et al. (2015) speak about four different approaches or business models as to how social entrepreneurs can generate their own income.

First, a large part of all social enterprises in Austria integrate their specific target group in the work or production process, by offering them employment and selling the products and services generated. Most work integration social enterprises pursue this approach, but also newly established organizations do so. For instance, the work integration social enterprise *Gabarage*[33] employs formerly drug-addicted persons and offers 1-year programs in order to qualify them for the first job market. Jobs in the production, administration, or sale of upcycling products are offered. Besides job, orientation is offered and social competencies are taught to facilitate the transition into the first labor market. The products are sold in their own shops.

Second, another approach is to offer products and services to a specific, often socially and economically deprived target group, for a fair price; in many cases, the products and services offered are not available or too expensive for the specific tar-

---

[32] https://www.threecoins.org/en/

[33] https://www.gabarage.at/%C3%BCber-uns/

get group. For example, *Helioz*,[34] an Austria-based social enterprise, falls in this category. It produces and sells a special device called WADI that allows solar water disinfection. It is mostly active in Asia and Africa, and helps governments and institutions there in their fight against waterborne diseases. While they charge a prize for the WADI, the prize is affordable for the people living in these regions.

However not all target groups can pay for the products and services offered. In these cases, products or services can be offered for free, while money is generated through separate, decoupled activities that cross-finance the social activity. For instance *Talentify*,[35] a network for education, offers a digital platform for student peer-to-peer tutoring. The aim is to bring together students with more and less learning experience. Via the platform, they can also figure out their personal strengths and book workshops. The platform allows a matchmaking with potential future employers. These employers thus receive access to young talents. While the platform is free for students, employers have to pay for the service and special workshops on employer branding and on how to access young people, allowing a cross-financing of the educational activities.

Fourth, some organizations do not have a specific target group in mind, but produce sustainable products, with the aim of changing consumption patterns and raising awareness for sustainability and other topics. They try to reduce negative externalities in their production process, through the usage of sustainable materials, upcycling, or reusage of materials. For instance, the social business *Erdbeerwoche*[36] produces sustainable sanitary products and in particular sustainable menstruation products. Additionally, they try to positively connote the topic and want to empower women to deal with this topic in a self-confident and positive way.

Overall, we can see that social entrepreneurship organizations are mostly involved in the provision of social services, at the expense of advocacy and community building (Schneider & Maier, 2013).

Relations to Other Sectors

Relationship between the Social Economy and the State

Austria is a corporatist welfare state, where many state-financed social service programs are implemented by nonprofit organizations (Pennerstorfer et al., 2013). As a general rule of thumb, a couple of large nonprofit organizations receive the major amount of available public funds. Thus it might be difficult for newly established social enterprises to acquire government funding. From the perspective of mostly newly established social enterprises, a study by Schneider and Maier (2013) indi-

---

[34] https://www.helioz.org/home/

[35] https://www.talentify.me/

[36] https://www.erdbeerwoche-shop.com/?gclid=EAIaIQobChMIvqatnKyq6QIVEYGyCh2kMwl9
EAAYASAAEgJIzfD_BwE

cates that they have a skeptical attitude towards the state. Two arguments are brought into play; first, state actors are seen as stolid, and second social enterprises do not believe that they have good chances to receive government funds. This is also reflected in the funding structure of social enterprises. Social entrepreneurs (on average) receive 30% of their funds from sales revenue; more than 50% from donations, investments, or personal savings; and only 13% from government subsidies or performance-based contracts. This is in stark contrast to more traditional nonprofit organizations that receive the majority of funds from public institutions: in total 50% of NPO income stems from contracts with public institutions and 17% from direct subsidies. Another 22% comes from sales revenues, and a relatively small share of 12% from private donations, sponsoring, and membership fees (Pennerstorfer et al., 2015).[37]

From the perspective of the state, until very recently there has not been much consideration of social enterprises on the political agenda as demonstrated in the reports of Mathis et al. (2014) and Benadusi et al. (2014). One exception has been the involvement of the government with work integration social enterprises, which until recently have been heavily supported by government funds (Leichsenring, 2001). This has changed in the years from 2017 to 2019, with the new policies of a rather right-wing government (Simsa, 2019). Regarding funding instruments within the new social economy, gradual change is on the way; with the first tailor-made instruments to fund and support social enterprises have been established by state-run/state-related funding agency, such as the Austrian federal promotional bank (AWS)[38] or the Austrian Development Agency (ADA).[39]

Additionally a first social impact bond called *PERSPEKTIVE:ARBEIT, with a duration of 3 years*, has been established by the Austrian Federal Ministry of Social Affairs, Health, Care and Consumer Protection in 2015. This bond involves a cooperation between the Ministry and a set of private foundations (e.g., Hil foundation, Schweighofer foundation, Familie Scheuch foundation) that finance the project and get reimbursed by the government if certain predefined impact dimensions and goals are met. Such a project also involves a set of intermediaries, coordinating the project and a nonprofit organization that is responsible for implementing the project on the ground. Social impact bonds allow experimentation with new social approaches, without having to spend government money if they are not successful. In this particular project the aim was to integrate women, who have been affected by domestic violence, into the job market. More than 300 women took part in the project. Experienced social workers worked with women to establish personal and career-related goals. While many involved women found a job and thus the program was partially successful, the overall impact goals in terms of duration of maintenance of job and the hereby earned income did not meet the initially set goals. While

---

[37] These figures concern the nonprofit sector as a whole and thus do not only include social services.

[38] http://www.awsg.at/Content.Node/foerderungen_alle/nationale-finanzierung/4067.de.php

[39] http://www.entwicklung.at/socialentrepreneurship/

overall this project allowed women to break free from the vicious circle of domestic violence, the government did not have to reimburse the founders, given that the predefined impact goals have not been met. A major learning from this project was that women need more time to settle in the job market, and thus the duration of such projects should be longer (Austrian Ministry of Social Affairs, Health, Care and Consumer Protection 2019[40]).

Relationship Between SE and Civil Society/Nonprofits

Within existing literature, SE is positioned at the intersection between the nonprofit and the market sector (Schneider & Maier, 2013). Depending on each individual case, they can lean more towards the market or nonprofit sector. Research so far indicates that social enterprises and traditional civil society/nonprofit organizations represent two different worlds, operating on different logics, and sometimes being skeptical towards each other (Benadusi et al., 2014; Schneider, 2017). Despite the skeptical attitude many social enterprises have towards the more established nonprofit sector, collaborations are forged in instances where access to important target groups would otherwise be difficult (Schneider, 2017).

Differences result from different educational and ideological backgrounds: many employees have an education in social work or related fields, and new social enterprises are often founded and run by business graduates. Additionally their approach to tackle societal challenges might differ. While traditional nonprofit organizations will work on the ground, social enterprises might work more indirectly on the topic, not necessarily working with vulnerable people directly (Benadusi et al., 2014). Additionally, in social enterprises there is more emphasis on an inspirational founder, while in the nonprofit sector collective actions stand in the foreground (Schneider & Maier, 2013). We do, however, see tendencies of a blurring of such boundaries, as when existing nonprofits establish social enterprises as spin-offs. For instance Magdas,[41] a hotel set up by Caritas, is an example going in this direction. In this case, a traditional nonprofit organization set up a separate legal entity, a hotel, in which people with a migration background are employed and trained. While it can rely on the expertise of the larger Caritas network, the long-term goal is that the hotel can sustain itself and is not dependent on government money.

---

[40] https://www.sozialministerium.at/Themen/Soziales/Soziale-Themen/Soziale-Innovation/Social-Impact-Bond.html

[41] http://www.magdas-hotel.at/home/

Relationship Between the Market and Social Enterprises

Many social enterprises forge strong networks and collaborations with profit-oriented enterprises (Schneider & Maier, 2013). Some argue that they operate on rather similar logics. Beyond that, many of the support institutions operate on a market logic. For instance, one of the first SE courses in Austria was offered by the Vienna University of Economics and Business Administration. Social branches of banks offer specific loans to social enterprises and incubation spaces and a small number of impact investors (such as Bonventure[42] or Toniic[43]) gradually conquered the Austrian market (see Mathis et al., 2014 for an overview of these actors). Additionally specific trainings are offered by support institutions that focus on training social entrepreneurs on business skills or on becoming investment ready (e.g., Investment Ready Program by the Austrian Impact Hub, special business-related workshops offered by the Social Impact Award). Due to these relationships, social enterprises are particularly aware or incentivized to adopt a management or investment logic (Schneider & Meyer, 2017).

Conclusion and Perspective

Quantitatively, experts estimate that the NSE or SE will gain in importance in the next decades. In the above-introduced study by Vandor et al. (2015), experts were asked to assess the future development of SE. There is a consensus among experts that the number of social enterprises (based on the test-based definition introduced in section "Existing Literature and Data") will at least double within the next 10 years. The first social entrepreneurial spin-offs by large established nonprofit organizations are another indicator of the increasing relevance of SE. For instance, the Magdas hotel founded by Caritas and where refugees can work is one example in this direction.

A couple of reasons/triggers can be linked to this emerging development.

- **New funding arrangements:** In a Delphi survey (Meyer & Simsa, 2013) focusing on the evaluation of future developments in the nonprofit sector, there was a consensus among experts that the resources available from government sources for social service provision will decrease; as a consequence, nonprofits will look for new types of funding. The trend of a quickly aging population, where more of the overall social protection spending needs to be allocated to retirement, health, and care-related expenses, puts the Austrian welfare state under great pressure. As a consequence, gradually, fewer public funds will be available for other activities (Österle & Heitzmann, 2009). Diminished economic growth rates, spread of atypical employment, and increasing unemployment rates (Talos

---

[42] http://www.bonventure.de/home.html

[43] https://www.toniic.com/

& Fink, 2005) weigh further on public budgets. It is likely that more actors will look for other sources of income. Against this background, financially autonomous organizations are highly welcomed and sometimes heralded as the new heroes that can bring about social change (Dey et al., 2016).

- **Changes in areas of activities:** In terms of specific areas of activities, changes are going on. Especially relevant were the large number of war refugees coming to Austria. Besides social movements, many ad hoc initiatives, volunteers (Simsa, 2017; Simsa, Rameder, Aghamanoukjan, & Totter, 2018), and also a set of social enterprises emerged that have dedicated themselves to this topic.
- **Support infrastructure:** The support infrastructure around SE and the policy-related issues have gained importance. In terms of financing options for SE, specific public funds for SE have been established.

What needs to be kept in mind is that despite this very optimistic outlook, the baseline is still very low, and one should not be seduced to believe that SE might or could replace social welfare actors. Rather, SE should best be seen as a complementary approach of actors that can bring about innovative solutions in specific niches. Schneider and Maier (2013) point out that SE could lead to selecting particular profitable projects while ignoring others. The heavy focus on service provision, compared to advocacy or community-building activities, is another example pointing towards the limits of SE.

Finally, it remains to be seen how the current COVID-19 pandemic will affect the NSE in the long term. Many of them are active in areas particularly affected by the crisis, such as in catering, sale of products, or coordination of physical events. While a public aid package[44] dedicated to nonprofit organizations was set up, only organizations that have a charitable tax status or are in possession of such an organization can apply for such aids, a criterion many organizations of the NSE do not fulfill. Some privately organized aid measures such as a solidarity fund[45] or crowdfunding campaigns were initiated. In the meanwhile, organizations of the new social economy have started to adapt their range of products and services (e.g., offering their services in a virtual format or producing protective masks instead of other products) and only few had to lay off staff.[46]

References

Anastasiadis, M. (2016). Work integration social Enterprises in Austria–Characteristics, evolution and perspectives. *Nonprofit Policy Forum, 7*(4), 541–564.

Anastasiadis, M. & Lang, R. (2016). Social Enterprise in Austria. A contextual approach to understand an ambiguous concept. In *ICEMS (The International Comparative Social Enterprise Models) Working Paper, 26.*

---

[44] https://npo-fonds.at/

[45] https://vienna.impacthub.net/solidarity-fund/

[46] https://www.derstandard.at/story/2000120259203/was-sozialunternehmen-jetzt-brauchen

BDV Austria (2008). *WISEs and their role in European policies. National Report – Austria.* Available at: http://www.arbeitplus.at/wordpress/wp-content/uploads/2012/06/WISE_Bericht_DE_2009_final.pdf

Benadusi, M., Schetelig, K. & Sapienza, R. (2014). *Social Enterprise, Social Innovation and Social Entrepreneurship in Austria: A national report.* Available at: http://www.fp7-efeseiis.eu/national-report-austria

Bertolini, R. (2012). *Allmeinde Vorarlberg.* Bregenz: Vertolini Verlag.

Bundesministerium für Arbeit, Soziales und Konsumentenschutz (2013). *Aktive Arbeitsmarktpolitik in Österreich. 1994–2013. Bericht BMASK.* Available at: https://www.sozialministerium.at/cms/site/attachments/5/9/0/CH3434/CMS1453972744490/arbeitsmarktpolitik_dokumentation_aktive_arbeitsmarktpolitik_in_oesterreich_1994-2013.pdf

Bundesministerium für Wissenschaft, Forschung und Wirtschaft (2014). *Mittelstandsbericht 2014.* Available at: http://www.bmwfw.gv.at/Unternehmen/UnternehmensUndKMU-Politik/Documents/Mittelstandsbericht2014.pdf

Dey, P., Schneider, H., & Maier, F. (2016). Intermediary Organisations and the Hegemonisation of social entrepreneurship: Fantasmatic articulations, constitutive Quiescences, and moments of indeterminacy. *Organization Studies, 37*(10), 1451–1472.

Esping-Andersen, G. (1990). *The three worlds of welfare capitalism.* Oxford: Polity Press.

Gschöpf, H. (2010). *The social economy sector and the situation of social enterprises in Austria. With special reference to "Work Integration Social Enterprises".* National report: Austria.

Leichsenring, K. (2001). Austria. Social enterprises and new childcare services. In C. Borzaga & J. Defourny (Eds.), *The emergence of social Enterprise. Studies in the management of voluntary and non-profit organizations* (pp. 31–46). London: Routledge.

Mathis, J., Heckl, E. & Senarclens de Gracy, R. (2014). A map of social enterprises and their eco-systems in Europe. Country Report Austria. European Commission. Available at: http://ec.europa.eu/social/keyDocuments.jsp?advSearchKey=socentcntryrepts&mode=advancedSubmit&langId=en&policyArea=&type=0&country=0&year=0&orderBy=docOrder

Mentschl, J. (1990). Mautner von Markhof, Adolf Ignaz Ritter. In *Neue Deutsche Biographie.* Available at: http://www.deutsche-biographie.de/pnd137978847.html

Meyer, M., & Simsa, R. (2013). Entwicklungsperspektiven des Nonprofit – Sektors. In R. Simsa, M. Meyer, & C. Badelt (Eds.), *Handbuch der Nonprofit – Organisation* (pp. 509–525). Stuttgart: Schäffer-Poeschel 5. überarbeitete Auflage.

Millner, R., Scholda, F., & Vandor, P. (forthcoming). *Impact investing – Wirkungsorientiertes Investieren in Österreich.* Working Paper. Social Entrepreneurship Center, WU Wien.

Millner, R., & Vandor, P. (2014). Neues Unternehmertum: Social Entrepreneurship und die Rolle des Umfelds. In A. Zimmer & R. Simsa (Eds.), *Forschung zu Zivilgesellschaft, NPOs und Engagement* (pp. 283–300). Wiesbaden: Springer.

More-Hollerweger, E., Simsa, R., Kainz, G., Neunteufl, F., Grasgruber-Kerl, R., & Wohlgemuth, F. (2014). Civil society index. In *Rahmenbedingungen für die Zivilgesellschaft in Österreich.* Available at https://www.wu.ac.at/fileadmin/wu/d/cc/npocompetence/downloads/civil-society-index_endbericht.pdf.

Neumayr, M., & Meichenitsch, K. (2011). Sind Non-Profit Organisationen die Guten? Qualitätsunterschiede zwischen gemeinnützigen und gewinnorientierten Alten-und Pflegeheimen. *Kurswechsel, 4*(11), 75–85.

Neumayr, M., Schneider, U., Meyer, M., & Haider, A. (2007). *The non-profit sector in Austria: An economic, legal and political appraisal.* Working Paper. WU Vienna.

Nowotny, C. (2013). Rechtliche Gestaltungsformen für NPOs. In R. Simsa, M. Meyer, & C. Badelt (Eds.), *Handbuch der Nonprofit – Organisation* (pp. 183–205). Stuttgart: Schäffer-Poeschel, 5. überarbeitete Auflage.

Obinger, H., & Tálos, E. (2010). Janus-faced developments in a prototypical Bismarckian welfare state. Welfare reforms in Austria since the 1970s. In B. Palier (Ed.), *A long goodbye to Bismarck? The politics of welfare reform in continental Europe* (pp. 101–128). Amsterdam: Amsterdam University Press.

Österle, A., & Heitzmann, K. (2009). Welfare state development in Austria: Strong traditions meet new challenges. In K. Schubert, S. Hegelich, & U. Bazant (Eds.), *The handbook of European welfare systems*. (pp. 31–48). London: Routledge.

Pape, U., Brandsen, T., Pahl, J., Pielinski, B., Baturina, D., Brookes, N., et al. (2019). Changing policy environments in Europe and the resilience of the third sector. *Voluntas: International Journal of Voluntary and Nonprofit Organizations, 31*, 238–249.

Pelinka, A., & Rosenberger, S. (2007). *Österreichische Politik: Grundlagen-Strukturen-Trends*. facultas. wuv/maudrich.

Pennerstorfer, A., Schneider, U., & Badelt, C. (2013). Der Nonprofit-Sektor in Österreich. In R. Simsa, M. Meyer, & C. Badelt (Eds.), *Handbuch der Nonprofit – Organisation* (pp. 55–76). Stuttgart: Schäffer-Poeschel, 5. überarbeitete Auflage.

Pennerstorfer, A., Schneider, U., & Reitzinger, S. (2015). *Nonprofit Organisationen in Österreich 2014. Forschungsbericht 01/2015*. WU Wien: Institut für Sozialpolitik. Available at: https://www.wu.ac.at/fileadmin/wu/d/i/sozialpolitik/FB_01_2015_gesamt.pdf.

Schneider, H. (2017). Social entrepreneurship: Wie ein Feld mit Bedeutung erfüllt wird. Doctoral Thesis, Vienna University of Economics and Business. Unpublished.

Schneider, H., & Maier, F. (2013). *Social entrepreneurship in Österreich*. Working Paper. Institut für Nonprofit Management, WU Wien.

Schneider, H., & Meyer, M. (2017). Social entrepreneurship as institutional work: The interplay between identity framings and identity work. In *European Group for Organizational Studies: EGOS colloquium*. Kopenhagen: Dänemark.

Simsa, R. (2017). Leaving emergency Management in the Refugee Crisis to civil society? The case of Austria. *Journal of Applied Security Research, 12*(1), 78–95.

Simsa, R. (2019). Civil society capture by early stage autocrats in well developed democracies – The case of Austria. *Nonprofit Policy Forum, 10*(3), 1–10.

Simsa, R., Auf, M., Bratke, S. M., Hazzi, O., Herndler, M., Hoff, M., et al. (2016). *Beiträge der Zivilgesellschaft zur Bewältigung der Flüchtlingskrise–Leistungen und Lernchancen*. Available at: https://www.wu.ac.at/npocompetence/research/laufendeforsch/studie-beitraege-der-zivilgesellschaft-zur-bewaeltigung-der-fluechtlingskrise-leistungen-und-lernchancen/

Simsa, R., Rameder, P., Aghamanoukjan, A., & Totter, M. (2018). Spontaneous volunteering in social crisis: Self-organization and coordination. *Nonprofit and Voluntary Sector Quarterly, 48*(2S), 103–122.

Simsa, R., & Schober, D., (2012). Nonprofit Organisationen in Österreich. Ein quantitativer Überblick über den Nonprofit Sektor In *Österreich. Projektbericht 2012,* Wien.

Talos, E., & Fink, M. (2005). The welfare state in Austria. In B. Vivekanandan & N. Kurian (Eds.), *Welfare states and the future* (pp. 131–150). Basingstoke: Palgrave Macmillan.

Vandor, P. (2014). *Annual Member Survey des Impact HUB Vienna 2013*. Unpublished results.

Vandor, P., Hansen, H., & R. Millner (2012). Supporting social entrepreneurs –the effects of organizational maturity. In *Paper for 10th International Conference of the International Society for Third Sector Research (ISTR) Siena, July 7–10, 2012*.

Vandor, P., Millner, R., Moder, C., Schneider, H., & Meyer, M. (2015). *Das Potential von Social Business in Österreich*. WU Vienna University of Economics and Business Working Paper.

Chapter 11
The Evolution of the New Social Economy in Sweden

H. T. R. Persson

Introduction

In this chapter, the new social economy is addressed from the point of view of the Swedish social economy. The Swedish social economy is appropriately described as the sole or the backbone of the Swedish society. It is a vast sphere containing several sectors and a melting pot of numerous organisations emphasising social values and has an effect on most Swedish citizens and denizens (for discussion on denizens see Hammar, 1990, p. 21) at some point, if not throughout their entire lives. Hence, it would be close to megalomania to set out to cover all aspects of the social economy sphere in this chapter. Instead, the main focus is on those aspects relating to the Swedish welfare state.

While the term—social economy—has been official within the European Union since 1989, it took until 1999 for Sweden to define the Swedish understanding of the concept. The concept had up to this point only been relevant in connection with the European Council's structural funds and programmes and the Swedish governments had shown little interest until they were forced to define the concept as a result of the Extra European Council Meeting on Employment in 1997. As a result, the government assigned a specific working group the task of defining the concept of the social economy. The working group was to pay special consideration to state measures facilitating the conditions of the social economy, various EC programmes and structural funds, and public sector cooperation and assignments, for example. The working group clarified that the social economy was a new way of looking at businesses and organisations with a long history and strong tradition in Sweden, but also containing new phenomena and opportunities yet to be explored. Hence, various

H. T. R. Persson (✉)
Department of Sport Sciences, Faculty of Education and Society, Malmö University, Malmö, Sweden
e-mail: thomas.persson@mau.se

© Springer Nature Switzerland AG 2021   225
B. Gidron, A. Domaradzka (eds.), *The New Social and Impact Economy*,
Nonprofit and Civil Society Studies, https://doi.org/10.1007/978-3-030-68295-8_11

existing definitions and descriptions were weighed against Swedish not-for-profit activities, cooperatives, popular movements, voluntary social work and more. As a result, the social economy and the civil society came to be more or less synonyms in the Swedish context.

The social economy was neither to be seen as a specific legal entity or method, nor as exclusive to a specific sector made up of specific organisations. Instead, the social economy was to be seen as part of the general economy with organisations founded and existing based on specific purposes. As such, an organisation should simultaneously be able to exist in several parts of the economy. 'What can be said to be at the "core" of the social economy is that the activities are primarily aimed at a good life for the individual, within specific delimited areas' (Näringsdepartementet, 1998, p. 8 [Ministry of Enterprise and Innovation]). It was supposed to be freestanding from the public sector, its basic values to focus on people and society both in terms of its 'recipients' and participants and be open to society and for those that wish to take part, insofar as the ability to fulfil the purpose permits. This follows the long and strong Swedish tradition of membership associations. In Sweden, 6.2 million, or 77.5%, of the Swedish population, 16 years and older, are members of one or more associations, and more than 60% of these, or 3.8 million people, are members of a trade union or entrepreneurial organisation (SCB, 2016). As a result, the social economy came to be defined as:

> organised activities that primarily have societal purposes, build on democratic values and are organized independent from the government. These social and economic activities are conducted primarily in the associations, cooperatives, foundations and similar organizations. Activities within the social economy have the public or its members' good, not the profit, as the main driving force.
> (Kulturdepartementet, 1999 [Ministry of Culture and Sport])

Hence, the concept of the social economy is best described as a sphere, made up of several sectors and organisations, primarily with societal purposes (see Fig. 11.1).

The evolution of the concept of the social economy is mirrored by the public, political and academic discourse, from little attention to almost none, simultaneously with the increasing attention paid to the not-for-profit sector and social enterprises, primarily understood as work integration social enterprises (here on WISEs).

The Prevalence of the Concept in Public and Academic Discourse

The concept of social economy is given little prevalence in the Swedish public, political and academic discourse. Nevertheless, it does have a presence in newspaper articles (news, business or debate articles)—online versions—commonly written by academics and representatives of interest organisation, but also by journalists, with headings such as *The furniture giant's billion will get refugees to work* (Frostberg, 2019b), *The state discriminates social enterprises* (Lundkvist Fridh,

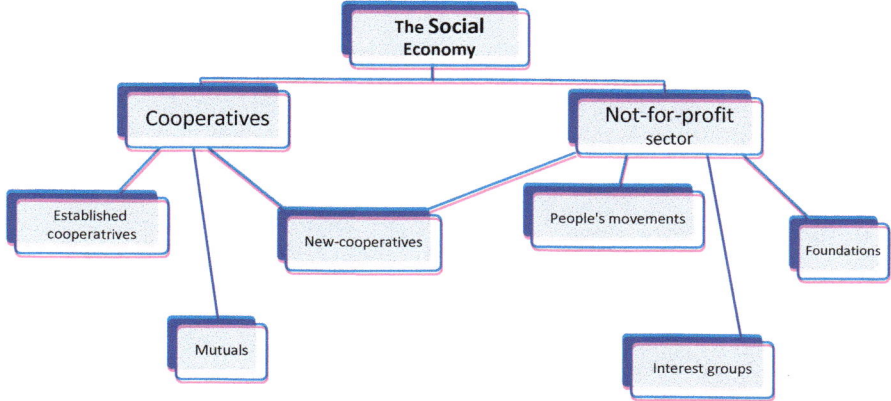

Source: Wijkström & Lundström, 2002, p. 99, authors translation

Fig. 11.1   Source: Wijkström & Lundström, 2002, p. 99, authors' translation

Svensson, Laurén, & Kowalewski, 2019), *Ikea aims to make social entrepreneurs grow globally* (Frostberg, 2019a), *Here, the social democrats raise venture capital for social projects* (Widehed, 2018), *Lund students train social enterprises in entrepreneurship* (Capuder, 2018) and *Rural associations must be able to obtain loans* (Nilsson, Hahn, Laurén, Thelander, & Herlitz, 2017). Zooming out, looking at the period between 2008 and 2018, the Swedish Agency for Economic and Regional Growth (from here on SAERG, Tillväxtverket, 2019b) shows how media's interest in the social economy—here defined by the keywords social enterprise, social innovation, social entrepreneurship, social entrepreneurs and work-integrated social enterprises (socialt företagande, social innovation, socialt entreprenörskap, samhällsentreprenör och arbetsintegrerade sociala företag)—has varied over time. The overall trend is positive, from 208 hits in 2008 to 763 in 2018, with a peak of 1091 in 2016 (see Table 11.1). Much can be said about keywords and the fact that the SAERG's report only made use of Veckans Affärer (economic journal), Upphandling24 (specific focus on public procurements) and Dagens Samhälle (focus on welfare issues), while leaving out for example the largest morning newspapers, but the trend seems to follow the growth in number of WISEs during the same period. Not being an analytical report, the peak in 2016 is left without explanation, but it would be logical to connect the steep increase in the number of articles with the refugee crises and the role played by social enterprises and not-for-profit organisations in assisting asylum seekers.

When the social economy surfaces in the Swedish political discourse it commonly does so with a focus on those individual sectors and organisations making up the social economy, such as the not-for-profit sector (idéburna sektorn) and not-for-profit welfare (idéburen välfärd), civil society, sport organisations, social entrepreneurship, social enterprises and social innovation (see SOU, 2019). That the concept of the social economy is given little attention is underlined by its absence from

Table 11.1 Compilation according to results from Retriever in Tillväxtverket, (2019b)

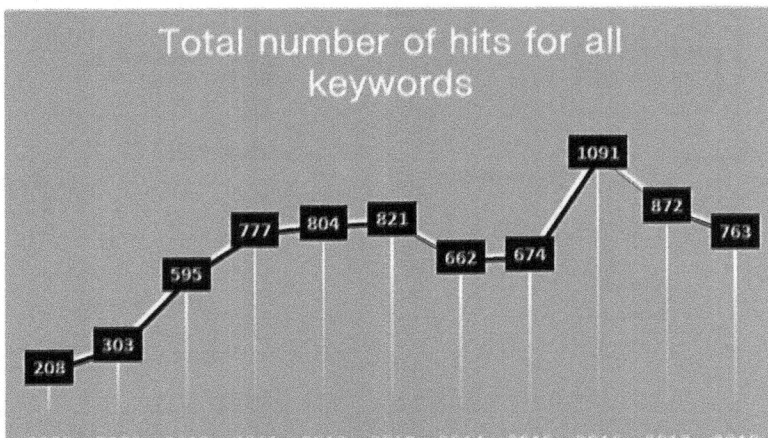

Sweden's national reform programme 2020: Europe 2020—A strategy for smart, sustainable and inclusive growth (Regeringskansliet, 2020). If it was not for the opinion input included in the report from organisations such as Coompanion (business advisory organisation for people who want to start businesses together, in cooperative activities, Coompanion, n.d.) and the European Youth Parliament Sweden (Regeringskansliet, 2020) the concept would not have been mentioned. The same pattern is repeated by the Forum for Social Innovation Sweden (FSIS: Mötesplats Social Innovation), the Swedish knowledge platform for social innovation and social enterprise, commissioned by the Swedish Government through Vinnova (the Swedish Governmental Agency for Innovation Systems). FSIS is in many ways the acting bridge between the political discourse and agenda, and the academic discourse and research. With its focus on creating spaces where actors across the social innovation and social enterprise field can meet, the concept of the social economy is only to be voiced indirectly on the web page (MSI, n.d.). Hence, it should come as little surprise that the academic discourse is simulating the political discourse. The research and discourse on the topic of the social economy is one of post-1999, insofar as it exists. However, this does not mean that some of the movements encapsulated by the concept of the social economy have not in their own right been researched pre-1999. Wijkström and Lundström (2002, p. 52) divide the pre-1999 social economy research into two main streams: *people's movement research* and research focusing on the corporate processes between the organisations and the state. As such it covers topics such as the people's movement, associations, foundations, civil society and corporatism (Heckscher, 1944, 1951; Hessler, 1952; Jansson, 1985; Thörnberg, 1943; for a summary on pre-1999 research see Wijkström & Lundström, 2002). The concept of social economy started appearing in publications—articles, books and reports—post-1999, but does not always follow the official definition and is sometimes put on par with the not-for-profit sector (see Westlund, 2003). Topics covered by the post-1999 research range from a social economy: as saviour of the welfare system (von Bergman-Winberg, 2005); saviour of the countryside from depopulation (Lundholm, 2002); a way to enter the labour market (Westlund, 2003; Wood, 2007); women's rights (Gawell, 2017); social capital, social economy and sustainable development (Gillberg & Stenberg, 2002); general conceptual discussions (Trägårdh, 2000), but also in larger international research projects where Sweden is but one of many cases studied and compared (Biggeri, Testi, Belluci, During, & Persson, 2018).

National Context

The history of the social economy in Sweden is partly also the history of the Swedish welfare state. Despite not being defined as one concept and sphere before 1999 (Kulturdepartementet, 1999), Salonen (2009) dates its birth to the period between 1880s and World War I, also referred to as the 'Liberal Reform Era'. This is the era when the seeds for future sickness benefits, injury insurance, and old age and invalidity pensions were sown, which all became central to the birth of the Swedish welfare regime. Besides being the era of a growing labour movement, this is also the period when modern popular movements in Sweden such as the temperance, cooperatives, women's and the Scandinavian sports movements (broader than the Anglo-Saxon concept of sport) were born. As well as representing the growth of the Swedish social economy, they all played a central role in making Sweden into a modern democracy (Einarsson, 2011; Hedenborg & Kvarnström, 2009; Klausen & Selle, 1996). Also, it is impossible not to attribute the roots of the social economy—popular movement, voluntary organisations and social enterprises—to different charitable activities by the Swedish state church (Pestoff, 2004), but also the latter's diminishing role as an agent for social prosperity which happened to coincide with the country suffering from high unemployment, poverty and misery (Eriksson, 2005; Hedenborg & Kvarnström, 2009). Although not fully implemented until the mid-twentieth century, due to the recession following upon World War I, '[m]any social ideas, such as universal security for all people, were already recognized as guiding policy principles' (Salonen, 2009, p. 132). Hence, it is fair to say that what we today call the social economy played an important role in the birth of the Swedish welfare state.

In modern times the Swedish state has always been supporting a broad voluntary sector, expressed for example in and by political, sport, cultural and religious associations, in Swedish referred to as the peoples' movement (Folkrörelser), popular movements or social economy (Lundqvist & Williams, 2010, pp. 25–26). More recently, social entrepreneurship and social enterprises have taken up an increasing part of the discourse on the social economy. However, when talking about social entrepreneurship in the Swedish social economy in a modern context, one needs to distinguish between at least four different streams of entrepreneurship with social and societal purposes. Some of these stem from older domestic traditions, while others spring from more recent foreign influences. The term societal entrepreneur-ship emerged as a description of those local, rather than centralised, counterstrate-gies and initiatives that developed during the late 1970s as a result of the decline of large corporate and industrial activities in smaller communities. As local strategies developed, early streams of Swedish research emerged around the phenomenon, which in international publications were labelled community entrepreneurship. From the 1990s onwards, the flora of prefix entrepreneurship increased to include civic, social and public entrepreneurship. A prominent feature of Swedish social entrepreneurship and social enterprises is that it commonly stems from a reaction to the state of the welfare regime and it breaks with traditional boundaries of the mod-ern industrial welfare state.

Despite this, it was the social democrat, ideologist and Minister of Finance, Ernst Wigforss (1925–196/1932–1949), who first during his time as Minister of Finance and then again at the 1976 LO Congress used the term social enterprise to describe a vision to nationalise large private corporations into social enterprises through *wage-earner funds*. The vision was one of where the state and unions in coopera-tion—as the employer—should be able to decide the level of employment (Henrekson & Jakobsson, 2003). Although this early ideological version of a social enterprise did carry some of the central ideas to a modern social enterprise—such as social, societal or solidarity purposes—and more specifically to a WISE, more mod-ern versions of Swedish social enterprises need to be understood as a phenomenon existing on a matrix with two sliding scales between exclusive and open forms, and between not-for-profit and for-profit forms.

If the social enterprises within the social economy are to be understood as coop-erative not-for-profit initiatives, which provide services that the public sector no longer is capable of delivering to the extent needed or quality demanded by the public, then social enterprises started to emerge during the 1970s and took off dur-ing the 1980s. The growth during the 1980s was primarily represented by coopera-tive childcare services. Around the same time, the first WISEs arose. This type of social enterprises was a response from those hardest hit at the time when the system of local employment offices eroded and a restructuring of the mental healthcare system took place, resulting in ever-larger number of openly marginalised groups. Although it is hard to find evidence supporting the purest form of this model—enterprises started and run by those long-term unemployed individuals who are per-ceived to be furthest away from the labour market—it has until recently been the only form with its own permanent state-funded 'start-up grant' through the Swedish unemployment offices. In 2010 social enterprises, and then only WISEs, were defined by SAERG commissioned by the Liberal-Centre-Right Alliance gov-ernment as:

> companies engaged in business with the overall purpose of integrating people who have great difficulty getting or keeping a job, in work and society. The companies are using the production of goods and/or services which are sold on a market as a tool to provide jobs but also to provide opportunities for job training, placement, rehabilitation and employment through participation in the company's production.
> (Tillväxtverket, 2010, p. 2)

On the other side of the same spectrum are the more open form of WISEs, initi-ated and 'run' by entrepreneurs with mainstream business ideas. While these may or may not express social or societal purposes as their premier goal, they integrate social and societal purpose by employing individuals who are marginalised/long-term unemployed and/or far removed from the labour market. To this should be added the social enterprise/economy intermediaries that are in business for social and societal purposes, such as Coompanion (Coompanion, n.d.) and Nätverket—Idéburen sector Skåne (Nätverket-Idéburen-sektor-Skåne, n.d.).

There is no fully reliable and comprehensible statistics over social enterprises in Sweden. Nevertheless, according to Sofisam (Sofisam, n.d.-b; Tillväxtverket, 2019a)—a collaboration between SAERG (Tillväxtverket), the Swedish Unemployment Office and the Swedish Social Insurance Agency—functioning as a knowledge bank for those interested in doing business with, starting up or work-ing in a WISE (Sofisam, n.d.-a)—Sweden has 353 WISEs that are employing 3741 individuals and providing jobs for another 9856. There is no common legal status or form among the social enterprises, but the most common one is cooperative economic association (two out of three or 64%, Tillväxtverket, 2019a). Others include joint-stock companies/limited companies (Aktiebolag), trading companies (Handelsbolag), not-for-profit associations (Ideella föreningar) and foundations (Stiftelser). The not-for-profit associations and limited companies accounted for 24% and 11% of the total amount of WISEs in the same year. As a result, the organ-isations in the social economy and the civil society are neither benefiting from the same type of public financial support, nor are all open calls and collaboration with municipalities and other public authorities accessible for all organisation in all cases, as a natural consequence of their legal status/form. The total turnover of the economic associations and stock companies in 2016 was SEK 817 million. In 2017 their turnover had increased by another SEK 69 million, to a total of SEK 886 mil-lion, out of which the majority, SEK 733 million, came from economic associa-tions (Tillväxtverket, 2019a).

While the WISEs make up the highest number of social enterprises, by default, within the healthcare sector the progress has been slower. Nevertheless, social enterprises do provide social care for elderly and home care, often in the shape of cooperatives (MKEF, n.d.; Personalkooperativet-Gullogården, n.d.; Omsorgskooperativet-Brännagården, n.d.). Other examples of social enterprises are found within the clothes sector where enterprises might focus on eco- and fair trade clothes, specifically for children, and use a percentage of their revenue to support specific aid purposes; recycling of children's toys to reduce the throw-away culture and develop an exchange economy, but also to distribute to those less well off; eco-city farming, where small-scale city farming is used as a tool for education; city beekeeping, where small-scale beekeeping is intended to help the ecosystem and sometimes is used as an education and integration tool by educating new Swedes in beekeeping; catering, sewing and cleaning services as tolls for empowering long-term-unemployed women; hotels using disabled per-sonnel; and homework or specific school subject support, aimed at, but not exclusively, helping children of parents with a non-Swedish background.

However, because the majority of aforementioned examples have more than one purpose it is neither necessarily easy to pigeonhole these social enterprises into one specific sector, nor whether to define them as just social enterprises or multipurpose WISEs (Persson & Hafen, 2015).

Although an increasing interest in social enterprises and how they may or may not contribute to the general welfare are shown, membership associations generally make up the largest part of the social economy and attract a constant interest by governments. The flora of different types and the number of membership associations makes for a prominent position in the sphere of the social economy. These associations range from the Swedish Association for Sexuality Education and women's shelters to associations for sustainable development, unions and the Swedish Red Cross. Nevertheless, the most typical membership association in the social economy is a sport association/club. The sport sector stands out as the most important representative among Swedish associations with state financial support primarily based on a belief of an inherent benefit in terms of social integration and public health (Persson, 2019). There are currently approximately 19,000 sport associations with approximately 3,249,000 members, which means that one-third of the Swedish population are involved in the life of a sport association, either as an athlete or trainer or in any other voluntary capacity supporting the association. Besides being involved in the core sport activity of the organisation, the sport association is perceived to personify an arena for social integration and as a result state-funded integration projects run by the individual sport association based on open calls have for a long time been a common activity and extra income for sport associations of different size. The number of integration activities and projects has increased as an aftermath of the 2015 migration crises. Moreover, several sport associations in the Swedish football premier league are in collaboration with the Swedish Employment Office running their own employment activities where they are utilising their business sponsor networks to find employments, jobs and internships for long-term-unemployed individuals (Ahonen & Persson, 2020; Persson, 2019).

However, many of the existing problems as well as the proposed solutions, such as labour market initiatives, are legacies from the era of industrialisation, when boundaries between different sectors of society were of greater importance than in today's post-industrialised societies. Current challenges are more complex in times of fewer traditional industries surviving, either closing down due to insolvency or moving abroad after being bought up or out of free will, and with unprecedented long-term unemployment and the current asylum situation in Europe. Hence, it is becoming apparent that traditional mainstream labour market measurement and programmes as well as traditional entrepreneurship may neither hold the key to the solution on their own nor together. Gradually it is being recognised that a diversity of solutions as well as entrepreneurship may be required to overcome various societal, economic and environmental challenges facing the society. A social entrepreneurship making use of mainstream entrepreneurial logic—discovery, evaluation and exploitation of opportunities creating future goods and services—has increasingly come into focus, as a potential stimulus for societal co-value creation in most EU member states (Santos, 2012; Moe, 2009, p. 7; Alvord, Brown, & Letts, 2004;

Lundqvist & Williams, 2010, pp. 24–25). This is also true for Sweden where politicians during the last decade once again have returned to discussing social enterprises in the context of employment, and more specifically in terms of long-term-unemployed individuals (def. more than 6 months). Today long-term-unemployed individuals make up 33.4% of all unemployed persons in Sweden (Ekonomifakta.se, 2019d). Here, the not-for-profit organisations, such as social enterprises, are seen as contributing to diversity and freedom of choice for users by providing custom or niche services, simultaneously as they often possess a stronger foundation and greater trust capital among the people who need welfare services due to addiction, homelessness, long-term unemployment and disabilities (SOU, 2019).

The Social Economy Responds to New Crises

Organisations in the social economy are per definition responsive to their nature, i.e. they react to social, socio-economic and environmental problems that exist in the societies in which they operate, but also to changing circumstances in terms of demography and funding schemes. They may or may not change what they do, but they certainly are accustomed to change how they do what they do best. In 2008/2009, a financial crisis originating in the USA hit the major part of the world. The impact was glocal, i.e. although with local origin it had global consequences. However, the crisis was neither felt the same in all societies, nor was the reaction the same or the same reactions needed in all societies. Partly, this was because the financial situation at the time of the crises was not the same all over the world. This seems to hold true for the social economy. At the time of writing, Sweden and the rest of the world are once again experiencing a global crisis, due to the corona pandemic. Whether one looks at it from a health or financial perspective, this is an unprecedented crisis. Countries around the world have once again chosen to respond to the pandemic in different ways. While many have closed down their society for a period of time, others such as Sweden have decided to stay open, albeit with restrictions. The long-term financial and psychological affect and end result are impossible to predict. The Swedish Economic Tendency Survey (Konjunkturbarometern), which measures the mood of the economy, fell by 34 units to 58.6 in April. This is the largest decline in the history of the survey. The indicator is now eight units lower than the previous bottom level from the financial crisis (Ekonomifakta, 2020a). To isolate the corona pandemic's effect on these numbers is of course impossible, but there is no doubt that it is a major contributor. The corona pandemic has already shown to affect all industries, albeit in different ways and to different extent, but the effect on individuals', families' and companies' financial situation is real, and companies are forced to lay off personnel. So far, since the beginning of March, companies have submitted 60,769 short-term layoffs (Ekonomifakta, 2020b), and a total of more than 71,000 people are under notice (Ekonomifakta, 2020c). Just like other companies, the social enterprises are facing difficult times, and specifically financial problems. The social economy's 'total sum of income loss and increase costs due to the crisis equals over 106 million Euro', according to SAERG (Tillväxtverket, 2020). Despite this, no special measures have been directed specifically for social enterprises. While social enterprises and other organisations in the social economy have been able to use general initiatives linked to green jobs, easier access to loans and reduced tax requirements for a few months, it has proven difficult accessing support due to the interest rate on loans being too high for the majority (Mail conversation, Section for Social entrepreneurship at the unit for Capital Support, SAERG, 8 October, 2020).

In difference to the corona pandemic, in 2008/2009 Sweden was relatively spared from the degree of hardship that many other countries endured due to the financial crises. Nevertheless, also Sweden had its fair share of increasing unemployment, which was worsened by the fact that the Swedish flagship car industry stood on the edge of bankruptcy and was in part dissolved and part sold out to foreign businesses that coincided with the financial crisis. The degree to which Sweden was affected by the global financial crisis can be measured in several ways, out of which the GDP is one. To provide a reasonably fair picture, excluding 2008 and 2009, the Swedish GDP between 1998 (4.3%), 10 years before the crises, and 2018 (2.2%), 10 years after the crises, has fluctuated between 0.6% and 6.2%. During the crisis years of 2008 and 2009 the GDP fell to −4.2% in 2009 (Ekonomifakta.se, 2019c). While this fall was substantial, in 2010 it was again at a level of 6.2%. Another way of looking at the outcome of a financial crisis is to look at social policies and unemployment numbers. Indeed, the crisis of 2008/2009 did result in a slight elevation in unemployment from 6.1 in 2007 to 8.6 in 2010 (age span 15–74, SCB, n.d.). However, in this context it is worth noting that employment numbers during the autumn of 2019, i.e. before the corona epidemic, once again showed a slight negative trend at 6.8% (Ekonomifakta.se, 2019a). With an unemployment distribution of 3.8% for Swedish born and 15.4% for foreign born, unemployment is as could be expected far from equally distributed over the population (Ekonomifakta.se, 2019b). The uneven distribution is explained partly by the time spent in the country, and partly by a matching problem based on perception of insufficient or wrong education and too little or wrong experience (Ekonomistyrningsverket, 2016). This is partially a legacy of the refugee crisis of 2015 and considering the short time having elapsed, this does not need to equal a long-term effect.

The so-called wheels of liberalism—deregulation, decentralisation, changes to the social security system, etc.—were initiated in 1980s, and kept on turning through and beyond the financial crises of 2008/2009, despite what could have been expected from a social democratic welfare state. Retrospectively, it should be clear that it primarily had been budgetary pressures that motivated and initiated the welfare reforms and spending cuts, rather than a liberal ideology. The Swedish social security system has over the last couple of decades been at the centre of critical debates of the welfare state, as well as through several reforms. Sprung from growing costs due to growing numbers of absentees, two different discourses came to dominate the debates of the 1990s: the *work environment discourse* and the *excessive use discourse*. Out of the two discourses, the latter came to dominate the discourse and form the basis for the *work strategy* (arbetslinjen), primarily associated with the Alliance government (Alliansen: Liberal-Centre-Right Alliance, 2006–2014). The work strategy has had an exclusive focus on making the social insurance more cost efficient and individuals more self-reliant and responsible for their own situation in relation to the labour market (Björnberg, 2012). The most current and fundamental changes to the social security system were implemented at the end of the first decade. These include a new work capability measurement and restriction to the number of sick leave days. The work capability measurement is supposed to esti-mate to what extent an individual is able to work. The lowest ability level is 25% and the compensation rate is adapted accordingly. Moreover, if not being able to return to one's employment within 181 days, the person is now transferred to the Unemployment Office to find a job in the remaining labour market (SOU, 2009). However, the most fundamental change to the sick leave period was the new sealing of 364 days. From no previous limit, the health insurance compensation is now terminated after 364 days when the person needs to return to work or he or she will be transferred to the Employment Office (Proposition, 2008). These are significant changes to a system with no previous limits to its sick leave period, and where long-term unemployed commonly were transferred into early retirement, but also for the individual who is at one and the same time demanded to have greater responsibility while being stripped of his or her own agency. The latter is because it is no longer up to the individual to conclude that or when he or she is in need of changing his or her occupation (Selmanovic, 2012).

While the Social Democratic-Green Party government in February 2016 removed the distal limit, it did not solve the problem with growing numbers of long-term unemployed. There are several reasons for this, but the inability to foresee the dra-matic increase in asylum-based immigration from an average of 4–5000 per month to 39,196 in October 2015, and a total of 163,000 at the end of the year (Migrationsverket, 2016), meant that all prognoses were largely irrelevant from the very start. The group of asylum seekers or newly arrived with granted residence permits (2015—36,630, 2016—71,562, 2017—36,531, 2018—25,114, 2019 Jan–Oct—26,443) likely run the risk of ending up among those categorised as long-term unemployed, where foreign born already are overrepresented (Migrationsverket, 2019; SCB, 2013). Although not yet clear how, the previous Social Democratic-Green Party government, today Social Democratic-Green Party with policy-influenced support by the Centre Democrats and the Liberal Party, seems to suggest a system where WISEs are to play part in solving the long-term unemployment problem. The WISEs that already have taken part in the previously existing 'FAS 3' programme are suggested to keep on providing the people furthest from the labour market a way back based on real work experience (Regeringen, 2015). This was reiterated by the working group delivering their SOU report on not-for-profit wel-fare (Swedish Government Official Reports, SOU, 2019). If materialised, i.e. put-ting social enterprises in the service of the welfare regime, this would be a most concrete example of the long-standing link between the social economy and the welfare regime. The similarity with the ideas of the Social Democratic party and LO in the first half of the twentieth century, suggesting that social enterprises were to solve the idea of full employment, is more of footnote than a real case. Hence, the idea of full employment is not about to be revived. To rely on organisations from the social economy to fill the gap of the inadequacy of the state institutions will in some ways be to repeat what happened during the actual refugee crises of 2015. Now based on a call for help, during the financial as well as the refugee crises it was a spontaneous reaction by organisations and volunteers of the social economy. In a similar fashion, the role of the social economy, potential collaboration and hybrid forms between social enterprises, municipalities and companies that will grow out of and as a reaction to the impact of the corona epidemic is in part already taking place. Among these examples are initiatives focusing on assisting the risk group, so-called older-older citizens (äldre-äldre, 80+), with food and medicine transports to their homes. This type of activity is run by everything from individuals in their own neighbourhood to small as well as larger football clubs, such as Malmö FF in collaboration with Skane City Mission (Skåne Stadsmission, MFF, 2020); housing associations such as KKB (Sehlin, 2020); and municipalities such as Trelleborg in collaboration with organisations in the social economy (Trelleborg, n.d.).

New Hybrid Funding Instruments

New problems sometimes need new solutions and the problem of funding is no exception, although a new solution sometimes is like old wine in a new bottle. Possible funding schemes for the social economy differ greatly depending on the sector, type of organisation and legal entity within the social economy sphere. While all associations based on specified preconditions can apply for and obtain a number of different types of financial support—normally based on number of members— sport associations, the largest part of the social economy, receive annual state financial support earmarked for organising sport, and municipality-based activity support for children and youth sport activities. If one instead equates the social economy with social enterprises, existing public funding schemes are irregular. Periodical state investments and calls are announced. One such example is 150 million between 2008 and 2020 to projects by social entrepreneurs and social enterprises to meet societal challenges, such as equality, environment, integration, health, education, climate and work integration (Tillväxtverket, n.d.).

The number of funding instruments is increasing and several of these are of a hybrid nature. Among these alternatives are venture capital, such as Almi and Microfonden (Almi, n.d.; Microfonden, n.d.); banks with alternative models for granting loans that differ from those of traditional commercial banks, such as Ekobanken and Jak (see: Jak, n.d.; Ekobanken, n.d.); impact investment or social impact investment, such as Impact Invest (Impact_Invest, n.d.), Centre for Social Entrepreneurship Sweden (CSES, n.d.) and Mikrofonden (Microfonden, n.d.); and crowdfunding, such as Funded by Me (Funded-by-Me, n.d.) and CrowdCulture (CrowdCulture, n.d.), but also both social impact and hybrid bonds (hybridobligationer), such as the collaboration between Trianon and Yalla Trappan (Trianon, 2020).

The majority of these funding alternatives with a more or less hybrid nature are relatively new to the Swedish context. Social impact bonds were discussed in the Swedish Parliament (Riksdagen) for the first time in 2013 (Motion, 2013), but was not put in the limelight and did not reach public attention until the collaboration between the Municipality of Norrköping, Leksell Social Ventures and SKL Uppdrag Psykisk Hälsa och Health Navigator with the overall aim of improving the situation for children and young people (socialt utfallskontrakt, Norrköping, 2015). The most recent addition is the hybrid bond. In 2017 the government assigned a special investigator to look into new and improved financing conditions for new housing and redevelopments and one of the suggested options in the context where social sustainability was hybrid bonds (Bard, Hägred, Song, & Hammes, 2017). Real Estate AB Trianon's (Trianon, 2020) rental and cooperation agreements for a café and catering business with Yalla Trappan in Malmö are one example of this. While Trianon invests in the project by granting properties and buying services from Yalla Trappan, Yalla Trappan in their turn undertakes to receive and train job-seeking women living in Trianon's properties. The overall aim is getting more immigrant women into employment through work integration, but also contributing to increased security and service in the immediate area. None of these funding instruments has been around long enough in the Swedish context to have been evaluated. Several of the mentioned examples potentially fall into more than one funding scheme category, but also as corporate social responsibility from the point of view of the company. This certainly applies to both IKEA's and Trianon's collaborations with Yalla Trappan.

Conclusions

The Swedish social economy has been described above as a vast sphere containing several sectors and a melting pot of numerous organisations emphasising social values and that has effect on most Swedish citizens and denizens. How to define the new Swedish social economy, if this is such a thing, in contrast to the *old* is not straightforward. The new and old are in several ways one and the same. The type of organisations still falls within the original definition from 1999 (Kulturdepartementet, 1999) as

> organised activities that primarily have societal purposes, build on democratic values and are organized independent from the government. These social and economic activities are conducted primarily in the associations, cooperatives, foundations and similar organizations. Activities within the social economy have the public or its members' good, not the profit, as the main driving force.
> (Kulturdepartementet, 1999 [Ministry of Culture and Sport])

together with the social enterprise specific definition by SAERG (Tillväxtverket, 2010):

companies engaged in business with the overall purpose of integrating people who have great difficulty getting or keeping a job, in work and society. The companies are using the production of goods and/or services which are sold on a market as a tool to provide jobs but also to provide opportunities for job training, placement, rehabilitation and employment through participation in the company's production.
(Tillväxtverket, 2010, p. 2)

Hence, the variety of actors within the social economy is great, ranging from not-for-profit professional football clubs with children and youth sections, as well as social responsibility agendas and ventures (see MFF, n.d.), and small village cooperatives working for local rural development and the social economy (see Hela-Sverige-ska-leva, n.d.) to smaller organic urban cultivation activities, that is, involving and teaching local residents, housing associations, property owners and municipal organisations about long-term sustainable city cultivation (see Odla-i-stan, n.d.) and WISEs helping disadvantaged individuals with integration in terms of the labour market and society by job opportunities and employment by selling goods and services, such as the day dog care centre Hundstund (, n.d.). There are numerous examples of these types of organisations and many more, but whether these organisations are new or have a long history is not what makes them potential examples of the new social economy. Instead, that which is new in terms of a new social economy in Sweden is new takes on organising activities and new types of collaboration and cooperation within the social economy and across economies. In the case of Sweden, this has less to do with the financial crises of 2008/2009 and more to do with finding new means to enable organisations to achieve their goals.

What is *new* in terms of organising can be categorised as cyber organising and switching identity. Although Facebook has in principle been open for everyone since 2006, 2 years prior to the financial crises of 2008/2009, the use of Facebook as a communication channel has enabled the organisation to reach everyone from already existing to potentially new customers, members and colleagues, collaborators and organisations from the social economy, and supporters (see Nätverket-Idéburen-sektor-Skåne, n.d.; Samhällsentreprenörskap-och-socialt-företagande, n.d.; Hela-Sverige-ska-leva, n.d.). While it is by no way specific to organisations within the social economy, it has become an important platform on where to share knowledge and experience, but also where to find inspiration and building bridges between different sectors of society, such as between the social economy and academia. That this also applies to the individual level proved to be the case in the midst of the refugee crisis of 2015 when people used Facebook to organise both people and collections of basic necessities for those in need. The second example of the new organising is related to funding streams and legal status. As mentioned above, there is no common legal status among social enterprises and the same applies to the rest of the organisations within the social economy. For researchers and state institutions this might be viewed as a problem in our quest to categorise, although for different reasons. However, social entrepreneurs seem to be divided on the issue. While the *wrong* legal status sometimes is a hinder for certain public funding schemes, the same legal status might be an advantage in terms of tax reason, for example. As a result, today many social enterprises practise the game of dividing their organisations into several legal statuses to enable them to apply for funding in streams that would otherwise be closed to them due to the wrong legal status (Focus group interview with Swedish social entrepreneurs, January 14, 2015).

New types of collaboration and cooperation, or at least more common to the new than the *old* social economy, can be divided into the private and public sector collaborations. Yalla Trappan (Yalla-Trappan, n.d.) with its established collaboration with IKEA personifies the success of the former. Yalla Trappan is a work-integrating social enterprise and women's cooperative which uses the production of goods and services—catering, sewing and cleaning—as tools to provide jobs but also to provide opportunities for job training, placement, rehabilitation and employment through participation in the company's production. Yalla Trappan's and IKEA's collaboration was started by Yalla Trappan sewing veils matching the IKEA uniforms for Muslim women employees. This was later followed by table clothes to their restaurants. The real collaboration, however, was established by IKEA providing Yalla Trappan with a pop-up space at IKEA-Malmö where they provided sewing services, such as custom-made curtains and different types of alterations to IKEA customers. This resulted not only in Yalla Trappan securing income, but also Yalla Trappan and their formerly long-term-unemployed women gaining a window to the public, while IKEA has acknowledged that they have made a substantial profit from happy customers and that they are engaging in similar collaborations on an international basis (Interview with chairperson and founder of Yalla Trappan, January 22, 2018). Similar types of collaboration are found elsewhere, such as the property company Byggvesta which cooperates with Yalla Rinkeby (AH, 2019) and the aforementioned collaboration between the property company Trianon and Yalla Trappan. Much due to Yalla Trappan's IKEA success, they have for several years, both in Sweden and internationally, been used not only as an example of a successful WISE, but also as an example of a new type of collaboration. While public sector collaborations have been strangely difficult to establish, there are existing exceptions and possible future possibilities. In 2010 the first local and regional agreements with the not-for-profit sector—common expression of will for cooperation and commitment—were signed between Region Skåne and the not-for-profit sector in Skåne in the south of Sweden. While Region Skåne guaranteed financial support, both parts agreed on five areas of development: collaboration; participation and influence; idea-driven entrepreneurship; not-for-profit sector; and learning and research. In 2014, the second generation of the agreement was signed (Region Skåne, n.d.). Today, similar agreement exists on a number of places in Sweden. The exact outcome of these collaborations is hard to evaluate, but Region Skåne is today buying more services and products from the not-for-profit sector than prior to the agreement. A second example is the above-mentioned collaboration between several not-for-profit sport associations in the Swedish football premier league and the Swedish Unemployment Office to facilitate job opportunities, internships and employments, primarily for long-term-unemployed individuals. While collaboration between the social economy and the welfare sector has proven slow in terms of healthcare services, with some exceptions within the social care for elderly and home care, the recent Swedish Government Official Reports, SOU2019:56, suggest alteration to the existing procurement law, for example, which gives some hope to the social economy of being able to compete on more equal terms with private and often much larger companies in the future.

A fifth example might be categorised as collaboration, as well as switching identity. This is not about changing legal form, but something that could be described as a new ball game. It will be about surviving the impact economy. In 2019 the Swedish National Advisory Board for Impact Investing was established and the impact economy with different type of impact investors gives the impression that it is here to stay. At the time of writing, it is too early to evaluate its true impact on the social economy. Most likely it will be welcomed among those that will be financed and successfully live up to the expectations of the investors. What the impact of the impact economy will be for all of those organisations that most likely will not even appear on the radar of the impact investors, either because their organisations' focus is not attractive enough or because their potential impact is viewed too small, is something for the future to tell.

References

AH. (2019). Jobba med sociala företag - win-win för alla. aktuellhallbarhet.se. Retrieved from https://www.aktuellhallbarhet.se/artikel/jobba-med-sociala-foretag-win-win-for-alla/. Accessed 30 Nov 2019.

Ahonen, A., & Persson, H. T. R. (2020). Social entrepreneurship and corporate social responsibility in team sport clubs. In V. Ratten (Ed.), *Sport entrepreneurship and public policy: Building a new approach to policy-making for sport* (pp. 7–21). Springer Nature, Cham. https://doi.org/10.1007/978-3-030-29458-8.

Almi. (n.d.). Almi. Retrieved from https://www.almi.se/vara-tjanster/tjanster. Accessed 11 May 2020.

Alvord, S. H., Brown, L. D., & Letts, C. W. (2004). Social entrepreneurship and societal transformation. *The Journal of Applied Behavioral Science, 40*(3), 260–282.

Bard, S., Hägred, U., Song, H.-S., Bard, S., Hägred, U., Song, H.-S. Lindsten, A. M. & Hammes, K. (2017). SOU 2017:108, Lån och garantier för fler bostäder. Betänkande av Utredningen om förbättrad bostadsfinansiering [Loans and guarantees for more housing. The study on improved housing financing] Government. p. 393. Retrieved from https://data.riksdagen.se/fil/461BFE2F-C1D5-4213-95ED-7AD3DB7F0EF1

Biggeri, M., Testi, E., Belluci, M., During, R., & Persson, H. T. R. (Eds.). (2018). *Social entrepreneurship and social innovation: Ecosystems for inclusion in Europe*. Milton Park, Abingdon, Oxon: Routledge.

Björnberg, U. (2012). Social policy reforms in Sweden: New perspectives on rights and obligations. In B. Larsson, M. Letell, & H. Thörn (Eds.), *Transformations of the Swedish welfare state: From social engineering to governance?* (pp. 71–85). Houndmills, Basingstoke, Hampshire: Macmillan.

Capuder, A. (2018). Lundastudenter utbildar sociala företag i entreprenörskap. Sydsvenskan. Retrieved from https://www.sydsvenskan.se/2018-02-28/lundastudenter-utbildar-sociala-foretag-i-entreprenorskap

Coompanion. (n.d.). Coompanion. https://coompanion.se. Accessed 9 May 2020.

CrowdCulture. (n.d.). CrowdCulture. Retrieved from https://crowdculture.se/se. Accessed 11 May 2020.

CSES. (n.d.). Center för socialt entreprenöskap Sverige. Retrieved from http://cses.se/finansier-ing/. Accessed 11 May 2020.

Einarsson, S. (2011). The Revitalization of a Popular Movement. Case Study Research from Sweden: *Voluntas, 22*(4), 658–681.

Ekobanken. (n.d.). Ekobanken. Retrieved from https://www.ekobanken.se/forening-foretag/. Accessed 11 May 2020.

Ekonomifakta. (2020a). Konjunkturen - Barometerindikatorn. Retrieved from https://www.ekonomifakta.se/Fakta/Ekonomi/Tillvaxt/Konjunkturen%2D%2D-Barometerindikatorn/. Accessed 14 May 2020.

Ekonomifakta. (2020b). Korttidspermittering. Retrieved from https://www.ekonomifakta.se/Fakta/Arbetsmarknad/Arbetsloshet/korttidspermittering/. Accessed 14 May 2020.

Ekonomifakta. (2020c). Varsel om uppsägning. Retrieved from https://www.ekonomifakta.se/Fakta/Arbetsmarknad/Arbetsloshet/Varsel/. Accessed 14 May 2020.

Ekonomifakta.se. (2019a). Arbetslöshet. Ekonomifakta.se. Retrieved from https://www.ekonomi-fakta.se/Fakta/Arbetsmarknad/Arbetsloshet/Arbetsloshet/. Accessed 30 Nov 2019.

Ekonomifakta.se. (2019b). Arbetslöshet - utrikes födda. Ekonomifakta.se. Retrieved from https://www.ekonomifakta.se/Fakta/Arbetsmarknad/Integration/arbetsloshet-utrikes-fodda/. Accessed 30 Nov 2019.

Ekonomifakta.se. (2019c). BNP - Sverige. Ekonomifakta.se. Retrieved from https://www.eko-nomifakta.se/Fakta/Ekonomi/Tillvaxt/BNP%2D%2D-Sverige/. Accessed 30 Nov 2019.

Ekonomifakta.se. (2019d). Långtidsarbetslöshet. ekonomifakta.se. Accessed 30 Nov 2019.

Ekonomistyrningsverket. (2016). Prognos: Statens budget och de offentliga finanserna. Ekonomistyrningsverket. Retrieved from http://www.esv.se/contentassets/97dd2dc6c698461a86bca4525fe79ba4/prognos-april-2016-korr.pdf. Accessed 26 May 2016.

Frostberg, T. (2019a). Ikea ska få sociala entreprenörer att växa globalt. Sydsvenskan. Retrieved from https://www.sydsvenskan.se/2019-04-26/ikea-ska-fa-sociala-entreprenorer-att-vaxa-globalt

Frostberg, T. (2019b). Möbeljättens miljard ska få flyktingar i arbete. Sydsvenskan. Retrieved from https://www.sydsvenskan.se/2019-12-16/mobeljattens-miljard-ska-fa-flyktingar-i-arbete

Funded-by-Me. (n.d.). Funded-by-Me. Retrieved from https://www.fundedbyme.com/en/. Accessed 11 May 2020.

Gawell, M. (2017). *Socialt entreprenörskap för kvinnors rättigheter. Genus och företagande: Ymer 2016* (pp. 129–143). Stockholm: Svenska Sällskapet för Antropologi och Geografi.

Gillberg, G., & Stenberg, J. (2002). Livsformsanalys och lokalt utvecklingsarbete: En pilotstudie om analysmetodens potential vid studier av socialt kapital, social ekonomi och hållbar utveck-ling. Göteborgs Universitet & Chalmers Arkitektur: Göteborgs Universitet, Institutionen för Arbetsvetenskap & Chalmers Arkitektur, Byggd miljö & Hållbar utveckling, p. 70.

Hammar, T. (1990). *Democracy and the nation state: Aliens, denizens, and citizens in a world of international migration*. Aldershot: Avebury.

Heckscher, G. (1944). Folkrörelser och intresseorganisationer. Några problemställningar. In A. Brusewi (Ed.), *Statsvetenskapliga studier. Till statsvetenskapliga föreningens i Uppsala tju-gofemårsdag*. Uppsala & Stockholm: Almqvist & Wiksells Boktryckeri AB.

Heckscher, G. (1951). *Staten och organisationerna*. Stockholm: Kooperativa förbundet.

Hedenborg, S. & Kvarnström, L. (2009) Det svenska samhället 1720-2006. Böndernas ocharbetar-nas tid. Lund: Studentlitteratur.

Hela-Sverige-ska-leva. (n.d.). Hela Sverige ska leva. Retrieved from https://www.facebook.com/pg/HelaSverige/about/?ref=page_internal. Accessed 16 May 2020.

Henrekson, M. & Jakobsson, U. (2003). The transformation of ownership, policy and structure in Sweden: Convergence towards the Anglo-Saxon model? *New Political Economy, 8*(1), 73–102.

Hessler, H. (1952). *Om stiftelser*. Lund: Berlingska Boktryckeriet.

Hundstund. (n.d.). Hundstund. Retrieved from https://www.hundstund.com. Accessed 2015 2020.

Impact_Invest. (n.d.). Impact invest. Retrieved from https://www.impactinvest.se/. Accessed 11 May 2020.

Jak. (n.d.). JAK Medlemsbank. Retrieved from https://jak.se/vardagstjanster/foretag/. Accessed 11 May 2020.

Jansson, T. (1985). Adertonhundratalets associationer. In *Forskning och problem kring ett sprängfullt tomrum eller sammanslutningsprinciper och föreningsformer mellan två samhällsformationer c:a 1800–1870*. Stockholm: Almqvist & Wiksell.

Klausen, K. K. & Selle, P. (1996). The third sector in Scandinavia: *Voluntas, 7*(2), 99–122.

Kulturdepartementet. (1999). *Social ekonomi – en tredje sektor för välfärd, demokrati och tillväxt? Rapport från en arbetsgrupp*. Stockholm: Fakta info direkt, Kulturdepartmentet, Regeringskansliet.

Lundholm, E. (2002). Den sociala ekonomin i glesa miljöer: En teoretisk diskussion. Retrieved from http://www.diva-portal.org/smash/get/diva2:227300/FULLTEXT01.pdf. Accessed 6 May 2020.

Lundkvist Fridh, Y., Svensson, J., Laurén, A., & Kowalewski, J. (2019). Staten diskriminerar sociala företag. Svenska Dagbladet. Retrieved from https://www.svd.se/staten-diskriminerar-sociala-foretag

Lundqvist, M. A., & Williams, K. L. M. (2010). Promises of societal entrepreneurship: Sweden and beyond. *Journal of Enterprising Communities, People and Places in the Global Economy, 4*(1), 24–36.

MFF. (2020). TV: Här levererar MFF mat till Skåne Stadsmission. Retrieved from https://www.mff.se/tv-har-levererar-mff-mat-till-skane-stadsmission/. Accessed 15 May 2020.

MFF. (n.d.). MFF. Retrieved from https://www.mff.se/. Accessed 16 May 2020.

Microfonden. (n.d.). Microfonden Sverige. Retrieved from https://mikrofonden.se/. Accessed 11 May 2020.

Migrationsverket. (2016). Migrationsverket - mitt i världen 2015. Retrieved from http://www.migrationsverket.se/Om-Migrationsverket/Fakta-ommigration/Migrationsverket---mitt-i-varlden-2015.html.

Migrationsverket. (2019). Beviljade uppehållstillstånd översikter. migrationsverket.se. Retrieved from https://www.migrationsverket.se/Om-Migrationsverket/Statistik/Beviljade-uppehallstillstand-oversikter.html. Accessed 30 Nov 2019.

MKEF. (n.d.). Mångkulturell Kunskap Ekonomisk Förening. http://www.mkef.se/. Accessed 12 May 2020.

Moe, E. (2009). Vi behöver fler samhällsentreprenörer! M. Gawell, B. Johannisson, & M. Lundqvist *Samhällets entreprenörer: En forskarantologi om samhällsentreprenörskap*. 24 March 2016. kks.se: Stiftelsen för kunskaps- och kompetensutveckling, p. 296. Retrieved from http://www.kks.se/om/Lists/Publikationer/Attachments/150/samhallets-entreprenorer-2009-publ.pdf

Motion. (2013). Social impact bonds. Motion 2013/14:Fi275 av Stefan Svanström. Retrieved from https://www.riksdagen.se/sv/dokument-lagar/dokument/motion/social-impact-bonds_H102Fi275. Accessed 13 May 2020.

MSI. (n.d.). Mötesplats Social Innovation. Retrieved from https://socialinnovation.se. Accessed 7 May 2020.

Näringsdepartementet. (1998). Social ekonomi i EU-landet Sverige – tradition och förnyelse i samma begrepp (Ds 1998:48) Näringsdepartementet. Retrieved from https://www.regeringen.se/rattsliga-dokument/departementsserien-och-promemorior/1998/01/ds-199848/. Accessed 13 Oct 2019.

Nätverket-Idéburen-sektor-Skåne. (n.d.). Nätverket - Idéburen sektor Skåne. https://www.facebook.com/natverketideburensektorskane/. Accessed 16 May 2020.

Nilsson, S., Hahn, G., Laurén, A., Thelander, J., & Herlitz, U. (2017). Landsbygdens föreningar måste kunna få lån. Svenska Dagbladet. Retrieved from https://www.svd.se/landsbygdens-foreningar-maste-kunna-fa-lan

Norrköping. (2015). Sveriges första sociala utfallskontrakt. För förbättrade skolresultat och minskad risk för återplacering för HVB- och SiS-placerade barn och unga. Retrieved from https://www.norrkoping.se/organisation/ekonomi/norrkopings-sociala-investeringsfond/socialt-utfallskontrakt.html. Accessed 13 May 2020.

Odla-i-stan. (n.d.). Odla i stan. Retrieved from http://www.odlaistan.nu/. Accessed 16 May 2020.
Omsorgskooperativet-Brännagården.   (n.d.).   Brännagården.   http://www.brannagarden.se/.
    Accessed 12 May 2020.
Personalkooperativet-Gullogården. (n.d.). Äldreboendet Gullogården. Retrieved from http://www.
    gullogarden.se/. Accessed 12 May 2020.
Persson, H. T. R. (2019). CSR eller idrottens samhällsansvar: för såväl stora som mindre organisa-
    tioner. In Å. Bäckström, K. Book, B. Carlsson, & P. Fahlström (Eds.), Styrning och samhällsen-
    gagemang inom svensk idrott (pp. 164–188). Stockholm: SISU Idrottsböcker.
Persson, H. T. R., & Hafen, N. (2015). New generation of social enterprises - Sweden. Retrieved
    from http://www.fp7-efeseiis.eu/new-generation-of-social-enterprises/. Accessed 25 March
    2016.
Pestoff, V. (2004). The development and future of the social economy in Sweden. In Evers, A. &
    Laville, J.-L. (Eds.) The third sector in Europe. Cheltenham, UK: Edward Elgar.
Proposition. (2008). (Government Bill) Proposition 2007/08:136 En reformerad sjukskrivning-
    sprocess för ökad återgång i arbete. Regeringen. Retrieved from http://www.regeringen.se/
    contentassets/b0cf04fc987642e7975e522c3c4bca31/en-reformerad-sjukskrivningsprocess-
    for-okad-atergang-i-arbete-prop.-200708136. Accessed 02 June 2016.
Regeringen. (2015). Regeringen vill stärka de arbetsintegrerande sociala företagen. Regeringen.
    se.   Retrieved   from   http://www.regeringen.se/artiklar/2015/10/regeringen-vill-starka-de-
    arbetsintegrerande-sociala-foretagen/. Accessed 15 March 2016.
Regeringskansliet. (2020). Sveriges nationella reformprogram 2020. Europa 2020 - EU:s
    strategi för smart och hållbar tillväxt för alla. p. 105. Retrieved from https://www.regerin-
    gen.se/499741/contentassets/6abdb3b31ed14e05906f97ee21760f36/sveriges-nationella-
    reformprogram-2020.pdf
Region-Skåne. (n.d.). Överenskommelse Skåne. Retrieved from http://overenskommelsenskane.
    se. Accessed 6 May 2020.
Salonen, T. (2009). Sweden: Between model and reality. In P. Alcock & G. Craig (Eds.),
    International social policy (pp. 130–147). Basingstoke: Palgrave Macmillan.
Samhällsentreprenörskap-och-socialt-företagande. (n.d.). Samhällsentreprenörskap och socialt
    företagande. https://www.facebook.com/groups/socialtforetagande/. Accessed 16 May 2020.
Santos, F. M. (2012). A positive theory of social entrepreneurship. Journal of Business Ethics,
    111(3), 335–351.
SCB. (2013). Långtidsarbetslöshet bland personer i åldern 15–74 år. Statistiska Centralbyrån.
    Retrieved   from   http://www.scb.se/Statistik/AM/AM0401/2011K03Z/AM0401_2011K03Z_
    SM_AM110SM1103.pdf. Accessed 24 May 2016.
SCB. (2016). Det civila samhället 2014: sateliträkneskaper. Civila samhället Rapport 2016:1. p. 76.
    Retrieved   from   https://www.scb.se/contentassets/4a04d0ef03714ae084c368b845389877/
    nv0117_2014a01_br_x105br1601.pdf
SCB. (n.d.). Arbetslösheten tog fart under finanskrisen. Statistiska Centralbyrån. Retrieved from
    http://www.sverigeisiffror.scb.se/hitta-statistik/sverige-i-siffror/samhallets-ekonomi/arbet-
    slosheten/. Accessed 24 May 2016.
Sehlin, M. (2020, 9 April). Bostadsbolag erbjuder matleverans till äldre. Sydsvenskan. Retrieved
    from https://www.sydsvenskan.se/2020-04-09/bostadsbolag-erbjuder-matleverans-till-aldre
Selmanovic, A. (2012). Den nya tidens AK-arbeten? En granskning av FAS 3. Enheten för eko-
    nomisk politik och arbetsmarknad. Retrieved from http://www.lo.se/home/lo/res.nsf/vres/
    lo_fakta_1366027492914_fas3_rapport_pdf/$file/Fas3_Rapport.pdf. Accessed 02 June 2016.
Sofisam. (n.d.-a). Om Sofisam. sofisam.se. https://sofisam.se/om-sofisam.html. Accessed 30 Nov
    2019.
Sofisam. (n.d.-b). Sofisam. Retrieved from https://sofisam.se/. Accessed 11 May 2020.
SOU. (2009). (Swedish Government Official Reports) SOU 2009:89 Gränslandet mellan sjuk-
    dom och arbete. Arbetsförmåga/Medicinska förutsättningar för arbete/Försörjningsförmåga.
    Regeringen. Retrieved from http://www.regeringen.se/contentassets/e27bdf19940f4ff687b44
    13b4d941474/granslandet-mellan-sjukdom-och-arbete-sou-200989. Accessed 02 June 2016.

SOU. (2019). (Swedish Government Official Reports) SOU 2019:56, Idéburen välfärd - Betänkande av Utredningen om Idéburna aktörer i väldfärden. p. 470. Retrieved from https://www.regeringen.se/4aeada/contentassets/978c3f825a704a9696e10dbb5ce40086/ideburen-valfard-sou-201956.pdf

Thörnberg, E. H. (1943). *Folkrörelser och samhällsliv i Sverige.* Stockholm: Albert Bonniers Förlag.

Tillväxtverket. (2010). Rapport av uppdrag till Tillväxtverket med anledning av regeringens handlingsplan för arbetsintegrerande sociala företag. N2010/4265/ENT. Retrieved from http://www.sofisam.se/download/18.3453fc5214836a9a47297c69/1443046935783/Tillväxtverket,+Rapport+till+regeringen+−+handlingsplan.pdf. Accessed 14 March 2016.

Tillväxtverket. (2019a). Ny statistik om arbetsintegrerande sociala företag. tillväxtverket.se. Retrieved from https://tillvaxtverket.se/statistik/foretagande/sociala-foretag.html. Accessed 30 Nov 2019.

Tillväxtverket. (2019b). Sociala företag och social innovation i media 2008-2019. p. 23. Retrieved from https://tillvaxtverket.se/download/18.49bc21ee16e0f8de7dc74597/1572861444176/Sociala%20f%C3%B6retag%20och%20social%20innovation%20i%20media.pdf

Tillväxtverket. (2020). Covid-19 effects on social enterprises and social economy in Sweden. Respons to GECES as input to the EU recovery plan.: Not published.

Tillväxtverket. (n.d.). Socialat företagande. Retrieved from https://tillvaxtverket.se/amnesomraden/affarsutveckling/socialt-foretagande.html. Accessed 12 May 2020.

Trägårdh. (2000). Utopin om den sociala ekonomin. In F. Wijkström & T. Johnstad (Eds.), *Om kooperation & social ekonomi* (pp. 1–21). Stockholm: Föreningen Kooperativa studier.

Trelleborg. (n.d.). Inköp på nätet. Retrieved from https://www.trelleborg.se/globalassets/files/socialforvaltningen/filer/digitalisering/infoblad-handladigitalt.pdf. Accessed 15 May 2020.

Trianon. (2020). Yalla Trappan och Trianon i nytt långsiktigt samarbete. Retrieved from https://news.cision.com/se/fastighets-ab-trianon/r/yalla-trappan-och-trianon-i-nytt-langsiktigt-samarbete,c3109394. Accessed 13 May 2020.

von Bergman-Winberg, M.-L. (2005). Kan den sociala ekonomin rädda välfärden? In B. Fjæstad & L.-E. Wolvén (Eds.), *Arbetsliv och samhällsförändringar* (pp. 299–312). Studentlitteratur: Lund.

Westlund, H. (2003). Social economy and employment: The case of Sweden. *Review of Social Economy, 61*(2), 163–182.

Widehed, M.. (2018). Här tar socialdemokraterna in riskkapital till sociala projekt. Dagens Nyheter. Retrieved from https://www.dn.se/ekonomi/global-utveckling/har-tar-socialdemokraterna-in-riskkapital-till-sociala-projekt/

Wijkström, F., & Lundström, T. (2002). *Den ideella sektorn: organisationerna i det civila samhället.* Stockholm: Sober Förlag.

Wood, A. (2007). Den sociala ekonomin: En väg till arbete. *Integrationsverkets stencilserie.* p. 21 2007: 08. Retrieved from https://mkcentrum.se/wp-content/uploads/2019/05/2007_08Den_sociala_ekonomin.pdf

Yalla-Trappan. (n.d.). Yalla Trappan. yallatrappan.se. Retrieved from https://www.yallatrappan.com/. Accessed 16 May 2020.

Chapter 12
International Social Economy Organizations

Ignacio Bretos, Anjel Errasti, and Aurélie Soetens

Introduction

Social economy organizations (SEOs) are commonly portrayed in the scholarly literature and public imagination as small-sized enterprises that tend to carry out their economic activity exclusively within the local context (Amin, Cameron, & Hudson, 2002). What is more, SEOs are seen as antagonistic organizations to conventional multinational corporations (Burke, 2010), and serve as buffers against the economic, social, and ecological imbalances and issues generated by transnational capitalism and its hypermobility (Imbroscio, Williamson, & Alperovitz, 2003). This is due to the fact that SEOs are "place-based enterprises" (Shrivastava & Kennelly, 2013): they tend to be established as locally owned and democratically controlled enterprises that serve as a vehicle for their members to meet the economic, social, environmental, and/or cultural needs of their surrounding community (Peredo & Chrisman, 2006). Small size and local scale of SEOs are argued to be crucial for these organizations to preserve local ownership structures and democratic decision-making mechanisms, create sustainable jobs, promote social cohesion and social capital, and strengthen community resilience (Lukkarinen, 2005; Sonnino & Griggs-Trevarthen, 2013).

I. Bretos (✉)
Faculty of Economics, University of Zaragoza, Zaragoza, Spain
e-mail: ibretos@unizar.es

A. Errasti
GEZKI Institute of Cooperative Law and Social Economy, University of the Basque Country (UPV/EHU), Leioa, Spain
e-mail: a.errasti@ehu.eus

A. Soetens
HEC Liège Management School, University of Liège, Liège, Belgium
e-mail: aurelie.soetens@uliege.be

© Springer Nature Switzerland AG 2021
B. Gidron, A. Domaradzka (eds.), *The New Social and Impact Economy*,
Nonprofit and Civil Society Studies, https://doi.org/10.1007/978-3-030-68295-8_12

While SEOs have been traditionally seen to be reluctant to grow and expand operations beyond national borders (Rothschild & Whitt, 1986; Smith, Gonin, & Besharov, 2013), this has significantly changed in the last few decades. A key trend in the social economy sector at a global level lies in the growing adoption of internationalization strategies by SEOs (Bretos & Marcuello, 2017), often through partnerships with public organizations and business corporations (McMurtry & Reed, 2009). The main drivers of international expansion in the social economy sector are the growing pressures faced by many SEOs to internationalize if they are to maintain their competitive position in increasingly globalized and dynamic markets (Bretos, Errasti, & Marcuello, 2020), and the growing demand to scale their social impact and innovations across borders in a context of growing economic, social, and environmental problems that are not being effectively addressed by the market and the state (André & Pache, 2016; Bretos, Díaz-Foncea, & Marcuello, 2020; Lindenberg, 1999).

Indeed, some studies suggest that international expansion of SEOs is far from a marginal phenomenon. For example, in a recent study on 300 of the largest co-ops and mutuals in the world, Bretos, Díaz-Foncea, and Marcuello (2018) found that the vast majority of them operate across borders through different strategies ranging from contractual typologies such as direct exports, franchising, and licensing to equity typologies such as greenfield investments, joint ventures, and full acquisitions. These strategies are not confined to just a few large enterprises though. Smaller SEOs and social ventures are equally producing and offering their goods and/or services on a global scale. Information and communication technologies (ICTs) are critical for these organizations to achieve a global dimension and scale social impact across borders: ICTs allow SEOs to identify and exploit global social entrepreneurship opportunities, access a wider range of funding sources (e.g., crowdfunding), and create social networks and entrepreneurial alliances to drive international growth (Torres-Coronas & Vidal-Blasco, 2013; Zahra, Rawhouser, Bhawe, Neubaum, & Hayton, 2008). Not surprisingly, many of the new international SEOs and social ventures are born global from their inception (Marshall, 2011).

This scenario raises some important questions for a better understanding of the nature and evolution of the *new social economy*. What strategies do SEOs deploy to expand their operations across borders and how scaling social impact is related to each strategy? What are the challenges for international SEOs in preserving and extending their socially oriented practices and values? What approaches can international SEOs adopt to maintain a sustainable balance between social and economic performance? Do they embody a genuine alternative in the international business arena to corporate managerialism and conventional multinationals? The chapter aims to shed some light on these questions. Being aware of the important national differences that exist in the world regarding the concept of social economy and the specific organizations that are part of this sector, in this chapter we adopt a broad and inclusive international approach that conceptualizes SEOs as organizations which, regardless of their legal form, engage in commercial activities to sustain their operations while pursuing a social mission and involving different stakeholders in decision-making.

In the next section, we identify three major scaling strategies and provide some relevant examples of how high-profile SEOs are adopting these strategies. We also discuss the potential of these strategies to address different social and environmental issues on a global scale as well as to scale social impact and innovations across national boundaries. The third section discusses the main challenges faced by international SEOs not only to preserve their community orientation, cooperative practices, and social values in the parent organization, but also to extend them across their international networks made up of branches, partners, and/or implementers. The fourth section illustrates how SEOs can manage the challenges associated with international expansion. In particular, we draw on insights from five cutting-edge SEOs that are operating successfully on a global scale while engaging in social values and cooperative and communitarian practices. The last section is devoted to conclusions.

Cross-Border Scaling Strategies in SEOs

Drawing on a review of the literature on social enterprise growth and scaling (e.g., André & Pache, 2016; Bauwens, Huybrechts, & Dufays, 2019; Dees, Anderson, & Wei-Skillern, 2004; Heinecke & Mayer, 2012; Lyon & Fernandez, 2012; Nazarkina, 2012; Vickers & Lyon, 2012), we distinguish three major typologies of cross-border scaling strategies: control based, altruism based, and hybrid. As illustrated in Fig. 12.1, these strategies can be placed along a continuum in terms of increasing degree of central control and resource requirements.

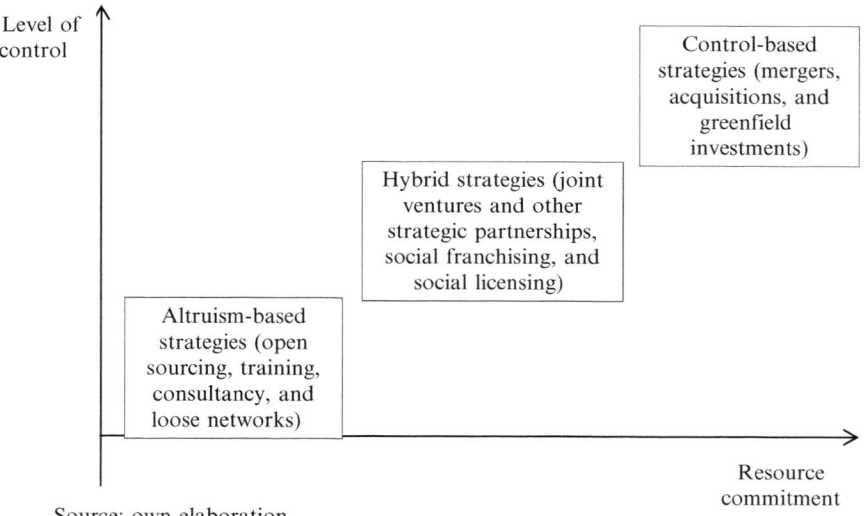

Source: own elaboration

Fig. 12.1 Three major typologies of international scaling strategies. Source: own elaboration

Control-Based International Scaling Strategies

Control-based international scaling strategies rely on a considerable degree of centralized control and coordination, and generally require the greatest investment of resources by the parent organization (Dees et al., 2004). These strategies, which basically include cross-border mergers, acquisitions, and greenfield investments, involve the parent organization creating branch structures beyond its national borders in the form of company-owned stores, offices, or plants (Heinecke & Mayer, 2012), that is, all units legally belong to the parent organization. Control-based strategies are often pursued by SEOs seeking to increase the scale of operations, to acquire new capabilities and access resources while entering new geographic markets (Nazarkina, 2012), many times as a way to preserve or stimulate their competitive position in highly globalized and dynamic markets (Bretos & Marcuello, 2017).

Many of the organizations included in the World Co-operative Monitor's list of the 300 largest cooperatives and mutuals in the world embody relevant examples[1] (Bretos, Díaz-Foncea, & Marcuello, 2018). For instance, some industrial cooperatives from the Basque Country have pursued extensive acquisitive growth in international markets since the mid-1990s in order to maintain their competitiveness and safeguard the jobs of the worker-members at the parent Basque plants (Bretos, Errasti, & Marcuello, 2019). These multinational co-ops tend to centralize major strategic, technical, financial, and commercial decisions in the parent cooperative (Errasti, Bretos, & Etxezarreta, 2016). They combine the exercise of direct control by enforcing policies and practices in the subsidiaries with indirect control mechanisms based on monitoring by way of expatriate personnel and communication between headquarters and key managers in foreign plants (Bretos, Errasti, & Marcuello, 2018). Internationalization strategies with similar degrees of central control have been equally adopted by SEOs in other sectors such as the banking industry (e.g., Crédit Agricole, Raiffeisen Banking Group, Crédit Mutuel, and Rabobank) and agri-food industry (e.g., Danish Crown, Fonterra, Arla Foods, and FrieslandCampina) (Birchall, 2014; Bretos, Díaz-Foncea, & Marcuello, 2018).

Other prominent examples beyond cooperatives and mutuals include large international nonprofit organizations such as the well-known cases of BRAC and Ashoka. Bangladesh-based BRAC, which is the largest nongovernmental development organization in the world, provides microloans, self-employment opportunities, health services, education, and legal and human rights services. With branches and operations in 14 countries, BRAC International was set up in 2009 to govern and manage all BRAC entities outside Bangladesh, the UK, and the USA (Hossain & Sengupta, 2009). Ashoka, meanwhile, is a nonprofit organization dedicated to identifying and supporting outstanding social entrepreneurs worldwide, providing them with living stipends, professional support, and access to a global network of peers in more than

---

[1]The World Co-operative Monitor has been published annually since 2011 by the International Cooperative Alliance and the Institute Euricse, and can be downloaded from https://www.monitor.coop/en

60 countries. The international board centralizes decision-making on the selection of social entrepreneurs to ensure consistency and accomplishment of quality standards across all Ashoka subsidiaries (Heinecke & Mayer, 2012).

The other two strategies—altruist and hybrid—are more likely to be deployed by international social ventures of a more entrepreneurial nature, which identify and exploit opportunities across national borders to create new businesses, models, and solutions for value creation, including financial, social, and environmental (Zahra, Newey, & Li, 2014). In these expansion strategies, the primary goal of the organization is to increase social value creation.

Altruism-Based International Scaling Strategies

Altruist strategies involve a disseminating organization that makes its social innovation internationally available by actively sharing information and/or providing technical assistance to one or more recipient organizations that seek to replicate the approach or model (Heinecke & Mayer, 2012; Sezgi & Mair, 2010). Also referred to as dissemination, scaling across, diffusion, or spread, altruist strategies rely on few resources, and there is little or no centralized control by the source organization over the replication of the social innovation by the adopter (Dees et al., 2004), which tends to use the shared information and knowledge as it deems appropriate. Hence, the source organization is not interested in owning and appropriating the value created using its approach but in altruistically spreading its model, ideas, or tools to generate broader social impact, that is, the focus of these strategies "is on replication, diffusion by other actors, and adoption rather than organizational control" (Bauwens et al., 2019, p. 5). Common mechanisms for the diffusion of knowledge and information in altruist strategies include open sourcing, training, consultancy, and loose networks (Berelowitz, Chopra, Coussa, et al., 2015; Lyon & Fernandez, 2012; Uvin, Pankaj, Jain, & Brown, 2000).

Open sourcing involves an organization that creates and shares resources, materials, and publications (e.g., brochures, best practice booklets, manuals, and online videos) guiding and advising others on how to implement the social innovation. In the case of training, the disseminating organization provides formal training to others, generally through courses, workshops, or seminars, in order to teach how to replicate the social innovation. Consultancy, meanwhile, usually involves providing long-term expert advice on specific aspects/issues of the replication of the social venture or innovation in definite contexts (Berelowitz et al., 2015). KaBOOM! illustrates how SEOs can combine these different mechanisms. This US-based nonprofit organization is dedicated to giving all kids—mainly in low-income communities— safe and accessible play opportunities. In 2004 KaBOOM! started offering different free or low-cost resources in order to disseminate its model more widely. These included toolkits, training seminars, and technical assistance. The nonprofit organization also made accessible for free the project's handbooks, as well as different publications, guidelines, and best practices on its website (Dees et al., 2004; McLeod

& Fulton, 2010). This dissemination strategy has enabled the construction of 3100 playgrounds and rehabilitation of 17,000 play spaces both in the USA and abroad.[2] Similarly, many SEOs encourage creation of spin-offs by providing training and technical support to the implementers. Indian nonprofit organization Urmul, which is engaged in different areas of action including health, basic education, rural craft and weaving, and savings and credit, actively promotes creation of spin-offs through training and support of former staff (Uvin et al., 2000).

Lastly, in loose networks different individuals or organizations that pursue the same social mission form a network, but with little coordination or control. The originator shares resources with the network, which are used by the implementers under no formal agreement or contract to adopt the social innovation and adapt it to their local context (Berelowitz et al., 2015). Food Assembly can be considered an example of expansion through the use of loose networks. This organization operates an online platform enabling a direct trade between communities and local farmers and producers. Anyone can set up their own local branch. Food Assembly operates as a central body which provides the technological platform and support, as well as guidance and assistance to implementers, but with no formal contract or agreement (Berelowitz et al., 2015). Indeed, the central association is small and reports no shared results. Originated in France, today, the Food Assembly model is spread across Europe in different countries such as Spain, Italy, Belgium, and Germany.[3]

Another relevant case is REScoop.eu, a European network of renewable energy cooperatives (REScoops). This network was informally established in 2011 in Belgium when the founders of six met to explore ways of promoting the REScoop model across Europe (Huybrechts & Haugh, 2018). Today the network comprises 1500 REScoops owned by about 1 million citizens from a wide variety of European countries. REScoop.eu basically coordinates the collaboration between members in different thematic working groups, aiming to provide their members direct access to experts and to build a forum for exchange. More specifically, the aims of the federation are (1) to represent the voice of citizens and renewable energy cooperatives to European policy makers; (2) to support the start-up of new REScoops by providing them with useful tools and contacts; (3) to provide services for the European REScoops; and (4) to promote the REScoop business model throughout Europe.[4]

Hybrid International Scaling Strategies

Hybrid international scaling strategies offer the broadest range of possibilities for SEOs to expand across borders and scale social impact (Dees et al., 2004). They rely on long-term contractual organizational arrangements in which both the parent

---

[2] https://kaboom.org/playgrounds

[3] https://laruchequiditoui.fr/fr

[4] https://www.rescoop.eu/federation

organization and the partners maintain their autonomy (Nazarkina, 2012), although they usually imply a commitment of both parties to share information and pool some level of resources (Smith & Stevens, 2010). In hybrid strategies, the relationship between the parent organization and the partners can range from loose cooperation to strongly linked structures (Heinecke & Mayer, 2012). Hybrid strategies represent an intermediate solution in terms of resource commitment and control. In comparison to altruist strategies, hybrid modes allow the source organization to gain greater control over its adopters and the process of transfer of knowledge and information (Uvin et al., 2000). However, hybrid strategies also require more resources and support from the source organization. In addition, hybrid strategies are also capable of achieving more varied impact increments, as they can scale social impact both directly, by reaching a larger number of users, and indirectly, in a process through which the partners of the alliance or network can induce each other to carry out new activities and processes aimed at increasing social value creation (Sezgi & Mair, 2010). Hybrid strategies can originate either from a single organization that builds or becomes a parent organization to allow for further scaling up or replication (e.g., Berelowitz et al., 2015; Chen, 2012; Giudici, Combs, Cannatelli, & Smith, 2018) or from different ventures or institutions teaming up in order to create, scale up, and/or diffuse a common social innovation or model (e.g., Davies, Haugh, & Chambers, 2019; Jiwa, 2007; Rattalino, 2018). Common hybrid forms of scaling include social franchising, social licensing, joint ventures, and other strategic partnerships.

International social franchising is basically the application of a commercial franchising approach on an international scale to achieve greater social impact, rather than profit (Tracey & Jarvis, 2007). This involves an organization systematizing and packaging its proven model or social innovation in a way that enables others to replicate it under a franchise agreement. A prominent example is Impact Hub, the largest global network of business incubators and co-working spaces for social businesses. Launched in London in 2005, this project quickly expanded in the early years through an innovative social franchising strategy that put the social mission at the very heart of expansion (Giudici et al., 2018). Today, the Impact Hub network comprises over 100 hubs with 16,500 members, located across 55 countries. Each hub is set up by local entrepreneurs who enjoy substantial autonomy to adapt the concept and model to their local contexts, while an Impact Hub global team provides them with know-how, solutions, and procedures (Impact Hub, 2019). Another example is VisionSpring, a social enterprise whose mission is to ensure affordable access to eyewear for disadvantaged individuals and which embodies an alternative social micro-franchising system. Relying on the essence of the microcredit model, VisionSpring loans franchisees the necessary materials and resources to launch the business, and the latter repays only once they have activity and sales (Chen, 2012).

International social licensing involves turning an innovation with social impact into intellectual property that can be licensed for use by others across borders. One example is the case of Green Gyms, run by the UK charity The Community Volunteering (TCV). These are outdoor sessions aimed at imparting a health and fitness focus to conservation projects. This model has been replicated in other countries such as Australia under the same trademark and the exclusive license from TCV, whose use requires the implementer (licensee) to pay an initial one-off fee. The license package includes training, evaluation, manuals for operations and management, and consultancy to start the Green Gym according to a set of quality standards (Berelowitz et al., 2015).

An international joint venture is an alliance formed by two or more independent entities based in different countries that aims to achieve common objectives. This implies the creation of a new entity, business activity, or project (the joint venture) in which profits, losses, and control are shared by the partners. Many SEOs form joint ventures and partnerships among them to scale their social impact. For example, Cafédirect, a well-known British farmer-owned, fair-trade social enterprise, was founded as a joint venture of four UK organizations involved in poverty alleviation: Oxfam, Traidcraft, Equal Exchange, and Twin Trading (Davies et al., 2019). What is more, much of the subsequent national and foreign expansion pursued by Cafédirect has been achieved through partnerships with other organizations (Davies, Doherty, & Knox, 2010). Another example is Divine Chocolate, which operates in the UK and the USA. This company is owned by Kuapa Kokoo, a Ghanaian cocoa farmers' cooperative; Twin Trading, a UK-based NGO working on market access for smallholder farmers; and the Dutch development finance cooperative Oikocredit.[5]

International public-private partnerships between organizations from the public and the not-for-profit sectors are also commonly used to address social concerns and unresolved needs more effectively, as well as to increase the efficiency and quality in the provision of public services (Quelin, Kivleniece, & Lazzarini, 2017). For instance, the German federally owned international cooperation enterprise GTZ and the British social enterprise Cafédirect set up AdapCC, a public-private partnership that operated between 2007 and 2010 in Kenya, Mexico, Nicaragua, and Peru, and whose aim was to support small coffee and tea producers in their developing strategies to cope with the risks and impacts of climate change. Another relevant example is Honey Care, a Kenyan social enterprise that strives to raise incomes for rural farmers through apiculture. This organization has been particularly successful in raising funds via international aid grants and loans to scale social impact. In partnership with local NGOs, national governments, and international development and financial institutions, Honey Care has extended its venture to countries such as Tanzania and Malawi (Jiwa, 2007).

Lastly, social purpose partnerships between not-for-profit organizations and large multinational corporations have also attracted notable interest in the last two decades (Shumate, Hsieh, & O'Connor, 2018). These partnerships undertake commercial activities that allow for economic sustainability while implementing a social mission either through its processes or through the provided good/service. A good example is the Common Threads Initiative, which was launched through a partnership between the clothing B corporation Patagonia and the multinational e-commerce company eBay. This initiative aims to make, buy, and use clothes more sustainably,

---

[5] https://www.twin.org.uk/projects-partnerships/divine/

specifically by reducing, repairing, reusing, and recycling the apparel that customers buy (Rattalino, 2018).

Challenges for International SEOs in Preserving and Extending Socially Oriented Practices and Values in International SEOs

International growth and scaling imply great challenges for international SEOs to maintain a sustainable balance between social and financial performance (McMurtry & Reed, 2009). This involves not only preserving their community embeddedness and socially oriented practices and values, but also extending these across their international networks made up of branches, partners, and/or implementers (Flecha & Ngai, 2014). When operating on an international scale, SEOs have to pursue the societal needs of a broader range of local communities and mutual benefits of the diverse stakeholders affected by their activities. At the same time, some SEOs must meet the increased efficiency and financial performance requirements associated with competing in highly globalized markets, while others are urged to implement their social innovations in culturally and institutionally distant contexts (Bretos & Marcuello, 2017).

Achieving such balance is extremely complex. Indeed, many SEOs have been found to be exposed to degenerative pressures whereby they depart from their original cooperative practices, communitarian purposes, and/or social values to focus on market orientation (Smith et al., 2013). Degeneration mechanisms include premium on technocratic managerial expertise at the expense of rank-and-file participation; prioritization of profit-seeking goals; prevalence of a managerialist rhetoric that privileges concepts such as quality, customer service, efficiency, growth, and competitiveness; and reshaping of cooperative culture and practices in line with managerial prerogatives and concerns (Bretos, Errasti, & Marcuello, 2018; Heras-Saizarbitoria, 2014).

Some SEOs have also experienced processes of demutualization or transformation into conventional investor-owned multinationals due to different problems such as those related to financial performance, access to capital, member engagement, and governance (Sousa & Herman, 2012). In some cases, demutualization occurs via a merger, takeover, or buyout of a SEO by a multinational corporation looking for new niche markets and, many times, pursuing a "clean-wash" strategy. Some well-known cases include purchases of cruelty-free beauty products company The Body Shop by L'Oréal, organic beverage company Honest Tea by Coca-Cola, natural body care products company Tom's of Maine by Colgate, and organic yogurt maker Stonyfield by Danone Group (Austin & Leonard, 2008).

In the case of SEOs pursuing organizational growth through control-based and hybrid scaling strategies demutualization can also take place through the conversion of equity into investment shares. A prominent example is Kerry Co-op, an Irish food company that demutualized in order to respond to market challenges and obtain capital required for future growth and development of the organization. In 1986 the co-op created a public limited company Kerry Group PLC and exchanged the bulk of its assets for a majority shareholding in Kerry Group (Juliá, Melià, & García, 2012). Since then, Kerry has achieved extraordinary expansion, regularly issuing shares, until having 147 manufacturing plants in 32 countries and selling its products in over 140 countries. Today, Kerry Co-op is a minority shareholder of Kerry Group, with only a 13.6% share in the PLC.[6] In extreme instances, international growth and global competition can result in the dissolution of a SEO (Sousa & Herman, 2012). This is the case of the Basque household appliances manufacturer co-op Fagor Electrodomesticos, which went bankrupt in 2013. Fagor Electrodomesticos, a weak and small company in comparison to its competitors and with a large part of its production activity located in high-cost countries, pursued a risky strategy of international growth that reached its peak with the takeover of the French giant Brandt for €165 million in 2005. Fagor Electrodomesticos finally collapsed due to the severe economic downturn of 2008, after steadily accumulating debt and experiencing a drastic fall in sales (Errasti et al., 2016).

We now turn to discuss some challenges that are more specifically associated to each of the cross-border scaling strategies discussed in the previous section.

Challenges Associated to Control-Based Strategies

Organizational growth associated to control-based strategies can challenge the participatory governance practices that characterize many SEOs. As the organization grows in size, members might find it more difficult to perceive a direct and tangible effect of their participation in decision-making. Likewise, the cultural, geographical, or motivational heterogeneity of large memberships may result in the interests of some groups of members not being addressed. Overall, these factors may lead to a decline in members' involvement in the organization and delegation of decision-making power in management (Bretos & Errasti, 2017; Errasti, Bretos, & Nunez, 2017; Nilsson, 2018). Other mechanisms are equally relevant. As the organization grows it becomes more difficult to establish an efficient flow of information between rank-and-file members and management, and organizational social capital can decline because trust and personal relationships are harder to foster (Nilsson, Svendsen, & Svendsen, 2012).

Employee-centered practices can also be endangered due to organizational growth. This is evident, for example, in the case of Digital Divide Data, a global social enterprise that provides disadvantaged people with economic opportunities through training and employment in an information technology outsourcing business. The company initially supported employees' training through grants. However,

---

[6] https://www.kerrygroup.com/annual-report/

as the number of employees increased, the company had to look for alternatives to finance training, such as replacing outright grants to employees with loans (Smith et al., 2013). Likewise, growth can translate into the weakening of the embeddedness in the local community. In this regard, trust and social networks built through local ties with community actors become harder to preserve as the organization increases in size (Smith & Stevens, 2010). This has been evident, for example, in microfinance social enterprises that have significantly scaled operations under a more commercial approach while losing some communitarian social capital, as is the case of Grameen (Bateman, 2010).

Many international SEOs deploying control-based strategies to expand across borders have also been criticized for not being willing to replicate their hallmark socially oriented practices and values in their branches. This is the case, for example, of nonprofit groups owning for-profit offshoots to generate revenue and strengthen their competitiveness and market position (Skelcher & Smith, 2015; Smith, 2010), or multinational cooperatives that have turned into "coopitalist" hybrids formed by a parent cooperative and a capitalist periphery of noncooperative subsidiaries abroad (Bretos & Errasti , 2018). In the latter, reasons behind the non-transfer of the cooperative model to overseas subsidiaries include institutional barriers such as absence of a legislation covering cooperatives and potential lack of a collectivistic culture and cooperative tradition in the recipient region. However, this might be more critically influenced by headquarters-subsidiary power relations, as well as by core co-op owner-members looking to protect their own interests (Bretos, Errasti, et al., 2018). In this regard, parent co-op owners tend to perceive the "coop-erativization" of foreign subsidiaries as detrimental for their own control over the business group and risky for the viability of the co-op because the subsidiary might take decisions that go against the former's interests (Bretos et al., 2019).

Challenges Associated with Altruism-Based Strategies

A key challenge associated with altruism-based scaling models lies in the fact that the source organization lacks control mechanisms regarding who replicates the approach or social innovation, for which purpose it is implemented, and whether its quality and essence are preserved (Heinecke & Mayer, 2012). This can result in the distortion of the approach and consequent damage to the brand image of the source organization, or of the social innovation in question, if the approach/innovation is not adequately applied, that is, if the social mission or innovation is perverted by pursuing purely economic goals or other personal concerns that go against general interest or the interest of the target audience.

This is illustrated to some extent by the case of Hippocampus Learning Centres (HLC), an Indian social enterprise whose mission is to transform the lives of under-served children through high-quality education. This SEO experienced some problems related to the distortion of its original approach during its initial dissemination across India, because some educational programs were not being replicated with the expected quality and some centers were not financially sustainable. When this experience was replicated in Mexico in 2016, however, HLC partnered with Connovo, a local social business specializing in the replication of social ventures to scale impact. With notable adaptation of the approach to the Mexican local context, for example, regarding the way in which the project was funded, the replication was highly successful (Conway & Dávila-Castilla, 2018), and Hippocampus is now targeting to operate 100 centers by 2021 in this country.[7]

Alternatively, the initial lack of control stemming from the altruism-based replication strategy might lead some SEOs to consolidate autocratic monitoring models that stifle the adaptation of the approach/innovation to the local context in which it is being replicated, thereby seriously damaging ties between the initiative and local community. The Freecycle Network exemplifies this transition. Founded in the USA in 2003 to promote a gift economy by connecting people to exchange free items for reuse or recycling in their local area, this initiative was quickly replicated in many countries, and hundreds of decentralized local groups were set up worldwide with substantial autonomy to implement the model. However, in 2009 most UK local groups broke away to set up the alternative network Freegle against accusations of increasing tight control from the US Freecycle parent and little room of maneuver for local adaptation, as well as growing concerns over the gradual erosion of Freecycle's grassroots ethos (Martin, Upham, & Budd, 2015). Overall, this reveals how enforcing a model or approach in recipient communities according to the standards of the region of origin does not work, as well as how important it is for implementers to have autonomy to adapt the model/innovation to the local context, as they know its characteristics better. In addition, it illustrates how preserving the autonomy of the (replicated) local groups may be a way to counteract the erosion of social values and practices at the parent company and ensure the survival of a community orientation.

Challenges Associated with Hybrid Strategies

Similar to the case of altruism-based scaling, purposeful distortion or misinterpretation of the original approach or social innovation can also emerge in hybrid scaling strategies such as franchising and licensing agreements, as the source organization does not have total control over the implementer (Heinecke & Mayer, 2012). Another potential problem is the lack of alignment between the interests of the source organization and the franchisee or licensee. These challenges were visible in the case of Aspire Group, a UK social enterprise that was founded in the late 1990s with the aim of providing employment for homeless people. This social enterprise experienced notable expansion through a social franchising strategy, but it failed due to different reasons including the lack of an efficient franchisee monitoring

---

[7] https://hippocampus.in/about/snap-shot/

system and the fact that the goals of economic viability and social service provision were not successfully aligned in the franchising network (Nazarkina, 2012). In the early stages of Aspire's expansion, the franchisees enjoyed notable autonomy in implementing the approach. As financial difficulties emerged, however, Aspire Group attempted to exercise greater centralized control over the franchisees and, moreover, its concerns shifted to financial survival, while the franchisees' priorities remained providing employment and support to homeless people (Tracey & Jarvis, 2007).

Tensions to maintain a sustainable balance between potentially contradictory goals are particularly prone to arise in cross-sector joint ventures and partnerships between corporations and SEOs (Di Domenico, Tracey, & Haugh, 2009). This is due to the fact that profit-seeking and competitiveness concerns typical of corporations might clash with the social and/or environmental performance interests that characterize SEOs. A major problem for SEOs engaging in partnerships with mainstream corporations might lie in the adoption of businesslike practices and approaches at the expense of social mission due to the latter's influence, as well as in the lessening of organizational legitimacy from stakeholders (Huybrechts & Nicholls, 2013) such as beneficiaries and donors who might perceive partnering with conventional businesses as a "pact with the devil" (Huybrechts, Nicholls, & Edinger, 2017).

The purchase of the American ice cream B corporation Ben & Jerry's by the British-Dutch transnational consumer goods behemoth Unilever illustrates these challenges. While this was not a partnership but a takeover, this case is relevant because Ben & Jerry's board retained total autonomy within Unilever to make decisions and pursue its own agenda, thus enjoying much more independence than any other Unilever's subsidiaries. Despite this special status, the co-op has been criticized both internally by employees and externally by customers and social activists for drifting away from its original social and ecological roots while embracing, influenced by Unilever, market values and a more pronounced commercial orientation. For example, Ben & Jerry's had to stop using their brand in political campaigns, such as anti-war demonstrations, because Unilever's ethical code required the company to remain apolitical (Haski-Leventhal, Roza, & Meijs, 2017).

Innovations in International SEOs for Balancing Social and Financial Performance

We now turn to discuss how international SEOs can manage the tensions, competing demands, and ethical dilemmas associated with international growth, both by preventing mission drift trends and by refinding the expected equilibrium between financial and social performance. In this regard, we draw on insights from five cutting-edge SEOs operating in different industries and countries that have been particularly successful in engaging with social values and practices while generating financial value. The selected SEOs are Aravind, Mondragon Corporation, Up Group, Arla Foods, and Rabobank.

Aravind Eye Care System

Aravind Eye Care System is an Indian-based nonprofit organization that provides eye care services to poor people. It is the world's largest provider of eye care, attending two million patients and performing 270,000 surgeries per year, most of them provided either free or steeply subsidized for the patient (Sezgi & Mair, 2010). Only in South India, Aravind's eye care facilities include 13 eye hospitals, 6 outpatient eye examination centers, and 75 primary eye care facilities. Its manufacturing unit, Aurolab, produces two million lenses per year, which are exported to more than 120 countries.

Aravind has actively promoted the dissemination of its model beyond India. Its expansion illustrates how SEOs can deploy altruism-based strategies to scale social impact across borders and prevent distortions of the original approach by the implementer while, at the same time, avoiding exertion of the excessively centralized control that might hinder the replication and local adaptation of the approach beyond the national borders. Aravind's solution was the creation of the Lions Aravind Institute of Community Ophthalmology (LAICO) in 1992 in order to support eye care programs globally through consultancy and capacity building, management training, and research. LAICO, which is Aravind Eye Care System's training and consulting arm, provides accompaniment and support for the replication of the model through a 2-year consultancy process that includes assessment, capacity building and strategic planning, implementation training, and monitoring (Berelowitz et al., 2015).

As noted by Sezgi and Mair (2010), Aravind's diffusion model has been based on four mechanisms: (1) training of organizational members to teach them skills and instill values; (2) rotation among organizational members to spread values in newly established hospitals; (3) ensuring communication between hospitals both to monitor performance and to reinforce maintenance and spread of values; and (4) providing updated templates containing their best practices to be shared with third-party hospitals. Today, Aravind's approach has been replicated in more than 30 countries (Berelowitz et al., 2015).

Mondragon Cooperative Corporation

The Basque Country-headquartered Mondragon Cooperative Corporation (MCC) is the largest worker-owned and -governed federation in the world. MCC employs nearly 81,000 workers across the world, most of them in 98 co-ops that control nearly 143 subsidiaries abroad. Operating in highly dynamic and globalized industries, many Mondragon co-ops have been compelled to pursue extensive growth both in the domestic and international markets since the early 1990s in order to maintain their competitive position vis-à-vis large multinational corporations and safeguard worker-members' jobs in the Basque plants (Bretos et al., 2019).

MCC illustrates how SEOs can reverse mission drift trends and refind a more balanced equilibrium between social and financial performance. After decades of tremendous growth that distanced MCC from its original communitarian approach, cooperative practices, and social values in favor of managerial prerogatives and market orientation, the group has been enveloped, since the mid-2000s, in a process of reflection directed at restoring essential aspects of the cooperative experience along three key areas: participation and cooperation, cooperative training and education, and social transformation.

Regarding participation and cooperation, many Mondragon multinational co-ops are boosting more democratic dynamics by opening up spaces for deliberation and more active participation of shop-floor workers, thus countervailing oligarchic trends that had been consolidated with international expansion and growth in the size of the co-ops. Some best practices include preparatory meetings held in small groups prior to the general assemblies in order to stimulate participation in those spaces; inclusion of members from all strata and hierarchical levels of the cooperative in the discussion and elaboration of the strategic plans; reconfiguration of mini-councils to strengthen information sharing; and creation of new spaces to broaden the workers' involvement, such as "social plant meetings" and "social business councils" in which information concerning management is shared, general cooperative matters are discussed, and social affairs are dealt with. Where cooperative training and education are concerned, MCC has introduced and renovated training courses for the cooperative members. Courses readdress philosophical, social, and practical aspects of the Mondragon cooperative movement, which had taken second stage for the benefit of the technical training in the last years. New courses also focus on social skills such as leadership and teamwork as well as management competencies in order to tackle a critical problem in many Mondragon multinational co-ops: many rank-and-file worker-members lack strategic and business skills to decide on highly complex strategic issues associated with operating in highly globalized and competitive environments. The social transformation area, meanwhile, includes very diverse policies directed at reconnecting Mondragon co-ops with their commitment to community development. The actions in this field are very varied. Some relevant examples include the introduction by many industrial co-ops of environmental sustainability policies and circular economy practices, or the alliance between Mondragon and United Steelworkers, the largest industrial trade union in North America, to promote Mondragon-like industrial cooperatives across the USA and Canada (Bretos, Errasti, et al., 2020).

Up Group

Up Group is the second largest co-op in France in terms of revenue and members. It is engaged in developing payment methods and management solutions that improve the vitality of companies and territories, as well as purchasing power and a better life for employees and citizens. Its services for employees include access to food, culture, recreation, education, home help, and social assistance. Up Group serves 1.1 million clients (which include companies and public and social actors), while 26 million employees and citizens are beneficiaries of Up's services and products. This international cooperative group employs about 3600 people across France and other 19 countries located in Western and Mediterranean Europe, Eurasia, and the Americas.[8]

Up has grown significantly through noncooperative subsidiaries both in France and abroad. However, Up's trade union tradition—the co-op was created by a score of French trade unionists in the 1960s and, today, all of the co-op's senior managers are required to be members of some trade union—has greatly influenced the company's strategy. Entry into some countries has been made by the hand of the trade union and cooperative movement. In other cases, decisions about whether and how to access new markets have been significantly shaped by Up's European Works Council and trade unions. For example, the Italian subsidiary was launched in partnership with the local cooperative movement, while in Spain the subsidiary was opened with notable help from Spanish trade unions (Poulnot & Matray, 2016). What is more, in the last years Up has attracted notable interest for designing and implementing a strategy of re-mutualization through the cooperativization of capitalist branches. Denominated as "Roots and Wings," this long-term project aims to develop employee ownership across the subsidiaries, and thus strengthen the Group's cooperative model. This is part of a broader strategy in Up to revitalize its original democratic principles and to re-engage with the Social and Solidarity Economy movement after a period of extraordinary international expansion and business development.

The first step in the Roots and Wings project was taken in 2016. Three French domestic subsidiaries were transformed into worker co-ops and their 250 workers were integrated as owner-members in Up. Thus, Up's cooperative membership base grew from 394 to 710 worker-member-owners (Up Group, 2018). Where foreign subsidiaries are concerned, meanwhile, Up is pursuing a different strategy. Aware of the specific social, cultural, legal, financial, and governance features of each country where the subsidiaries are located, Up has designed a series of common, exportable principles and commitments to be applied by its foreign subsidiaries in order to bring them closer to the cooperative management model of the French parent company (see Table 12.1).

---

[8] https://groupe.up.coop/en/who-are-we/up-an-independent-and-international-group

Table 12.1   Up's principles and commitments in introducing the cooperative model in the foreign subsidiaries

Better cooperative	Better bank
• Enhanced countervailing power of members on Rabobank as a whole • Increased transparency of roles and responsibilities in organization • Increased distinctiveness, enhanced visibility, tangible participation in local communities • Streamlined decision-making process and consultative structure	• Full and prompt compliance with new regulatory, supervisory and resolution requirements • More efficient internal processes due to the abolition of delegated supervision and more effective monitoring of management performance • Improved cost efficiency • Annual accounts and income statement reflect more strongly the financial solidity of Rabobank Group

Source: Up Group (2018)

Arla Foods

The co-op Arla Foods is the largest organic dairy producer in the world, employing 19,190 people all over the world. Born from the merger of Danish MD Foods and Swedish Arla, today, Arla Foods is owned by 10,319 dairy farmers from Denmark, Sweden, Germany, the UK, Belgium, Luxembourg, and the Netherlands. Arla has significantly expanded until becoming a major global player in the food and beverages industry. It controls production plants in 12 countries and sales offices in 30 countries, and exports its products to 105 countries.[9] Arla is in fact one of the few European agri-food cooperatives whose membership base consists of farmers from different countries.

Arla stands out for designing and implementing the strategy "Good Growth" in 2015, as a route to shared value creation for the stakeholders and the company. This integral strategy combines the development of Arla as a global food company through business growth and expansion, with a strong commitment to social responsibility and environmental sustainability. More specifically, in the Good Growth strategy, three key pillars can be distinguished: responsible international growth, cooperative expansion, and concern for environmental sustainability (Høvring, 2017).

Responsible international growth includes a wide variety of commitments and actions concerning, for example, respect of human rights and international principles, workers' well-being and inclusion, and increased transparency and communication with stakeholders. Cooperative expansion involves, on the one hand, growth through cooperation. Arla's expansion largely relies on strategic alliances and partnerships. On the other hand, this strategy pursues the enlargement of cooperative membership and extension of democratic control. In this regard, farmers in acquired or newly created Arla's subsidiaries outside the country of origin have become owner-members of the co-op. What is more, the company is trying to move towards a "One Global Arla," that is, a company in which the cooperative business culture is shared by employees across all the subsidiaries (Arla Foods, 2018). Environmental

---

[9] https://www.arla.com/company/

concerns in Arla's growth strategy include, among others, the commitment to reduce the company's carbon footprint, maintenance of animal welfare and biodiversity in the farms, and production and distribution of high-quality, natural-source products. These elements of social responsibility and cooperative identity are reinforced in Arla not only through a powerful corporate discourse that emphasizes generation of shared value (Høvring, 2017 but also by implementing social performance and environmental indicators to monitor advances and assess their impact.

Rabobank

Rabobank is an international financial services provider operating on the basis of cooperative principles. Its main activities include retail and wholesale banking, private banking, leasing, and real estate services. In particular, it has specialized in financing activities for the agri-food sector. As a cooperative bank, Rabobank is owned by 101 local Rabobanks in the Netherlands which, in turn, belong to 1.9 million of client-member-owners. Rabobank Group employs nearly 42,000 people across 40 countries worldwide and serves approximately ten million customers.[10]

The case of Rabobank reveals the importance of participatory governance in aligning prescriptions from distinct institutional logics to maintain a joint accountability to both social and economic goals, and thus preventing mission drift. In 2014 the co-op embarked in the Great Governance Debate, a broad internal discussion about the revision of the governance structure and mechanisms to achieve a more decentralized organization. All local cooperative Rabobanks and Rabobank Nederland started operating as one cooperative bank. Among other issues, membership base also increased, and today more than 25% of Rabobank's clients are member-owners of a local bank. Meanwhile, local bank member councils became more specifically focused on the bank's local services and its role in the community. Their influence and control also extended to Rabobank as a whole, as each local Rabobank directly represents its members in the supreme management body of the co-op: The General Members Council (Rabobank, 2019).

Above all, this new configuration sought to turn Rabobank into a better co-op and a better bank, allowing a better alignment and monitoring of the relationship between social and trading activities (see Table 12.2). Financial performance has been enhanced, for example, through the improved cost efficiency and introduction of more effective control strategies for monitoring management performance. At the same time, local Rabobanks operate now with a higher degree of independence so they can better align their activities with local communities' interests, member-owners' power in Rabobank's decision-making has been enhanced, and a shared cooperative culture has been spread across employees in both the co-op and subsidiaries (Groeneveld, 2016). Furthermore, the impact of social responsibility practices

---

[10] https://www.rabobank.com/en/about-rabobank/profile/index.html

Table 12.2 Main results of the governance revision in Rabobank. Source: Groeneveld (2016, 20)

Better cooperative	Better bank
• Enhanced countervailing power of members on Rabobank as a whole • Increased transparency of roles and responsibilities in organization • Increased distinctiveness, enhanced visibility, tangible participation in local communities • Streamlined decision-making process and consultative structure	• Full and prompt compliance with new regulatory, supervisory and resolution requirements • More efficient internal processes due to the abolition of delegated supervision and more effective monitoring of management performance • Improved cost efficiency • Annual accounts and income statement reflect more strongly the financial solidity of Rabobank Group

has also been more precisely evaluated. For example, in 2018 Rabobank assessed its contribution to the achievement of the Sustainable Development Goals, drawing results that show a substantial positive impact of its economic and social activities on 8 Goals (Rabobank, 2019).

It is also worth noting that all the international SEOs analyzed have shown an extraordinary capacity to innovatively adapt their production processes, organizational structures, and services in order to respond to the ongoing Covid-19 crisis. For example, Up Group has signed an agreement with the global humanitarian organization Action Against Hunger to donate meal vouchers and hygiene kits to vulnerable people. Several Mondragon industrial cooperatives temporarily restructured their manufacturing processes to produce and supply face masks and ventilators to combat the Covid-19 disease in Spain, in a context of medical equipment shortage and national emergency. Among other measures, Aravind has disseminated through its website a series of videos and resources with information to prevent the spread of the virus. Rabobank has launched a specific loan program with advantageous conditions to support small and medium-sized enterprises and social entrepreneurs affected by the coronavirus downturn. Arla Foods is involved in several projects with public organizations to send out grocery packages to people at higher risk of severe illness. In sum, these cases illustrate how globally oriented SEOs and social entrepreneurs are mobilizing a wide range of resources and designing diverse solutions to provide communities with greater resilience to weather Covid-19's dramatic consequences (Zahra, 2020).

Conclusions

Contrary to the conventional wisdom and mainstream theory depicting SEOs as small-sized organizations that exclusively operate on a local scale and suffer from different barriers and limitations for their growth, recent studies show that international expansion has become a key trend in the evolution and diffusion of the social economy sector globally. As this chapter illustrates, SEOs can operate successfully across borders, playing a key role in addressing growing environmental and social issues that are global in nature, such as poverty, worsening of health and living conditions, social exclusion, impoverished labor conditions, biodiversity depletion, and climate change.

Two main drivers of SEOs' international expansion can be distinguished. First, growing globalization and international competition in many sectors have pressured some SEOs to adopt internationalization strategies in order to maintain their competitive position and safeguard their contribution to social welfare. Second, the fact that global economic, social, and environmental problems are not being effectively addressed by the public and private capitalist sectors has created a growing demand for SEOs to implement solutions and scale up their social impact across borders.

These different drivers and rationales are critical in determining the choice of the scaling strategy by the SEO. As we have seen, SEOs looking to stimulate their competitive position in highly globalized and dynamic markets tend to adopt control-based scaling strategies, as these offer greater opportunities to increase the scale of their operations, access new capabilities and resources, and appropriate the financial value generated by the organization as a whole. SEOs primarily looking to scale their social impact beyond national boundaries, meanwhile, tend to adopt altruism-based strategies because these are prone to enable a rapid diffusion and wide replication of social innovations and solutions across different sectors and countries. ICTs are particularly relevant for these SEOs to scale their social impact because they enable dissemination of the information and sharing of the resources, materials, and best practices with other organizations or entrepreneurs interested in replicating the social innovation or model, as well as providing the necessary online training and technical support. Lastly, SEOs deploying hybrid strategies combine social welfare and market logics in their international expansion and seem to seek both scaling social impact and enhancing financial performance. Indeed, these SEOs usually expand across borders through cross-sectoral partnerships with public organizations and mainstream businesses, reflecting how these SEOs blend different demands.

International scaling in SEOs is not exempt from tensions and risks, as they face unique challenges for balancing social welfare and commercial goals effectively. These organizations confront different problems in preserving and extending their socially oriented practices and values. SEOs deploying control-based scaling strategies are exposed to degenerative pressures that might lead these organizations to embrace purely profit-seeking goals, market values, and managerialism practices. This is due to the fact that these SEOs face increased economic requirements and pressures for greater efficiency and financial performance associated with operating on the international scale, often in highly globalized and competitive markets. In the case of SEOs utilizing altruism-based scaling strategies, the main challenge is that the external implementer might distort and pervert the nature and values of the former's original model or solution. SEOs expanding across borders through hybrid scaling strategies mainly risk departing from their original practices and values when engaging in partnerships with public and private sector organizations that pursue different, often competing, objectives.

Nonetheless, the different case studies presented in this chapter illustrate how international SEOs can mobilize resources and activate processes of organizational change not only to prevent mission drift, but also to counterbalance degenerative processes and thus recover the expected equilibrium between social welfare and financial logics. The main mechanisms include recovery of countervailing social discourses emphasizing democracy, social transformation, and community development; reinforcement of social accounting and participatory governance; updating and institutionalization of education and training in the organizational culture; support from the source organization concerning the correct replication of the solution or innovation by the third parties; and dissemination of the parent organization's original social practices and values among its overseas branches or subsidiaries. The adaptability to changing international conditions also seems to be a critical feature of SEOs. As we have seen, the international SEOs analyzed in this chapter have successfully adapted their structures, approaches, and services in order to respond to the societal, public health, and environmental issues generated by the ongoing Covid-19 crisis.

In conclusion, the evidence collected illustrates how international SEOs can sustain and promote over time the distinctive social values, cooperative practices, and communitarian approaches that make them genuine alternatives to corporate managerialism not only in their local, national contexts, but also in the international business arena.

Acknowledgement   Research for this paper was supported by grants from the Basque Autonomous Government (GIC 18147/IT 1327-19) and the Spanish Ministry of Science and Innovation the PID2019-109252RB-I00.

References

Amin, A., Cameron, A., & Hudson, R. (2002). *Placing the social economy*. London: Routledge.
André, K., & Pache, A. C. (2016). From caring entrepreneur to caring enterprise: Addressing the ethical challenges of scaling up social enterprises. *Journal of Business Ethics, 133*, 659–675.
Arla Foods. (2018). *Annual report 2017*. Viby: Arla.
Austin, J., & Leonard, H. (2008). Can the virtuous mouse and the wealthy elephant live happily ever after? *California Management Review, 51*, 77–102.
Bateman, M. (2010). *Why doesn't microfinance work?* London: Zed Books.
Bauwens, T., Huybrechts, B., & Dufays, F. (2019). Understanding the diverse scaling strategies of social enterprises as hybrid organizations: The case of renewable energy cooperatives. *Organization & Environment.*, in press. https://doi.org/10.1177/1086026619837126.
Berelowitz, D., Chopra, P., Coussa, G., et al. (2015). *Social replication toolkit*. London: Spring.
Birchall, J. (2014). *The governance of large co-operative businesses*. Manchester: Co-operatives UK.
Bretos, I., Díaz-Foncea, M., & Marcuello, C. (2018). Cooperativas e internacionalización: Un análisis de las 300 mayores cooperativas del mundo. *CIRIEC-España, Revista de Economía Pública, Social y Cooperativa, 92*, 5–37.

Bretos, I., Díaz-Foncea, M., & Marcuello, C. (2020). International expansion of social enterprises as a catalyst for scaling up social impact across borders. *Sustainability, 12*(8), 3262. https://doi. org/10.3390/su12083262.

Bretos, I., & Errasti, A. (2017). Challenges and opportunities for the regeneration of multinational worker cooperatives: Lessons from the Mondragon corporation – A case study of the Fagor Ederlan group. *Organization, 24*(2), 154–173.

Bretos, I., & Errasti, A. (2018). The challenges of managing across borders in worker cooperatives: Insights from the Mondragon cooperative group. *Journal of Co-operative Organization and Management, 6*(1), 34–42.

Bretos, I., Errasti, A., & Marcuello, C. (2018). Ownership, governance, and the diffusion of HRM practices in multinational worker cooperatives: Case study evidence from the Mondragon group. *Human Resource Management Journal, 28*(1), 76–91.

Bretos, I., Errasti, A., & Marcuello, C. (2019). Multinational expansion of worker cooperatives and their employment practices: Markets, institutions, and politics in Mondragon. *ILR Review, 72*(3), 580–605.

Bretos, I., Errasti, A., & Marcuello, C. (2020). Is there life after degeneration? The organizational life cycle of cooperatives under a 'grow-or-die' dichotomy. *Annals of Public and Cooperative Economics, 91*(3), 435–458.

Bretos, I., & Marcuello, C. (2017). Revisiting globalization challenges and opportunities in the development of cooperatives. *Annals of Public and Cooperative Economics, 88*(1), 47–73.

Burke, B. (2010). Cooperatives for "fair globalization"? Indigenous people, cooperatives, and corporate social responsibility in the Brazilian Amazon. *Latin American Perspectives, 37*, 30–52.

Chen, S. (2012). Creating sustainable international social ventures. *Thunderbird International Business Review, 54*(1), 131–142.

Conway, M., & Dávila-Castilla, J. A. (2018). *Modelando el emprendimiento social en México.* Ciudad de México: LID Editorial.

Davies, I. A., Doherty, B., & Knox, S. (2010). The rise and stall of a fair trade pioneer: The story of Cafédirect. *Journal of Business Ethics, 92*, 127–147.

Davies, I. A., Haugh, H., & Chambers, L. (2019). Barriers to social Enterprise growth. *Journal of Small Business Management, 57*(4), 1616–1636.

Dees, J. G., Anderson, B. B., & Wei-Skillern, J. (2004). Scaling social impact. *Stanford Social Innovation Review, 1*(4), 24–32.

Di Domenico, M. L., Tracey, P., & Haugh, H. (2009). The dialectic of social exchange: Theorizing corporate-social enterprise collaboration. *Organization Studies, 30*, 887–907.

Errasti, A., Bretos, I., & Etxezarreta, E. (2016). What do Mondragon Coopitalist multinationals look like? The rise and fall of Fagor Electrodomésticos S. Coop. and its European subsidiaries. *Annals of Public and Cooperative Economics, 87*, 433–456.

Errasti, A., Bretos, I., & Nunez, A. (2017). The viability of cooperatives: The fall of the Mondragon cooperative Fagor. *Review of Radical Political Economics, 49*, 181–197.

Flecha, R., & Ngai, P. (2014). The challenge for Mondragon: Searching for the co-operative values in times of internationalization. *Organization, 21*(5), 666–682.

Giudici, A., Combs, J. G., Cannatelli, B. L., & Smith, B. R. (2018). Successful scaling in social franchising: The case of Impact Hub. *Entrepreneurship Theory and Practice.*, in press. https:// doi.org/10.1177/1042258718801593.

Groeneveld, J. M. (2016). *The road towards one cooperative Rabobank.* Utrecht: Rabobank.

Haski-Leventhal, D., Roza, L., & Meijs, L. (2017). Congruence in corporate social responsibility: Connecting the identity and behaviour of employers and employees. *Journal of Business Ethics, 143*, 35–51.

Heinecke, A., & Mayer, J. (2012). Strategies for scaling in social entrepreneurship. In C. Volkmann, K. Tokarski, & K. Ernst (Eds.), *Social entrepreneurship and social business* (pp. 191–209). Wiesbaden: Gabler Verlag.

Heras-Saizarbitoria, I. (2014). The ties that bind? Exploring the basic principles of worker-owned organizations in practice. *Organization, 21*(5), 645–665.

Hossain, N., & Sengupta, A. (2009). Thinking big, going global: The challenge of BRAC's global expansion. *IDS Working Paper*, (339).

Høvring, C. M. (2017). Corporate social responsibility as shared value creation: Toward a communicative approach. *Corporate Communications, 22*(2), 239–256.

Impact Hub (2019). *Impact Report*. Available at www.bepartofthechange.impacthub.net/.

Huybrechts, B., & Haugh, H. (2018). The roles of networks in institutionalizing new hybrid organizational forms: Insights from the European renewable energy cooperative network. *Organization Studies, 39*(8), 1085–1108.

Huybrechts, B., & Nicholls, A. (2013). The role of legitimacy in social enterprise-corporate collaboration. *Social Enterprise Journal, 9*(2), 130–146.

Huybrechts, B., Nicholls, A., & Edinger, K. (2017). Sacred Alliance or pact with the devil? How and why social enterprises collaborate with mainstream businesses in the fair-trade sector. *Entrepreneurship & Regional Development, 29*(7–8), 586–608.

Imbroscio, D. L., Williamson, T., & Alperovitz, G. (2003). Local policy responses to globalization: Place-based ownership models of economic enterprise. *Policy Studies Journal, 31*(1), 31–52.

Jiwa, F. (2007). Honey care Africa. In J. Fairbourne, S. W. Gibson, & W. G. Dyer (Eds.), *Microfranchising* (pp. 149–163). Northampton, MA: Edward Elgar.

Juliá, J. F., Melià, E., & García, G. (2012). Strategies developed by leading EU agrifood cooperatives in their growth models. *Service Business, 6*(1), 27–46.

Lindenberg, M. (1999). Declining state capacity, volunteerism and the globalization of the not-for-profit sector. *Nonprofit and Voluntary Sector Quarterly, 28*(4), 147–167.

Lukkarinen, M. (2005). Community development, local economic development and the social economy. *Community Development Journal, 40*(4), 419–424.

Lyon, F., & Fernandez, H. (2012). Strategies for scaling up social enterprise: Lessons from early years providers. *Social Enterprise Journal, 8*, 63–77.

Marshall, R. S. (2011). Conceptualizing the international for-profit social entrepreneur. *Journal of Business Ethics, 98*, 183–198.

Martin, C. J., Upham, P., & Budd, L. (2015). Commercial orientation in grassroots social innovation: Insights from the sharing economy. *Ecological Economics, 118*, 240–251.

McLeod, H., & Fulton, K. (2010). Breaking new ground: Using the internet to scale. A case study of KaBOOM! Monitor Institute.

McMurtry, J., & Reed, D. (2009). *Co-operatives in a global economy: The challenges of co-operation across Borders*. Newcastle: Cambridge Scholars Publishing.

Nazarkina, L. (2012). How sustainable are the growth strategies of sustainability entrepreneurs? In G. Mennillo (Ed.), *Balanced growth*. Berlin: Springer.

Nilsson, J. (2018). Governance costs and the problems of large traditional cooperatives. *Outlook on Agriculture, 47*, 87–92.

Nilsson, J., Svendsen, G. L. H., & Svendsen, G. T. (2012). Are large and complex agricultural cooperatives losing their social capital? *Agribusiness, 28*, 187–204.

Peredo, A. M., & Chrisman, J. J. (2006). Toward a theory of community-based enterprise. *Academy of Management Review, 31*, 309–328.

Poulnot, J. L., & Matray, M. (2016). Promoting social and solidarity economy: The up group experience. In *31st CIRIEC international congress*. Reims: CIRIEC International.

Quelin, B. V., Kivleniece, I., & Lazzarini, S. (2017). Public–private collaboration, hybridity and social value: Towards new theoretical perspectives. *Journal of Management Studies, 54*(6), 764–792.

Rabobank. (2019). *Annual Report 2018*. Utrecht: Rabobank.

Rattalino, F. (2018). Circular advantage anyone? Sustainability-driven innovation and circularity at Patagonia, Inc. *Thunderbird International Business Review, 60*(5), 747–755.

Rothschild, J., & Whitt, J. A. (1986). *The cooperative workplace: Potentials and dilemmas of organisational democracy and participation*. New York: Cambridge University Press.

Sezgi, F., & Mair, J. (2010). To control or not control: A coordination perspective to scaling. In P. Bloom & E. Skloot (Eds.), *Scaling social impact: New thinking* (pp. 29–44). New York: Palgrave Macmillan.

Shrivastava, P., & Kennelly, J. J. (2013). Sustainability and place-based enterprise. *Organization & Environment, 26,* 83–101.

Shumate, M., Hsieh, Y. P., & O'Connor, A. (2018). A nonprofit perspective on business–nonprofit partnerships: Extending the symbiotic sustainability model. *Business & Society, 57*(7), 1337–1373.

Skelcher, C., & Smith, S. R. (2015). Theorizing hybridity: Institutional logics, complex organizations, and actor identities: The case of nonprofits. *Public Administration, 93*(2), 433–448.

Smith, B. R., & Stevens, C. E. (2010). Different types of social entrepreneurship: The role of geography and embeddedness on the measurement and scaling of social value. *Entrepreneurship & Regional Development, 22*(6), 575–598.

Smith, S. R. (2010). Hybridization and nonprofit organizations: The governance challenge. *Policy and Society, 29*(3), 219–229.

Smith, W. K., Gonin, M., & Besharov, M. L. (2013). Managing social-business tensions: A review and research agenda for social enterprise. *Business Ethics Quarterly, 23*(3), 407–442.

Sonnino, R., & Griggs-Trevarthen, C. (2013). A resilient social economy? Insights from the community food sector in the UK. *Entrepreneurship & Regional Development, 25,* 272–292.

Sousa, S., & Herman, R. (Eds.). (2012). *A co-operative dilemma: Converting organizational form.* Saskatoon: Centre for the Study of Co-operatives.

Torres-Coronas, T., & Vidal-Blasco, M. (2013). *Social E-Enterprise: Value creation trough ICT.* Hershey, PA: IGI Global.

Tracey, P., & Jarvis, O. (2007). Toward a theory of social venture franchising. *Entrepreneurship Theory & Practice, 31*(5), 667–685.

Up Group. (2018). *Annual report 2017.* Gennevilliers: Up Groupe.

Uvin, P., Pankaj, S., Jain, L., & Brown, D. (2000). Think large and act small: Toward a new paradigm for NGOs scaling up. *World Development, 28*(8), 1409–1419.

Vickers, I., & Lyon, F. (2012). Beyond green niches? Growth strategies of environmentally-motivated social enterprises. *International Small Business Journal, 32,* 449–470.

Zahra, S., Newey, L., & Li, Y. (2014). On the frontiers: The implications of social entrepreneurship for international entrepreneurship. *Entrepreneurship Theory and Practice, 38,* 137–158.

Zahra, S. A. (2020). International entrepreneurship in the post Covid world. *Journal of World Business.*, in press. https://doi.org/10.1016/j.jwb.2020.101143.

Zahra, S. A., Rawhouser, H. N., Bhawe, N., Neubaum, D. O., & Hayton, J. C. (2008). Globalization of social entrepreneurship opportunities. *Strategic Entrepreneurship Journal, 2*(2), 117–131.

Chapter 13
Towards a 'Wellbeing Economy': What Can We Learn from Social Enterprise?

Michael J. Roy

Introduction

This chapter looks at how social enterprises—organisations that work to improve wellbeing, rather than for the personal enrichment of owners or shareholders—could provide lessons and inspiration for those looking to transform to a 'wellbeing economy'. It has been argued that laissez-faire economic policies lay at the root cause of many of the cataclysmic upheavals of the early twentieth century, including the First World War, the Great Depression, the rise of fascism and the horrors of World War II. As Karl Polanyi (1944, p. 3) explains, such a 'self-regulating market' 'could not exist for any length of time without annihilating the human and natural substance of society'. Once again, we seem to be living through a time rife with 'grand challenges' (Ferraro, Etzion, & Gehman, 2015), particularly since the Great Financial Crisis of over a decade ago which precipitated an admittedly fairly short-lived crisis of confidence in the capitalist system and some well-needed reflections on what we believe the economy should be *for*. It was in such a context that Amin (2009, p. 4) was writing of renewed interest in the social economy, understood to mean 'commercial and non-commercial activity largely in the hands of third-sector of community organizations that gives priority to meeting social (and environmental) needs before profit maximisation'. It is timely to reflect on the 'new' social economy that has emerged since then, not least because of the nature and scale of the challenges that confront us today, which have been so brutally exposed during the COVID-19 pandemic of 2020, the social and economic effects of which will be felt for many years to come. Inequality has grown to such an extent that half of the entire wealth of the planet has come to be concentrated into the hands of just 26

M. J. Roy (✉)
Yunus Centre for Social Business and Health, Glasgow Caledonian University, Glasgow, Scotland, UK
e-mail: Michael.Roy@gcu.ac.uk

© Springer Nature Switzerland AG 2021
B. Gidron, A. Domaradzka (eds.), *The New Social and Impact Economy*, Nonprofit and Civil Society Studies, https://doi.org/10.1007/978-3-030-68295-8_13

people (Elliott, 2019). Populist politics and 'strongman' politicians can now be found in (and, indeed, leading) many countries across the world from the USA to Hungary, Turkey, Brazil, India and the Philippines. A decade of austerity policies in the UK has been blamed for precipitating Brexit (Dorling, 2016) while we have seen climate crisis becoming evermore acute and pronounced, accompanied by refugee crises, civil unrest and even the spectre of fascism re-emerging (Mouffe, 2018).

Partly in response to such global phenomena, and quite distinct from ongoing conversations about the *social* economy, the idea of a 'wellbeing economy'—an economy that is designed to work for people and the planet, rather than the other way around (Coscieme et al., 2019; Costanza et al., 2018)—has captured the imagination of politicians and policymakers across the globe. A shift in emphasis 'from measuring economic production to measuring people's wellbeing' (Stiglitz, Sen, & Fitoussi, 2009, p. 12) has been sought for decades and Scotland, alongside Iceland and New Zealand, has been at the forefront of recent international efforts, with the formation of the Wellbeing Economy Governments (WEGo) initiative. The First Minister of Scotland and the Prime Ministers of both New Zealand and Iceland (all three of whom are female, perhaps not coincidentally) have taken a lead in trying to reshape the conversation around the need for economic policies that emphasise wellbeing over a narrow focus on gross domestic product (GDP) (see Coscieme et al., 2019; Hough-Stewart, Trebeck, Sommer, & Wallis, 2019; Trebeck, 2020). But Scotland is also recognised internationally for the maturity and sophistication of their social economy ecosystem and for being at the forefront of social enterprise policy and support (Roy, McHugh, Huckfield, Kay, & Donaldson, 2015), the first country in the world to develop a 10-year social enterprise strategy co-produced with the sector (Scottish Government, 2016). This strategy, operationalised through three 3-year action plans, fully acknowledges the role of social enterprise and the social economy in generating the so-called inclusive growth in Scotland to ensure that 'there is fairness in how Scotland's wealth, resources and opportunities are distributed' (Scottish Government, 2016, p. 14) underpinned by 'a commitment to fairness, equality and solidarity'. Scotland's National Performance Framework (NPF)[1] is a deliberate 'operationalisation' of the United Nations Sustainable Development Goals (SDGs) at a national level. At the heart of the NPF, the stated purpose of the Scottish Government is to secure 'opportunities for all, improved wellbeing and sustainable and inclusive economic growth', underpinned by values of kindness, dignity and compassion. While recognising that economic progress is important, the Scottish Government set out in their 'Wellbeing Report for Scotland'[2] that they believe 'success' to be about more than growing GDP. We also saw the 'world-first' wellbeing budget unveiled by New Zealand's Labour coalition government in 2019, to widespread international attention (Roy, 2019).

---

[1] See https://nationalperformance.gov.scot/

[2] See https://nationalperformance.gov.scot/scotlands-wellbeing-report

This chapter is organised as follows: I will initially set out the latest thinking on the idea of the 'wellbeing economy' with a brief overview of the history of the concept, and the context in which it has emerged. I will then turn attention to social enterprise, with a key focus on research explaining the role of social enterprise in achieving (health and) wellbeing gains, particularly for vulnerable individuals and communities. I will then attempt to bring both lines of inquiry together and argue that the social enterprise is a key organisational form on which to influence the shaping of a wellbeing economy. I will then explore the challenges faced—practically, conceptually and methodologically—in providing inspiration for shaping a wellbeing-focused 'new' social economy for the twenty-first century. First of all, however, what is meant by a 'wellbeing economy'? Where did it come from?

What Is a Wellbeing Economy?

The idea of a 'wellbeing economy' is arguably as old as discussions on economics itself. Aristotle gives over a good proportion of his works to the relationship between *oikonomia* ('householding' or 'household management')—the origin of the word economics—and *eudaimonia* (Leshem, 2016; Polanyi, 1957) roughly translated as the 'good life' or 'flourishing'. The idea of *eudaimonia*, particularly as set out in the *Nicomachean Ethics* (Peters, 1906), is not too inconsistent with many contemporary notions of wellbeing, particularly those that stress the importance of living a long, happy, healthy, fulfilled life. We organise and fulfil our material needs and wants to such ends, it is reasonably argued, and it is actually the unlimited pursuit of wealth that is unnatural and an obstacle to living the 'good life' (Peters, 1906).

At the very real risk of indecently compressing a very long and complex process that occurred over the course of several centuries, the idea of 'utility' came to stand in for wellbeing, and then, subsequently, wealth for utility.[3] The idea of *homo economicus*, of a consistently rational, narrowly self-interested agent, who works optimally to pursue their subjectively defined ends, has emerged to dominate thinking. Why such a narrow and reductive perspective on human nature has come to the fore, and why the pursuit of economic growth and the maximisation of measures such as GNP and GDP are the overriding concern of economic policies more or less everywhere, is well outside the scope of this chapter (albeit a fascinating tale in itself—see Mirowski & Plehwe, 2015). But critiques of the primacy of pursuing growth above everything else stretch back many decades, not least from Karl Polanyi's (1944) seminal work *The Great Transformation* to the Club of Rome's *Limits to Growth* report (Meadows, Meadows, Randers, & Behrens, 1972). In different ways, both of these warned of the impossibility of infinite growth on a finite planet and

---

[3] I should doubly caveat this statement by acknowledging that 'economists have long understood that the primary purpose of the discipline is to contribute to enhanced wellbeing of persons' (Dalziel, Saunders, & Saunders, 2018, p. 3) and this tradition does continue to this day, most prominently within the sub-discipline of welfare economics.

offered prescient warnings of societal breakdown and environmental devastation if we do not amend our trajectory, a change of course that has never been meaningfully embraced.

Inequality, at levels unprecedented since the last Gilded Era, is bad for all of us, both rich *and* poor alike (Wilkinson & Pickett, 2010, 2018), not least because it corrodes the ties that bind us, undermines societal cohesion and creates the idea of 'winners' and 'losers'. The 'losers' are far more likely to seek someone to blame for their predicament and engage in 'othering' groups such as people on welfare, minorities, immigrants, asylum seekers and refugees, thus allowing space for populist policies and politicians to come to the fore (hence Trump, Brexit). We know too that while people *overall* are healthier, wealthier and live longer than ever before (Deaton, 2013), ever-widening inequality is inevitable under the present system (Piketty, 2014) and, with the barest veneer of democracy, the political apparatus has been shown to be rigged to ensure the ongoing benefit of elites (Gilens & Page, 2014). Gains in GDP do not necessarily translate to wellbeing advances for people beyond a fairly basic level of income (Easterlin, 1974, 1995) and GDP inadequately recognises many of the aspects that make life worthwhile, which humans and our natural environment depend upon to thrive. And yet the pursuit of unsustainable growth has remained entrenched in the economic policy mindset (Lang & Marsden, 2018). As a result, we are experiencing various forms of crises simultaneously. In her impassioned plea to the United Nations climate summit, the young Swedish climate activist Greta Thunberg captured it thus:

> 'People are suffering, people are dying. Entire ecosystems are collapsing. We are at the brink of a mass extinction and all you can talk about is money and fairy tales of eternal economic growth. How dare you!' (Thunberg, 2019)

The idea of a 'wellbeing economy' has emerged in such a context. Coscieme et al. (2019) explain that the idea of a wellbeing economy means to live within planetary ecological boundaries; ensure the equitable distribution of wealth and opportunity; efficiently allocate resources (including environmental and social public goods); and bring wellbeing to the heart of policymaking and in particular economic policymaking. Moving from the macro level to the meso and micro levels, Lang and Marsden (2018, p. 496) argue for an 'intelligent, efficient, sustainable and place-based approach' to wellbeing economy initiatives. This, I argue, is where social enterprise comes into play.

However, before I turn attention to social enterprise, I need to briefly discuss what we mean by 'the economy'. Whether wellbeing based, or otherwise, we cannot think of the economy in its *formal* sense, that is, in the same way as contemporary economics tells us to. We need to apprehend the economy in a 'substantive', pluralistic or holistic sense (Hopkins, 1957; Laville, 2010; Rotstein, 2014; Roy & Hackett, 2017) where the economy not only consists of goods and services produced and sold in the market by capitalist firms (in other words, the sorts of activity that GDP is restricted to counting) but also takes account of the role of both the state and community for providing for our material needs and wants. By definition, this is far wider than the types of goods and services that are exchanged on the principle of market exchange alone. The economy therefore cannot be apprehended by restricting our lens only to the market, but by also taking adequate account of the economic principles of redistribution and reciprocity. Conceptualising the economy in such a way also reframes 'non-market' actors as vital *economic* actors: from the mother and caregiver; the volunteer and the moonlighter; in spaces such as communities, schools, churches and prisons; and within families, and between friends and neighbours (Gibson-Graham, 2008; Gibson-Graham & Cameron, 2007; Pearce, 2003). It is in such contexts that we can begin to understand the role that social enterprises play in supporting wellbeing.

How Do Social Enterprises Impact Wellbeing?

In recent decades, we have seen how 'social enterprise' has come to be promoted as a mechanism through which people can be transitioned out of disadvantage, address poverty and unfulfilled capabilities and mitigate against social exclusion (Barraket, 2014; Farmer et al., 2016; Muñoz, Farmer, Winterton, & Barraket, 2015; Teasdale, 2012). But 'social enterprise' is one of those 'essentially contested' concepts (Gallie, 1955) that are almost impossible to define accurately: 'a fluid and contested concept constructed by different actors promoting different discourses connected to different organisational forms and drawing upon different academic theories' (Teasdale, 2012, p. 99). In essence, though, we can say that social enterprises aim to 'create wealth in communities and keep it there. They trade on a "not-for-personal-profit" basis, re-investing surplus back into their community … effecting social, economic and environmental … outcomes' (Teasdale, 2012, pp. 105–106). In effect, social enterprises are a (potential) means of unlocking the 'social and economic capacities latent in even the most deprived communities' (Amin, Cameron, & Hudson, 2003, p. 27). They have been known by a variety of names in the past: terms such as community business, community enterprise, social venture or even 'affirmative business' (particularly in North America) have been commonly used at various times. Muhammad Yunus (2010) has his own brand of 'social business' and countless other labels have been used to denote roughly the same idea. Francophone and Hispanophone countries often use terms such as *'economie sociale'* ('social economy') or *'economie solidaire'* ('solidarity economy') (Utting, 2015) to describe their own traditions of trading for social purpose, and there are at least two clear traditions of 'social enterprise' that are apparent in academic discourse today (Defourny & Nyssens, 2010) which, although they have developed independently, have only recently been brought together.

Some of the more common reasons for establishing a social enterprise include providing jobs, skills, work experience and income in fragile local economies (e.g. rural areas, disadvantaged places, low-income country contexts); providing work experience, and improving the skills and education of people experiencing disadvantage, or who come from disadvantaged backgrounds; creating, mobilising and enhancing resources within communities (e.g. drawing on volunteers); and tackling important areas of the economy often characterised by low profitability (e.g. recy-cling). However, we should not overlook that many social enterprises (almost irre-spective of whether they have been labelled as such) have come to be founded to emphasise the importance of collectivism and solidarity apparent in alternative or 'popular' forms of economic organising, particularly in areas that have suffered from colonial oppression (e.g. in Latin America) (Calvo & Morales, 2017; Esteves, 2014).

Social enterprises act on wellbeing through addressing local social vulnerabili-ties faced by individuals and communities, the factors in the social environment that we know favour or harm health and wellbeing (Marmot & Wilkinson, 2006; Solar & Irwin, 2010). These range from poverty, poor education and lack of confidence to social isolation, loneliness or exclusion. Despite the fact that I have framed social enterprise as an organisation designed to improve wellbeing, rather than for per-sonal enrichment for owners or shareholders, conceptual and empirical research that adopts such a standpoint, and which looks to examine how, and in what ways, social enterprises work in such a way, is relatively recent, and still fairly thin on the ground.

That said, arguments for bringing the (sub-) fields of social enterprise and (health and) wellbeing together, roughly in the manner I have described, but particularly in relation to addressing entrenched health inequalities, have been set out (Donaldson et al., 2011; Roy, Donaldson, Baker, & Kay, 2013; Roy, Hill O'Connor, McHugh, Biosca, & Donaldson, 2015; Roy, Lysaght, & Krupa, 2017), with the first scoping reviews recently emerging (Suchowerska et al., 2019). Importantly, the first fully blown systematic reviews (Mason, Barraket, Friel, O'Rourke, & Stenta, 2015; Roy, Donaldson, Baker, & Kerr, 2014) related to the topic have been undertaken, which show from a robust examination of the 'state of the art' of evidence that some—albeit quite weak and not especially well developed—evidence exists that social enterprises can be effective in reducing stigmatisation, particularly of marginalised groups, and they can work to build social capital, improve health behaviours and build health 'assets' (Alvarez-Dardet, Morgan, Cantero, & Hernan, 2015; Roy, 2017). Some of these 'assets' include sustainable local economies, good work, qual-ity social networks and relationships, stable employment (Poveda, Gill, Junio, Thinyane, & Catan, 2019), shared public spaces with plenty of access to green and blue spaces (Song et al., 2018), existence of emotional support mechanisms, and enhancing feelings of confidence and/or feelings of trust and safety (Roy et al., 2014). As the conceptual base has developed further (Macaulay, Roy, Donaldson, Teasdale, & Kay, 2017; Roy, Baker, & Kerr, 2017) and as our nascent subfield has matured somewhat, we have seen empirical research starting to emerge which assesses different impacts on different groups of beneficiaries in different contexts (Macaulay, Mazzei, Roy, Teasdale, & Donaldson, 2018). Some of these include the following: longitudinal work undertaken in a Work Integration Social Enterprise setting (Elmes, 2019); in rural settings (Kelly, Steiner, Mazzei, & Baker, 2019); with asylum seekers and refugees (Barraket, 2014); addressing the needs of older people (Henderson, Steiner, Mazzei, & Docherty, 2019); and addressing the stigma of mental illness (Krupa, Sabetti, & Lysaght, 2019). We have also started to see excellent examples of theoretical and methodological innovation, including empirical research (Farmer et al., 2016, 2020; Muñoz et al., 2015) that utilises 'spaces of wellbeing theory' (Fleuret & Atkinson, 2007) to assess how social enterprises build and maintain the capabilities of individuals, including in regional community settings (Farmer et al., 2019). We have even seen work that examines how actions at the local level can be thought about as having potential for systemic change at the level of the political economy itself (Roy & Hackett, 2017). However, we know that meaningful, systemic change at the level of the political economy is exceptionally challenging, and it is to such challenges that I now turn.

Challenges to Building a Wellbeing Economy

Social enterprise, by itself, is unlikely to be able to turn around how we think about, organise and talk about the wider mainstream economy, particularly if we recognise the scale and persuasive power of the actors who are setting contemporary discourse on the topic. That said, the scale of the social economy and the contribution of social enterprises to the social and economic fabric of countries themselves are often impressive and should not be so easily dismissed. In Scotland, for example, there are 6025 social enterprises, employing over 88,300 FTE workers (CEiS, 2019). While it may feel as if we are trying to turn around the metaphorical supertanker, the shift to a wellbeing economy at least starts to feel less impossible when we are aware of the firm foundations on which we can start to build.

Just like social enterprise, however, 'wellbeing' is a notoriously slippery, contested concept. It is also highly subjective: 'what matters' to you in terms of your wellbeing may not matter much to me, or at all (see Sayer, 2011). A 'wellbeing economy' is thus different things to different people, or maybe even all things to all people. Although this flexibility has its advantages, particularly in trying to 'sell' the concept to politicians across the political spectrum, this potentially puts the idea at severe risk of dilution or co-option. It is perhaps unsurprising that there is a vast array of challenges to face in shifting to a wellbeing economy. I have tried to set out the most obvious challenges that immediately come to mind. For ease of organising these, I have split them into three categories—practical, conceptual and methodological challenges—but, in reality, these categories inevitably overlap and bleed into one another.

Practical Challenges

This first practical challenge is connected to the idea of whether the 'wellbeing economy'—just like regular ongoing conversations about the social economy—represents an *alternative* (Amin et al., 2003; Baum, 2009) means of organising the economy, or whether it is seen as *complementary* to (or even a somewhat marginal or quirky component of) the mainstream capitalist system. Social economy activity, particularly historically, has often been presented as operating at the margins of the mainstream economy (Utting, 2015), albeit somewhat 'antagonistically' (Chatterton, Dinerstein, North, & Pitts, 2019) at times, so not necessarily representing a viable alternative *system*, but rather to serve as an inspirational example that alternatives are possible *within the present system*. The *wellbeing* economy debate, perhaps in contrast to how the social economy may have been presented in the past, looks to be offering an alternative economic paradigm altogether: to radically reshape the global political economy. The need for such a radical approach was expressed by Amin (2009, p. 3) just after the Great Financial Crisis, that

> 'The critics of capitalism see the present time as an opportunity to move on, to alter radically the meaning and social status of the economy, so that the inequality, egotism and recurrent crises built into capitalism can be overcome … the current finance-led meltdown is the symptom of a deeper systemic flaw, necessitating a different kind of economic system.'

How, then, do we deal with powerful agents who, at least on the surface, look like they are trying to change the conversation but, in reality, are not changing it at all? Instead they are (perhaps unwittingly, to give them the benefit of the doubt) merely reinforcing or 'doubling down' on maintaining the existing growth-focused trajectory and discourse that support this. Whether they are simply 'not getting it', or whether there are powerful forces at work which do not allow them to step outside of the market fundamentalist mindset, remains purely speculative at present. But we have seen over the years how 'challenges to the status quo have regularly been met with assimilation, co-option or repression' (Roy & Hackett, 2017, p. 89; see also Roy & Grant, 2019). We know that bringing challengers, and challenging ideas, into the realm of the 'authority system' (Coy, 2013), whether formally or discursively, is a regular tactic for maintaining the 'common sense' narrative that underpins the hegemony of market fundamentalism (Crouch, 2011). To give a recent example, the Secretary-General of the OECD (Gurría, 2019) recently defined an 'economy of wellbeing' as the

> 'capacity to create a virtuous circle in which citizens' wellbeing drives economic prosperity, stability and resilience, and vice-versa those good macroeconomic outcomes allow to sustain wellbeing investments over time'.

Under the Finnish Presidency, the Council of the European Union (2019) recently adopted the conclusion that 'while people's wellbeing is a value in itself, it is also vitally important for the Union's economic growth, productivity, long-term fiscal sustainability and societal stability'. Gurría (2019) goes on to explain how an 'economy of wellbeing' should be built upon four main pillars: education and skills; health; social protection and redistribution; and gender equality. Now while it would be churlish to suggest that a wellbeing economy should *not* focus on addressing such aspects in a positive way, the health and wellbeing of people and the planet are too important to be reduced to a mere 'positive externality' (that is, a useful spin-off benefit) of economic activity. Instead they should be the *focus* of economic activity itself. But both the European Council and the OECD frame their arguments for focusing on wellbeing *as a means to increase GDP*, therefore missing the point completely, or positing a dangerous compromise. As has been argued, the economy is not the end, but the *means* by which wellbeing benefits for our citizens are often achieved.

It is very difficult to challenge such intentions, however, without sounding churlish and pedantic. At least they are doing *something*, which is more than many other powerful transnational actors are doing. But perhaps we need to be brave and say that such work is not good enough, and poor or slipshod (intentional or otherwise) linguistic framing may even represent a danger to the whole idea through subtle dilution and assimilation of the whole 'wellbeing economy' concept. We have seen frequent examples of terms for practices that started off as posing a challenge to the status quo and ending up by furthering it.

Conceptual Challenges

I mentioned previously that the Scottish National Performance Framework has clear line of sight to the UN SDGs. But there has been consternation in some quarters regarding the wording of several of the goals, particularly in relation to SDG8: 'promote sustained, inclusive and sustainable economic growth, full and productive employment and decent work for all'[4] because of the focus on perpetual growth, and the lack of recognition that 'market fundamentalism' (Block & Somers, 2014; Stiglitz, 2009), with an uncompromising focus on growth, may lie at the heart of why we need the SDGs in the first place. For example, Wahl (2019) outlines that:

> 'A fundamental dilemma underlying all of the world's most pressing problems is the obsession, or let's say the illusion, of perpetual quantitative growth on a finite planet. This is pursued virtually by all of our politicians and economists. It is a real detachment from reality, the ecological reality! This seems to be enshrined in SDG 8 …'

In response, it is considered that:

> 'We need to reframe SDG8 as "Good Work and Qualitative Growth". That alone would start a conversation about what kind of growth we want. … of course we want forests to grow and healthy grasslands to grow … we need to pay attention to the linguistic framing of the goals …'

As has been stated earlier, when a focus on economic growth prevents us from achieving wellbeing enhancements and, it turns out, is actually harming people and the planet, then we need to imagine, and *meaningfully* consider, alternative trajectories. This includes the idea of degrowth and a 'postgrowth' economy[5] as a potential pathway to social and environmental wellbeing (Büchs & Koch, 2017). However, the very idea of 'postgrowth' is anathema to those with an unshakeable belief in both perpetual economic growth and sanctity of markets. One major conceptual challenge has always been that it is often easier, in the words of Mark Fisher (2009),

---

[4] See https://sustainabledevelopment.un.org/sdg8

[5] See https://www.postgrowth.org/about-post-growth-economics

to 'imagine the end of the world than the end of capitalism': that no alternative does—or even can—exist. But social enterprises *do* exist: they provide an example of what the sociologist Erik Olin Wright referred to as a form 'real utopia' (Wright, 2009, 2012): presently existing institutions that are grounded in their potential for redesigning social systems and institutions, the existence of which allows us to sustain and deepen discussions of the potential of radical alternatives to current realities. Utopian thinking allows us to break out of our conceptual straitjacket to imagine what might be possible, including the whole idea of a wellbeing economy.

Methodological Challenges

The third challenge that requires to be discussed relates to methodological issues. Analytically speaking, moving from the level of the organisation (the micro) to the level of the global political economy (the macro) is not only conceptually challenging, but methodologically demanding too. Methods able to cope at different conceptual levels, and which can take sufficient account of both structural *and* agential factors, are not especially well developed in the social enterprise field. However, methods rooted in, and inspired by, the critical realist philosophical stance (Archer, 1995; Bhaskar, 1975) may well hold promise in this regard.

Indeed, methodological pluralism and working across disciplines, particularly drawing upon methods employed in public health for the development and evaluation of complex forms of public health intervention, are undoubtedly required to allow us to better explore the impact of social enterprises on the wellbeing of individuals and communities. But establishing a control or comparator group to undertake the kind of research that is usually used to confirm whether or not an intervention 'works', such as we see in randomised controlled trials, is notoriously difficult in community settings. Identifying a control group also presents a number of ethical challenges to overcome, particularly when working with vulnerable people: What might the consequences be of 'no treatment' for example? The use of natural experiments, on the other hand, where differences in context, policy or practice, or between different nations or regions, exist, may prove more appropriate, albeit they will never *unequivocally* determine causation. Realist evaluations (Pawson & Tilley, 1997), on the other hand, which are designed to assess what works, for whom and in what circumstances, use the idea of generative causality to develop configurations of context, mechanism and outcomes, but—again—have rarely been used to evaluate the work of social enterprises.

There is also an opportunity to draw upon various philosophies of wellbeing. Recently Blake (2019) utilised the work of Alasdair MacIntyre to understand how social enterprises may facilitate wellbeing, while the 'capabilities approach' (Nussbaum, 2011; Sen, 1999) is regularly employed in development studies, public health and a wide range of other fields. Methods inspired by this approach (e.g. Coast et al., 2008) have been utilised in a variety of public health contexts, but rarely with social enterprises. Employing methods that employ proxy measures such as

Satisfaction with Life (Diener, Emmons, Larsen, & Griffin, 1985; Pavot & Diener, 1993) or which employ some variety of subjective wellbeing measure (see McHugh, Biosca, Baker, Ibrahim, & Donaldson, 2019) will also take us further down the road that we are presently on.

One note of caution, however, is that methods, particularly those originally used in medical settings, can adopt an individualised focus, where impacts upon individuals are often aggregated to say something about communities, or to whole populations. This is, of course, problematic when we are talking about community wellbeing, since communities are comprised of far more than atomised individuals.

To build on this note of caution further, and again summoning the work of Polanyi and his 'substantive' view of the economy, we are reminded that human economies organise themselves differently in different contexts, but there is always

> 'an institutionalized pattern of relationships by which individual social units are linked together to form a social whole. Different patterns always coexist within the same society, but there is usually a dominant one' (Block & Somers, 2014, p. 66).

These different patterns of relationships involve different combinations of market, state and community. Bruni and Zamagni (2007, p. 19) observe that these involve different economic principles that are distinct, but not independent. They argue that 'if this "triadic" structure is sustained – if all three of these principles are active and well-combined – then societies develop in a harmonious way'. In other words, their argument goes that to maximise wellbeing, we need to find the optimum balance of different types of institution, each fulfilling different functions. While aggregation can often be useful, we cannot simply fall into the trap of 'aggregating up' the numbers of social enterprises or their impacts to say anything especially meaningful about a society or economy, especially the sort of economy or society we aspire to. We also cannot say much about the 'correct' number of social enterprises suitable for maintaining wellbeing presently. We are aware that in places where the state and civil society are far stronger than in the UK or the USA, such as we see in the Nordic states, there are apparently far fewer social enterprises (Andersen, Gawell, & Spear, 2016) and yet the Scandinavian people often report among the highest wellbeing levels on earth. If 'market fundamentalism', or too firm a focus on markets, is detrimental to society as a whole, we need tools that help us establish what the correct *balance* of different types of institution should be in any given society, with a view to maximising wellbeing overall, and for different groups.

Conclusion

In this chapter I sought to introduce the idea of the 'wellbeing economy' and advance debates on what role social enterprises may have in furthering this agenda. I outlined what is known presently about the role that social enterprise has in maximising wellbeing, particularly for vulnerable individuals and communities, albeit we are probably in the midst of the 'first wave' of conceptual and empirical research on the topic. But bringing the social enterprise and health and wellbeing (sub-) fields closer together presents an exciting range of opportunities for policymakers, practitioners and researchers alike.

There are, however, a number of formidable challenges, which are practical, conceptual and methodological in nature, and/or probably a combination of all three. What is clear, though, is that overcoming such challenges, and building a new social economy designed to address the twenty-first-century challenges, requires new methods, new approaches, new conversations and new alliances. It is at the nexus of various fields that exciting new science often emerges. If we are serious about changing the trajectory of our economy to avoid catastrophe—and by all accounts we are almost past the point of no return—then this requires leadership, imagination and foresight. Above all we need action that brings scientists, policymakers and practitioners together to shape a shared vision of the type of economy and society that is best suited to the needs of everyone, not just a few.

References

Alvarez-Dardet, C., Morgan, A., Cantero, M. T. R., & Hernan, M. (2015). Improving the evidence base on public health assets-the way ahead: A proposed research agenda. *Journal of Epidemiology & Community Health, 69*, 721–723.

Amin, A. (Ed.). (2009). Locating the social economy. In *The social economy: International perspectives on economic solidarity* (pp. 3–21). London: Zed Books.

Amin, A., Cameron, A., & Hudson, R. (2003). The alterity of the social economy. In A. Leyshon, R. Lee, & C. C. Williams (Eds.), *Alternative economic spaces* (pp. 27–54). Thousand Oaks, CA: SAGE Publications Ltd.

Andersen, L. L., Gawell, M., & Spear, R. (Eds.). (2016). *Social entrepreneurship and social enterprises: nordic perspectives*. Abingdon, Oxon: Routledge.

Archer, M. S. (1995). *Realist social theory: The morphogenetic approach*. Cambridge: Cambridge University Press.

Barraket, J. (2014). Fostering wellbeing of immigrants and refugees? Evaluating the outcomes of work integration social enterprise. In S. Denny & F. Seddon (Eds.), *Social Enterprise: Accountability and evaluation around the world* (pp. 102–120). Abingdon, Oxon: Routledge.

Baum, G. (2009). The social economy: An alternative model of economic development. *Journal of Catholic Social Thought, 6*(1), 253–262.

Bhaskar, R. (1975). *A realist theory of science*. London: Verso.

Blake, J. (2019). Utilising a MacIntyrean approach to understand how social enterprise may contribute to wellbeing. *Social Enterprise Journal, 15*(4), 421–437.

Block, F. L., & Somers, M. R. (2014). *The power of market fundamentalism: Karl Polanyi's critique*. Cambridge, MA: Harvard University Press.

Bruni, L., & Zamagni, S. (2007). *Civil economy: Efficiency, equity, public happiness*. Bern: Peter Lang.

Büchs, M., & Koch, M. (2017). *Postgrowth and wellbeing: Challenges to sustainable welfare*. Berlin/Heidelberg/New York, NY: Springer.

Calvo, S., & Morales, A. (2017). *Social and solidarity economy: The world's economy with a social face*. Abingdon, Oxon: Routledge.

CEiS. (2019). *Social enterprise in Scotland: Census 2019*. Glasgow: CEiS/Scottish Government/ Social Value Lab. Retrieved November 26, 2019, from https://www.ceis.org.uk/wp-content/ uploads/2019/09/Social_Enterprise_in_Scotland_Census_2019_Full_Report.pdf.

Chatterton, P., Dinerstein, A. C., North, P., & Pitts, F. H. (2019). *"Scaling up or deepening? Developing the radical potential of the SSE sector in a time of crisis", UNTFSSE, presented at the implementing the sustainable development goals: What role for social and solidarity economy?* Geneva: UNTFSSE.

Coast, J., Flynn, T. N., Natarajan, L., Sproston, K., Lewis, J., Louviere, J. J., et al. (2008). Valuing the ICECAP capability index for older people. *Social Science & Medicine, 67*(5), 874–882.

Coscieme, L., Sutton, P., Mortensen, L. F., Kubiszewski, I., Costanza, R., Trebeck, K., et al. (2019). Overcoming the myths of mainstream economics to enable a new wellbeing economy. *Sustainability, 11*(16), 4374.

Costanza, R., Caniglia, B., Fioramonti, L., Kubiszewski, I., Lewis, H., Lovins, L. H., et al. (2018). Toward a sustainable wellbeing economy. *The Solutions Journal, 9*(2), 5.

Council of the European Union (2019, 24 October). Economy of wellbeing: The council adopts conclusions., Available at: https://www.consilium.europa.eu/en/press/press-releases/2019/10/24/economy-of-wellbeing-the-council-adopts-conclusions/

Coy, P. G. (2013). Co-Optation. In *The Wiley-Blackwell encyclopedia of social and political movements*. Malden, MA: Wiley-Blackwell. https://doi.org/10.1002/9780470674871.wbespm054.

Crouch, C. (2011). *The strange non-death of neoliberalism*. Cambridge: Polity Press.

Dalziel, P., Saunders, C., & Saunders, J. (2018). *Wellbeing economics: The capabilities approach to prosperity*. Cham, Switzerland: Palgrave Macmillan.

Deaton, A. (2013). *The great escape: Health, wealth, and the origins of inequality*. Princeton, NJ: Princeton University Press.

Defourny, J., & Nyssens, M. (2010). Conceptions of social enterprise and social entrepreneurship in Europe and the United States: Convergences and divergences. *Journal of Social Entrepreneurship, 1*(1), 32–53.

Diener, E. D., Emmons, R. A., Larsen, R. J., & Griffin, S. (1985). The satisfaction with life scale. *Journal of Personality Assessment, 49*(1), 71–75.

Donaldson, C., Baker, R., Cheater, F., Gillespie, M., McHugh, N., & Sinclair, S. (2011). Social business, health and well-being. *Social Business, 1*(1), 17–35.

Dorling, D. (2016). Brexit: The decision of a divided country. *BMJ, 354*, i3697.

Easterlin, R. A. (1974). Does economic growth improve the human lot? Some empirical evidence. In P. A. David & M. W. Reder (Eds.), *Nations and households in economic growth: Essays in honor of Moses Abramovitz*. New York: Academic Press.

Easterlin, R. A. (1995). Will raising the incomes of all increase the happiness of all? *Journal of Economic Behavior & Organization, 27*(1), 35–47.

Elliott, L. (2019, 21 January). World's 26 richest people own as much as poorest 50%, says Oxfam. In *The guardian*. Retrieved October 23, 2019, from https://www.theguardian.com/business/2019/jan/21/world-26-richest-people-own-as-much-as-poorest-50-per-cent-oxfam-report

Elmes, A. I. (2019). Health impacts of a WISE: A longitudinal study. *Social Enterprise Journal, 15*(4), 457–474.

Esteves, A. M. (2014). Decolonizing livelihoods, decolonizing the will: Solidarity economy as a social justice paradigm in Latin America. In M. Reisch (Ed.), *Routledge international handbook of social justice* (pp. 74–90). Abingdon, Oxon: Routledge.

Farmer, J., De Cotta, T., Kilpatrick, S., Barraket, J., Roy, M., & Munoz, S.-A. (2019). How work integration social enterprises help to realize capability: A comparison of three Australian settings. *Journal of Social Entrepreneurship*, 1–23. https://doi.org/10.1080/19420676.2019.1671481.

Farmer, J., De Cotta, T., McKinnon, K., Barraket, J., Munoz, S.-A., Douglas, H., et al. (2016). Social enterprise and wellbeing in community life. *Social Enterprise Journal, 12*(2), 235–254.

Farmer, J., Kamstra, P., Brennan-Horley, C., De Cotta, T., Roy, M., Barraket, J., et al. (2020). Using micro-geography to understand the realisation of wellbeing: A qualitative GIS study of three social enterprises. *Health & Place*. https://doi.org/10.1016/j.healthplace.2020.102293.

Ferraro, F., Etzion, D., & Gehman, J. (2015). Tackling grand challenges pragmatically: Robust action revisited. *Organization Studies, 36*(3), 363–390.

Fisher, M. (2009). *Capitalist realism: Is there no alternative?* Ropley, Hants: Zero Books.

Fleuret, S., & Atkinson, S. (2007). Wellbeing, health and geography: A critical review and research agenda. *New Zealand Geographer, 63*(2), 106–118.

Gallie, W. B. (1955). Essentially contested concepts. *Proceedings of the Aristotelian Society, 56,* 167–198.

Gibson-Graham, J. K. (2008). Diverse economies: Performative practices for 'other worlds'. *Progress in Human Geography, 32*(5), 613–632.

Gibson-Graham, J. K., & Cameron, J. A. (2007). Community enterprises: Imagining and enacting alternatives to capitalism. *Social Alternatives, 26*(1), 20–25.

Gilens, M., & Page, B. I. (2014). Testing theories of American politics: Elites, interest groups, and average citizens. *Perspectives on Politics, 12*(3), 564–581.

Gurría, A. (2019, 8 July). The economy of Well-being. In *Remarks by the OECD secretary-general*, Brussels. Retrieved November 25, 2019, from http://www.oecd.org/social/economy-of-well-being-brussels-july-2019.htm

Henderson, F., Steiner, A., Mazzei, M., & Docherty, C. (2019). Social enterprises' impact on older people's health and wellbeing: Exploring Scottish experiences. *Health Promotion International, 35,* 1074–1084.

Hopkins, T. K. (1957). Sociology and the substantive view of the economy. In K. Polanyi, C. M. Arensberg, & H. W. Pearson (Eds.), *Trade and market in the early empires: Economies in history and theory* (pp. 270–306). Glencoe, IL: Free Press.

Hough-Stewart, L., Trebeck, K., Sommer, C., & Wallis, S. (2019, December). What is a well-being economy? In *Wellbeing economy alliance*. Available at: https://wellbeingeconomy.org/wp-content/uploads/2019/12/A-WE-Is-WEAll-Ideas-Little-Summaries-of-Big-Issues-4-Dec-2019.pdf

Kelly, D., Steiner, A., Mazzei, M., & Baker, R. (2019). Filling a void? The role of social enterprise in addressing social isolation and loneliness in rural communities. *Journal of Rural Studies.* https://doi.org/10.1016/j.jrurstud.2019.01.024.

Krupa, T., Sabetti, J., & Lysaght, R. (2019). How work integration social enterprises impact the stigma of mental illness. *Social Enterprise Journal, 15*(4), 475–494.

Lang, M., & Marsden, T. (2018). Rethinking growth: Towards the Well-being economy. *Local Economy: The Journal of the Local Economy Policy Unit, 33*(5), 496–514.

Laville, J.-L. (2010). Plural economy. In K. Hart, J.-L. Laville, & A. D. Cattani (Eds.), *The human economy* (pp. 77–83). Cambridge: Polity Press.

Leshem, D. (2016). Retrospectives: What did the ancient Greeks mean by 'Oikonomia'? *Journal of Economic Perspectives, 30*(1), 225–238.

Macaulay, B., Mazzei, M., Roy, M. J., Teasdale, S., & Donaldson, C. (2018). Differentiating the effect of social enterprise activities on health. *Social Science & Medicine, 200,* 211–217.

Macaulay, B., Roy, M. J., Donaldson, C., Teasdale, S., & Kay, A. (2017). Conceptualizing the health and well-being impacts of social enterprise: A UK-based study. *Health Promotion International.* https://doi.org/10.1093/heapro/dax009.

Marmot, M. G., & Wilkinson, R. G. (2006). *Social determinants of health.* Oxford: Oxford University Press.

Mason, C., Barraket, J., Friel, S., O'Rourke, K., & Stenta, C.-P. (2015). Social innovation for the promotion of health equity. *Health Promotion International, 30*(suppl 2), ii116–ii125.

McHugh, N., Biosca, O., Baker, R., Ibrahim, F., & Donaldson, C. (2019). Innovating on methods to understand the relationship between finances and wellbeing, In *Wealth(s) and subjective well-being* (pp. 129–144). New York: Springer

Meadows, D. H., Meadows, D. L., Randers, J., & Behrens, W. W. (1972). *The limits to growth: A report for the Club of Rome's project on the predicament of mankind.* New York: Universe Books.

Mirowski, P., & Plehwe, D. (Eds.). (2015). *The road from Mont Pèlerin: The making of the neoliberal thought collective.* Cambridge, MA: Harvard University Press.

Mouffe, C. (2018, 10 September). Populists are on the rise but this can be a moment for progressives too. In *The guardian*. Retrieved October 18, 2018, from https://www.theguardian.com/commentisfree/2018/sep/10/populists-rise-progressives-radical-right

Muñoz, S.-A., Farmer, J., Winterton, R., & Barraket, J. (2015). The social Enterprise as a space of wellbeing: An exploratory case study. *Social Enterprise Journal, 11*(3), 281–302.

Nussbaum, M. C. (2011). *Creating capabilities: The human development approach*. Cambridge, MA: Belknap Press of Harvard University Press.

Pavot, W., & Diener, E. (1993). Review of the satisfaction with life scale. *Psychological Assessment, 5*(2), 164.

Pawson, R., & Tilley, N. (1997). *Realistic evaluation*. Thousand Oaks, CA: Sage.

Pearce, J. (2003). *Social enterprise in anytown*. London: Calouste Gulbenkian Foundation.

Peters, F. H. (Tran.). (1906). *The Nicomachean Ethics of Aristotle*. London: Kegan Paul, Trench, Trübner & Co Ltd.

Piketty, T. (2014). *Capital in the twenty-first century, (A. Goldhammer, Trans.)*. Cambridge, MA: Harvard University Press.

Polanyi, K. (1944). *The great transformation: The Political and economic origins of our time*. Boston, MA: Beacon Press. Second Beacon Paperback Edition Published in 2001.

Polanyi, K. (1957). Aristotle discovers the economy. In K. Polanyi, C. M. Arensberg, & H. W. Pearson (Eds.), *Trade and market in the early empires: Economies in history and theory* (pp. 64–94). Glencoe, IL: Free Press.

Poveda, S., Gill, M., Junio, D. R., Thinyane, H., & Catan, V. (2019). Should social enterprises complement or supplement public health provision? *Social Enterprise Journal, 15*(4), 496–518.

Rotstein, A. (2014). Innis and Polanyi: The search for the substantive economy. *Journal of Economic Issues, 48*(1), 229–240.

Roy, E. A. (2019, 30 May). New Zealand 'wellbeing' budget promises billions to care for most vulnerable. In *The guardian*. Retrieved November 27, 2019, from https://www.theguardian.com/world/2019/may/30/new-zealand-wellbeing-budget-jacinda-ardern-unveils-billions-to-care-for-most-vulnerable

Roy, M. J. (2017). The assets-based approach: Furthering a neoliberal agenda or rediscovering the old public health? A critical examination of practitioner discourses. *Critical Public Health, 27*(4), 455–464.

Roy, M. J., Baker, R., & Kerr, S. (2017). Conceptualising the public health role of actors operating outside of formal health systems: The case of social enterprise. *Social Science & Medicine, 172*, 144–152.

Roy, M. J., Donaldson, C., Baker, R., & Kay, A. (2013). Social enterprise: New pathways to health and well-being? *Journal of Public Health Policy, 34*(1), 55–68.

Roy, M. J., Donaldson, C., Baker, R., & Kerr, S. (2014). The potential of social enterprise to enhance health and Well-being: A model and systematic review. *Social Science & Medicine, 123*, 182–193.

Roy, M. J., & Grant, S. (2019). The contemporary relevance of Karl Polanyi to critical social enterprise scholarship. *Journal of Social Entrepreneurship*. https://doi.org/10.1080/19420676.2019.1621363.

Roy, M. J., & Hackett, M. T. (2017). Polanyi's 'substantive approach' to the economy in action? Conceptualising social enterprise as a public health 'intervention'. *Review of Social Economy, 75*(2), 89–111.

Roy, M. J., Hill O'Connor, C., McHugh, N., Biosca, O., & Donaldson, C. (2015). The new merger: Combining third sector and market-based approaches to tackling inequalities. *Social Business, 5*(1), 47–60.

Roy, M. J., Lysaght, R., & Krupa, T. M. (2017, 20 March). Action on the social determinants of health through social enterprise. *Canadian Medical Association Journal (Journal de l'Association Medicale Canadienne), 189*, E440–E441.

Roy, M. J., McHugh, N., Huckfield, L., Kay, A., & Donaldson, C. (2015). 'The Most supportive environment in the world'? Tracing the development of an institutional 'ecosystem' for social enterprise. *Voluntas: International Journal of Voluntary and Nonprofit Organizations, 26*(3), 777–800.

Sayer, A. (2011). *Why things matter to people: Social science, values and ethical life.* Cambridge: Cambridge University Press.

Scottish Government (2016). Scotland's social enterprise strategy 2016–26. Edinburgh: Scottish Government. Retrieved January 27, 2017, from http://www.gov.scot/Resource/0051/00511 500.pdf

Sen, A. K. (1999). *Commodities and capabilities.* Delhi/New York: Oxford University Press.

Solar, O., & Irwin, A. (2010). A conceptual framework for action on the social determinants of health, World Health Organisation, Geneva. Retrieved April 16, 2014, from http://whqlibdoc. who.int/publications/2010/9789241500852_eng.pdf

Song, J., Fry, R., Mizen, A., Akbari, A., Wheeler, B., White, J., et al. (2018). Association between blue and green space availability with mental health and wellbeing. *International Journal of Population Data Science, 3*(4) Available at: https://doi.org/10.23889/ijpds.v3i4.921.

Stiglitz, J. E. (2009). Moving beyond market fundamentalism to a more balanced economy. *Annals of Public and Cooperative Economics, 80*(3), 345–360.

Stiglitz, J. E., Sen, A., & Fitoussi, J.-P. (2009). *Report by the commission on the measurement of economic performance and social progress.* Retrieved February 25, 2020, from https:// ec.europa.eu/eurostat/documents/118025/118123/Fitoussi+Commission+report

Suchowerska, R., Barraket, J., Qian, J., Mason, C., Farmer, J., Carey, G., et al. (2019). An organizational approach to understanding how social enterprises address health inequities: A scoping review. *Journal of Social Entrepreneurship, 11*, 1–25.

Teasdale, S. (2012). What's in a name? Making sense of social enterprise discourses. *Public Policy and Administration, 27*(2), 99–119.

Thunberg, G. (2019, 23 November). Transcript: Greta Thunberg's speech at the U.N. climate action summit. In *NPR.Org.* https://www.npr.org/2019/09/23/763452863/transcript-greta-thunbergs-speech-at-the-u-n-climate-action-summit?t=1574683271899

Trebeck, K. (2020). Agenda: Working towards an economy that is focused on wellbeing. In *The herald.* Retrieved January 27, 2020, from https://www.heraldscotland.com/opinion/18177452. agenda-working-towards-economy-focused-wellbeing/

Utting, P. (Ed.). (2015). *Social and solidarity economy: Beyond the fringe?* London: Zed Books.

Wahl, D. C. (2019, 25 November), A systems approach to the SDGs and the need to reframe SDG8. In *Medium.* Retrieved November 26, 2019, from https://medium.com/@designforsustainability/ a-systems-approach-to-the-sdgs-the-need-to-reframe-sdg8-6c4853118f82

Wilkinson, R., & Pickett, K. (2010). *The spirit level: Why equality is better for everyone.* London: Penguin.

Wilkinson, R. G., & Pickett, K. E. (2018). The inner level: How more equal societies reduce stress. In *Restore sanity and improve everyone's well-being.* London: Penguin.

Wright, E. O. (2009). *Envisioning real utopias.* London/New York: Verso.

Wright, E. O. (2012). Transforming capitalism through real utopias. *American Sociological Review, 20*(10), 1–25.

Yunus, M. (2010). *Building social business: The new kind of capitalism that serves humanity's most pressing needs.* New York: Public Affairs.

Chapter 14
From Crises to a Social and Impact Economy

Anna Domaradzka and Benjamin Gidron

In Chap. 1 we started the discussion on whether the "new" social economy is actually a continuation of the "old" one or it represents a different phenomenon and a new set of values. We asked our contributors to present their national case studies and compare diverse approaches to social economy, both inside and outside of the European Union. We were particularly interested in discovering new forms or processes emerging within the social economy field as a result of the structural shocks provided by crisis.

Indeed, the country chapters cover a wide array of geographical regions (Europe, Asia, South and North America) and welfare regimes (from developed to nonexistent). By putting those country cases side by side, we can offer a reflection on the nontraditional and novel processes emerging in the social economy domain, highlighting the role of new actors as well new sources of funding worldwide. Moreover, many of the authors, as members of FAB-MOVE project seconded to partner institutions, had a unique opportunity to study social economies while immersed in different national contexts.[1] This allowed us to see more clearly the specificities of our own countries, experience differences firsthand, as well as discover new trends in the social economy worldwide (see also Dietz & Jager, 2019; Domaradzka & Żbikowska, 2019; Obuch & Zimmer, 2019).

With this collection of international chapters, we wanted to contribute to widening the discussion concerning the changes both within and outside the social econ-

---

[1] For more information about the project, country reports, and case studies see the project website: https://fabmove.eu/

A. Domaradzka (✉)
Robert Zajonc Institute for Social Studies, University of Warsaw, Warsaw, Poland
e-mail: anna.domaradzka@uw.edu.pl

B. Gidron (✉)
Professor Emeritus, Business Administration, Ben-Gurion University of the Negev, Beer-Sheva, Israel

omy sector stemming from the subsequent waves of economic crises. While we started this volume focusing on the aftermath of 2008/2009 crisis, we are wrapping it up in the middle of COVID-19 crisis. In our conclusions we will try to reflect on the worldwide trends concerning the possible outcomes of both waves of economic shocks that we witnessed.

The Emerging Field of New Social Economy

As a result of this volume of collected chapters, we posit that at the moment, only the initial stage of new social economy emergence can be observed. This can be partly explained by the inertia of the European welfare systems that promotes certain forms of social economy, dependent on the public support rather than competitiveness or innovativeness. However, the "crawling crisis" of the welfare model, as well as the more disruptive COVID-19 crisis, creates new openings for social economy, based on its links with the business sector, as well as new forms of service provision and fundraising enabled by Internet technologies. In other words, recent developments seem to be stimulated by both the weakening of the state authority and successful spread of the information and communication technologies, the Internet of Things, and new modes of funding made available by companies willing to expand their investment portfolio (and often boost their PR).

While there are not enough arguments to analyze the new social economy as a sector, we suggest using the concept of "field" to analyze its dynamics and identify actors and norm entrepreneurs. As a strategic action field (Fligstein & McAdam, 2011), new social economy is where the actors representing civil society, business, and public authorities meet to negotiate new solutions to social challenges. Influenced by the field of public policies from the one side and the trends in the global economy from the other, the social economy becomes a fertile ground for new social enterprises and social start-ups. It is significant that many of them base their competitive advantage on the digital competences and tools.

What seems to be at stake within the social economy field is the place and role of social enterprises and other hybrid forms within the overall economy and civil society. Those adjacent or overlapping fields have an important impact in shaping strategies and norms within the social economy field, which still remains fluid compared to the more established fields. The new global strategies of impact investors as well as social economy organizations have been shaping the field as well. It can be said that these global actors played a role of norm entrepreneurs (Finnemore & Sikkink, 1998), promoting a new way of creating social impact through responsible business practices.

The state of affairs presented here has a quality of liquidity, due to the exogenous shocks created by both the 2008 and 2020 crises, as well as the underlining climate crisis. Although some historians (De Witte, 2020; Scheidel, 2018) point out that throughout history, pandemics have been effective levelers of social and economic inequality, the corona crisis may not bring the same outcome. We can already observe that the promise of the transforming power of the crisis remains hard to fulfil. However, the preservation of the status quo seems unlikely as well. This is because of the long-term implications of the work-from-home patterns, as well as the pandemic effect on the educational systems and teaching methods. What seems sure is that the governments will have to cut services and deal with tremendous deficits due to the rise in unemployment and costs of small businesses' support. This will call for new approaches and create opportunity for smarter solutions, focused on social impact rather than profit.

On the other hand, the crisis did not (yet?) undermine the forces of corporate hegemony, nor the Plutarchic political systems. To the contrary, some of the economic and political forces use the chaos and fear as an opportunity to strengthen their position. While the populistic parties gain traction in many of the studied countries, the consumption is often advertised as more vital than rethinking and redesigning the supply chains. Also, while we tend to think of science and technology as drivers of innovation, in the case of the pandemic pharmaceutical companies may slow down the societal change, by offering effective treatments and vaccines. Making the crisis less disruptive and shorter has the potential to bring the not-so-good normalcy back and help preserve the structural inequalities.

What seems new, however, is that as a result of the global pandemic, there is a possibility that the world will face the prospect of de-globalizing and returning to more local self-sufficient economy model. After COVID-19 has affected communities, businesses, and organizations globally, the uncoordinated governmental responses and lockdowns have broken the weak links in the global supply chain. If most governments can overcome the current crisis within the next year, the world will likely return to a—slightly revised—path of globalization. The countries most hit by the crisis will have to fight hard to regain their place in the global market while dealing with long-term negative effects at home. This scenario creates openings for those investors and entrepreneurs who did not become fully specialized or dependent on external actors and can fill the new niches or design fast solutions to the problems brought by the crisis. However, there is a threat that more "entrepreneurs of necessity" than "entrepreneurs of opportunity" will emerge, creating business models that are not sustainable, nor desirable from the impact point of view.

The current situation favors ICT-based social innovations, thus creating an opportunity for social start-ups, digital cooperatives, and social tech ventures. In the meantime, the crisis pushed various countries toward technological solutions, to control the spread of virus as well as provide services with minimal risk of person-to-person transmission. In various countries, chatbots, drones, contact tracing apps, and fifth-generation wireless networks are being adopted. While COVID-19 has helped to accelerate the automation and digitalization of services it has also enabled the widespread invigilation of citizens (Couch, Robinson, & Komesaroff, 2020; Gasser, Ienca, Scheibner, Sleigh, & Vayena, 2020, Wnuk, Oleksy, & Maison, 2020). Some citizens-led technical solutions are therefore severely needed to create more acceptable and trustworthy alternatives (Domaradzka & Roszczyńska-Kurasińska 2021). With the threat of pandemic due to shape the future economic and political strategies, social economy role as a field of ethical innovations and ground-up resilience should be more widely recognized.

From the grassroots perspective, we observe some signals that the new reality is slowly but surely emerging. People become increasingly conscious of global interdependencies and more frustrated with the traditional economy solutions that treat them as consumers, not vulnerable humans. It is often said that the COVID-19 crisis makes us more equal, but the effects of the pandemic are still more deadly in the global South and the access to vaccines is not ensured even in more developed countries. As a result, we may be soon looking at an even more divided world, with higher stakes and inequalities or injustices becoming more visible.

It is difficult to find answers and patterns in the middle of a huge uncertainty created by COVID-19. Following the logic of our analysis, this crisis, as the previous one, has the potential to open up the new path of development of social economy. While looking at country-specific stories about new trends within social economy we were asking ourselves if this new social economy has a potential to change power relations. By forcing to include social considerations into economic activity, it obviously is part of certain value shift. But does it have the potential to amend power relationships in society? In the aftermath of the pandemic, the world should prepare itself to prevent the next global catastrophe, namely the climate crisis. This calls for tremendous investments in long-term projects, which will likely change the lifestyle of consumerism and should bring considerations of sustainability and communitarianism to our lives, which in turn should decrease the power of economic interests. The social economy can be a central framework where these developments occur.

New Social Economy and the Three Crises Combined

It can be said that the subprime mortgage crisis, the climate crisis, and the COVID-19 pandemic emphasized the negative impact of the neoliberal economy on the society and the environment. It therefore gave rise to new forms of economic and social response to the shortages, uncertainty, and value shifts. In both the economic and civil society field the idea of hybridity gained traction, blurring the lines between nonprofit and for-profit activities. Suddenly, the idea that social goals can be pursued via economic means became an obvious response to the weakening of the welfare systems. The less economic power the government has, the more open to hybrid solutions to public problems it becomes, which may explain the underdevelopment of social economy in countries like Sweden, and its flourishing in countries like Italy.

The COVID-19 pandemic has created new type of uncertainties, not experienced before. Suddenly, the basic social security structure is being tested worldwide, the health sector becomes crucial for the survival of the whole generation, and the traditional economy sector has to reinvent itself to last. Even the climate crisis that has been shaping the international policies in the last decade became marginalized during the virus outbreak. However, some of the authors already point out the relation between all three crises: the economic, the environmental, and the pandemic. For example, Vidal (2020) highlights how the economic progress leading to the destruction of biodiversity, rapid urbanization, and population density, with a growing global interconnectedness, creates a favorable condition for the transition of both coronavirus and other pathogens. According to Vidal, the expansionary economic regime disrupts the balance between human and ecosystem health and generates "a hidden cost of human development."[2]

While we are yet to fully experience the effects of the second wave of pandemic, the perspectives seem grim worldwide and the strain on the economy and the health system comes at the price of human lives from both the disease and lack of financial means of survival. At the same time, major industries strive to invent new ways of producing, transporting, and selling their products, while smaller enterprises find themselves in the new landscape, where they can compete with big (and less flexible) competitors and where their innovative ability becomes their greatest strength. While crises certainly create new opportunities for the social economy, it also weakens their ability to count on nation-states, which already are under huge financial stress to protect basic services and safety of the citizens. However, outside the European context we could observe the growing importance of impact investors in stimulating the development of the social economy.

As mentioned above, as a result of the economic strain and collapse of both 2008 and 2020 a new field emerged that we termed the *new social economy*, to underline its roots in the ideological underpinnings of a known social economy concept. The impact economy concept is also fitting here but is more relevant in countries where the social economy is not as institutionalized as in most European countries. As we could see from the analysis of Gabriel Berger or Maria Radyati, in countries like Argentina or Indonesia, the social economy is based on the big investors' involvement, rather than public institutions.

Where there is no welfare state, the alternative solutions to social problems much often grow from the grassroots, with support of CSR or impact investment funds. This creates a different ecosystem of social enterprises, social start-ups, and impact initiatives than the one we could observe in Europe. Importantly, the development of SEs in Indonesia and Argentina is often a response to societal and environmental challenges that the states are not able to address, and which are becoming visible also in Europe. The results of the economic and climate crisis and sanitary restrictions create an additional strain on the welfare systems and undermine the economic stability of the whole region. Therefore, we posit that the slowly evolving European new social economy could take inspiration from the countries, where the highly innovative impact investment sector developed in a less friendly environment.

As we mention in the beginning, the concept of social economy is a construct and hence gives us an opportunity to discuss and update its meaning according to new realities emerging after major transforming events. However, even more diversity can be observed between countries studied by our book's contributors. While

---

[2] Vidal, J. (2020, March 17). Destruction of habitat and loss of biodiversity are creating the perfect conditions for diseases like Covid-19 to emerge. Retrieved from https://ensia.com/features/covid-19-coronavirus-biodiversity-planetary-health-zoonoses/

we expected to see some differences stemming from the national versions of welfare system or historical underpinnings of legal and economic systems, we can now say that described crises made those differences even more complex. One of the most important factors defining the local flavors of social economy is the strength (or weakness) of two actors of new social economy—investors and entrepreneurs.

Interestingly, although maybe not surprisingly, we find more ferment and innovations outside the European context. Countries like Argentina, Israel, or Indonesia present themselves as fertile ground for cooperation between social entrepreneurs, private investors, and public actors. As our book shows, in these countries we cannot really apply the social economy concept developed in the European context, which helps us to go beyond a traditional approach to social economy and focus more on the impact investment role in developing new socially focused businesses.

The current crisis related to COVID-19 highlighted not only the need for non-state solutions but also the potential of start-ups (especially the medical and technological ones) and social businesses to mitigate the crisis results. Many point out that the demand for the social economy has never been greater. In the current crisis, the social economy organizations turn out to be a trusted partner, addressing urgent social and health-related needs.

Traditionally, the goal of the social economy has been seen to address and repair social problems, such as exclusion, unemployment, or homelessness. However, in the post-COVID world, social economy can develop a much larger role in the transformation to a more inclusive and sustainable economy and society. Up to now, it has proven to be a pioneer in identifying and implementing social innovations and alternative ways of organizing economic activities. Some of these innovations, related to organic food production, fair trade, or ethical banking, have been adopted by the mainstream economy. Still, their focus on social impact does not make them immune to the consequences of lockdown faced by other economic actors. Moreover, traditional legal forms of social enterprises like associations or foundations make them ineligible for the government support measures addressed to companies, not CSOs.

Despite these shortcomings, we believe that the social economy impact can be expanded to address both environmental and societal challenges, by involving local stakeholders in designing and implementing new practices of production and economic exchange. However, new legal frameworks are needed to support these promising forms of social innovation and collaboration, to create meaningful impact.

As OECD points out, the role of the social economy in response to the current crisis has been important and allowed to mitigate some of the short- and long-term impacts of the COVID-19 crisis on economy and society. During the first wave of the pandemic, social economy actors have provided innovative solutions aimed at strengthening public services to complement government action. In the long term, social economy organizations are seen as actors who can help reshape the post-crisis economy by promoting inclusive and sustainable economic models. In OECD words, it can bring in an important value shift into the economic mainstream: "Relying on decades of experience, its specific features and underlying principles, the social economy can inspire models of social innovation and a sense of purpose to firms operating in the market economy."[3]

However, the pandemic has undoubtedly posed a major challenge to the new social and impact economy. On the one hand it has created a whole host of immediate problems, related to health, social isolation, and economic hardships for billions of people in the world. These problems needed to be addressed without delay, and while different societies have used social economy systems to deal with such problems, it is much too early to assess these modes of intervention and their success.

On the other hand, once the health threat of the virus will be removed (not at the time these lines are written) and the focus will shift from the immediate and urgent problems to planning the economic recovery, the role of the new social and impact economy will be put to its real test. We asked our contributors to reflect on those issues in their respective countries. These reflections were all written during the acute phase of the pandemic, before it was controlled and before humankind clearly understood its dynamic, so obviously the world was mostly concerned with solving immediate problems, not dealing with the long-range implications.

The Effect of the COVID-19 Crisis on the Social and Impact Economy in Different Countries

By and large, our contributors found relatively little unique patterns of involvement by the social and impact economy organizations and their ecosystems in the fight against the COVID-19 pandemic and its health, economic, social, educational, and cultural consequences. In general, what we observe is an involvement of these bodies in measures taken by governments in alleviating immediate problems emanating from the pandemic and utilizing their specific characteristics and abilities in doing so. Thus, all contributors stress the involvement of new social and impact economy organizations in efforts to alleviate immediate problems, with a special focus on the vulnerable populations, such as refugees, the elderly, women with low income, and small businesses. Those efforts included entrepreneurial and creative responses, such as crowdfunding and use of other virtual channels. This has been reported in Sweden, Austria, Argentina, and Indonesia as well as by the international SEOs. Also, along these lanes, certain new social economy organizations have been created, some of them based on new technologies. Their range of services was indeed very wide, from dealing with loneliness to encouraging people to develop home gardens.

In some countries, France and Canada in particular, the new (and old) social economy actors have taken steps and called upon to be included in the plans for the "world after." This is indicative as in these two countries there is a long tradition of

---

[3] http://www.oecd.org/coronavirus/policy-responses/social-economy-and-the-covid-19-crisis-current-and-future-roles-f904b89f/

a social economy presence and involvement in policy processes. For example, in Canada, the crisis has raised issues pertaining to the welfare state and the role of government in tackling the difficult consequences of the pandemic. It also demonstrated the strengths of the traditional social and solidarity economy structures and is testing the resiliency of the new social economy ones.

Italy too has a long social economy tradition, but the authors of the Italian chapter lament the fact that leaders of social economy organizations are not involved enough in planning the recovery and the future reality. In Austria as well, the social economy organizations are mostly involved in dealing with the consequences of the current crisis, namely providing a range of services with the use of virtual tools as well as privately organized solidarity funds and crowdfunding for specific projects. Similarly, in Sweden, while social economy actors have been a part of the efforts to help vulnerable populations during the pandemic, they have not been a part of efforts to plan the future social economic reality.

In other countries however, the pandemic has brought out certain structural attributes, which are crucial to successfully fight the pandemic as well as plan the future economic recovery. In Israel, Poland, and Spain, COVID-19 came at a time of major political divisions and crises, with low levels of trust in the country's leadership. Such a situation obviously hampers the taking of effective steps in order to fight the pandemic and the ensuing economic recovery.

According to our authors the international social economy organizations have quickly adapted to the new situation and initiated various local and immediate programs to deal with the effect of the pandemic. These included the produce and supply of face masks, loan programs to support small businesses, or sending of food packages to people in need.

While looking in more detail to specific country developments we could observe that in several countries, while some new social economy initiatives were unable to continue their operations, other initiatives thrived. In France the pandemic has raised the visibility of certain local social economy organizations working in the fields of transport, food production, and care. The latter, namely elderly homes, nurseries, and home help, were forced to create new methods to provide their services. In Poland several initiatives emerged to deal with people's needs for information as well as support in specific areas like childcare or access to food. The technological know-how of such initiatives gave them an edge in comparison to traditional forms of social support and allowed for widening the clients' base. Similarly, in Argentina, Israel, and Indonesia we could observe some entrepreneurial responses to emerging needs and the wider use of virtual channels to reach suffering businesses. The importance of the virtual tools was visible also in Indonesia, where millions of COVID-19 victims recorded on the Internet were provided with direct and indirect help, often in the form of crowdfunding.

As Michael Roy points out in his chapter on the "well-being economy," social enterprises have an important role not only during pandemic, but also in furthering the post-crisis economic and social agenda. By focusing on maximizing well-being instead of income, they are ideally positioned to quickly respond to crisis-related challenges, setting new standards and alliances with policymakers, practitioners, and researchers.

Conclusions: With the Next Crisis in Sight

Does the economic recovery mean to go back to what was a neoliberal economy we knew? Or will the world seize the opportunity to plan a different type of an economy—one that is people and environment oriented, one that will intervene in the world and in society so as to sustain it and thus prevent the next global crisis.

There will undoubtedly be forces to push in both directions. The economic interests behind the preservation of fossil fuels and systems which are based on it, as well as those responsible for destroying rainforests in order to plant palm trees for the cosmetic industry, will clearly be pushing for bringing back the previous and known order. Yet the long periods of lockdowns have taught us that humans can survive in the twenty-first century with much less consumerism and if one needs a certain article, it can be purchased online, which turns large shopping centers unnecessary. While online shopping started long before, the pandemic intensified its usage. Similarly, the pattern of working from home, needed during the pandemic, will not escape large as well as small businesses that pay expensive rent for their office spaces and are already reflecting whether at least some of their workers can continue to work from home (at least part-time) after the crisis. These are just two examples of the long-term effects, directly emanating from the pandemic, with tremendous social and environmental oriented impact on our way of life. They are likely to alter certain economic systems in the right direction, because of economic considerations, without any ideological transformation. Can such changes be a precursor for more fundamental changes needed in order to prevent the next global crisis—the climate crisis?

Apparently, there are signs that even the staunch supporters of the neoliberal economy have some second thoughts on the fit of the neoliberal economy to deal with the world in the twenty-first century in a way that will sustain it. The fact that the current system enriches a minute fraction of the population—those controlling the big corporations—and deprives the vast majority and that it depletes the world's natural resources did not escape certain leaders of the neoliberal economy. Kristalina Georgieva of the International Monetary Fund (IMF) and Klaus Schwab of the World Economic Forum (the Davos Conference) have recently expressed the opinion that the time has come to rethink some conventional truisms[4]. The book by Melleret and Schwab (2020), following Piketty (2019), questions some key elements in the neoliberal economy such as the GDP indicator for economic well-being, and calls for a change in our mindset regarding the notion that humans are

---

[4] See https://www.bloomberg.com/news/audio/2020-10-04/bloomberg-best-heads-of-the-imf-and-world-bank-podcast

intrinsically selfish; it calls for creating new metrics to measure what matters and build new genuine connections between people, between society and its leaders, as well as between humans and nature. The London Financial Times has also started a campaign entitled "Capitalism: Time for a Reset,"[5] suggesting that while businesses must make a profit, they should serve a purpose too. Furthermore, Walmart, the world's largest retailer, has set a goal to become a "regenerative company," which is translated into zero emissions by 2040, and the company aims to protect, manage, or restore at least 50 million acres of land and one million square miles of ocean by 2030.

Ideas about what needs to be done to create a more social and human economy have been discussed many times in the past two decades. The economic recovery from the pandemic can take the form of investment in sustainable energies, in recycling systems, and in introducing social considerations in planning housing projects, to name a few examples. The changes in the business sector's strategies will have to be expressed in their governing structures, which should include not only shareholders but also stakeholders such as those representing the interests of the environment, the dispossessed, and the future generations (Elkington, 2020).

The major thrust by the UN's Sustainable Development Goals (SDGs),[6] launched in 2017, laid the foundations for this transformation. The test will be their implementation, namely the commitment of governments to meet those goals by the next decade. Project Drawdown[7] is an example of such an attempt. Success will undoubtedly help save humanity as we know it.

To move the world into such a new direction obviously calls for visionary (rather than populist) leadership, one that understands the dangers the world faces and has the ability to communicate those to the population. It also calls for international bodies to oversee the transformation, which will not be even, with lots of bumps along the way. It can benefit tremendously from an international movement, based on civil society, to give it popular and symbolic backing.

An example of such a direction can be the recent call by the European Commission (EC) President Ursula von der Leyen for adopting a Green Deal European Project entitled New European Bauhaus. The idea is to launch an architectural style of a climate-neutral Europe.[8] The EU could build a "European Bauhaus" as part of

---

[5] https://www.b2bmarketing.net/en-gb/resources/news/financial-times-launches-first-campaign-global-financial-crisis#:~:text=With%20its%20slogan%2C%20'Capitalism%3A,future%20of%20the%20corporate%20world

[6] https://sdgs.un.org/goals

[7] https://drawdown.org/

[8] Named after the famous architecture style developed after World War I, with the slogan "Form follows Function" that revolutionized architecture and design last century. The thinkers and actors of the original Bauhaus movement "were responding to opportunities offered by novel construction materials such as steel and poured concrete, technologies such as electrification, telephones and motor cars, and the new requirements of life in mass-industrial society. Today, it is the climate transition that demands new materials, construction processes and planning for changing lifestyles …. The Bauhaus school wanted design to make consumer goods functional and pleasing, and architecture to raise the quality of life for the masses — artistic precursors to the social market economy and liberal democracy enshrined in the EU's values."

coronavirus recovery. The idea is to fuse pandemic-recovery initiatives with the environmental programs that were already on the agenda when the coronavirus struck. A big part of that green plan relates to the energy efficiency of buildings and investing in circular solutions. The refurbishment of buildings is a worthy but generally too technical and often misunderstood subject. That is why the authors state, "This is not just an environmental or economic project: It needs to be a new cultural project for Europe … Every movement has its own look and feel. And we need to give our systemic change its own distinct aesthetic—to match style with sustainability … This is why we will set up a new European Bauhaus—a cocreation space where architects, artists, students, engineers, designers work together to make that happen."[9]

Another innovative project along these lines is the National Park City movement, London being an example of it.[10] National Park City is a movement to make cities greener, healthier, and wilder, using a variety of spaces, including rooftops for example, and turn them into green ones. Another move in that direction comes from the idea of the circular city championed by Italian researchers (Gravagnuolo, Angrisano, & Fusco Girard, 2019) as well as Michel Bauwens' ideas of collaborative economy and peer production (Bauwens, 2005; Bauwens, Kostakis, & Pazaitis, 2019). Such projects, with their imposing titles, are examples of the far-reaching thinking needed to create the transformation. It requires symbols and aesthetic innovation that have a key role in making both the economic and the cultural transformations we face go more smoothly.

New social and impact economy organizations have a tremendous role in such a transformation. Having a hybrid structure, they can serve as a microcosmos of the larger, macro change, upholding principles needed to save the planet and create a conscious society.

The outbreak of COVID-19 virus already exposed how the profit-centered economical model leads to commercialized and dysfunctional society, prone to pandemic and crises. As Rubinić (2020) points out, the global health crisis and the resulting economic collapse reveal the ultimate market failure. This failure creates an opening for a change and a paradigm shift that will deprioritize the economic growth driven by commodification of social relations to the alternative model of economy. Together with the climate crisis, current situation brings focus to the sustainable and equitable increase in societal well-being.

According to Rubinić (2020), the excessive pre-pandemic inequality is both the cause behind and the cure for the current state of economy. Given this logic, the pandemic could and should become the new "great equalizer," leading to a value shift and the departure from the egoistic consumerism and maximization of profits toward a system which focuses on collective good and humans in all economic dealings. As a result of "putting the basic needs of the many ahead of the insatiable

---

[9] *Financial Times*, Sept. 18, 2020.

[10] https://www.nationalparkcity.london/?gclid=CjwKCAjw0On8BRAgEiwAincsHPb5GtaRWPq VJwKJNYUSAmMRjghaXZpGctHM0vTZ_JuQhMx_9TZX9xoC1W4QAvD_BwE

wants of a few" a new economic model could emerge, much better prepared to address the ecological threats to planet and the society.

If we agree that the coronavirus pandemic can be considered a market failure, we may conclude that it has the potential to create a shift from the profit-centered neoliberal paradigm toward the society focused on efficient, sustainable, and equitable development. Social economy actors could be leaders in that regard. As Rubinić (2020) suggests, we should not let this crisis go to waste and miss another opportunity to rethink and redesign the global power relations, business models, and local approach to human welfare.

We already observe that consumers are undergoing a fundamental change in behavior driven by health, privacy, and hyper-localization (EY report, 2020). New openings for virtual services and online sales of goods are emerging, because people have learned to use them during the pandemic. More opportunities for local providers versus global ones appear, due to breaking of supply chains and lockdown restrictions. There are also multiple new needs resulting from lockdown—virtual childcare, online learning, self-care, healthy and sustainable lifestyle, catering services, and many health-related goods and services. Importantly, new meeting platforms and linking apps become a necessity allowing to sustain social relations as well as clients' loyalty and satisfaction.

We know already that despite all restrictions, the pandemic has been amplifying innovation to historic levels. However, it was followed by the tech-clash, resulting from the misalignment of business value with people's values. The COVID-19 exacerbates the fact that the digital-age technology models are increasingly out of sync with shifting societal values. This is why it is so critical that businesses think about mitigating uncertainty and proposing solutions in line with new value systems.

The full extent of COVID-19's impact on social economy is not yet known. Already, this crisis has become a catalyst for change, where need for innovation is greater than ever, to face new disruptive factors. The question remains: Can the new social economy actors become central players in shaping the new economic order that seems to be evolving?

References

Bauwens, M. (2005). The political economy of peer production. *CTheory*, 12–11.

Bauwens, M., Kostakis, V., & Pazaitis, A. (2019). *Peer to peer: The commons manifesto*. London: University of Westminster Press.

Couch, D. L., Robinson, P., & Komesaroff, P. A. (2020). COVID-19—Extending surveillance and the panopticon. *Journal of Bioethical Inquiry*, 1–6.

De Witte, M. (2020). *Past pandemics redistributed income between the rich and poor, according to Stanford historian,* Stanford News. Retrieved April 30, 2020, from https://news.stanford.edu/2020/04/30/pandemics-catalyze-social-economic-change/

Dietz, T. & Jager, U. (2019). *Driving forces of Social Enterprises in weak-welfare States: comparative study of four Developing Countries*. Retrieved from https://fabmove.eu/comparative_reports/comparative-report-iii-driving-forces-of-social-enterprises-in-weak-welfare-states-comparative-study-of-four-developing-countries/

Domaradzka, A. & Żbikowska, A. (2019). Dancing with the state or the market? Social enterprises relation to other sectors in international perspective. Retrieved from https://fabmove.eu/comparative_reports/comparative-report-ii-dancing-with-the-state-or-the-market-social-enterprises-relation-to-other-sectors-in-international-perspective/

Domaradzka, A. & Roszczyńska-Kurasińska, M. (2021). The Impact of ICT on Citizens' Well-being and the Right to the City. An Introduction. In *Proceedings of the 54th Hawaii International Conference on System Sciences,* 2474–2476.

Elkington, J. (2020). *The green swans: The coming boom in regenerative capitalism.* New York: Fast Company Press.

EY. (2020). Beyond COVID-19: How a crisis shifts cultural and societal behaviors. Retrieved April 24, from https://www.ey.com/en_us/consulting/beyond-covid-19-how-a-crisis-shifts-cultural-and-societal-behaviors

Finnemore, M., & Sikkink, K. (1998). International norm dynamics and political change. *International Organization,* 887–917.

Fligstein, N., & McAdam, D. (2011). Toward a general theory of strategic action fields. *Sociological Theory, 29*(1), 1–26.

Gasser, U., Ienca, M., Scheibner, J., Sleigh, J. & Vayena, E. (2020). Digital tools against COVID-19: Taxonomy, ethical challenges, and navigation aid. *The Lancet Digital Health.*

Gravagnuolo, A., Angrisano, M., & Fusco Girard, L. (2019). Circular economy strategies in eight historic port cities: Criteria and indicators towards a circular city assessment framework. *Sustainability, 11*(13), 3512.

Melleret, T., & Schwab, K. (2020). *Covid 19: The great reset.* Geneva: Forum Publishing.

Obuch, K., Zimmer, A. (2019). *Social Enterprises in FAB-MOVE partner countries; evolution, discourses and characteristic features.* Retrieved from https://fabmove.eu/comparative_reports/comparative-report-i-social-enterprises-in-fab-move-partner-countries-evolution-discourses-and-characteristic-features/

Picketty, T. (2019). *Capital and ideology.* Cambridge, MA: Harvard University Press.

Rubinić I. (2020). Pandemic paradigm shift. Labor and Society 1–15. https://doi.org/10.1111/wusa.12486. Retrieved from https://www.ncbi.nlm.nih.gov/pmc/articles/PMC7436549/#wusa12486-bib-0035

Scheidel, W. (2018). *The great leveler: Violence and the history of inequality from the stone age to the twenty-first century.* Princeton, NJ: Princeton University Press.

Vidal, J. (2020). Destruction of habitat and loss of biodiversity are creating the perfect conditions for diseases like Covid-19 to emerge. Retrieved March 17, from https://ensia.com/features/covid-19-coronavirus-biodiversity-planetary-health-zoonoses/

Wnuk A, Oleksy T, Maison D (2020) The acceptance of Covid-19 tracking technologies: The role of perceived threat, lack of control, and ideological beliefs. PLoS ONE 15(9): e0238973. https://doi.org/10.1371/journal.pone.0238973

Index

© Springer Nature Switzerland AG 2021
B. Gidron, A. Domaradzka (eds.), *The New Social and Impact Economy*,
Nonprofit and Civil Society Studies, https://doi.org/10.1007/978-3-030-68295-8